Midhurst WW2 Memoirs:
2. 'Evil' Rising: 'Good' Awakening

Dr Peter H Sydenham

Previous Midhurst WW2 Memoirs Books

Sydenham, Peter H., *Midhurst WW2 Memoirs: The Evacuee's Story.* Companion book. Red Robin Publishing, Adelaide, 2018.

Sydenham, Peter H., *Midhurst WW2 Memoirs: 1. A Place Close to My Heart,* Book 1. Red Robin Publishing, Adelaide, 2018.

Both available as e-books and on-line POD hard copy

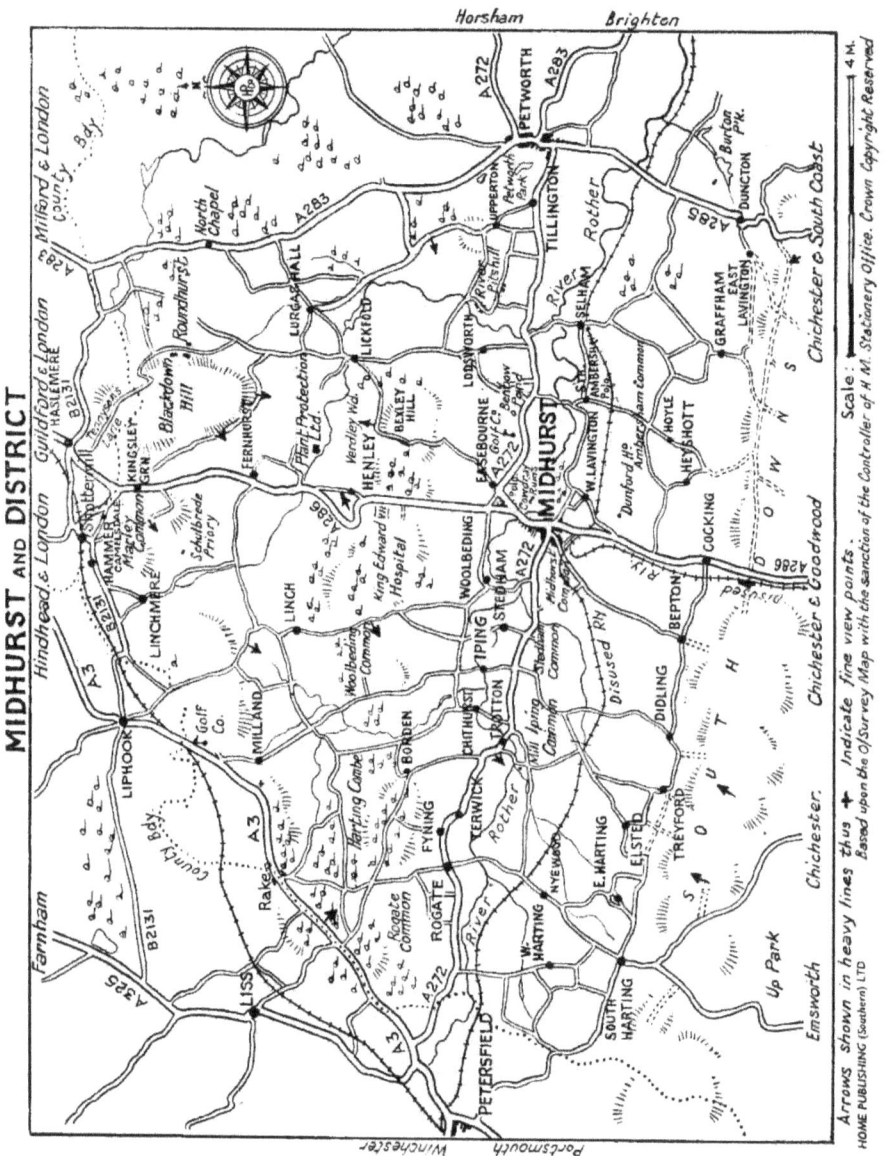

Frontispiece: Map of the Midhurst Rural District, c1967. This would be very much the same as in WW2 times. (MRDC)

Midhurst WW2 Memoirs:
2. Evil Rising: Good Awakening

by

Peter H Sydenham
Midhurst Memoirs Project

Front Cover: *Hans, Marching and Heiling, Heiling and Marching.*
From Walt Disney cartoon, 1943

Red Robin Publishing

First Published 2020 by
Red Robin Publishing Pty Ltd
8 Weemala Crescent Rostrevor
South Australia 5073
Tel: + 61404083339
Email: sydenham@senet.com.au
Web: www.midhurstmemoirs.com

Copyright © 2020 Peter Sydenham
All rights reserved. No reproduction permitted
without prior permission of the copyright holders

**Midhurst WW2 Memoirs:
2. Evil Rising: Good Awakening**

ISBN 978-0-6481713-6-2
Printed on demand by IngramSpark

Disclaimer
The publisher of this book has made every effort to ensure the accuracy of the information contained in it but such accuracy cannot be guaranteed. If errors have nevertheless crept in, the publisher apologises, but cannot accept liability for loss or inconvenience resulting from inaccurate information.

Dedication

*Book 2 is dedicated to
Sue Edwards of the Midhurst
Society. These Memoirs resulted
from her encouragement and
subsequent support given to me
starting in 2013.*

Preface

To understand the aims of these Midhurst WW2 Memoirs books, consult the Introduction given at the start of Book 1.

That first book provides a comprehensive history of over 500 years of the Midhurst District. It shows how it came to be a beautiful rural area, maintaining its features, and not being urbanised. It provides the foundation for appreciating what happened to the Midhurst District during WW2.

It needs a solid foundation to appreciate those times. WW2 did not just happen, but was the result of many events that impacted heavily on the lives of millions of people over the 1930s.

It answers questions, the first being 'who caused the war'? And, who were the Good and the Evil countries, and what were their long-term aims? Who resisted the Evil elements and what was their build-up to the war over the last half of the 1930s? What kind of negative effects took place globally? Where were the Nazis in Britain before the war on Germany was declared by Britain?

That background in place, the book turns attention on how the people in Midhurst District reacted. Where were the wealthy estates? How did the growing presence of a seriously bad conflict affect the daily lives and influences on their pastimes such as sport, film, music, and art? What did families experience and what memories did they leave for us today?

War was getting close. What was taking place as it came to be? How did the British Government react in its latter days of being the world's most powerful nation?

In the late 1930s, photographs and films were easily made allowing these memoirs to include the reference to such materials. Many of the topics given here have been recorded in documentaries and pseudo-docs. Films are mentioned that are well worth spending time viewing to get the fuller story and to really 'feel' the mood of times during WW2.

Contents for Book 2

Preface
Contents
1 Storm Clouds are Forming
1.1 WW1 Treaty Sets in Place WW2
1.2 Joachim Liebschner's Experience as a German
1.3 The Feuchtwanger Family Suffer Anti-Semitism
1.4 Deterioration of World Order
1.5 Enter, Stage Front, Evil
2 Nazi Germany; the First Arch enemy of Britain
2.1 Germany
2.2 Bonhoeffer's Life of Discipleship
3 Others of the Evil Camp
3.1 Russia - Good and Evil
3.2 Italy and Spain
3.3 Japan
4 The Goods Respond
4.1 Peaceful Moves
4.2 Elements for Good - the Democracies
5 The Allies
5.1 Britain and its Commonwealth
5.2 Canada
5.3 Australia
5.4 USA in the 30s
5.5 European and Nordic Countries
5.6 China
5.7 Russia
5.8 Other Good Contributions
6 War Approaches
6.1 Unable to Comprehend
6.2 "Goering stayed here" Fact or Fiction?
6.3 Goering and Ribbentrop Unravelled
6.4 Pre-war life in Germany – Love Story Extraordinaire
7 Persons without Essentials
7.1 Kinder Transport and Midhurst
7.2 On Being a Recognised Citiz

8 Money Makes the World go Around
8.1 Currency Guidance; from Midhurst
8.2 Barbara Ward: Voice in the Wilderness
9 Glimpses of a Then Possible Future
9.1 Fascists in West Sussex
9.2 Creation of Lord Haw-Haw
9.3 William Joyce's Story
9.4 Midhurst Connection with Fascism
10 Midhurst Life with War Imminent
10.1 The 30s - a Time of Changes for the Worst
10.2 The Rich Play On
10.3 Life with War Imminent
10.4 The World is Invaded
11 Where the 'Other Half' lived in the District
11.1 Cowdray
11.2 Stedham Hall
11.3 Wispers/St Cuthman's School/Durand Academy
11.4 Fitz Hall
11.5 Bignor House
11.6 Bohunt Manor
11.7 Uppark House
11.8 Stansted Park
11.9 Parham House
11.10 Leonardslee Estate
11.11 Woolbeding House
11.12 Petworth Estate and House
11.13 West Dean House
11.14 Goodwood House and Estate
11.15 Other Country Houses
12 Entertainment and Sport
12.1 Music and Film
12.2 Art Collecting
12.3 Sport in the District: Stoolball

13 Some Local Memories
13.1 Heroes of WW1 - in Submarines
13.2 Experiences of Nearby Persons
13.3 Local Midhurst Memories as War Arrived
14 War Begins in Britain
14.1 War is Declared; September 1939
14.2 Plans go into Action
14.3 BoB Pilots in the Making
14.4 The Midhurst Region Sends Sons and Daughters
14.5 Life will Never be the Same Again
Appreciations and Acknowledgements
About the Author
List of Illustrations
References for Book 2
Index

Chapter 1. Storm Clouds are Forming

1.1 WW1 Treaty Sets WW2 in Place

It was the day when Britain was expected to declare war on Germany; that is, on 3 September 1939.

Jonah Barrington was looking out from his workplace, a primitive hut in which was installed privately-owned radio receiving station equipment. *Radio Towers,* near Leatherhead, was some 35 miles to the northeast of Midhurst. Jonah was a leading British journalist who had been directed to listen for any breaking news he could get from foreign radio broadcasts to use in his employer's newspaper. His fuller story is covered later in this book; he had an unexpected link to Midhurst.

In his field of view from that hut is a remarkable sight. Jonah writes:

"And then the B.B.C. announcement - Chamberlain to speak at 11 a.m. So, it had come! I walked across the field and stared out across the fifteen miles of clear air to London - the capital which, in a few hours' time might be burning from end to end. And then my heart turned over! For there, in the sky, motionless and noiseless above the city, and outlining the city's contours, was what appeared to be a gigantic oval field of white, shimmering thistledown . . ., [like in Fig. 1.1], - hundreds of them - glinting in the morning sun! The sight, so long expected and yet so utterly unexpected, brought a lump to the throat. A great city at bay! Defenceless, probably, down below, yet so gaily and gallantly defenceless . . . Barrage balloons - pennons of modern warfare." Barrington (1948)

Fig.1.1 Squad getting a barrage balloon under control. Dame Laura Knight's famous painting *Balloon Site at Coventry*, (Imperial War Museum)

An oval layout of balloons could be safely flown over to drop bombs on London so a clearly visible ring shape was never implemented. Instead, the balloons were located in a random pattern, thus looking like many thistle seed-bods would be in a field, Christopher (2004).

The first book of these Midhurst WW2 memoirs started when my mother was staring, with sheer amazement and fright, at Crystal Palace burning in late 1936. That must surely have been the worst fire she would ever witness in her life.

Now, however, in a few short years, the whole of central London might soon be engulfed in fire and destruction brought about by a madman in Germany - Adolf Hitler.

How did the world get to this hapless state of affairs in a few short years? The Great War of 1914-1915 had been said to be the 'war to end wars'. The League of Nations had been created specifically to stop this sort of situation happening; by keeping the Peace across Europe.

WW2 did not start in September 1939; that was when Britain entered it. Germany, Japan, and Italy were already well into warfare, as will be explained below.

The Second World War had been festering ever since WW1 ended. This second book looks into the forces at play during the 1930s and how the Evil players were growing their capacity and experience to make war; comparing that with the life of those living in the sleepy, beautiful, Midhurst Rural District that was also being caught up in the conflict as it prepared for such a contingency during that 30s decade.

World War Two is far too complex, and extensive, to report in detail. Here we develop an overview that helps to understand its protagonists. Then we can look into how it impacted the Midhurst District. Along the way, some accounts are given of lives and endeavours of individuals who were right up close to the way Hitler was acting to create his vision of how the world should be.

It is suggested that well over 60,000 books have been published about WW2, and they keep coming. Wikipedia's *WW2 Portal* lists the pathways into a staggering amount of material.

In my learning journey of life, I was fortunate to visit Professor R V Jones at his home university in Aberdeen; that was in 1967. I only knew of him as an outstanding scientist, me then being a just-completed

Chapter 1 Storm Clouds are Forming

PhD student, in the same science and engineering field as RV.

Upon entering his room on campus, I saw very extensive bookshelves packed to capacity with books about WW2 - all round the room, from floor to ceiling. This colonial bumpkin just had to ask why RV was interested in the topic.

His reply took me aback for it showed my total ignorance of recent history. "Yes", he said. Being the Assistant Director of Intelligence (Science) for the British War Office he had been actively involved at the coal face of British 'secret' knowledge on the operations being directed in the war bunkers of power. Due to that experience, he was constantly being asked to review books.

An appreciation is essential for the key events that inexorably led to this great time of change for the world. Our need here is to paint the background situation, with examples, that relate to the life and times of my life then; and how the war years impacted those of the Midhurst District as the conflict made its cruel way across the world after September 1939.

Loss of life in WW2 was staggering; 300,000 British armed forces personnel did not return from active overseas war service.

Many more did not even need to leave Britain to lose their lives. For example, some 500 men and women were killed as the result of their service in Balloon Command, operating the barrage balloons for the protection of London and other major cities in Britain. Civilians killed numbered around 43,000 in the 1940 Blitz on London, and that was the situation in but one of many areas across the rest of Britain, wherein civilians died from enemy action, Hill (2010).

Midhurst District residents made local WW2 sacrifices with some 30 people being killed by air-raids on Midhurst and Petworth. However, their personal, direct experience of the effects of the war was initially more like being in a mist of war hovering around, with seemingly little to worry about.

The glorious British Empire, with the enormous strength of its Commonwealth, was constantly telling itself, and the world, it was all-powerful in a benevolent manner. It was a period of *Pax Britannica (British Peace):* Britain was keeping relative peace between the Great

Powers of the times in the role of a global police force, Fig.1.2.

Fig. 1.2 The British Empire kept the Peace for the World during the 1930s.

It could afford to be complacent, or at least it thought it could! The mood seems to have been that as the build-up of Nazism was not happening in direct view, it could be left to the Europeans to sort out their problems. It would not spread to British soil or its Commonwealth possessions!

Ronnie Boxall (see Ch. 9 in Book 1) wrote up his childhood memories in Midhurst until the summer of 1938. He says little of the sudden change from a mist of war becoming the blackening storm clouds that began to hit the home front from 1936 onward.

Adults were being told of the changes taking place in Germany via newspapers, radio, and even for some on television; for those with this, still experimental, wondrous magic box.

The older generation must have been most concerned about a large war brewing but they would have dismissed the short reports on how the Nazis were changing German life under a dictatorship. The reports coming into those in Britain could not be true. Britain was so strong that they could not be challenged!

The major problem for the Western nations of the 1930-33 period was mass unemployment. Numerous working-class people lived in fear of hunger, cold, ill-health and, the worst, ingrained despondency. Would it ever get better? How could it, when the debt of WW1 and other factors had left Britain with a huge financial deficit?

"You can't command the spirit of hope in which anything has got to be created, with that dull evil cloud of unemployment hanging over you," Orwell

Fig. 1.3 Hunger march of unemployed men, somewhere in Britain c1935. (Telegraph, 4 Dec.)

The *Local Histories* web-site reports that in 1933 unemployment had risen to 1 in 4 being out of work, see Fig. 1.3. However, things did start to improve! As was happening in Germany with great economic effect, preparing for war and the slow climb out of the Depression resulted in improved employment figures dropping from a maximum of 22% in 1932, to 14% in 1936, and 10% in 1939.

The threat of war started another boom time need for the production of materials and men and women to fashion them. Living standards rose from 10% of people being at a subsidence level to 4% in 1936.

As we have seen in Book 1, Midhurst was one of those places with destitute people. During the mid-1930s, improvements in housing standards were happening in the town; but not in all villages and hamlets of the Midhurst District.

This declining situation in the Western World had been brewing for decades. It was not helped toward peace by the conditions imposed on Germany by the Armistice that ended WW1. The German Imperial

Command had no option but to accept the terms given to them for by the time they agreed to stop fighting they had few bargaining chips left.

The ensuing peace, resulting from the *Treaty of Versailles* imposed by the Allies, was punitive to the extreme. Its first step, the signing of the Armistice ending WW1, was signed in the Compiegne Forest in Northern France in November 1918.

It took 6 months to thrash out an acceptable treaty wording and in it, took a most vengeful approach to Germany. It had caused WW1 so it would pay dearly! There was no room then in political thinking for consideration of how Germany would be able to rise from its ashes to be a peace abiding nation with its dignity restored.

The terms presented to the Germans are today, seen as being poorly chosen in many important ways. They were used as the way to, presumably, subjugate any more world leadership ambitions of the German nation. The Treaty carried political implications.

US President, Woodrow Wilson, wrote:

'If the Government of the United States must deal with the military masters and the monarchical autocrats of Germany now, or if it is likely to have to deal with them later in regard to the international obligations of the German Empire, it must demand not peace negotiations but surrender'

By 1918 the German nation had used up all its material and human resources to the point where life there had become abysmal for all of its people - civil and military. That country was decimated in all respects. The Allies had no well worked out plans for rebuilding a stable new Germany that harmonised with its neighbours. People of that country were left to it, to find a way back to prosperity from such a parlous state.

Reparation dictates were very harsh. The 34 terms included:

- Removal of German troop and armaments presence from all occupied countries and colonies.
- Surrender of its remaining war machine including all railway stock.
- Renunciation of all treaties it had made.

- Release of French, British and Italian prisoners of war, but not German POWs until later - they were needed to work on restitution projects.

The Germans were not permitted any voice in the treaty development and, when they would not accept the terms, they were threatened with a return to war.

They also would not accept the *War Guilt* clause as it was too humiliating and made them out to be fully responsible for that war.

Little was left to them with which to rebuild a nation. They also had lost their few overseas colonies, that had been providing them with the many essential resources they lacked within their landmass. The situation built up massive resentment throughout the decimated population. We will explore their civilian situation in the next sections.

WW1 did not turn out to be 'a war to end all wars'. Far from it. Once the Treaty of Versailles was signed, troops and civilians on both sides were not inclined to celebrate for long: everyone had lost significant things and gained little from the immense loss of life and human dignity.

That festering mood provided the foundation for Hitler to come to total dictatorial power in 1933, promising his people a 1000 year Third Reich of great standing and glorious developments. It was, indeed, very attractive to the German people.

To see how his power was rising in Germany, it is sobering to now consider two opposite views on how the vanquished Germans and the unwanted Jewish people were coping.

1.2 Early Experiences as a German

As the internal German politics developed under the Nazi party set up by Hitler, it was those living close to the home situation in Germany who were coming to see the totalitarian and anti-Semitic stance being rapidly adopted.

Across the German *Fatherland* in the mid-30s, German lives were coming under threat on their very doorsteps as the result of the way the Nazis ran the country; the deteriorating social environment could be seen by simply looking out of their windows!

One post-war Midhurst town resident knew a lot about the post-WW1 conditions in his German Fatherland. Fortunately for us, he wrote his autobiography giving us descriptions, in great detail, of his experiences as a young man. He was initially brought up to have great respect and pride in his country; but only to lose that love as time passed, Liebschner (2006).

Joachim Liebschner was born in Germany in 1925. In 2016 he passed away, in near anonymity, in Midhurst where his immediate family had lived for most of his post-war years. I was saddened to have been unable to meet him in time. His published story is picked up as these following memoirs books cover the WW2 period. Here are covered his post WW1 childhood experiences.

His father had been a musician playing the tuba in the band of the German 51st Infantry Regiment when the First World War erupted. He served as Red Cross bearer field medic, in which capacity he was awarded the Iron Cross for valour under fire.

As a child before WW2, Joachim's family lived in a typical town flat situated in 3, or 4, storey buildings. Each floor housed 2 flats. He was brought up to appreciate honour, courage, gentleness, and have respect and wholesome pride in being a German.

From this background, for instance, he believed that local families assisted each other in keeping their collective building clean and bright. His family's two-bedroom flat was home for his parents and their four boys. They were cramped quarters, but compared with many others he lived quite well.

He especially remembered his days in primary school, Fig. 1.4, led by schoolmaster Lehrer Kade who instilled in the children that all people deserve to be respected:

> 'He was a man of the highest integrity, in command of a wide range of knowledge, he genuinely cared about his homeland, the plants and living creatures, the grown-ups and the children.' Liebschner (2006)

Joachim lived in Leignitz, which is now (again) part of Poland, being then known by one of its earlier names *Legnica*. That area has had many changes of nationality over its tumultuous history.

Chapter 1 Storm Clouds are Forming

It became part of the German Empire when Germany undertook unification in 1871.

Fig.1.4 Primary School class in 1931. Joachim is the top row, fifth from the left. Liebschner (2006).

The Treaty of Versailles had resulted in this essentially German town being part of the newly created Province of Lower that remained as such from 1919-1938. Joachim's family were Germans!

During the early 1930s, Joachim's formative years, even in their small 55,000 inhabitant city, changes were being implemented in the country by this man Herr Hitler. It soon became clear, to all who opened their eyes even a little, to see that he was not honouring the principles of living that Joachim and his parents had been practising.

Boys scrapping in the street were commonplace, but to witness adult members of the Hitler movement behaving like children - with fists, sticks, and stones; it was a shock to Joachim.

Then the 7 years old Joachim was becoming confused about this movement for they acted just like thugs, not models of showing those Fatherland principles of honour.

You will probably not know that similar public behaviour by Fascists was also present, to a limited degree, in England at the time; a matter to be taken up when we look, later in this book, into their presence in Sussex and London, right up to the outbreak of WW2.

Even more startling to Joachim was the fact that these were members of the recently formed *Sturmabteilung,* (SA for short, and translated as

'Storm Department'). They wore, Fig. 1.5, neat brown shirts (hence their common name of such), shiny black boots and had short haircuts. They were very militaristic and looked most menacing.

Fig. 1.5 Brownshirts parading, as people *Heil Hitler*.

In his book, Joachim suggests that this experience was the first time he began to doubt the new regime was upholding the Fatherhood ideals he had been brought up to believe in.

His adolescent years saw the changes, but he recalled little use of teachers being used to indoctrinate school children with Nazi thinking, at least until the all-out war came. Nevertheless, it could be argued indoctrination was a subtle long-term process.

Later, we will see that many schools were indeed training boys to serve their leader as soldiers ready to die; and with girls to be mothers of babies, to also be so persuaded in use of their lives.

Joachim was an upstanding young man carrying out civic duty as expected by the Nazis of a suitable person. Boys at 10-13 joined the *Deutsches Jungvolk* (German Young People), Fig. 1.6, and then transferred to the *Hitler Jugend* (Hitler Youth) until their 18th year. They were then of the age for call-up into military service for the Führer; ready to fight for the Hitlerian idea of a Glorious Reich.

Fig. 1.6 *Jungvolk* members were being indoctrinated to be fighting soldiers.

Hitler had always seen children as most important to his ideals of the Third Reich. This was his idea for them:

Chapter 1 Storm Clouds are Forming

'The weak must be chiselled away. I want young men and women who can suffer pain. A young German must be as swift as a greyhound, as tough as leather, and as hard as Krupp's steel.'

His movement was partially modelled on the ideals of Baden-Powell's Scouting movement that started in Britain in 1907. The difference is seen in their missions. Hitler's ideal, above, differs from that of Scouting, that organisation's intentions being:

'a movement that aims to support young people in their physical, mental, and spiritual development, that they may play constructive roles in society, with a strong focus on the outdoors and survival skills.'

Around Joachim, people generally shunned being associated with the Hitler Youth movement; but that was not as all saw it. The Versailles Treaty had carved away some one-eighth of the former nation's landmass, taking a tenth of its population with it. To Joachim, the need was to 'put it right again'.

The Hitler Youth was for him; its ideals fitted his upbringing. When he was nine, in 1934, he joined the part-time activity of the Jungvolk. He had been encouraged by his brother to do this for it was all great fun.

'We held our twice-weekly meetings (in an old brickworks) sang, talked, played musical instruments, enjoyed physical and mental games, duelled with long canes instead of sabres, and planned our future activities.' (Duelling was a long-standing practice in Germany).

They attended talks on politics by their older Hitler Youth members and spent time marching and drilling. These militaristic things were, however, done under some sufferance by Joachim and his friends.

In 1933 a directive came from their new Chancellor, Herr Hitler: all should assist those in need, as was occurring with the rapid build-up of the several million unemployed; Joachim did his bit there. The rewards for this community contribution by the Jungvolk were major and impressive to him. He was still living the dream of the old German traditions.

When 14 years old he moved on: see Fig, 1.7. Hitler Jugend members became the auxiliary part of the German Army.

Fig. 1.7 "The German Student Fights for the Führer and the People".

By that time, Hitler was well into his mission of taking over local nations to create the Third Reich.

The wholesome physical activity of the Hitler Youth had become more militaristic including military skills; throwing hand grenades went with ball throwing and air rifle shooting was in. Precision marching, en masse, was also a feature.

At the outbreak of war with Germany, Joachim was still too young to be conscripted, but his experience, from his pseudo-military training with the Hitler Youth, made him ready and keen to fight for his country when he turned 18 years in 1941.

Joachim's story is of a non-Jewish German, one caught up with the Nazi ways, but less close to them in his local small town as those in the major cities were.

The published autobiography, Liebschner (2006), is of a kind, nationally proud, considerate, and 'thinking' German who made Midhurst his home sometime after the war. It sheds insight into the pre-war life of the ordinary German people in a small country town.

His school years at secondary level were not a happy time for him for they included 'experiences that filled him with dread'. He was good at the sciences and history, but languages of Latin and French were his problem subjects. Despite some additional tutoring he failed to do well

Chapter 1 Storm Clouds are Forming

overall. In his fourth year, he failed both subjects. Failure in two subjects was a reason to not proceed at school so he went into an apprenticeship. Whilst he records that much has been said about Nazi teachers 'poisoning the minds of youths' he experienced none of that himself,

His apprenticeship was with an insurance company dealing with fire, accident, and life. Whilst working there, in September 1939, the news that war had broken out had 'dazed' crowds. National papers immediately took the place of the usual French newspaper. The national papers told readers that German troops had entered Poland:

'to protect German nationals from harassment and ill-treatment by Polish citizens'

He did not appreciate what that meant but did recall the oppressive moment and fear of foreboding those around instilled in him. Much later, when writing his autobiography, he then realised the relevance of the streams of refugees they had seen during the previous month who told of 'persecutions, lootings, burning and killings' carried out against them by his countrymen.

Things then changed for everyone. The adult staff of his employer went into war service so he had to carry more responsibility.

Polish street sweepers appeared wearing the yellow band on their arms. Local newspapers became filled with little else but court cases about Jewish people in cases of fraud, illegal stock market dealings, and currency infringements.

Local Jewish bank links to British and US banks were intimated to be the reason for the German economy doing so badly; 'they were bleeding the nation white'.

Jews were banned from public office and encouraged to leave the country.

The persecution of the Jews took a big step for the worst on 9 November 1938... on the 'Night of the Broken Glass', called such as the riots against them left broken glass on the streets. Hundreds of synagogues were destroyed, along with as many shops and businesses. All over Germany, brutality against Jews was implemented by the Nazi

Midhurst WW2 Memoirs: 2. 'Evil' Rising: 'Good' Awakening

Fig. 1.8 Synagogue burning; buildings around were hosed, but not this one.

paramilitary, and also the many taken-in German citizens who took to the streets to fire up fear and hate toward the Jews at large.

Joachim, at the age of 13 years, was at home at the time with a broken arm and had not been to school that day. In the evening he saw, in the distance, the lights of burning shops and the local synagogue.

Hitler had given orders that if civil disorder broke out no one was to intervene. Fire engines were not put to use; the fires burned. The German morning News explained that a diplomat, Ernst Vom Rath, had been shot in Paris (see Chapter 7.1) by a Jew and that German people were enraged to the point of burning synagogues.

Elsewhere in the world newspapers flashed scenes of this happening along with headlines such as that of *The New York Times*:

'NAZIS SMASH, LOOT, AND BURN JEWISH SHOPS AND TEMPLES UNTIL GOEBBELS CALLS HALT'.

These continuous lies by the Nazi regime were excuses for ever-increasing escalation in the persecution of the Jews. The deaths of Jews increased in many fields of misery - privation, suicide, murder by civilians and the military, and in the concentration and work camps that were increasingly being established at that stage to provide forced labour to support the German war machine and the building of Hitler's civil works toward his new *Germania* city.

Of the next-door Jewish family to Joachim, they left one night never to be heard of again. They might have been lucky enough to have been given an hour's notice to pack a small suitcase before being taken to the German border and told to leave the country. They may instead have been sent to work camps; hopefully, they escaped all that. The work camps were shown in the films seen by the German populace as being

Chapter 1 Storm Clouds are Forming

reasonably furnished, had libraries, flower and vegetable gardens, and even their orchestras. Joachim recalls these films and found it hard not to believe they were as it was.

We do not have a photograph of Joachim at the age of 13, but there is one, Fig. 1.9, of him in charge of a Hitler Youth camp at 16 years old.

Fig. 1.9 Joachim Liebschner, centre rear, age 16, with his Youth camp colleagues.
Liebschner (2006)

At the camp, they would have enjoyed the companionship and fun, along with a not so obvious undercurrent of being groomed to suit Hitler's ambitions. One has to wonder how many of this group of bright-eyed lads survived the war without serious harm.

> 'Great ambition is the passion of a great character. Those endowed with it may perform very good, or very bad acts. All depends on the principles which direct them'. Napoleon Bonaparte

Despite all of the unusual and horrific activity seen at the time it had not sunk into Joachim's mind that the invasion of Poland was not the good and noble action they were reading about in the newspapers.

In 1939 Joachim joined the Hitler Youth; he was 14 years old. For all that he had, by then, seen and heard, he was still keen to join the German army to serve his Fatherland. He tried to join up by increasing his age but they soon sent him home to wait. It was not until 1942 that he would be called up to military service - just before he was to turn 18 years old.

His active service experience is for Book 3 covering the start of his fighting part of Hitler's war. We leave this account of his childhood formation with a clear idea of how the Nazi-led nation was grooming physical fitness, leadership, basic military skills, and inbuilt obedience into the youth to make them ready for war-making (not defence!); and for great reverence for their leader.

In stark contrast at that time, the children of Britain had not had prior indoctrination on how to fight for 'or to believe they were part of a great mission to rebuild their mighty nation and follow a power-hungry leader. Their childhood formation was concerned with living in a democracy where the people made their decisions in a Parliament of elected representatives.

German children had a quite different formation; they subsequently manned the massive German Army. They had been led to believe that a dictatorship was the best way to decide every aspect of their lives.

Whilst children in 1930s Britain played with daisy-chains and skipped hopscotch, those of Germany spent their time getting superbly fit and trained ready to die for the great cause.

More is given about this process for creating fighting German soldiers from early childhood in the following chapter on Nazi Germany.

Now we need a contrasting account of life in pre-war Germany. We find that with a lad who was not at all enamoured with the idea of a Third Reich. His family was Jewish!

1.3 The Feuchtwanger Family Suffer Antisemitism

Another account, of considerable difference to that of Joachim Liebschner, details the childhood of Edgar Feuchtwanger. His record of Germany of the 1930s paints the situation of people who saw themselves as Germans, but who was soon to be persecuted to the limit because they were of Jewish descent. In 1933 there were 500,000 Jewish people with German citizenship in the overall population of 67 million.

Edgar had been born in 1924, a year before Joachim. He lived, not in the rural areas but some 500 miles from him, in a major city of Germany. His family lived in Munich having been in Germany for a century before; they were German Jews. His family was very successful in publishing and authorship so he was well known in Germany. They enjoyed a very good life and truly felt they were German.

Surprisingly, Edgar lived in a fine flat opposite 16 Prinzregentenplatz in Munich. Why be so specific? Opposite their home was the private flat

Chapter 1 Storm Clouds are Forming

of Hitler; he had moved there when Edgar was 5 years old, Fig.1.10.

Fig. 1.10 Hitler's apartment, as it is today, was rented in this building in Munich.

Edgar saw him regularly and may have spoken to him. His story is published in French but has been made into a YouTube documentary film *Hitler was my Neighbour.*

What we are to consider here is how the life of Jewish people in Germany changed very much for the worse.

In 1928 the emerging Nazis, led by Hitler, only managed to get some 3% of the vote in the Reichstag's parliamentary elections; that was just 12 seats. His party did not gain any power at that first attempt.

Hitler had published in 1925 *Mein Kampf* (My Struggle), laying bare his ambitions and plans for a 'New Order' in Germany. Despite being an insignificant man with little charisma and few skills, he was so sure he would rise to power.

By the use of numerous methods, many not acceptable to a large part of the German citizens, plus being buoyed up by the plight of the German people at the time, he rapidly achieved the ultimate where he, and he alone, was able to do what he liked with a major nation of the time – as its absolute dictator.

The effects of the USA's, 10 year long Great depression, flowed into Germany in 1929. Hitler had been promising solutions to the severe level of unemployment that had risen from 650,000 to 6,000,000 over 3 years. By 1930 his party had won 107 seats in the national parliament to become the second most powerful, and feared, presence in ruling the country.

The bulk of people in Germany and across the world considered his ideas and success would be short-lived. His ideas and methods were so far-fetched and abhorrent! The wealthy class in Germany did not expect Hitler to become their Fuhrer as a tyrannical leader. He was grossly underestimated. 'Who was this little man' they must have asked!

So often people realised, too late, what could evolve from the many terrible things Hitler was doing as he made life increasingly intolerable for Jews and other unwanted minority groups of people. He wanted to get a super-race in place as soon as possible, for that was a need of his Third Reich. Natural birth was a slow way to get there. Ridding Germany of his unwanted people, by any means, was a relatively quick first step!

Edgar Feuchtwanger recalls, in his film, the brutal manner of that political party with its violent bullying presence infiltrating every walk of a life that once had been free, dependable, and honourable.

His brother, Lion, was one of the first to recognise and warn against the dangers of Hitler and the Nazi party. His constant criticism of Nazi methods was eventually recognised by a 1974 postage stamp, Fig. 1.11.

Fig.1.11 East German stamp in memory of Lion Feuchtwanger.

Well before the Nazis came to absolute power, Lion wrote books that portrayed how the future of Germany might become. He wrote of this around 1920:

'Towers of Hebrew books were burned, and bonfires were erected high up in the clouds, and people burnt, innumerable priests and voices sang: Gloria in Excelsis Deo. Traits of men, women, children dragged themselves across the square from all sides, they were naked or in rags, and they had nothing with them as corpses

Chapter 1 Storm Clouds are Forming

and the tatters of book rolls of torn, disgraced, soiled with faeces and they followed men and women in kaftans and dressed the children in our day, countless, endless.' [in places this quote is 'corrected']

Despite constantly attracting increasing Nazi attention, he again wrote prophetic words in a book, Feuchtwanger (1925), based on the real-life of an 18th century, much corrupted, person of the German nobility.

It was written about 1916, but not released then, as a play study of the 'human weaknesses of greed, pride and ambition and where all of that might lead'. A film was made of it in the English language in 1934.

Being aimed against the long-standing establishment it was, incredibly, taken by the embryonic Nazis in 1925 to be aiming at the anti-Semitic movement actions, then gaining a considerable following in Germany.

Later, in 1940, Hitler's propagandist, Hermann Goebbels, used this very story in his propaganda campaigns, but then rewriting it, Fig.1.12, as that person being a Jew who stealthily and corruptively, wheedled his way up the ladder of leadership to become the leader of the Jews taking over that country.

Fig. 1.12 *Jud Süß* poster. The worst antisemitic film made by the Nazis, 1940.

It was said to be the most heinous film ever made attacking the Jews. It was a great hit with the much mind-muddled German audience, making a huge profit from its box office! The YouTube version is 90 minutes long; and very frightening to watch!

By 1929 Lion considered the Nazi party to be a spent entity and in 1930 he published another book, *(Success* in English), Feuchtwanger (1930), that was about real life in Germany, masked behind a facade of fiction.

This was about the state of Bavaria in the 1930s; it covered the political rise of a fictional character Rupert Kutzner, (that is, Hitler!) who created a party of 'true' Germans.

Bertold Brecht, possibly influenced by Lion Feuchtwanger's works, also later wrote a play like this in 1941, Brecht (1981). His opposition to Hitler's movement is covered in the following Book 3.

The *Erfolg* book is large and complex and a challenge to read. If you were living in that environment then, you would have seen the numerous parallels taking place that were covered throughout the work.

> 'It was a contemporary roman à clef, a novel of a gloriously liberal but doomed Weimar Republic moving inexorably toward fascism. Published just three years before Hitler's rise to power, the novel is not only prophetic of Germany's, but uncanny in its multi-level depiction of the corruptive process'
> http://biography.yourdictionary.com/lion-feuchtwanger.

> 'constitutes a conspectus of Germany in the 1920s, brilliantly dissecting the private and public tensions that were building to a national crisis and, ultimately, to a European calamity.'

> 'Hitler is represented in the novel as a character named Rupert Kutzner, leader of a lunatic-fringe right-wing group whose power grows and moves centre-ward as ministers and industrialists find the group useful.'

As would be expected, by what we now know was happening in Nazi Germany, Lion's book again attracted Hitler's attention! When Hitler became Chancellor in 1933, Fig. 1.13, one of his first tasks was to strip Lion of his German citizenship.

Fig.1.13 Hitler appointed Chancellor in 1933. Absolute power!

Chapter 1 Storm Clouds are Forming

By pure chance, Lion was in the USA (still not at war then with Germany) when this happened; he returned to Germany to find his assets confiscated by the Nazis.

He fled to France but was taken to a concentration camp in 1940. Escape to the USA came when he disguised himself as a woman. During his wartime period in the USA, he produced more novels about how leaders, like the Nazis, swindled Jews in all manner of ways.

Remarkably. the Feuchtwanger family members all survived the war. Lion died in Los Angeles in 1958. Edgar appears to be still alive.
Another close friend of the family who suffered under the Nazis was Michael. It was not long after Hitler gained absolute power in 1933 that the Brown Shirts began serious public humiliation of Jews.

A famous picture. Fig. 1.14, that circulated the world press of the time, was of the lawyer, Michael Siegel, being marched along the street in his underwear carrying a placard over his shoulders that read:

'I am a Jew and I will never again complain to the police.'

Michael had gone to the police to complain about the conditions imposed on a client! The globally distributed photograph truly alerted the world to what Hitler's regime was becoming. The signs were there, but no country had the will at that stage to try to stop Hitler's ambition.

Fig.1.14 Lawyer Michael Siegel being forced marched in a street in Munich, 1933

All of these incidents almost certainly meant another war, that was just not wanted at that time. We will see in the next Chapter that many brave individuals were prepared to give their lives resisting the new order in Germany.

1.4 Deterioration of World Order

The deterioration in world order was not due to the situation in Germany alone. A stable world of individual sovereign countries was existing in reasonable harmony but the concept of - 'we are doing this to you for your own good!' was the way it had been for centuries for those under oppression, even still existing in the more liberated 1930s. By the early 20th century the immorality of this, however, was emerging. Colonised countries wanted their freedom back and were acting on that.

How this all came about has been well explained by Dr Christopher Clark, an Australian working in England. He headed up the 2018, 6-part TV series, *The Story of Europe*. Part 3, *Ambitions and Conquests,* covers the state of play by various European political ambitions.

From the earliest days, men have known what they should aim for in society. As early as 1776, in the of the foundling USA, the concept was recorded that 'all men are created equal'; but it was not always driven to be for all men; to wit, the situation of the slaves taken from Africa to the US.

Restorative morality toward human dignity, as a right, was slowly being realised before the 30s decade, but the ongoing poor conditions of people's lives provided the social setting for a few strong dictatorial, power-hungry, leaders to gain sole leadership.

With their own, much worse, forms of imperialism they instituted systems of control that were forced, often under threat of death, causing people to do what was wanted of them to realise the personal desires of the few fanatical leaders.

For example, in 1884-5, European Heads of State met at the West African Conference, held in Berlin; they were there to divide up the remaining side of Africa that had not then been colonised by a European country. Needless to say, the Africans affected were not invited! This is when the Germans were emerging and wanting their colonies; just to be like the others!

The competitive nature of this colonisation was a constant source

Chapter 1 Storm Clouds are Forming

of minor war-making. It may appear to have solved the discordant situation, but in the longer term, it led to Hitler's and Mussolini's ideas of conquest.

Looking back now it may, at that time, have been a plausible reason for world powers to state they were helping their colonised countries to enjoy a better life with their kind of government rule. History, however, shows that by this decade many of these European states were having their power over their colonies seriously contested.

By the middle of the 1930s, the World was moving most certainly toward deep inter-country problems. Another world war could not be ruled out.

So how did it come to World War II?

On top of the social decline, another unintentional and largely unforeseen evil was about to burst forth to hasten the work of the Devil.

Wikipedia summarises the 30s decade as follows:

'After the Wall Street Crash of 1929, the largest stock market crash in American history, most of the decade was consumed by an economic downfall called 'The Great Depression' that had a traumatic effect worldwide.

In response, authoritarian regimes emerged in several countries in Europe, in particular, the Third Reich in Germany. Weaker states such as Ethiopia, China, and Poland were invaded by expansionist world powers, ultimately leading to World War II by the decade's end.'

The reasons for Germany taking the course it did following its humiliating defeat in WW1, have been explained in Strachan (2014).

The victors had behaved appallingly. They had stripped the German people - just pawns in their leader's plans - of their dignity. Their centuries-old, homeland heritage had been divided up. They were left with only a meagre national resource with which to rebuild their everyday lifestyle and global standing.

After that war, they were ready to follow any leader who had a grand plan for restoring their prior greatness! Vengeance by the victors on everyone in the population was not needed at that time. Fig.1.15 is an expression of the result of the treaty. Britain and her partners are carving

up Germany into parts and shredding its dignity.

Fig.1.15 Decimating the dignity of the 1920s German nation was not the way to go.

Social conditions were then fertile growing fields of discontent. Anyone who offered a plausible solution to their plight and resurrection of the nation – such as the Third Reich - would find strong favour with their people, who were then close to starving and living in very poor conditions.

Terms in the Armistice agreement were very harsh when considering the political and social state of Europe. The humiliation alone spawned many of the vanquished to become the most barbarous Nazi leaders.

It was not well enough understood at that time that the victorious nations needed to consider the effect that a subjugated Germany would have on future nations who were involved. Being vindictive and revengeful has now been seen to not be appropriate if the victorious need long term peace.

The First World War led to the creation of the *League of Nations* (LN), charged with preventing war by the peaceful intervention. Unfortunately, its toothlessness being to the 'left', showed that harsh regimes can be effective. The brutality and carnage of harsh authoritarian regimes do work for the higher ideals, but they usually regard human life as a dispensable item to be sacrificed for the better good of the whole.

At the time of the armistice, Frenchman Marshall Ferdinand Foch,

Chapter 1 Storm Clouds are Forming

a highly respected military theorist, declared that because Germany was allowed to stay as one united country, the war would come about again.

'This is not peace. It is an armistice for twenty years.'

He was out with that prediction by only 65 days. Post-war, the civilians suffered as much as soldiers, especially in the German-held territories. The Germans had far less access to resources than the Allies.

The 1914-1919 British naval blockades of German shipping traffic, from the tip of Cornwall to north-eastern Scotland, led to a massive need to find every available resource in the Axis controlled countries. So much was stripped; many of the people were forced to live at starvation levels. To make matters worse there were major crop failures and more severe than normal, winters. Farm animals and seeds were eaten, leading to diminished production.

Starvation and poorly controlled disease led to high levels of deaths and much privation in the countries involved. This situation was still in force when rebuilding began after WW1. People easily flocked to authoritarian regimes that declared they could lead the people to prosperity again by bringing in major developments.

In the UK, some of this situation was experienced during WW1 when farms were vacated by their men, and women were pushed into harsh work conditions in munitions factories and other war tasks.

Gradually those in power, and under them, on both sides of the long and bloody conflict, realised the uselessness of the war. A great groundswell at home, and in the trenches, indicated their desire for the war to end.

The leaders, however, on both sides wanted to keep squeezing their populations even more. The German High Command was too proud to stop warring; the Allied leaders wanted to make sure that opposition was totally crushed.

Near the end of WW1 manufacture of war machine products, and killing on the war fronts, were still more important to the leaders than the overall welfare of the people fighting for their lives and existence.

Ultimately Germany had only paid about an eighth of its war

reparations - around £1 billion - when they were suspended in 1932. The failure of major banks in Germany and Austria in 1931 had worsened the worldwide banking crisis.

In the midst of all this, my tiny part in the story starts. I was born in 1937. The 30s decade set the scene that moulded the circumstances of my earliest formative years and the lives of countless millions of people.
    Unlike many of the other kids born at that time I was one of the lucky ones, for although living rather close to some of the enemy actions of World War 2, I narrowly missed its devastating effects. There were some close shaves for our family.

We need to develop an understanding of the mood of the nations and the common peoples in the 30s; it has relevance to memoirs of the Midhurst District.

1.5 Enter Stage Front - Evil.

The time came when *Good* was forced to battle *Evil* of great strength, initially on the latter's terms.
    The portrayal of *Good* vs. *Evil* as an image if not easy to create: many visual artists have tried. These will be based on various belief systems and are, therefore, different. Darth Vader and Luke Sky Walker, locked in a laser sword battle, will spring to mind to some.
    In Christian terms, it is *Christ* versus the *Devil*. The image, Fig. 1.16, sums it up well in my mind. This is a mood in which peoples of Britain and other countries lived during the 1930s and the WW2 period of 1939-1945.

Fig.1.16 Depiction of the Battle between *Good* and *Evil*

In WW1 the combatant countries had grouped into

Chapter 1 Storm Clouds are Forming

the Good side, the *Allied Powers,* with those that fought against them being the Evil grouping, the *Central Powers.* In WW2 these became the *Allies* and the *Axis* powers. There exist rules of war - the G*eneva Convention* - that was supposed to give guidance of humane activities, but these were greatly ignored in WW2 by the Axis.

In both wars, some countries declared themselves *neutral* powers. The *rules of war* defined their behaviour. If they were not occupied by an *Evil* country against their will, it was not so much because of international law, but the fact that it suited the likely invaders to keep them in that state.

A perfect state of Goodness seems to be impossible for society; it was certainly often blurred at times in the 1930s and 1940s when the distinction, in global country terms, between the combatant nations was relatively easy. The partner countries of each side settled out as we shall soon see.

Do you want the *Evil* news or the *Good* news first? How would one decide in what group a country fit? I choose based on which country went to war with the goodness of the global family at heart and did not suppress their own people in horrific ways.

Let's start with the state of *Evil* in the world for it explains why people in Britain and elsewhere had eventually come to see that another world war was unavoidable and that they were well and truly trapped as participants on the *Good* side.

One expression of this is from the Adelaide *Advertiser*, South Australia, 7 May 1938:

'The age in which we live has been described as "the most impersonal in history". In the nineteenth century, a Swinburne [an exceptional person] could sing "Glory to man in the highest" for thus he saluted the triumphs of scientific discovery and the blessings which applied science had showered on a grateful world. The mood of the twentieth century is very different. The cynics of this generation are more inclined to echo Swift's description of human beings as "the most odious little vermin that ever crawled on the face of the earth". One might almost say that we are dwelling in an iron cage. Persons seem to be at the mercy of processes. We are the victims of the mechanisms we have ourselves created. The individual appears to be no more than a cog in the machine or a unit in the mass.'

The 30s decade is remembered for being the 'swinging thirties', an age of relaxing social standards, of greater freedom of expression, and of the 'upstairs' and 'downstairs' societal divide beginning to break down toward more equality. At the same time, general living conditions had fallen.

Thinking about the daily diet of bad news delivered to those in Britain, as Germany was making its heavy stamp on Europe, the trends of that era would seem to have been more about finding a means for gaining consolation for, and ability to cope with, the issues of the times.

The reality was that a small handful of madmen had decided to take over parts of the world to fulfil their evil dreams of personal greatness and restored empires.

Due to lack of interest and slow acceptance by the *Good* side that war would come, the *Evil* ones were able to make considerable progress before the elements of *Good* finally prevailed!

It is thus necessary to describe how things were on the world stage that was deciding how people lived, despite what they might have desired.

This chapter mainly uses Wikipedia sources to achieve its basic description. It is not claimed to be a scholarly account of the history of the 30s but presents facts to show how large proportions of the world were caught up in a highly twisted and complex moral decline that seemed to be unavoidable.

To me, as I write, a question of interest is how might that have affected myself and other children when I joined this world in 1937.

By the 1930s bitter memories, some so bad that they could not be spoken of by many in the First World War, remained with citizens all over Britain, the British Empire, the USA, and the nations in Europe.

Minds were still raw with the horrors of the Great War and its needless massive loss of human life. So many families lost sons, fathers,

Chapter 1 Storm Clouds are Forming

and uncles. Some aristocratic estates lost almost all of their 'in-service' male staff. Hamlets, villages, towns, and cities lost population ranging over both the common people and the privileged classes.

That this did happen cannot - indeed, must not - be forgotten. We constantly come across many WW1 memorials found in numerous places, from Whitehall down to the smallest of hamlets; from the cities to the tiniest bush towns in Australia and other British Empire countries. In Midhurst, the main war memorial is on Church Hill.

Fig.1.17 Every 1930s home had its set of WW1 history books.

In the 1930s many British homes had a set of leather-bound volumes recording the gory history of the Great War that had ended a decade and a half before.

They, Fig. 1.17, were full of images that were hard to accept by the faint-hearted. Thank goodness they were edited and not rendered in full colour! The pictures were quite unbelievable to those who had not been there. I read some of these volumes in my early teens. They left dreadful images in my mind!

It is now time to appreciate the nature of those major nations involved in this global conflict. The worst of the *Evil* nations are covered first - Germany.

Chapter 2. Nazi Germany: The First Arch Enemy of Britain

2.1 Germany

From time to time I include references to videos available on the Internet, to gain background about a very complex global situation. A good thing to do at this stage is to view the 135 minutes run of Episode 1 *Inside World War II*, a 2012 TV movie by Kristen Akers and Nicolas Zimmerman. Its introduction states:

> 'Firsthand accounts of World War II are shared in this documentary, which includes archival footage and more than 50 testimonies from American, British, German and Soviet service members.'

The German nation that took to war in the late 1930s had a population of some 66 million people in 1935.

The, as yet to be properly identified, arch-enemy devil of mankind that burst forth before this time was Herr Adolf Hitler. His climb to being a dictator had been going on for many years.

To most of his people, he was their saviour; their leader in a climb back to again being a great nation. Each year they assembled, en masse, to hear him speak at his annual Nuremberg Rallies. One estimate suggests that around 1 million children and adults were involved in the 1937 rally.

Fig. 2.1 1935 'Come to Germany' travel poster.

Midhurst WW2 Memoirs: 2. 'Evil' Rising: 'Good' Awakening

To the outside world publicity drives by the famous Thomas Cook's travel company and others, Fig. 2.1, were in place to attract people to holiday in Germany from overseas. It all seemed to be going so well!

A useful, recent, account of how this the evil came into being, apparently without serious notice in other countries, is Boyd (2018). The book surveys the life of local people and tourists to that country. In 1937 Hitler was at the zenith of his popularity. Many aristocrats in Britain then also admired his achievements, pushing for working relationships with such a great and emerging country.

There was, however, another side to this that had been developing since the 1920s. Herr Hitler seized upon the declining global situation to support his empire-building intentions, eventually taking the German nation to complete disintegration over 20 years - along with several millions of souls of his own, and many other nations.

Fig. 2.2 Adolf Hitler; early Party Day held in Nuremberg, 1927. (Orbis)

Fig. 2.2 shows him giving his infamous *Heil* salute. This picture was taken at his third, Party Day, 1927 annual Nuremberg Rally. It shows a march past of his *Sturmabteilung* Brownshirts. This group had been formed in 1920 to guard, and bully meetings, having developed out of the

Chapter 2. Nazi Germany: The First Arch Enemy of Britain

prior *Freikorps*; 'illegal' right-winger military units that came together after WW1 to combat communist uprisings and defend the German borders. Its membership was far from controlled and lacked discipline, Snyder (1998).

Hitler's ideas for global governance were already well exposed and published in the two volumes of his book, *Mein Kampf,* Hitler (1925, 1926). In these, he explained his anti-Semitic views and justifications, whilst expounding the concept of a glorious *Greater Germanic Reich* of the German Nation - the Third Reich to last at least 1000 years.

His long-term plan was to make the European area a huge Reich with only cleansed persons in it of Aryan descent; long head and blond hair. To him, all others had "lost their sense of racial pride". He admired the Spartans who, with just 7,000 men, were said to have held back an estimated 150,000 Persian Army men at the pass of Thermopylae in 480BC. They were eventually outflanked, leaving a small force to guard their retreat, fighting to the death of the last man.

In the 1930s there existed a highly fashionable 'science' exploring which race had the highest intelligence and then, what factors gave them that ability. Hitler believed these were the ancestors of those with the right kind of German blood.

One eminent British scientist declared, in an early 1900s book on the knowledge of science, that it was the cold and a darker climate of the region that allowed the Europeans to excel at high science discovery in the 19th century. He compared them with peoples from the hot climates, such as in Africa. This kind of racial argument was put up in all sincerity by many eminent people of the time. Hitler just picked it up to suit his arguments.

The Jewish peoples have long been singled out by society. As well as the records of numerous assaults on them that are recorded in the Old Testament Bible, actions against them in these last two millennia are to be found in the Christian Crusades of the 11th century, and many times after that. Anti-Semitic ideas had become strong in the German national thinking before the turn of the 19th century.

His declared ideas about the Jews were not all Hitler's. Evidence of this intended brutal conquest starting up with its anti-Semitic aspect, was seen in the cruel writings of the *Jewish Peril,* Nilus (1920). On face value this hateful document, Fig. 2.3, seems to be a truly startling document about the Jews, supposedly working for world domination.

Fig. 2.3 A cover of *The Jewish Peril: Protocols of the Learned Elders of Zion*.

Another pictorial depiction of the situation portrayed is that of a mythical serpent circling the earth in an ever-tightening squeeze.

This document was first published, in parts, in a Russian newspaper in 1903. Thereafter, numerous authors became involved with views of its authenticity ranging from total debunking it as a very cleverly fabricated conspiracy fraud, to those supporting it as 'fact' that can be always, somehow, be aligned to world events since then. It is said to be:

> 'the minutes of a late 19th-century meeting where Jewish leaders discussed their goal of global Jewish hegemony by subverting the morals of Gentiles, and by controlling the press and the world's economies.' This version from Wikipedia; others exist.

In 1920, it was researched extensively by *The Times* newspaper proving that its structure, and numerous parts, could be attributed to the existing fictional writings of many earlier, well-known, authors. It was declared to be a forgery. Their reporter in Constantinople called it 'clumsy plagiarism'.

It is an early example of a 'false document'. Many modern novels use facts that are strategically woven into a fictional story, thereby creating the document as apparently being entirely about true circumstances. This breaks no ethical rules of authorship if it is portrayed as such, but does if it is passed off as being all true and all original work when, in reality, it is

Chapter 2. Nazi Germany: The First Arch Enemy of Britain

plagiarised from many prior documents.

Its publication has had an enormous following in one way or another. An account of its disturbing influence, even in recent times, is covered in several YouTubes on people's views of the *Protocols of Zion*.

One of its committed adherents was Henry Ford who published many aggressive stories in his newspaper, the *Dearborn Independent,* and who distributed 500,000 copies throughout the US in the 1920s. You got a copy with your new Ford car!

He subsequently published a large collection of the most popular articles as several volume books, *The International Jew*. Hitler was a great admirer of Ford, honouring him with the *Grand Cross of the German Eagle* in 1938.

During that time many well-known people in the Western world nations still felt the need to keep up relationships with Germany, an issue taken up again in the account on the Fascists on West Sussex - covered in Chapter 9.

The authenticity of the *Protocols* document does not matter here; the fact is, it was available to aid Hitler's propaganda machine! One commentator suggested it became a compulsory study for all German youth in the early 1930s.

This was all good fodder for Hitler and his propaganda machine led by Joseph Goebbels, who as the head of the German *Ministry of Public Enlightenment and Propaganda*, took this kind of hate talk to its most evil level.

As soon as Hitler gained absolute power as Chancellor of Germany on 30 January 1933, he immediately began instituting a whole range of directives that would soon affect the half-million plus Jews in Germany and, later, others elsewhere. Events against Jews in Germany became world news, letting the people of Britain know of many of the horrors being perpetrated under Hitler's occupations. The Jewish Holocaust-era was well and truly in place, as he had already declared in 1922.

'my first and foremost task will be the annihilation of the Jews'.

Starting with the Dachau Camp in 1933, by 1939 seven concentration camps had been created over the continent of Europe, ostensibly to hold political prisoners. Dachau was a former ammunition factory, Fig, 2.4.

Fig. 2.4 The ruins used as the Dachau Concentration Camp in 1933. (US Holocaust Museum)

It was initially set up by Heinrich Himmler to hold prisoners with adverse political views to those of Hitler's Reich. Soon, unwanted races and groups, and hardened criminals were also sent there. This was the thin edge of the wedge for it soon became used to hold Jews; simply for being Jewish.

These often became harsh forced labour camps where lives were not precious. Indeed, in some cases, people were deliberately left to die through overwork, poor nutrition, torture, murder and woeful living conditions where medical attention was minimal and diseases rife.

Deaths rose sharply. Estimates suggest that 273,000 inmates were murdered by 1945 by these above conditions alone. Readers with very strong dispositions to horror may care to view the evidence films made as the hundreds of camps were liberated. The evidence film *Nuremberg: Nazi Concentration and Prison Camps,* shown at the Nuremberg trials, is

Chapter 2. Nazi Germany: The First Arch Enemy of Britain

shocking to the greatest degree.

Even more monstrous (there must be a harsher word than *dreadful* with which to describe these!) were the extermination death camps set up by the Nazi killing machine before the war ended. These are explained in depth in Wikipedia. Jews were the primary target of elimination, but virtually every European nation felt the effects of this Nazi inhumanity.

On 24 March 1933 Hitler was granted the *Enabling Act* by the German parliament. By this, he gained total dictatorial power. He lost no time in setting in place his relentless attack on the Jewish people as we have seen in the Feuchtwanger family story in Chapter 1, section 1.3.

The mood was that they, and other marginalised groups such as the disabled, mentally ill and gipsies, all had to be eliminated from the country to 'make room'. Others made the case for removal of these groups as them being sub-humans that did not fit the ideal person profile needed for a renewed German Empire.

Examples of this inhuman treatment were a national boycott of Jewish businesses, reduced access to university entrance for Jews, removal of German citizenship for Jewish Polish migrants, and the opening of the first concentration camp in Dachau on 22 March 1933: in readiness for the imprisonment of such undesirables.

It was just a start of the *Devil* in Hitler; he was ready and waiting to act that role.

He continued to take the harshest action on those who opposed or criticised him, not just to stop them but to eliminate those he 'felt' were not supporting him in his insane plans.

The so-called *'Night of the Long Knives,'* (Operation Hummingbird) from 30 June 30 to 2 July 1934, was a short sharp and bloody, violent purge of thousands of his political enemies in Germany, including those who tried to stop Hitler in his tracks.

The list of acts against humanity by the Nazis was large indeed. Later there took place, in November 1938, the *Kristallnacht* or *Night of the Broken Glass*.

Anything and everything Jewish under Nazis control were attacked and destroyed, leaving masses of broken glass in the streets as hundreds of Jewish businesses were vandalised. Tens of thousands of Jews were sent to concentration camps. Many were murdered in the streets; no one was prosecuted for these crimes.

Fig. 2.5 Hitler's *Time* cover; 2 January 1938.

'From the unholy organist, a hymn of hate'

Chapter 2. Nazi Germany: The First Arch Enemy of Britain

Hitler's previously published intentions were eventually made very clear. The Times newspaper published a most damning cover picture on 2 January 1939, Fig. 2.5. It is almost too horrible to face. A description of it was:

'On January 2, 1939, Time Magazine published its annual *Man of the Year* issue. For the year 1938, Time had chosen Adolf Hitler as the man who "for better or worse" (as Time founder Henry Luce expressed it) had most influenced events of the preceding year.

The cover picture featured Hitler playing 'his hymn of hate' in a desecrated cathedral while victims dangle on a St. Catherine's wheel and the Nazi hierarchy looks on.'

This picture was drawn by Baron Rudolph Charles von Ripper, a German Catholic who had fled Hitler's Germany.

The 'Man of the Year' cover had been a Time tradition since 1927 when Charles Lindbergh became the first Man of the Year. Ironically, Lindbergh was an admirer of Hitler and Nazi Germany; he became active in the America First Organisation which opposed America entering World War II in the fight against Adolf Hitler.

That article in the Times is worth reading in full to capture the mood of the times. Against this violence, many things done by Hitler seemed to progress acceptably.

In August 1936, Germany staged the 1936 Summer Olympics in Berlin, Fig. 2.6. This grand international event suited Hitler's plans well for it allowed him to show-piece the growing architectural grandeur and achievements of the Third Reich under his development.

Fig. 2.6. Artist's view of Germany's 1936 stadium and Hindenburg airship.

'It seemed as though the basic design of commonly practised architecture at the time was to be either left in place or modified within Germany's dominion. The new building style may have been intended to give the idea to the rest of the world and to the unconverted Germans that the era of the thousand-year Reich had dawned'. Wikipedia

By 1936 it was painfully clear to the international communities that his regime was not so peaceful and the games should not be held there. However, the die had been cast for this event in 1931 when Germany won the right to stage the games.

At that time in his rise, Hitler was seen as a great leader to many for he was doing well in the political and national leadership spheres. His national achievements were outstanding for which he had then attracted many admirers in foreign countries. He seemed to be the leader to follow; he was overcoming the ills of his country and giving it back its pride after their humiliating loss in WW1.

By 1936 it was a very much different situation, and others overseas were seeing it!

Just weeks before the Games commenced, the Nazis, on 16 July 1936, cleared the city of Romani gipsies, placing them into a newly used labour camp, the Berlin-Marzahn concentration camp. This camp was set up in the East of Berlin between a cemetery and a sewage plant.

Initially, for the events of the games, the Germans banned sporting participation by Jews and Blacks, but as the result of a serious threat of a global boycott, Hitler relented.

Being forced to do this must have galled him in a major way. Interestingly this shows the Olympic movement was more able to change national opinion than could the League of Nations! This Nazi-led 'Master Race' would still have its day on the international scene.

Preparing for the world attendance, and massive media presence, all anti-Semitic posters and notices were removed: they knew they were wrong! What was strange is that the Nazi members wore their uniforms on the leader's balcony! The Olympic Flame was run into the stadium through corridors formed by massed Jong Folk and Brownshirts in uniform. They *Sieg Heiled*, which to us now seems quite inappropriate,

Chapter 2. Nazi Germany: The First Arch Enemy of Britain

but the term comes from the words meaning 'Victory! Hail'.

The organisers deployed the very latest in broadcast equipment using closed-circuit TV and numerous loudspeakers as 'proof of supremacy'. Hundreds of microphones and many broadcast vans, all of the latest design, were set up for the 'good news' to be sent to overseas homes via the many international journalists in attendance. It was a most impressive achievement, Fig. 2.7.

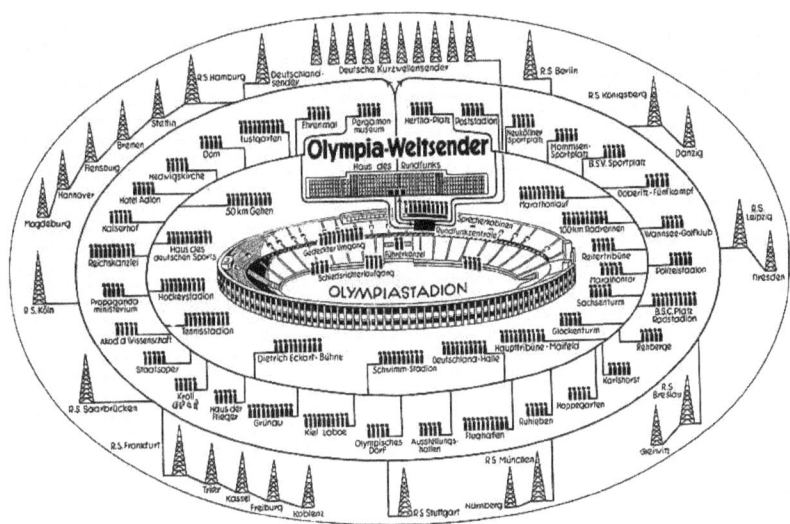

Fig. 2.7 Broadcasting network created by the Germans for their hosting of the 1936 Olympic Games.

Over the days, winning an event that Hitler wanted badly, fell flat for he did not get it! Germany's main track star Lutz Lang, blue-eyed with blond hair, as all racially perfect Aryans were supposed to have, was well out-run and out-jumped by Jesse Owens, an African-American from the US. A black man indeed!

Hitler had preached that the Blacks were racially inferior to his competitors. Owens won more medals by himself than any country apart from his own; other African-Americans also won them. However, Germany did win the most medals; 33 golds to 24 of the USA.

It is often stated that Hitler refused to place the Gold Medal around

Owens' neck. However, there is evidence that this was not as it appeared to be; there had been a change in the protocol of who performed that task. Hitler was also said to have chosen not to shake hands with Jesse; a 2014 documentary reported that the British Naval Fighter pilot Captain Eric Brown, in his youth, saw them shake hands, Fig, 2.8. It is left to the reader to delve into the information available on the Internet. Reports on Hitler were often very biased – the Victor gets to tell the story!

Fig. 2.8 Did he, or didn't he? This artist's impression shows Hitler congratulating Jesse Owens.

The History Learning website states Balder von Schirach, head of the Nazi youth movement, Hitler Jugend, claimed Hitler had said, following the 100m victory of Jesse Owens:

"The Americans should be ashamed of themselves, letting Negroes win their medals for them. I shall not shake hands with this Negro.......do you really think that I will allow myself to be photographed shaking hands with a Negro?"

It was not only Hitler that had the conviction that the Germans were a super-race. Hans von Tschammer und Osten, of the Reich Sports Office, played a major role in the structure and organisation of the Olympics. He promoted the idea that the use of sports would harden the German spirit and instil unity among the German youth. At the same time, he also believed that sport was a 'way to weed out the weak, Jewish, and other undesirables'.

Anti-Semitic sentiments of some kind or another in the 30s were not restricted to the Germans alone but they took it way, way, beyond the

Chapter 2. Nazi Germany: The First Arch Enemy of Britain

others. Evidence of undercurrents of 'Jew-haters' can be found in many of the Allied country's histories. This was to do with democracy working as its freedom of speech regime, allowing small factions to shout out loudly. In effect, this bad press was little more than 'grumblings and rumblings' within nations.

According to Research Guides of the National Archives of Australia, *Safe Haven: Records of the Jewish Experience in Australia* in the 1930s, Britain and Australia were, in fact, well recognised as having long traditions of Philo-Semitism (appreciation of the Jewish people's history). Outcomes from this, that became Midhurst events, are discussed later in this volume.

My own experience with my Midhurst primary schooling was that, in WW2, I was being taught handcrafts, reading and writing, combined with learning songs, hymns, prayers, fairy tales and nursery rhymes that stirred the heart in generous ways. In sharp contrast, at that time Hitler was having his children taught to become war fodder.

Confirmation that this was true is seen in the writings of Gregor Ziemer, an American author and educator who lived in Germany from 1928 to 1939. In 1941 he published a non-fiction book, *Education for Death,* shortly after fleeing Germany; on the eve of World War II.

'This work presents first-hand descriptions of the indoctrination and race-purification processes undertaken in the prenatal clinics, sterilisation hospitals, mental institutions and educational facilities of pre-war Germany.' Google books on Ziemer (1941)

It showed that the education of German children progressively changed them from being innocent, kind boys and girls into chained, muzzled, Nazi drones.

When the war ended Germans knew only the Nazi Socialist form of national governance. It had been inculcated for too long, in an environment of fear, to be questioned by the majority.

This thinking had become so ingrained within the concept of Hitler's dictatorial kind of socialism that German POWs and citizens needed to be rehabilitated into the ways of democracy when the war was over.

With the attack on Pearl Harbour in December 1941, the USA declared war on Japan; thereby resulting in Germany declaring war on the USA. Until that date US citizens could still visit and live in Germany; there existed several centuries of a tradition of enjoying good German-USA relationships.

Gregor Ziemer was the Head Master of the American Colony School in Berlin from 1928 - 1939. A few of the students were Jews. The Prologue in a book he published, Ziemer (1941), explains how the Western World got to learn of the Nazi education methods. This is the background.

Around 1936, opposite his school in Germany was a *Volksschule* (a Nazi State school). One day, Brownshirt-adorned youngsters threw rocks at his students shouting anti-Jewish slogans; in short - 'Meddlesome Jews go home'.

He told his students to put up with it for any complaint would bring in the dreaded Gestapo. He then spoke with his opposite Head Master asking for it to stop. The reply was to tell him his students were not controllable, and anyway, he would not be allowed to admonish them! He said, "They taught the German children that the Jews are their greatest enemies".

Gregor was not a Nazi supporter in any way, but decided to find a way to learn of its education process; he had been most interested in these new ways of teaching since 1933.

He slowly developed the confidence of the authorities into believing that he was genuine in this interest by expressing his admiration for their work. He eventually was given a permit that allowed him access to classes and the educational materials. Numerous aspects of conventional teaching classes were doctored to be war-like. For example, he states that students were persuaded to pull other students into line where they strayed from the Nazi party policy; as was fed into the teaching materials. One example is from the manual he was given:

> 'The German school in the Third Reich is an integral part of the National Socialist order of living. It has the mission, in collaboration with other phases of the Party, to fashion and mould the National Socialist Being according to Party Orders'

Chapter 2. Nazi Germany: The First Arch Enemy of Britain

Students were taught and rewarded more for their adherence to the Party line than for the usual educational merits. Class materials were fashioned that way. In physics teaching the projectile path of an object is given in terms of the path of a bullet. The time to do a task is framed as how long will it take to dig a slit trench.

The book is hypnotic reading for it is full of such twisted materials. It is fantastical, like a horror tale of a madman wanting to shape the world, with himself at the pinnacle. It is unbelievable; but, taken in perspective with the enormity of many other Nazi national practices, it was very real.

It also covers the glory parades held to present honours to students. These were staged in historic places that were cloaked in the history and trappings of the former Roman Empire's glory. Hundreds of students of impressionable age were at these gatherings.

In short, Ziemer stated in his long prologue:

"And I drew one conclusion. Hitler's schools to their job diabolically well. They are obeying the Führer. They are educating boys and girls for death. They are preparing them as a sacrifice for Hitler, who hath said, LET THE CHILDREN COME UNTO ME - FOR THEY ARE MINE UNTO DEATH"

Hence the title of his book - *Education for Death: The Making of a Nazi.*

In the early part of WW2, after the US had joined the war, its propaganda machine wanted to make the point that the Nazis were monsters. Amusing for its cartoon characters, yet chilling, is the animation of this education of German children, commissioned of the studios of Disney (1943), as *Education for Death.* Being released in 1943, it was based on the facts given in Ziemer (1941). The same subject matter was also used to make the film, *Hitler's Children.*

In Disney's cartoon, the stages in the life of little boy Hans, the subject of the film, are shown in blackened humour.

First, to be given German citizenship his parents had to prove Ayran bloodlines with documents and swear that Hans would follow Hitler with service to the Fatherland. The parents' passport included space for 12 children as a hint that they should provide support for the struggle with more offspring.

Next, if Hans became ill with a long-term complaint, he would be taken into care by the State … with potentially dreadful treatments, including euthanasia!

As Hans develops, he constantly hears romantic tales of a knight in shining armour (Hitler) taking the Fatherland (a very large woman) to new and better heights.

At one stage Hans gets humiliating punishment in the classroom for feeling pity for a rabbit being eaten by a fox on a class exercise. He must toughen up for 'weakness has no place in a soldier'. Hans has to agree.

He then takes part in a book burning exercise in which the *Holy Bible* is replaced by a copy of *Mein Kampf* and the Cross of Crucifixion is replaced by the Nazi sword.

By then Hans had had years of 'marching and heiling, heiling and marching', Fig. 2.9.

Fig. 2.9. Hans had years of 'marching and heiling' to become a good Nazi soldier! (Disney)

That the theme of *Education for Death* was not just a propaganda promoted by the Allies, was well proven when Hitler was fast running out of troops for the war in 1944 and 1945. He ordered boys, including some as young as 12 years old, and old men to be conscripted.

Chapter 2. Nazi Germany: The First Arch Enemy of Britain

Some youths had already been sent to the Eastern Front in 1942, Fig. 2.10. Others manned the infantry force defending the 6 June 1944 invasion.

Fig. 2.10. Hitler's young soldiers at the Eastern Front, 1942.

To end this summary of Germany leading the world into war in the 30s, there is another instance of the arrogant, egomaniacal ambitions of the senior Nazi leaders.

It concerns the *Spear of Destiny.* Fig. 2.11 shows the artefact held in the Imperial Treasury, Hofburg Palace, Vienna.

Fig. 2.11 The Holy Lance (Spear of Destiny).

To rule the world Hitler was creating, he just had to have this relic. This was claimed to be the lance that pierced the side of Jesus as he hung on the cross. Several churches across the world claim to possess this lancehead!

It was said, from centuries of knowledge of it, that it has 'phenomenal talismanic power' and whoever possessed it would have the power to conquer the world; but losing it would bring immediate death.

Hitler is said to have had visions

of his own destiny unfolding before him when he first saw it. He set up a special team of academic historians to find the true one and to organise a snatch of it. In 1912, when Hitler first saw it in the Hofburg Treasure House in Vienna, he is purported to have said:

> "I knew with immediacy that this was an important moment in my life...I stood there quietly gazing upon it for several minutes, quite oblivious to the scene around me. It seemed to carry some hidden inner meaning which evaded me, a meaning which I felt I inwardly knew, yet could not bring to consciousness...I felt as though I myself had held it in my hands before in some earlier century of history - that I myself had once claimed it as my talisman of power and held the destiny of the world in my hands. What sort of madness was this that was invading my mind and creating such turmoil in my breast?"
> http://antarctica.greyfalcon.us/highjump1.html

On 12th March 1938, the day Hitler annexed Austria, he arrived in Vienna as a conquering hero. He first port of call was to the Hofburg Museum where he took possession of the Spear which he immediately sent to Nuremberg, the spiritual capital of Nazi Germany.

At 02.10 on 30th April 1945, during the final days of the war, that Spear fell into the hands of the American 7th Army under General Patton. Later that day, in fulfilment of the legend, Hitler committed suicide.

Many YouTube videos are available on this topic. Other senior Nazis also had illusions of gaining inordinate power from a religious artefact. Graham Keeley in the *Independent*, 6 February 2007, tells the story of another Nazi leader with these delusions of power.

Heinrich Himmler, *Reichsführer*, the head of the Nazi SS, believed Christ was descended from Ayran stock, via Jacob. If he could only possess the *Holy Grail* (the cup used by Christ at the Last Supper) it would help Germany win the war and give him supernatural powers. He did not find it!

To end this description of Nazi affairs in Germany as war was looming, Churchill, in his memoirs, wrote of Hitler thus:

Chapter 2. Nazi Germany: The First Arch Enemy of Britain

'It had been a long struggle, difficult for foreigners, especially those who had not known the pangs of defeat, to comprehend. Adolf Hitler had at last arrived. But he was not alone. He had called from the depths of defeat the dark and savage furies latent in the most numerous, most serviceable, ruthless, contradictory, and ill-starred race in Europe. He had conjured up the fearful idol of an all-devouring *Moloch* of which he was the priest and incarnation. It is not within my scope to describe the inconceivable brutality and villainy by which this apparatus of hatred and tyranny had been fashioned and was now to be perfected.'

(A word of explanation is needed here. Tradition says that the *Moloch* was a horrific Canaanite statue made of bronze heated with fire into which children were thrown as sacrifices.)

By the time that Britain declared war on Germany, that nation had been massively indoctrinated with incorrect views of the Allied Nations situation, Fig. 2.12.

Fig. 2.12 British 1936 cartoon sums up the thinking of Hitler. (D Low)

At an interview after his defence at Normandy in June 1944 the German soldier Marten Eineg, just 18 years of age then, a Soldat

(Private) with the 726th Infantry regiment, 716th Static Infantry Division, stationed in the area of La Riviere, recorded what he had been taught during his youthful training:

> 'We saw the British as an outdated Imperial force, organised by Freemasons, who sought to turn the clock back one hundred years to the days when their word was the law around the world. Why should they be entitled to install their Freemason puppet, De Gaulle, in France, to rule as a proxy? The Vichy government had three consistent points in its propaganda regarding the threats to the French people: these were De Gaulle, freemasonry and communism. As for the American State, we perceived that as controlled by the forces of international finance and banking, who wished to abolish national governments and have the world run by banks and corporations. And there was the definite sentiment that both these countries, England and the USA, were being manipulated, controlled, by the Bolsheviks in Moscow. I stress that these were my views, and they were very common views, at the time.' Eckhertz (2015).

Heinrich Runder, a Grenadier (Rifleman) with the German 709th Static Infantry Division, was also manning defences on the Cotentin Peninsula on D-Day June 1944.

Asked, "You saw your role as protecting Germany?" His reply was:

> 'Our training had impressed this on us. The idea was that the Western Allies were in the pay of the Bolsheviks in the East, who were orchestrating world events against us. I remember that phrase clearly from some of the officers: "They are orchestrating world events." To us, this meant that the Reds were closing in on Germany in the East, and their partners the Americans and the English were trying to crush us in a pincer from the West, by attacking through France. This is another phrase I recall: 'We are in a *clamp*, and Germany is caught between the Anglo-Americans and the Slavic races.' Eckhertz, (2015)

Chapter 2. Nazi Germany: The First Arch Enemy of Britain

For all of the explanations of negative issues of Germany's evil, there were those putting a different, more favourable, viewpoint. These are worthy of viewing as an aside for there were circumstances behind the major war issues that coaxed Hitler to drive things as he did, to begin with.

This is the appropriate place to briefly introduce the close members who implemented Hitler's *directives*, these being his instructions on specific topics and strategy plans. These were very short documents that simply had to be obeyed under pain of execution; that was not just a threat. Hitler did this to many of his subordinates.

Some were simple statements, others major such as directing military plans. For example, the **Plan of Attack of Poland**, their first major active war operation, was his first directive. It had just 4 clauses:

'The Supreme Commander of the Armed Forces.
OKW/WFA Nr. 170/39 g. K. Chefs. L1.

MOST SECRET
Senior Commanders only
By hand of Officer only

Berlin,
31st August 1939.

8 copies
Copy No. 2

Directive No. 1 for the Conduct of the War

1. Since the situation on Germany's Eastern frontier has become intolerable and all political possibilities of the peaceful settlement have been exhausted, I have decided upon a solution by force.
2. The attack on Poland will be undertaken in accordance with the preparations made for 'Case White', with such variations as may be necessitated by the build-up of the Army which is now virtually complete.

The allocation of tanks and the purpose of the operation remain unchanged.

Date of attack 1st September 1939.

3. In the west, it is important to leave the responsibility for opening hostilities unmistakably to England and France. Minor violations of the frontier will be dealt with, for the time being, purely as local incidents.

The assurances of neutrality given by us to Holland, Belgium, Luxembourg, and Switzerland are to be meticulously observed.

The western frontier of Germany will not be crossed by land at any point without my explicit orders.

This applies also to all acts of warfare at sea or to acts which might be regarded as such.

The defensive activity of the Air Force will be restricted for the time being to the firm repulse of enemy air attacks on the frontiers of the Reich. In taking action against individual aircraft or small formations, care will be taken to respect the frontiers of neutral countries as far as possible. Only if considerable forces of French or British bombers are employed against German territory across neutral areas will the Air Force be permitted to go into defensive action over neutral soil. It is particularly important that any infringement of the neutrality of other States by our western enemies be immediately reported to the High Command of The Armed Forces.

4. Should England and France open hostilities against Germany, it will be the duty of the Armed Forces operating in the west, while conserving their strength as much as possible, to maintain conditions for the successful conclusion of operations against Poland. Within these limits enemy forces and war potential will be damaged as much as possible. The right to order offensive operations is reserved absolutely to me.

The Army will occupy the West Wall and will take steps to secure it from being outflanked in the north, through the violation by the western powers of Belgian or Dutch territory. Should French forces invade Luxembourg the bridges on the frontier may be blown up.

The Navy will operate against merchant shipping, with England as the focal point. In order to increase the effect, the declaration of danger

Chapter 2. Nazi Germany: The First Arch Enemy of Britain

zones may be expected. The Naval High Command will report on the areas which it is desirable to classify as danger zones and on their extent. The text of a public declaration in this matter is to be drawn up in collaboration with the Foreign Office and to be submitted to me for approval through the High Command of The Armed Forces.

The Baltic Sea is to be secured against enemy intrusion. The Commander in Chief of the Navy will decide whether the entrances to the Baltic Sea should be mined for this purpose.

The Air Force is, first of all, to prevent action by the French and English Air Forces against the German Army and German territory.

In operations against England, the task of the Air Force is to take measures to dislocate English imports, the armaments industry, and the transport of troops to France. Any favourable opportunity of an effective attack on concentrated units of the English Navy, particularly on battleships or aircraft carriers, will be exploited. The decision regarding attacks on London is reserved to me.

Attacks on the English homeland are to be prepared, bearing in mind that inconclusive results with insufficient forces are to be avoided in all circumstances.

Adolf Hitler.'

Knowing now of the forthcoming conflict, and the so-called diplomacy that preceded it, the actual phrases are worth consideration for its duplicity and sense of Hitler's rationale. It is chilling to realise this statement on paper was all that was needed to start WW2.

Hitler's 'Inner Circle of Evil' (from a film series of that name) that carried out his orders, has been characterised:

'All were psychologically unbalanced and fanatical individuals'.

The Members were:

Adolf Hitler (Führer, meaning 'leader')
Joachim Von Ribbentrop (Ambassador 11 August 1936 to 11 March

1938 when he became the Foreign Minister of Nazi Germany)
Hermann Goering (Commander-in-Chief Luftwaffe - the German Air force; named successor to Hitler)
Heinrich Himmler (Reichsfuhrer in charge of Waffen-SS; Gestapo; Interior affairs; Home Army; and supreme leader of the entire Third Reich)
Joseph Goebbels (German Minister of Propaganda)
Martin Borman (Head Nazi Party Chancellery. Deputy Fuhrer at one stage)
Walther Funk (Reich Minister of Economics)
Albert Speer (Chief Architect of civil works)
Karl Donitz (Commander-in-Chief, German Navy)
Erich Raeder (Grand Admiral, German Navy)
Wilhelm Keitel (Field Marshall, Germany Army)

Hitler, von Ribbentrop and Goering were attributed, by the war trials held after the end of the war, to have been the prime group that brought WW2 into existence.

The totalitarian, overpowering authoritarian, way of ruling a country was that introduced by the Nazi party - meaning, by Hitler. He was resisted by numerous individuals and groups. He did not take kindly to criticism.

Some went as far as deciding to assassinate him, but they always failed. These attempts started in 1921 when a young radical made a fiery speech in the beer hall; it incited the crowd into an all-out brawl. Shots were fired toward Hitler standing in the speaker's podium. He was unhurt. More than 30 assassination attempts on Hitler's life were to follow.

Many individuals decided to fight back, through resistance to his directives. Most eventually paid the price by being executed. One brave person was the German priest, Dietrich Bonhoeffer.

2.2 Bonhoeffer's Life of Discipleship.

We have seen how Hitler took over Germany and how he did it in a manner that not only destroyed the lives of the minorities that he

Chapter 2. Nazi Germany: The First Arch Enemy of Britain

considered were little more than vermin, but also the lives of the German people at large.

We have so far explored how Germans, such as the Feuchtwanger family, who considered themselves to be German, and their close friends, suffered deeply simply because they were born into the Jewish faith.

We have also started to see how a good upright loyal German boy, Joachim Liebschner, was educated and made virtually into a robot soldier of the State; and how, in his teens, was beginning to appreciate that the Nazi way was not the classical German way.

To start with, Lion Feuchtwanger chose to fight with his pen, and from within the Nazi State, later continuing that in the safety of exile in the USA.

Joachim's realisation was not yet upon by him at the time he went to war; the fortunes of war decided all of his fears for him; a matter for the next Memoirs book.

The Western nations decided to cope with Hitler in their usual way... by being led to war as the last resort: and only at the very latest moment of Hitler's already long and brutal rise to power. They kept thinking and hoping it would not come to that.

The external world seems to have tried nothing but diplomacy. There were no commando kidnap raids; no targeted bombing raids, at least in the early days.

Resistance and non-compliance with the Nazis were carried out by many Germans, most losing their lives for it. However, it seems there was no well organised German Resistance movement with external support from the Allies, as was the case for the French Resistance.

One brave and courageous German individual was Dietrich Bonhoeffer. His *Life of Discipleship*, as he called one of his books, well-illustrated the levels of courage and persistence showed. As we will see, he worked tirelessly opposing the Nazi *Evil*.

Following the general theme of these memoirs, Dietrich had a strong and useful direct connection to West Sussex via the Chichester Cathedral leadership.

Dietrich Bonhoeffer, Fig. 2.13, was born in Breslau, Germany on 4 February 1906 and died, by the evil hands of the Gestapo, on 9 April 1945. He was a Lutheran Pastor, a leading theologian and a working member of those resisting Hitler's policies in many areas against the oppression of the German peoples. Such was his endeavour that he became one of the ten Modern Martyrs chosen to be honoured in stone over the West Door at Westminster Abbey; unveiled in 1998.

Fig. 2.13 Dietrich Bonhoeffer statue at Westminster Abbey.

Here was one dedicated soul who worked tirelessly for better order in Germany. His life story is one of great protestation and immense courage as he, among other things, opposed the rising Nazis regime as they took control of the German Christian churches. He was martyred by the Gestapo for his actions.

This short account of his work against the German Nazis regime illustrates church and political life in Germany during the 30s and how the international Christian community played a part. Early in the 30s, despite knowing the situation in his native Germany, he voluntarily returned from safety to keep up the pressure on the German authorities.

At 14 years old, he decided his life was to be devoted to theology and church duty; he did not follow his father into psychiatry practice.

In 1927 he was awarded the research PhD of the University of Berlin. After a short period in Spain, he returned to Germany to complete the necessary Habilitation thesis.

Chapter 2. Nazi Germany: The First Arch Enemy of Britain

This, a second, higher, doctorate was and still is, the highest University qualification awarded. It is normally needed to ascend to Full Professorship posts in Europe and is necessary to supervise research doctorate candidates. It is not required for supervision in British Universities but they also award a doctorate of much the same standing, the second, higher research, doctorate, but in smaller numbers.

Well before the emergence of Hitler in Germany - that is, going back some 40 years before 1930 - the German Socialist Party, stemming from anti-Semitic roots, had inserted the *Aryan Paragraph* into German civil law. It stated that only those of Aryan descent, and without Jewish parentage, could obtain the strictly controlled Aryan Certificate needed to be a civil servant.

The trace of purity needed had to be at least back to 1800, sometimes further to 1750, to be able to join the *Schutzstaffel SS* officer Corp.

This restriction was extended to education in 1933 as a method of isolating the Jewish and other peoples in Germany. It was extended continuously to the point where their very existence became extremely difficult.

Due to the social circumstances of the times in Germany, this heinous paragraph was accepted with little protest. No democracy there! However, a major rejection did come from within the Christians of the *Evangelical Church*; it caused the *Confessing Church* to split from it.

This Confessing Church was created within the German Protestant churches in the early '30s. They were opposed to Hitler's actions where he was working to make the Christian churches an arm of National Socialist propaganda and politics. The German Protestant tradition was already to link the church and with state affairs, but not for the State to control Church affairs.

Political activities soon became an essential part of Bonhoeffer's theological work. He saw that political and religious beliefs had to live alongside each other in the same community in harmony, and not with the State deciding religious matters; the Hitler regime was certainly not following the ways of the past.

Hitler ascended to total power on 30 January 1933; this considerably changed the dynamics of Bonhoeffer's career and aspirations. His strong convictions compelled him to speak out. He immediately broadcast a radio speech in which he denounced, in very positive and clear terms, Hitler's intentions and his seductive power for organising evil.

Bonhoeffer's language was too strong; his broadcast was cut off mid-sentence. Shortly after this incident, he made a very provocative statement,

> 'the church must not simply bandage the victims under the wheel, but jam the spoke in the wheel itself.'

Hitler then made sure Bonhoeffer failed in his attempts to be elected to a Church governance post and worked to ensure that all the key posts went to Nazis sympathisers.

The Confessing Church went on to insist that Christ, not the Führer, was the Head of the church. They strongly opposed amalgamation of Nazi nationalism with the Christian gospel.

Because of Hitler's Aryan and anti-Semitic policies, by 1934 there had become two German Protestant churches, one under State control, the other not being recognised by the State.

Fig. 2.14 By the mid-1930s, Dietrich Bonhoeffer had become the target of Nazi oppression.

The latter, Confessing Church, proclaimed it was the true church. Dietrich Bonhoeffer, Fig. 2.14, was becoming a tireless worker fighting the Nazi regime over matters of religion using the Confessing Church as his identity.

Being unable to get traction with overcoming the complacency of the German Church to the regime's attempts to integrate the Reich with the church, Bonhoeffer, in late 1933, went to England for a two-year post as a Pastor in the Sydenham suburb of London. That building was destroyed by bombs during WW2. He was then chided by a church official for leaving Germany in its time of need for him, but he needed

Chapter 2. Nazi Germany: The First Arch Enemy of Britain

time to rethink things and develop opposition from afar. At that time Germans and the British were still free to travel between the countries. He soon had a visit by the German Bishop handling foreign activities for the Confessing Church; Bonhoeffer was advised to cease any actions not authorised by Berlin. He refused.

The overpowering climate of Hitler was steadily descending on him as they worked to stifle his views.

Hitler had reached his pinnacle of power but was still taking some care to keep up workable relationships with other nations and international organisations. For these reasons, he was not yet removing recalcitrant senior people from being able to work for the church by some pretext or another. Primarily, Hitler needed to keep up relationships whilst he was building up his military machine ready to invade Poland in September 1939.

When on that two-year trip to London, in April 1933, Bonhoeffer chanced to meet with George Bell, then the Anglican Bishop of Chichester in Sussex.

Bell had seen for himself, on a visit to Germany, the effects of the Nazi takeover in that year. He became the top foreign ally of the Confessing Church. In April he publicly expressed the international church's concerns for the anti-Semitic moves in Germany.

Bonhoeffer would keep Bell informed of the declining situation and he, in turn, would let those in Europe and the US know of this by various means, including letters to *The Times* newspaper of London.

People in Britain and the US were most certainly being informed of the methods of the Nazis! But they were powerless. They hoped the British government would see them through and avoid the apparent consequences to come.

In 1934, Dick Sheppard, canon of St Paul's Cathedral, had initiated a movement called the *Peace Pledge Union* (PPU). It is the oldest British secular pacifist non-governmental organisation. It had continuously campaigned for a warless world and was still a force. Anyone could sign their pledge:

"I renounce war and am therefore determined not to support any kind of war. I am also determined to work for the removal of all causes of war."

During events leading to war with Germany, the PPU supported Chamberlain in the use of appeasement with Hitler. Unfortunately, the 100,000s who signed the pledge could not persuade Hitler to change from being a doer of *Evil* to one for *Good*. Membership included many eminent thinkers who took that line: to no avail. A madman sees a different reason to the norm.

This resolve changed course when Hitler invaded the West of Europe. The Nazi sympathisers then moved to PPU support of those who objected to military service, and to support victims of war such as Jewish refugees.

Part of their problem was their doctrine, that seemed to be a close match with that of the *Blackshirts,* of the British Union of Fascists (BUF). That did not help its cause. They received bad press calling for them to be banned. They opposed conscription, the building of air raid shelters and other necessary issues. They put up banners stating:

"War will cease when men refuse to fight. What are YOU going to do about it?"

The problem is that war is not based on the sound reasoning of very long-term outcomes. It is a case of the human race being unable to control itself without the use of physical force.

It is a fact that individuals can take charge of people's minds in undesirable ways. The doctrine of Christianity 'turn the other cheek and love thy neighbour' is along sensible lines of individual thinking but individual achievement seems to not be useful in preventing war - only of creating it!

After his short, self-imposed, exile in London, Bonhoeffer returned to Germany in 1935 to set up illegal underground training of Pastors of the Confessing Church. Arrests were made by the Gestapo. Bonhoeffer was no longer allowed to teach at Berlin University. In 1937 the illegal Seminary was closed down.

In this year Bonhoeffer published his much-acclaimed book 'The *Cost of Discipleship'* Bonhoeffer (1937). He surely would have understood the depths of that topic by this stage in his life.

Persecution by the Gestapo, however, did not end his discipleship;

Chapter 2. Nazi Germany: The First Arch Enemy of Britain

he was not giving up. He had a cause and he was not going to relent.

His next move against the authorities was to create a 'seminary on the run', (a popup!) travelling around the eastern side of the country as its mentor. In 1938 he was banned from Berlin by the Gestapo. Following the outbreak of war with Britain in 1939 this seminary was also closed down.

Early in 1939, he decided to leave for the US for it seemed he might soon be conscripted and that would lead to him refusing to take the oath to fight for the Führer. That could easily lead to his death as that was a capital offence. Further, it might also damage the Confessing Church because refusing to serve would offend many German Christians at that time.

He, however, could not live with this 'desertion' of his duty to his country. He returned to Germany on the last ship to be given inward bound clearance. It was probably not a difficult decision to return to Germany, he said:

'I have come to the conclusion that I made a mistake in coming to America. I must live through this difficult period in our national history with the people of Germany. I will have no right to participate in the reconstruction of Christian life in Germany after the war if I do not share the trials of this time with my people... Christians in Germany will have to face the terrible alternative of either willing the defeat of their nation in order that Christian civilisation may survive or willing the victory of their nation and thereby destroying civilisation. I know which of these alternatives I must choose but I cannot make that choice from security.'

By 1940 he had so irritated the Nazis to the extent that he was not permitted to speak in public and had to report regularly to the police. Knowing of the already harsh ways the Nazis were using to silence any opposition he was still tolerated by the authorities!

In the previous year, an event took him in another, even more, dangerous direction, one that would eventually lead to his death for his cause.

Early in 1938, he had made contact with the disorganised German Resistance, via an introduction to a senior level group within the *Abwehr,* the German military intelligence. This group realised the way things were progressing and were looking to overthrow Hitler to make peace with the Allies.

Its Chief was German Admiral Wilhelm Canaris, Fig. 2.15, an enigmatic man who managed to keep control of the Abwehr despite internal battles with some of Hitler's cronies. From as early as 1939 he secretly turned against the Nazis and, by much cunning, held that high post whilst working for the German Resistance.

Fig. 2.15 Admiral Wilhelm Canaris. Master spy for the Allies whilst heading up German military intelligence.

Canaris was eventually found out when he became implicated as a major participant in the resistance against the Nazis and in the assassination plot of 20 July 1944, that took place in Hitler's Wolf's Lair. It became known as *Operation Valkyrie,* the title of a film on this attempt.

On one hand, he protected those in opposition to Hitler; but on the other hand, assisted the development of expansion plans. Perhaps this was the tightrope he needed to walk to achieve his goals of overcoming Hitler's aims? Direct and open opposition could not work as it was soon eliminated by execution.

Chapter 2. Nazi Germany: The First Arch Enemy of Britain

Looking back, unexpectedly this contact with the Abwehr led Bonhoeffer, in 1940, to being permitted into its ranks as an agent to make use of his many ecumenical contacts. These were used to collect information of use to the extensive intelligence community in the Third Reich. This also protected him from conscription. Again - walking a tight-rope to survive whilst carrying out his opposition.

There was little German Resistance effort in the early days of Hitler's rise for he was achieving many great things that benefited the general public. As things degenerated into crimes against humanity many people began to appreciate Germany needed to try to correct this state of affairs. As we have seen with the many attempts to assassinate Hitler, Germany had its share of individuals prepared to use their situation to carry out underground resistance against the regime.

To give scale to this, by the end of the war some 77,000 German resistance workers had been killed by order of military and civil courts. Unlike, however, most resistance fighters in other countries, the resistance movement in Germany had no central organisation but was built from many independent groups. The Church strand was not that effective using, in the main, only spoken disagreement with the regime. Bonhoeffer was in that group.

In 1943 there had been many attempts by Germans to assassinate Hitler. In 1942 Bonhoeffer had again met with Archbishop Bell, from Chichester, in neutral Sweden. He provided him with the names of people involved in one of the internal military assassination attempts. Bell passed this information on to the British Prime Minister, Anthony Eden. When the attempt failed Bell was unable to interest the British Government in supporting the German Resistance at large.

Arrested for his part in the assassination attempt in April 1943, the Gestapo incarcerated Bonhoeffer in the Tegel prison in Berlin, Fig. 2.16. He was then moved from prison to prison, ending up in the Flossenburg concentration and execution camp. Hitler had ordered 'all involved in that assassination attempt be destroyed'.

Following a drumhead court-martial by the Gestapo, that had no witnesses or records of its proceedings, he was condemned to death on 8 April 1945. He was executed at dawn by hanging, have been taken to the

execution yard naked!

Fig. 2.16 Cell 92 in the Tegel Military Prison.

Evil remained in force as the Nazis were, by then, just holding on to power. Dietrich's life was taken just 23 days before the German surrender! Admiral Wilhelm Canaris was arrested immediately after July 20, 1944, and was also executed at Flossenburg on April 9, 1945.

Bonhoeffer had been a very spiky thorn in the side of the Germans; his example and books hold high today. His cost of discipleship had been to give the ultimate; his life.

Regardless of the needs at the time, he had not always been free of guilt; he was often put in the situation wherein he had to condone *Evil* to do *Good*. He had joined the Abwehr! In a 1932 sermon, he had already foreseen how his life might map out,

> 'the blood of martyrs might once again be demanded, but this blood, if we really have the courage and loyalty to shed it, will not be innocent, shining like that of the first witnesses for the faith. On our blood lies heavy guilt, the guilt of the unprofitable servant who is cast into outer darkness'

Chapter 2. Nazi Germany: The First Arch Enemy of Britain

To end this person's story, it is with sadness to add that the name of Bishop George Bell, years after his death, despite the good he did over his life, has had his name expunged from some Chichester places because of alleged sexual abuse in the 40s and 50s. Compensation was paid. However, many have expressed the view that suggests he was the 'fall guy' for poor church responsibility in such matters in the past.

On 7 January 2016, *The Daily Telegraph* published a letter by Bishop Warner stating:

> 'that the church was mindful of the widely felt hurt about its decision, especially because of the bishop's great reputation. However, the church was seeking, "to move on from a culture in which manipulation of power meant that victims were too afraid to make allegations, or allegations were easily dismissed." In future, "we must provide safeguards of truth and justice for all, victim and accused alike".'

The whole matter is murky. Bell seems to also have paid the cost of discipleship; not at the hands of the Nazis, but by his countrymen.

A postage stamp, Fig. 2.17, featuring Dietrich Bonhoeffer, was published on July 20th, 1964, that date being the 20th anniversary of the Operation Valkyrie assassination attempt on Adolf Hitler's life. One can see and feel the anguish in his face!

Fig. 2.17 1995 postage stamp commemorating Bonhoeffer's life.

Dietrich's Bonhoeffer's life is permanently commemorated by a limestone statue placed, along with the other nine 20th century Modern Martyrs, over the West Door of the Westminster Abbey. These were unveiled in 1998, see Fig 2.13.

Midhurst WW2 Memoirs: 2. 'Evil' Rising: 'Good' Awakening

By now the *Evil* side of Hitler's direction was now out in the open. His goodness projects seem to be easily forgotten. His evil side had taken over.

The next step now is to look at the other nations of the Axis who were also forces of Evil. Each had its Empire building reasons for being in that unholy group.

Chapter 3. Others of the Evil Camp

3.1 Russia - Good and Evil

Russia, more correctly the Union of Soviet Socialist Republics (USSR), had about 170 million people in 1935. It had an evil leadership and yet was thought to be good for Britain. The USSR was on the Allies side before the war began, then changed to being with the Axis until they realised the Allies side was best for them again. This will become clear as Russia's history is examined.

Russia was a third huge empire stemming from the 17th and 18th centuries. That was the Tsardom period in Russia. It had close ties and bloodlines connected to the leadership of the Western empires, including Germany, and thus also to Great Britain.

This was one of the largest empires in man's history, being slightly smaller than the British Empire of that period. Its upper ruling class emulated the lifestyle and thinking of its rich cousins in Europe, but its peoples were more dreadfully treated and oppressed.

Its last Emperor was Nicholas II, Fig. 3.1, who lost power, being forced to abdicate as the result of a national revolution in 1917. Autocracy had lost its hold on this empire.

Fig. 3.1 Nicholas 11, captive after abdication in 1917. (L of C)

The wealth of the Russian Empire was produced not so much by the colonisation of foreign countries, as the other modern time's Empires had done, but by using its people in serfdom bondage.

Tens of millions of the Russian peasant class were treated as being little more than slaves to the ruling regime. Only a very small upper-middle class was formed, being the Tsarist Court that mainly followed orders of the Tsar on how to live, build, decorate, clothe, eat, fight, and so on. The capital city of this Russian empire was St. Petersburg. The majority of Russians formed a massive poor class who was always occupied with worry about their uncertainty of living adequately.

Severe discontent by them with the overpowering burden of working to create wealth for the aristocracy led to many signs of major revolt taking place became clear by 1900. Tsar Nicholas had started the internal political process for change to happen, but the upper classes resisted it for too long.

This action was too slow, too little and too late. It was not able to prevent a bloody revolution by the people. The Communist Party, supposedly the party of the people, gained power in 1917, thereby ending the reigns of the Tsars.

So strong was the hatred of Tsar Nicholas II, that he and his whole family were cruelly assassinated on 17 July 1918.

This situation had come about due to many internal shortages, the weariness of their subsistence lifestyle, loss of life from the actions of WW1, and total discontent with autocratic rule. Thus, were born the seeds of the Soviet Union in 1917; birth followed in 1922.

The northerly location of St. Petersburg is not a good area for carrying out construction works. Tens of thousands of serfs and conscripts built the beautiful city under the most dreadful conditions. For the privilege of that building work, they had to provide their tools!

I once asked a graduate student in St. Petersburg what it was like to live there. She replied:

'We have two seasons, both winters; the white one and the green one'.

By the start of the 20th century, St. Petersburg had become a major world city. During WW1, Russia was an enemy of Germany so Germanic names were expunged; the city was renamed Petrograd (Peter's City) to make it sound less German.

Later, in 1924, the honour of having a major city named after a person went to the communist hero Leningrad, thus removing the imperial dynasty name. Following the demise of communist party rule in 1991 it is now back to using the name of St. Petersburg again.

Chapter 3 Others of the Evil Camp

Thus, by authoritarian Imperial successions through the Romanov dynasty 1613-1917, the 18th and 19th centuries' ruling classes took on the same lifestyle of a great show, and abuse of wealth, as was being exercised by their Western cousins. Their social reformation was, however, not happening anywhere as fast as in the West.

From 1929 until 1953, Joseph Stalin ruled the Soviet Union as a cruel authoritarian dictator having no scruples or respect for the lives of his people. Shown in Fig. 3.2 is Stalin looking jovial in 1937, that being in the middle of what became known as his *Great Purge*.

During the Soviet history from 1917 - 1991, over 800,000 persons were shot for opposing the State, of which half were imprisoned over 1937 and 1938 - during the period of the Great Purge. And over a half were communists, the State's political party!

Fig. 3.2 Joseph Stalin, 1937. General Secretary of the Communist Party of the Soviet Union.

Stalin ruled by ultimate terror. People were much afraid, all of the time, lest they say something that was seen to be against his rule. Friends turned-in friends, family members turned-in family members. If they did not, they lived in fear for their lives from the Secret Police: if they did, they lived in fear from anti-establishment followers. Life was a case of trying to 'be invisible' in society.

Stalin put in place many national actions that often resulted in abject failure to protect human life and dignity. He is said to have set up the *Great Genocide* of the Ukrainian people that took place over 1932-1933. The actual number that died, as a result, was unknown but is estimated to be from 3-7 million. It became known as the *Holodomor*, Ukrainian for 'to kill by starvation'. Numerous people died of starvation and murder and had no death registered. For example, the horror of this is reported:

'One day in 1933 a street cleaning service in Kiev picked up 9,472 dead bodies'.

Once, Stalin wanted the population survey to declare a result higher than their 1937 census returns had shown. For political, and other reasons, only about half of the deaths were registered. Stalin simply tampered with clauses of the official census form used, detailing who should be counted. That led to dissent by the committee who were responsible for the census taking; many senior members were sent to the Gulags as being saboteurs! Such things happen under dictators.

Gulags were labour camps maintained in the Soviet Union from 1929 to 1955. For the first time in Russia, forced labour from a Gulag was used to dig by hand, and construct, the White Sea-Baltic Ship Canal that opened in 1933, Fig. 3.3. Records were broken for its completion time, but by the death of how many prisoners? Of the Gulag's 126,000 labour force on the project, an estimated 20,000 died.

Fig. 3.3 Digging the *White Sea-Baltic* Ship Canal in 1932.

As in German detention camps, these also employed brutal methods of control over detainees. The Gulags were used to maintain

Chapter 3 Others of the Evil Camp

fear in Stalin's people. By 1934 many millions were being held in them for sins as small as minor theft, to as large as murder. Political prisoners were also sent to these, often without trial. Life in them was horrific: hard labour, poor nutrition and dreadful living conditions. They were built in out-of-the-way places; the harsh weather of Siberia being well known.

Like Hitler, but not in the same way, Stalin also had strong ambitions and needed total control of everybody in his country. Starting in the mid-20s he created conditions to take absolute power using the most devious methods, including mass murder and purging of the Communist party, and all dissidents.

Purges were commonly taking place. Opposition leaders were accused of crimes against the State and executed. The more usual way of ridding himself of true, or perceived, disagreement with him was to simply 'disappear' people without trial or reports of their whereabouts.

To think I, and many others in London and Midhurst, were born into this period but fortunately not in Russia or Germany. In the mid-1930s most people of the Midhurst Rural District would not have known, or been able to piece together from newspapers and other sources, what was happening in Russia. It was too far away to bother most of them.

Despite the rent riots in London, strikes in the coalfields, poor wages, and troubles in India, Midhurst was a haven away from all that sort of thing.

Perhaps the acclaimed diplomat, Sir Arthur Grant-Duff, then 77 years old and living in Sheep Lane of Midhurst during his retirement, might have followed the reported events. He had had a very extensive senior experience involving numerous diplomatic posts in overseas countries. He would have understood the ebb and flow of diplomatic manoeuvres in dictatorships.

Stalin became another dictator extraordinaire. He could implement any policies he chose without opposition, such was the fear he had instilled in his people. No one dared to object for fear of death.

Politically, despite Stalin's well-deserved *Evil* reputation, he had to be kept on-side by the Allied nations because he commanded a huge army of 1.3 million, that grew to 3 million by WW2.

As Britain's war began with Germany in 1939, Russia was actually about to change sides from being with the Allies to join the Axis group.

In secret, at that time, the Soviet Union was engaged in talks with British diplomats on the threat arising to Russia by Hitler, who had made it clear he wanted to occupy that country.

Russia was then suggesting it was prepared to make an offer of support to persuade Britain and France into an anti-Nazi alliance with them in late 1939; that proposition took place just before Britain declared war on Germany.

'The Soviet offer - made by war minister Marshall Kliment Voroshilov and Red Army chief of general staff Boris Shaposhnikov - would have put up to 120 infantry divisions (each with some 19,000 troops) (2,280,000 in total), 16 cavalry divisions, 5,000 heavy artillery pieces, 9,500 tanks and up to 5,500 fighter aircraft and bombers on Germany's borders in the event of war in the west'

Nick Holdsworth, *The Telegraph*, 18 October 2008.

As it happened Britain failed to act on this, just two weeks before war broke out between Britain and Germany. The Russians, instead, agreed to a non-aggression pact with Hitler to keep the Germans at bay. Few knew of these high-level talks; they only became public knowledge some 70 years later!

So, at the start of WW2, Russia was an Axis partner on the *Evil* side. That changed later in the war.

Fig. 3.4 In 1939 and 1943 Stalin was *Man of the Year* on a Time magazine cover.

Stalin was certainly another person of great *Evil*. Some insist he was worse than Hitler because he was more ruthless; if that was possible. He is credited with the deaths of 20 - 60 million of his people. He bettered Hitler in another respect for he was twice the *Time Magazine's* Man of

Chapter 3 Others of the Evil Camp

the Year; in 1939 and again in 1943, Fig. 3.4. The 1939 one was for signing the *Non-Aggression Pact* with Germany. It was not in the World's interest but it qualified him as 'the public figure that had the most effect on world affairs over the year.'

The other time was for surviving the Nazi attack on Russia and grinding down Hitler's ambitions, with gigantic loss of life on both sides. At that time, he unlike Hitler, got credit for his good leadership. After all, he did lead his nation to a victorious defeat of Hitler's great force by beating the Nazis back out from his great land, Russia. Some suggest the British owe them a lot as that action meant the Nazis were not able to invade Britain with such a commitment as he did moving into France.

Returning to Stalin's leadership in his pre-war years:

> 'On the death of Lenin in 1924, Joseph Stalin took control of the Soviet Union, instituting policies of nationalisation and agricultural collectivisation that fomented civil war and famine as well as cultivating a cult of personality'.

In 1917, under the new communist doctrine, the Union of Soviet Socialist Republics USSR had taken power. This era had one distinctive difference to the other Western Powers; it still had dictatorial power over all of its controlled areas, including the vast area of Siberia.

Although it appeared that a kind of democratic rule was in place the policy-making Politburo had all authority and used the rule of fear to control its people. This era lasted until 1991.

As with most other industrialised countries, the 30s decade in Russia was tumultuous after Stalin took total dictatorial power in 1929 and put into action, massive modernisation of its industries. Stalin's life aims seem to have been to achieve ultimate power for himself in Russia, and to modernise his country at a fast pace.

There was no thrust for Russia to regain any previous empire, to rid the world of all impure races, or to evangelise communism into all countries. He was not trying to become a god but had a lust for the ultimate power. He was, however, most interested in making himself a personality of history. He wanted, and on face value got, unquestioning flattery and praise.

TIME magazine described this public worship:

> 'Joseph Stalin has gone a long way toward deifying himself while alive. No flattery is too transparent, no compliment too broad for him. He became the fountain of all Socialist wisdom'

He was a determined and quietly ruthless man. Russia did become a formidable third world power, but in gaining this status many millions of his subjects were killed by his policies, in one brutal way or another. Time Magazine, said of him in 1940:

> 'History may not like him but history cannot forget him'.

The early 30's decade saw the main world powers begin to respect the Russian nation. However, the Western powers began to fear the new and unique communism form of government for it seemed capable of undermining the class structure and ideals of Imperialism and Democracy.

Initially trying to slow the development of the USSR, Britain, Germany and France all had favourable diplomatic ties in place with the Soviet Union by the end of 1933. With these, they hoped to influence and temper the Soviets.

World events moved swiftly. By 1933 the Soviet Union leadership had become greatly alarmed by Hitler's acceptance and the announcement of the need for a long-stated ambition of Germanic leaders of the previous century. This was the German *Drang Nach Ostenor*, 'Push to the East', plan for conquest. Militaristic steps were being taken by the German nation towards fulfilling this mad desire of Hitler.

Relationships between Russia, Germany and the Allies varied greatly from the 1930s to 1945. Very much due to the slowness of developing technical progress in Russia, Germany was victorious over them in WW1. However, its relationship with Russia warmed in the 20s rising to be very close in the early years of WW2, when they were allies at the start.

In August 1939 Germany and Russia, two totalitarian regimes, signed the non-aggression *Molotov-Ribbentrop Agreement*, leaving Russia free to be part of the Axis force if that suited it.

Chapter 3 Others of the Evil Camp

Shortly after Germany invaded Poland, Russia took over areas to the east of Poland and then invaded several regional countries, that being a secret part of the above agreement.

Russia was very much in control of its actions in localised countries. Its position, however, was soon to become dire, putting it on the highest level of defence against invasion of all of its territory!

With time the two nations fell apart over various territorial demands, and Hitler's treachery. In 1941 Stalin experienced Germany ignoring their friendly agreement, invading his Russia in the German *Operation Barbarossa* campaign under Hitler's Directive 21. This 'bloodiest conflict in human history', in which Russia lost some 20 million men, pushed Russia to align with the Western Allies, that remaining as the situation for the rest of the war.

In its time of greatest need posters used old appeal methods to call to arms soldiers, sailors and women to defend Moscow. Advance patrols of the German Army got within 15 miles, being at the outskirts of the Moscow tram system.

However, due to extremely long supply distances and total use of all local Russian materials as they advanced, they had run out of strategic materiel. The Russians, on the other hand, just kept up the supply of more and more, men, women and machines. They were accustomed to the harsh 'white' winter of November 1941 and deployed over a million men and women, and a thousand tanks. They were able to mount counter-attack, after counter-attack, Fig. 3.5,

Fig. 3.5 Russia fights back to defend Moscow in late 1941.

By December the winter temperature dropped to -45C. The Germans were not equipped for that; many soldiers froze to death.

The Allies partnership with Russia was, however, always strained by it not being a democracy; having enforced collective communist ideals; its sheer strength and size; and largely growing self-sufficiency of resources. Matters were made worse by the dominance of Stalin's character that did not always follow reason. That clashed with Churchill's persona and his ability to 'see through' people.

It is, therefore, not that simple to put the Russians in the *Good* or the *Evil* category during WW2 for they changed sides mid-stream between the Allies and the Axis countries. Their impact on eastern European nations was much more significant than it was for the Western nations.

It could be said of Stalin that if he had been left alone, he might not have joined the Allies or the Axis in WW2. He would have stood in the wings picking off bordering countries when it was easy and safe to do so. Hitler's moves on the WW2 chessboard forced Stalin to align as he did.

The Soviet Union was an important country in ending the war of the Allies against Germany. In late 1940, Hitler had gained a firm foothold in France and, following the Dunkirk withdrawal by the Allies, had begun to prepare for a sea invasion of Britain.

Some say Russia saved Britain from invasion by the Germans when Hitler decided to invade Russia, Germany being then signed in as an ally of the Russians!

Starting the operation with 4.5 million German troops, Russian resistance to that invasion lost Hitler whole armies! Casualties for the Germans ran to 750,000, with 200,000 lives lost.

For the Russians, some 2.8 million Soviet POWs died in German hands in the 7 months following their invasion. They had 800,000 military deaths.

Other countries were caught up in this *perfect storm* of would-be dictator empire builders! Next, we look into the place of Spain and Italy

3.2 Italy and Spain

Italy had a population of about 44 million people in 1935. The earliest civilisation in Italy was the ancient world of the Roman Empire, that faded rapidly as parts of the country separated. War after war took place in the Italian region over the centuries. For all the turmoil in what we

Chapter 3 Others of the Evil Camp

now call Italy, it was the Western world cultural centre from the 13th to 16th centuries. In 1870 unification of Italy had been achieved. The Kingdom of Italy was created.

In WW1 Italy declared itself to be a neutral country for the reason that Germany was being offensive. It was disappointed that it did not gain much from it; the land given to it was not enough.

Enter another dictator, Benito (*Il Duce*) Mussolini. Using his own *Black Shirt* paramilitary force, being like Hitler's *Brown Shirt* force, he took advantage of the general discontent existing at the time by forming a Fascist political party to assist him to become the Prime Minister in 1922.

He beat both Hitler and Stalin to having his face on the cover of *Time* magazine as its *Man of the Year* in 1923, and again on covers in 1936 and 1943. In contrast to Hitler's decimating the *Time* front page, this award was for great things he was, at the time, doing for his country and regional peace.

Fig. 3.6 Mussolini as Time *Man of the Year, 1923*

Extracts from *The Journal of Historical Review,* May-June 1995 (Vol. 15, No. 3), pages 6-7 provide insight into his following at that time.

'Americans, in particular, saw in Mussolini certain enduring qualities which enabled him to qualify as a `great man' not only of his time but of the ages."

'President Franklin Roosevelt expressed admiration for the Italian leader and sent him cordial letters. In June 1933, Roosevelt praised Mussolini in a letter to an American envoy: "... I am much interested and deeply impressed by what he has accomplished and by his evidenced honest purpose of restoring Italy and seeking to prevent general European trouble."

In another letter a few weeks later, the President wrote:

> "I don't mind telling you in confidence that I am keeping in fairly close touch with the admirable Italian gentleman.'"

> 'America's Roman Catholic press reported sympathetically on Fascist Italy and its leader, encouraged by the signing in February 1929 of the Lateran treaty between Mussolini and the Vatican.'

But it later came apart:

> 'The American attitude toward Mussolini cooled considerably during Italy's military subjugation of Ethiopia, 1935-1936.'

Like other world powers, following unification the Italian Kingdom became engaged in major industrial developments, taking it into the global club of leading nations.

In 1922 the King of Italy entered into an Alliance with the National Fascist Party, led by Benito Mussolini. Over the following years, Mussolini eliminated all opposition parties, by fair and foul means. He took power as another tyrant dictator in 1929. He showed:

> 'how absolute power corrupts absolutely'.

Mussolini's ambition seems to have been to be a god-like leader, as is the case for those who use the personality cult line to gain the people's support; as did Stalin and Hitler. He had statues erected of him and was portrayed as a sportsman and a skilled musician.

He was always promoted as an intellectual and had won some acclaim for his political skill underpinned by his knowledge of contemporary philosophy and political literature.

As with the Nazi regime, he employed a hierarchy of youth membership stages, see www.historylearningsite.co.uk. The names stem from the ancient *Romulus and Remus* legend of the founders of Ancient Rome. These were *Sons of the She-Wolf*, formed as *Figli della Lupa* (4-8 years old); *Balilla* (8-14); *Avanguardista* (14-18), Fig. 3.7.

Chapter 3 Others of the Evil Camp

Fig. 3.7 Mussolini is pleased with his little *Sons of the She-Wolf.*
(Sturgis West History)

    He had a rule of thumb: when a country reached 20 million in its population it was capable of preparing and prosecuting a major war! Italy was ready. These groups gradually indoctrinated members to be fighting men, not just family men.

Their code of honour chant was:

> 'I believe in Rome, the Eternal, the mother of my country......I believe in the genius of Mussolini...and in the resurrection of the Empire'.

Girls also had their place defined; as mothers of lots of children who would become soldiers. Mussolini, in 1927, instituted a programme - the *Battle of Births*. He wanted a larger population as that better supported going to war. Despite the women being supported by financial incentives, the programme was not successful.

At the start of the 30s, Mussolini was a friend of France and Britain, but events of 1935-36 changed all that when Italy invaded the Ethiopian Empire, on a whim of Mussolini. By this action, he eventually aligned with Japan and the *Evil* Germany Axis in 1940.

He then thought that Britain and France were spent forces and that the war would be shortly opening up a chance to gain territories in Africa that were then French or British colonies.

Urged on by Hitler he interned Jews in a concentration camp. Overall, he does not appear to be particularly anti-Semitic.

The Italian people did not start major wars; they had no such tradition in modern times. Mussolini, to further advance his bully-boy corrupted mentality, was taking his people to their slaughter in battlefields afar. They did not want that!

By that time Mussolini had long held his eyes on colonising Ethiopia, (then called Abyssinia), one of the few remaining independent countries in Africa. By this, he emulated Hitler's view that he should 'acquire any territory he considered to be Italian'. Slim reasons were used to justify this invasion.

There had been attempts to mediate a border dispute by LN, (see later), but to no avail. This gave him the excuse to invade. However, he had underestimated the cost of doing so, taking his country into gross financial difficulties.

Four weeks after my Mum and Dad were married on 8 September 1935, Mussolini invaded Ethiopia. At home in Britain, Ethiopia was a long way off; and where was that country anyway?

The major German actions of 1939 made Mussolini believe he had become a lesser member of the Axis. When Hitler annexed Austria and moved against Czechoslovakia, Mussolini decided to have his way and invade Albania - without reference to Hitler! To impress Hitler, he rapidly took action against the Italian Jews by isolating them from the rest of Italian society.

Mussolini had severe racist views, somewhat differently directed than Hitler's. He regarded the black races of Africa as 'uncivilised savages, without ideals', Fig. 3.8. To him, the world was formed of hierarchies that had to struggle for Darwinian survival of the fittest.

Fig. 3.8 Mussolini's racial attitude, 1936. (Evening Standard)

This drove his view that he was simply implementing that line of thought by colonising parts of the continent of Africa. He rationalised that action as Italy badly needing space for its expanding population. Colonising of other 'lesser' countries was morally justified to him!

This was further supported by his views that Italy had rights to those lands anyway; his country was the heir of the long past ancient Roman Empire's assets.

For all the horror caused that we know of today, his policies and charm were persuasive. By the mid-30s the State, and thus Mussolini, was said to be in control of three-quarters of Italian businesses. In 1938 he brought about wage and price controls.

Churchill regarded southern Italy as Hitler's 'soft underbelly'. In 1943 the Allies invaded Sicily in southern Italy and parts of the landmass gradually became on the side of the Allies from September 1943. As they invaded, Italy progressively changed sides leaving the Germans as part occupiers with massively diminished support by the citizens. They had were joining the *Good* side from the bottom up!

It was on 24 July 1943 that Mussolini was arrested by order of King Victor Emmanuel III after the *Grand Council of Fascism* voted him out.

After Mussolini was deposed, he was imprisoned. His life was in high danger from the people; a German paratrooper *Fallschirmjager* unit of their air force extracted him and whisked him away to another hideout. This move saved him from being given over to the Allies.

Fig. 3.9 Mussolini saved at Mount Sasso in 1943 - to lead again in the *Evil* Axis (Bundesarchiv.)

Hitler then allowed him to set up the *Italian Social Republic* in the northern part of Italy that was still under Axis occupation and control.

This, in effect, led to civil war in Italy but with neither side being keen on involvement. The northern half became a puppet state collaborating with Hitler by using its 600,000 soldiers.

The south was then a monarchist region aligning with the Allies. They had 50,000 troops to offer plus a very strong resistance movement acting all over Italy; numbering some 350,000 partisans. However, for that subversive activity German administrators made Italian people, and whole villages, suffer dreadfully with numerous mass executions in

Chapter 3 Others of the Evil Camp

reprisals for German losses. These are given in more detail in a later book of these Memoirs.

Under Il Duce's reign, the Italian Social Republic lost many areas and whole territories to the Allies. Mussolini also lost still more favour by Italians when he, after Hitler's assertive suggestions, orchestrated executions of many of his former Fascist party members. Their Japanese ally was enraged that Italy had surrendered; to them, that state of acceptance was the ultimate humiliation.

At that point he was at his lowest ebb:

> 'Seven years ago, I was an interesting person. Now, I am little more than a corpse.'

By then he was in hiding in the Northern part, but eventually was physically recognised by the partisans as he was moving around in disguise. He and companions were summarily shot the next day along with his mistress.

The Italians had come to hate him so much, Fig. 3.10, that on 29 April 1945 they hung his body, on meat hooks, along with those of his companions, upside down at a very public motor gas service station in Milan. This was a message to other, still fighting, fascists to cease hostilities.

Fig. 3.10 'The Fascist Beast is Vanquished': WW2 poster after the fall of Mussolini. (Bauer)

Another dictator had been eliminated. He had sought to be accepted into the league of empire builders but he was more like a 'terrier biting at the heels' of everyone, hoping to get attention. Like both Hitler and Stalin, he had done much good for his country in the early days of his rule but that all changed as the authoritarian rule was imposed on a nation that had been dragged into war by an incompetent military leader, with a wild ambition to recreate a past empire.

Were the Italians in the *Good* or the *Evil* place? I think not quite either; their people just suffered purgatory as innocents. They had little interest in the whole war and, once Mussolini was gone, they had no one pushing them in that direction; but the upper regions of Italy were still with Nazi rule under which they suffered great cruelty by the occupying Nazi regime.

If they had not entered the war, little would have changed due to their absence. Italy ceased to be actively overt when it joined the Allies in 1943. As will be covered in a later book, they had many reasons to be furious at being dragged into it. Germans still occupied a diminishing part of the country right up to the end of the war.

Spain had a population of about 25 million in 1935. It was constantly suffering from its numerous internal unrests; it had 33 different governments from 1902 to 1923.

It remained neutral throughout the First World War, that being to its financial advantage for it could supply both the Allied and Axis with equipment and portage. The downturn of exports following the end of its WW1 supplier role; a spin-off from the Great Depression; Spanish Flu, and lack of modernisation all took their toll at the end of WW1, driving the country into serious debt.

After a coup in 1923, its governance moved to a bad dictatorship. In 1930 King Alfonso XIII removed that dictator, Miguel Primo de Rivera y Orbaneja, Fig. 3.11, who was not experienced to run a country in virtually any aspect.

Fig. 3.11 General Primo de Rivera. Prime Minister in Spain 1923-1930.

The Second Republic of 1931-1936 was led by a succession of leaders who all saw a serious decline in necessary reforms; the people became belligerent, responding with general strikes.

Chapter 3 Others of the Evil Camp

All this, following several most brutal murders of prominent leaders, led to the Spanish Civil War (1936-39), during and after which an estimated 300,000-1,000,000 people lost their lives.

The Spanish Civil War played an important part in the development of WW2. The civil war had its origins back in the 1920s after it became abundantly clear that the monarchy ruled by King Alphonso was corrupt and incompetent.

He was replaced in a bloodless coup by Primo de Rivera. His rule was partially beneficial to the country with many public works and better land-use schemes implemented. Sadly, for the nation, the Great Depression hit them hard and his leadership was not able to overcome the financial issues. He had to resign.

Elections were set up. Spain became a Republic. The Catholic Church, the Army, and the Government were at strong odds. There were many attempts to overcome social problems of the kind being reformed in Britain. Successive rulers failed to bring about stability. Political turmoil prevailed and anarchy erupted in parts of the country.

In July 1936, another leading politician was murdered, leading to General Francisco Franco Bahamonde, Fig. 3.12, assuming power. The bitter civil war had begun. Other countries mostly stayed overtly out of the Spanish Civil conflict, whilst covertly supplying support: these supporters were often at war with each other in other theatres! Germany and Italy used it to great effect for their purposes.

Fig. 3.12 A beaming Franco with Hitler, 1st April 1939.

Following the Nationalist victory in the Spanish Civil War, General Franco ruled Spain as a military dictator from 1939. He held this position until he died in 1975. With the same political persuasion as Hitler, it would have been expected that Spain would have sided with the Axis. Hitler and Mussolini tried hard to get Franco to join the Axis group, Fig. 3.13. As inducements, they promised him back Gibraltar; economic and military aid; and territory in Morocco. He resisted: more Spaniards would die if he joined them.

There seem to be many different opinions for Spain staying neutral through WW2. Their resources were depleted due to internal fighting.

Fig. 3.13 Hitler and Mussolini wooing Franco.

The people were tired of the killing that took place in their civil war. Also, Franco made it too hard for Hitler to be bothered to attempt an occupation. Through all of WW2, Spain declared itself to be non-belligerent. It was truly neutral, although they did have a continuing protectorate role in Morocco on the pretext that Italy would invade it as WW2 developed.

All of these events may appear to have been too isolated for Britain to be involved. That was not the case. Regional powers appeared likely to come under the Fascist rule if France was taken over by Germany, or Spain. They would be able to control shipping lanes.

In the Spanish Civil War Britain, France and the United States refused to sell arms to the conflict partners but did send, allow, or turn a blind eye to, volunteers to fight in this war.

Chapter 3 Others of the Evil Camp

Russia supplied arms. Communist parties across the world sent 'International Brigades', as did Britain. Who was fighting for who is confusing! The left, and the many liberals, fought the Catholics and the Conservatives. This conflict has become known for its depth of brutality, with 'brother pitted against brother, and neighbour against neighbour'.

The country became severely split. The Nationalists, under General Franco, eventually won the day and fascism was implemented to be the case existing during WW2.

In WW2 Germany had no ambitions to occupy Spain even though, by 1943, Germany was in control of all shorelines from northern Norway to the south of France. It was convenient for them to have a haven shared with their enemies for that permitted clandestine dealings and intelligence gathering. Further, to the Germans, this was one country they did not feel threatened by and did not need an occupying force to keep it in their control.

This civil war broke out in July 1936. In August 1936 all regional nations considered a non-intervention agreement to contain the war to Spain alone. In November, Germany declined, saying it was not needed. Lies were told by the Nazis for it was known they were providing arms - but they insisted they were not, see Fig. 3.14.

Fig. 3.14 Spanish Civil War poster suggesting Hitler was the real leader in Franco's clothing.

Controls were attempted with little success. Germany stepped up its involvement, landing a considerable amount of heavy equipment and men, much of it being in secret.

Figures quoted later suggest they sent from their African bases tanks, aircraft, heavy and light guns, tons of ammunition, fuel, tens of thousands of troops, and submarines. It had been stated that the Germans would only be training Spanish Nationalists and not be involved with the fighting interface. They had other ideas in mind!

The result was a very real and bloody war in which the worst nature of man came to the fore. Fig. 3.15 shows the result of a bombing raid under Operation *Rugen*, by the Luftwaffe Condor Legion and the Italian Legionary Air Force, this being condoned by Franco's Nationalists. Hundreds were killed, the number is much debated.

Fig. 3.15 Bombing of Guernica city in 1937.

Russia sent some forces and France, Britain and others set up embargoes on munitions and troops making their way into Spain. These nations also gained some experience, but much less than the Germans who engaged in all-out, war-implementation trials!

Hitler was not ready to invade Spain so he stalled getting Mussolini from sending in Italian troops.

At the end of this contained civil conflict on 1st April 1939, Franco won out and Spain became an informal Fascist ally of Germany; but for all that Spain stayed neutral in WW2.

This had been a very fortuitous war for Hitler. He had been building up a highly modern war machine to a substantial level of power and combat readiness. Spain was an ideal theatre to exercise it all in real combat. Some 16,000 civilians fought in this war. He was prepared to sacrifice civilians of another country to further his ends.

This all took place with knowledge gained by British diplomats and parliamentarians. British leaders knew what Hitler was up to there. In 1936 they know about the International Brigade members going from Britain, including the British XV International Brigade.

Chapter 3 Others of the Evil Camp

Germany was stealing a march on the Allies by tuning its designs, methods, prototypes and tactics of a much-improved way to make war. This field and logistics experience served them well when war broke out with Britain. It was a case of the head in the sand, Fig. 3.16.

Fig 3.16. Cartoonist David Low's portrayal of the *Good* shrinking from the *Evil* Bully. (Evening Standard)

So, the question is, was Spain in the *Evil* or *Good* camp? Its people were at war within the State. The fascist Axis partners made use of their war to test Hitler's readiness with one faction, the Nationalists easily allowing that situation to exist.

It provided indicators for Britain to see what Hitler was doing. Peaceful diplomacy will win through, they hoped. After all, that was the gentleman's way to solve, living-together, State disagreements!

Surprisingly, war policy was relatively stagnant in early 1930s Britain. Today, Internet searches will come up with extensive material on *appeasement*, but little appears on how the British War Department was preparing for the appearance of Hitler's worst ideas.

The British Royal Navy seemed to be well able to keep the peace with its overwhelming global sea battle force. To some there appeared to be no threat to the British Commonwealth on land; wars would continue to be contained, as it was happening in Spain. However, before 1939, the British Army had only nine divisions compared with eighty-six for France. and seventy-eight for Germany: and it was an army that needed to be much stronger.

Air warfare was still in its infancy then: modest natural development of air force capability was in place in Britain wherein no one else seemed to be a threat. Hitler's stealthy activities were mostly discounted for that suited leaders in Britain to think so.

They did not realise the extent, tenacity, sheer cunning, overwhelming power, and fresh thinking entailed in Hitler's grandest of grand ambitions, to build the Thousand Year Third Reich.

3.3 Japan

Japan was another *Evil* element that had been at play for some time before the European war got underway. It was far away so was all but forgotten by the Western nations. Japan joined the Axis affray when it made a catastrophic mistake of invading US territory in late 1941.

Japan's population was about 70 million people in 1935. That was small compared with other major Axis partners: Russia 170 million, Germany 66 million, and Italy 44 million. Despite that Japan caused as much human misery and loss of resources and human life as did Germany.

In the European sector, there was much less attention given to them; their part in WW2 was yet to be felt. It was the USA, Australia and other Asian countries that suffered greatly at the hands of that *Evil* wind. Japan had good relations with Germany starting in 1860. They began to modernise after 1867, using German thinking to a large extent and via

Chapter 3 Others of the Evil Camp

'intense intellectual and cultural links'. Even in the 1960s, it was common for Japanese visitors to British technical establishments to photograph all that they saw to an amazing limit. They were quick to learn!

However, in WW1, for their gain, they aligned with the Allies, not Germany. Japan declared war on Germany in 1914 and in doing so took some German possessions in the Pacific region and China. They had started their path toward an Asian empire.

Germany and Japan joined forces in the 1930s when they each adopted aggressive militaristic actions. Global separation of the two wars - in Asia and Europe - resulted in what were essentially separate events.

Japan was relatively close to China and then played a large part in the development of China. When modernisation in that part of Asia began in the late 19th century China did not follow Japan, being much concerned with internal problems of the serious political instability of being run by warlords in around 10 regions. Almost all wars where China fought against external aggressions had been lost! China was, therefore, a large country rich with natural resources ready for others to carve up, Fig. 3.17.

Fig. 3.17 French cartoon of 1898. The China pie is being divided up by the global powers.

Britain, Germany, and Russia (with French influence) are there, hard at the carving up the task. The Japanese samurai warlord is contemplating what to take and the Qing dynasty official is hapless; see Wikipedia for more detail.

The First Sino-Japanese War took place from 1894-1895. Japan came out of it as a powerful nation and showed up the considerable weakness of

China to defend its sovereignty. Japan was a small country; modernisation demanded greater natural resources and they came easily by taking them from China. The first major engagement between them was at the Battle of Yalu, Fig. 3.18.

A report by a Commander of a Chinese Iron-Clad ship recorded problems:

> 'Though well drilled, the Chinese had not engaged in sufficient gunnery practice beforehand. This lack of training was the direct result of a serious lack of ammunition. Corruption seems to have played a major role; many Chinese shells appear to have been filled with cement or porcelain, or were the wrong calibre and could not be fired. Philo McGiffin noted that many of the gunpowder charges were "thirteen years old and condemned".'

GUERRE SINO-JAPONAISE
Combat naval du Yalu (25 Octobre 1894).

Fig. 3.18 The Battle of Yalu in October 1894 showed up the weakness of China to combat Japan.

Chapter 3 Others of the Evil Camp

By the mid-1930s China's resources were still easy pickings for the much more modern war forces of Japan. Japan defeated the incapable Qing Dynasty that had bankrupted the country.

Then came the *Second Sino-Japanese war* of the period of July 1937-September 1945. This time it commenced through involvement with Manchuria and Northern China.

It started as a Mexican stand-off over a missing soldier that rapidly led to Japan declaring war on China. Again, Japan was able to dominate in its early years because they were well experienced on a war footing whereas neighbours, such as China with a vastly larger population, had not modernised and had no ingrained ambition for war.

Unlike with the other Axis countries, it was not the Japanese Emperor taking Japan to war; it appears the Japanese Generals were always far too keen to go to war, especially for easily won battles. They did not always take 'no' from their Emperor, despite regarding him as a God.

Japan occupied Manchuria in China and the Korean Peninsula by 1932, advancing to occupy Inner Mongolia by 1937.

China was left with a country in depths of the internal struggle between the established Nationalist and the creeping Communists. The Chinese people suffered greatly. The Japanese occupation of parts of China left a trail of cruelty and human rights abuses.

Fig. 3.19 Chinese recruitment poster, c1937.

Despite the pride and courage shown in the poster, Fig. 3.19, it aimed to recruit pilots for their Air Force, the Chinese Air Force was not sufficiently up to date to match that of Japan when their war began. They lacked the organisation to get the best from what they had.

China's global isolation left them without enough experts to train their aircrews. Captain Claire Chennault, retired from the U.S. Army Air Corps., was asked to advise them. Over 1937-1940 he trained pilots and set in place, advance-warning systems to allow them to be strategically placed for prosecuting defence retaliation. The Battle of Britain also used this approach to effect, via the British Royal Observer Corps.

Another, later, US initiative for China against the Japanese was to recruit American pilots from 1941-42 to form the 1st American Volunteer Group, flying 90, or more, P-40 fighter planes against the incoming Japanese marauders. They began combat just days after the disastrous Pearl Harbour raid.

From the eyes and teeth painted on their Curtiss P-40 Warhawk aircraft, Fig. 3.20, that first flew in 1938, they became known as the *Flying Tigers*; Walt Disney created their insignia, based on its use on German aircraft. These became one of the most recognisable symbols of combat aircraft in WW2. This was a real success; downing nearly 300 Japanese planes for a loss of 14 pilots.

Fig. 3.20 *Flying Tigers* in formation over China in 1942.
(R T Smith)

Chapter 3 Others of the Evil Camp

Japan was finally challenged to the limit by the Allies when it made the fateful mistake of bombing Pearl Harbour in December 1941; that took the USA into the full war state that eventually won out in 1945. Japanese armies of that time left a long-time emotional scar from its inhumane treatment of prisoners of war.

Germany and Italy were not the only regimes with the ambition to implement partial world dominance at that time and rebuild long past empires. What was Japan's reason to be a raider of countries?

In the Far East of the globe, Japan had been a major aggressor since earlier times than the Germans under Hitler. As other nations industrialised, they became a threat to Japan because they would try to stop her ideas on the world stage. Japan needed to secure their sources of raw materials. Korea was an early first target for invasion and it provided a land link to Manchuria. Unlike the German and Italian nations, the blame for the Japanese conquests in the 1930 and 40s cannot be placed on the head of any particular individual leader's ambition.

Their leaders were driven by the basic need for resources, helped along by their genuine belief that their Emperor was an actual *God* in human form. They also wanted to create a non-whites Asian region by removing the European colonists from there.

We rarely hear the names of any individual Japanese military leaders being described as tyrants. There were key national leaders in earlier times. For example, it is said the three top military leaders of the 16th century were Oda Nobunaga, Toyotomi Hideyoshi, and Tokugawa Leyasu. They united the country. Most people are unlikely to have heard of these persons in the West.

It was much the same for WW2. The most responsible person was clearly:

- Emperor Hirohito, Supreme Commander in Chief of their Armed Imperial Forces - many times he sanctioned 'crimes against humanity' carried out by his rebellious military leaders, but was not tried for war crimes at the end of WW2. For example, at 375 times, he authorised the use of toxic gas against the Chinese in 1938.

Midhurst WW2 Memoirs: 2. 'Evil' Rising: 'Good' Awakening

The Japanese High Command comprised:

- General Hideko Tojo - called the *Dictator of Japan* and in charge of war operations, and was succeeded by Koiso, below, in 1944.
- Lt General Kuniaki Koiso - a senior member of the army, not involved with key military decisions for most of the early Japanese war-making.
- Kantaro Suzuki - an Admiral who became significant in 1944 and was in favour of peace toward the end. He agreed to their surrender in 1945.
- General Yoshijiro Umezu - the Chief of Army from 1944; he wanted to prosecute the war to the bitter end.
- Admiral Isoroku Yamamoto - Naval leader and architect of the Pearl Harbour attack in 1941. He died in 1943.

There being no obvious leader to incite hate against by the Allied nations, it was the Japanese nation that became the target of hostile animosity.

In the late 1930s, British people were given little general knowledge of the Japanese abuses of human rights or its military conquests; that history was not taught in mainstream British education. A strong reason they might have been interested was if they had family or business interests there, or in Australasia.

Japanese goods bought from them then were more of the 'amazing arts and crafts' kind, than for their cars, cameras and war materiel. Their local coastal ships, so often depicted in magazines, were so quaint with their 'junk' style, and appearance. A peaceful mood was given in their travel posters, Fig. 3.21.

Fig. 3.21 Romantic image of 1930s Japan. (Hatsusaburo Yoshida)

Chapter 3 Others of the Evil Camp

To the British 'man on the street', 1930s Japan was a romantic country very far away, that still used strong and stealthy men in leather armour, using long swords and martial arts to fight local territorial wars - the *Samurai*. There was nothing to worry about from there! They were not that smart!

However, that image was not how things were becoming. Japanese industry had been designing and building warships since the 1920s that paralleled those of the Western nations - aircraft carriers, battleships, corvettes and gunships, cruisers of all types, destroyers, submarines, and so on. It had rapidly become a major, technology-savvy country having a major military force and global economic presence.

The first 'modern' Japanese campaign success was in the First Sino–Japanese War (1894–1895) from which they emerged triumphant over the Chinese. It was fought over possession of Korea.

Next, the Japanese were victorious in the Russo-Japanese War (1904 – 1905). That conflict has been epitomised as 'the first great war of the 20th century'. It was a conflict between the ambitions of the Russian and the Japanese Empires, fighting for control of Korea and Manchuria.

Shortly after, Russia, France and the UK joined in the *Triple Entente* of 1907; this stood for 'friendship, understanding and agreement'. This was set up to counter ambitions of Germany, Austria and Italy. As with so many cross-country agreements, this one was not a happy alliance. The main reason for it was the defence of some of their overseas possessions.

At the start of WW1, these three members entered the Allies group, against the *Central Powers* of Germany and Austria-Hungary.

Then followed, in Asia, a more settled but not calm period. In that pause, Japan caught up with its industrialisation enabling the production of the materiel of war to be produced at a capacity that would allow the push for another land-grabbing expansion to be commenced again. Their war ambitions were almost continuous until 1942. They seemed to be unstoppable before then.

From 1901-1989 the overall Japanese leader was Emperor Hirohito, Supreme Commander in Chief of Armed Imperial Forces, Head of State and central government, and the representative of the *Imperial Sun Lineage* State. He was a god to his people and that was by an incredibly long succession back in history. His name meant 'abundant benevolence'.

The extent to which Emperor Hirohito was responsible for Japanese aggression is still debated. Some assert he was a 'virtually powerless constitutional monarch', merely a puppet under total control by his military generals. Others say he usually gave the final approvals, so was culpable.

He also was featured in a Time Magazine issue, that being on 19 November 1928. He was there not as 'Man of the Year'; after all, he was a God, not a man. He could trace back his paternal family tree back for some 123 generations! He was considered to be a direct descendant of the Sun Goddess.

Emperor Hirohito was featured many times on the front cover of Time Magazine, his first time being the first full-colour cover, Fig. 3.22, in 1928.

Fig. 3.22 Emperor Hirohito - *The Son of Heaven*, 1928.

This first article opened with these words:

'Supreme above every other man or woman in lineage, rank and sanctity combined is the Emperor of Japan, upon whose splendorous Enthronement world interests focused last week'

By 1930 the jubilant Japanese military leaders, leaning toward Fascism and intense nationalism, felt invincible as the result of many easy campaigns over much weaker countries. They saw the use of armed force was the way to expand their ideal of an Empire of Asia.

Assassinations were numerous as leadership fought for power over the next 10 years. Hirohito did not punish the straying generals. No one

Chapter 3 Others of the Evil Camp

dared challenge him; he was God! The Japanese military leadership saw themselves as ridding Asia of the white imperialists, them being the Asian leader.

This push for territory was not the ambition of a single man but of a country run by a group of military leaders and a few civilians, together acting as an authoritarian military dictatorship with several heads.

There was no one particular Japanese leader on which to pour the guilt of the nation for their WW2 part. That *Evil* lay on a cadre of military personnel who carried out the wishes of the Emperor who, in turn, got his ideas from these advisers. Emperor Hirohito, despite often clearly leaning to the side of *Good* on occasion, was not able to stop Japan's military ambitions.

He was not tried as a war criminal at the end of WW2 because he then still had the confidence of the people and so was left in his supreme position by the US Forces during post WW2 reconstruction. He did, however, have to repudiate his divine state, that act ending centuries of inheritance tradition and god status.

Japanese people of the early 20th century had been seriously conditioned from birth to be prepared to fight to the death for their Emperor, a god in their eyes.

Furthermore, not being the case in the other Axis members, it was more honourable to commit suicide for such a cause than to be taken a prisoner. That made them determined fighters. As their fighting against the liberating Americans came to an end, they often committed ritual suicide. Their disdain for being captured flowed into their dreadful treatment of Allied prisoners who, in their psyche, were the lowest form of humanity for allowing themselves to be captured.

This gradually hardening situation was forming the intentions of its military leaders. In 1931 Japan fully invaded Manchuria. By 1937 they had annexed land, north of Beijing, leading to full-scale attempt to invade China. The Second Sino-Japanese War (1937–1945) had begun. This initial period saw over 300,000 civilians killed! Unlike the Allies, at the time they, by then, had hardened war-fighting experience by the start of WW2.

There was a link between Germany and Japan through both being part of the Axis force; it was not that strong a bond for each had quite different territorial ambitions, and cared little for the legal and honourable sanctity of signed agreements. They did, however, have one common conquest in mind - the Russians; Germany from the west and Japan from the south-east. Starting in 1936, several agreements were signed, first between Japan and Germany, later Italy, that culminated in the *Tripartite Pact* of the Axis countries that were signed in September 1940, Fig. 3.23.

Other European countries joined it after that event. (Hungary, Romania, Bulgaria, Yugoslavia, Slovakia and Croatia.) Under this treaty they each would assist anyone of them who was being attacked by others, not in the war. The USA was still not at war by then, so they set in place economic sanctions. This did not help matters as it increased Japan's need to invade territories to obtain resources. A year on, found Hirohito permitting the bombing of Pearl Harbour in December 1941. Japan had aligned with Germany and Italy in 1941 to declare war on the United States.

That raid was rapidly followed by the Japanese invasion of Malaysia and then Singapore in January 1942. In their eyes, it was the beginning of the end of white 'supremacy' in Asia. This is when Britain, as well as the US and Australia, came to feel the sharp cutting edge of the cruel swords of Japan.

With the Allies well engaged in the European theatre of war, the Japanese seized the opportunity in February 1942 to finally remove white supremacy for good in Asia. Churchill was not prepared to garrison Singapore: 80,000 British and Australian troops were left to surrender to the Japanese and become POWs. They were used on cruel and inhumane projects as forced labour working under dreadful,

Fig. 3.23 The *Tripartite Pact* is signed by the Axis members in 1940.

Chapter 3 Others of the Evil Camp

conditions of overwork, scant rations, and with the cruellest of punishments.

From that time Japan became deeply in conflict with the Allies, especially the Americans. The Pearl Harbour bombing, in December 1941, had led to a second war region making it harder for the Allies to defend both Europe and Asia.

On 4th May 1942, the tide began to turn. The Japanese called off their intended invasion of Port Moresby. One of their many aircraft carriers was sunk on the same day. Carrier sea battles ensued in many locations. Bloody island invasions by US troops gradually pushed the Japanese homeward, their furthermost places from home being in September 1942.

As was the case with Germany, the Japanese would not lie down. Bitter fighting was needed before they were beaten back to their home boundaries.

It took nearly two more years to get the Japanese to surrender. This Pacific theatre of war was fought mainly by US fighters along with smaller, often very effective forces from Australia, Britain, China, British India, New Zealand, Dutch East Indies and other British colonies. Russian forces were also used.

The long battle against Japan continued until the two atomic bombs were dropped on Japan, by the Americans on 6th and then the 9th August 1945, to stop the war. V-J Day, the end of the war with Japan, was held on 14th August 1945, or 15th depending on location in the world time zones.

The European War had ended on V-E day on 8 May 1945. Unless families in Midhurst had relatives still fighting the Japanese, were Prisoners of War, or in forced slavery by them, people in Midhurst would probably have been pleased to learn it was over. The war was finally over, but reconstruction was another hard period for the world at large.

Before leaving the brutal *Evil* Axis regimes of the 1930s a few words are needed about the use of signed agreements by them.

The various Imperialist empires of Europe were not that familiar with getting on in real harmony with each other. They co-existed by keeping their boundaries and influences mainly under control for the common good. After all, they had carved up the World's peoples amongst themselves in previous centuries. By agreeing, via jointly signed documents, on how to keep their place in this board game did facilitate a kind of working peace, and thus prosperity for each.

They now, however, had to rethink their situations as one man, Adolf Hitler, did not want to play the honesty game. He wanted what they had and was preparing to take it all by force.

One apparent solution to the coexistence of these long-standing empires was to sign sheets of paper that laid down the top levels of things they accepted on each side of the bargaining table. They each had considerable power so that tended to moderate any undue ambitions for a while, but never for long.

The new game, when Hitler joined, was what I call 'treaty writing'. The amateur historian of the 1930s period can be excused if he or she fails to know of a treaty or two, here and there.

From the 1933 year the various countries were progressively being forced to take sides, forming into just two teams; the Allies for the *Good* side and the Axis for the *Evil* side. In military terms, the *Evils* had superiority at the time.

Treaties were signed between many different countries. Some were adhered to, others not. Hitler broke them in fast succession. They merely gave him time to build up his war machine to a level never seen before.

Germany and Japan signed the anti-communist, *'Anti-Comintern Pact'* on November 25, 1936. It stated in part:

> 'recognizing that the aim of the Communist International, known as the Comintern, is to disintegrate and subdue existing States by all the means at its command; convinced that the toleration of interference by the Communist International in the internal affairs of the nation's, not only endangers their internal peace and social well-being but is also a menace to the peace of the world desirous of co-operating in the defence against Communist subversive activities'

Germany was certainly not siding with Russia at that time! However, shortly after the Nazis invaded Poland in 1939 the USSR again became an ally of Germany for reasons of convenience. The declaration of Hitler

Chapter 3 Others of the Evil Camp

in the *Anti-Comintern Pact* was briefly ignored. That was short-lived: Germany invaded parts of Russia in 1941. Treaties were, indeed, merely as a tactical tool of war for Hitler. By 1938 there existed three-way involvement between Hitler, Hideki Tojo, (Supreme Military Leader of Japan) and Mussolini. Fig. 3.24 shows these leaders being celebrated in a Japanese poster of 1938.

Fig. 3.24 Children of their nations dancing in unison for the Axis leaders in 1938: Japanese propaganda poster.

Whereas Hitler and Mussolini led their armies toward massive Empire goals, in Japan, it was a small group of military generals, headed by Hideki Tojo, that had a common vision of an Asia with only Asians in it; and it was not well controlled by their Emperor.

By the end of 1939, the global situation had been dragged into the 'mother of all global takeover' attempts; a 'perfect storm' of dictatorial pursuits. Interestingly, all three Axis leaders never met together, face to face, but they were just bit players in the grand scheme, often pulled into the fight by expediency or coercion.

It is now time to explore key members of the *Good* Allies side that eventually overpowered the Axis forces.

Chapter 4. The Good's Respond

4.1 Peaceful Moves

We have seen how many countries came to a state of war due to the *Evil* elements causing it to occur. The next sections look at some circumstances and work for the *Good* in both German and the Allied countries.

A very dark era was emerging in the mid-30s, being brought on by Hitler's actions to build up a huge and powerful military force and to steadily clamp down on the lives of all Jews, in Germany and his occupied countries. Many minds were being exercised in this situation.

One person, of interest to Midhurst, who offered a scenario *future history* solution, was the author, H.G. Wells.

Wells was born in the London suburb of Bromley in 1866. He spent some of his early life in Midhurst as a student first enrolled in 1881 and then a little after that as an assistant teacher at the now gone, Midhurst Grammar School.

Maybe he got the ideas for his 1930s sci-fi books by observing the breaking news about German Nazi behaviour, and how it might develop?

In the early 1930 period, he wrote the *Shape of Things to Come* that was published in 1933, Fig. 4.1. It was soon made into a very popular film, *'Things to Come'*, that was released in 1936.

Fig. 4.1 *Shape of Things to Come*: Dust jacket of First Edition in 1933.

His scenario in that book involves a major force for *Good* coming down from a fleet of spacecraft in the sky, to correct the *Evil* on Earth. It predicted the 1939 start of WW2 with uncanny realism.

From the newspapers and the radio broadcasts, people knew facts about the world's politics and of the reported barbaric acts taking place; this film must have put fear into those that saw it, but also offered hope that there was a solution. Maybe they then held high hopes that a Saviour race would come to rid them of the Hitler's of the world.

At the time the nearest reality peace-making force, like that of Wells' sky dwellers, was the League of Nations (LN). Wells was skilled at pulling together ideas about contemporary issues, creating many books from them. One contribution was of a *World Brain* concept.

> 'His vision of the *World Brain*: a new, free, synthetic, authoritative, permanent "World Encyclopaedia", could help world citizens make the best use of universal information resources and make the best contribution to world peace.'

In 1937 a World Congress was held in Paris to explore the idea of *Universal Documentation.* Wells felt that:

> 'the creation of the encyclopaedia could bring about the peaceful days of the past, with a common understanding and the conception of a common purpose, and of a commonwealth such as now we hardly dream of'.

This was a remarkable event for at that time all recorded knowledge was stored only on paper, or photo film. Tape recorders, digital printers, computers and the Internet were not yet invented in practical forms. Indeed, the electronic solid-state technology needed to implement these ideas was then in its infancy. *Wikipedia* and the *Internet* form the first real embodiment of that ideal.

Sci-fi authors can dream up the future in terms of words and image representations well before its substance can be implemented. Wells was remarkable in that he was so right; so many times. He was able to extrapolate the then-current facts into the future happenings.

Returning to the League of Nations; this had been set up after WW1 to maintain world peace, Fig. 4.2. The methodology, chosen by democratic means, was intended to stop wars happening on a global

Chapter 4 The Good's Response

Fig. 4.2 The LN was intended to be the muzzle holding the mad dog in control.

scale. No more WW1 times! This ideal state of affairs would be obtained by exercising collective security and general disarmament, these to be achieved by arbitration and negotiation, not by physical force.

The LN, however, had no armed force of its own. It's stated aims incorporated ideals for many of the issues that lead to wars, such as working conditions, illegal trade, recognition of rights of minorities, and health issues. Major nations had to provide any armed forces needed, but that was not acceptable to all.

The LN does not exist today, having been replaced by the United Nation UN; with extended ideals. Its effectiveness at the time was not helped by the US not joining. Today the UN is more effective but still not the mechanism to gain the degree of peace desired when arbitration collapses.

Did the existence of the LN stop major wars? No! The aggressive Benito Mussolini of Italy said of it:

'The League is very well when sparrows shout, but no good at all when eagles fall out.'

As time soon proved, the LN failed to control the powerful rogue Axis nations bent on conquest. Nazi Germany, Italy, Japan and Russia, all merely terminated, or ignored, their membership. Pieces of paper did not work with them.

During the 1930s the peace-seeking countries, their nature being to be peaceful, kept procrastinating until the situation with things reached the point where the use of the strongest physical intervention was the only solution to bring the Axis nations to heel.

By 1938 the European situation had reached the point where Britain was preparing to 'do or die'.

I had been in the world for just a year. These events were already deciding how my life path, and that of millions, would follow. The events severely disrupted the lives of my parents in a way that would not have been if the war had not happened. In some ways, I was lucky to be born then, but that was indeed sheer luck for my case as it all went well. For many millions, it was for the worse.

The science fiction work of H. G. Wells, *'The Shape of Things to Come'*, was starting to fit the real-world events alarming well. For how long would his predictions hold? Could we use that as a crystal ball to see our fate ahead of time? His foretelling of total all-out war, with almost no limits of morality, was sheepishly dismissed by many as pure fiction. Who would act so badly? It was just not cricket!

Was anyone in Britain alarmed enough to take serious action, to put their life on the line, to try and prevent what should not have been occurring?

In this period when *Good* and *Evil* became well defined, the last book authored by Charles Dickens was eventually published. He had written a family work *The Life of Our Lord* for the instruction of his children over the period 1846-1849. They used it at special times, such as at Christmas. He never intended it to be published in their lifetime giving advance permission for its publication to be only after the death of his last child. It eventually became available to the world, Dickens (1934).

However, the sentiment of universal kindness expressed there was not heard by leaders, of what became the Axis power of evil in WW2!

Before covering the nature of the *Good* nations, it is a time to introduce the elements of democratic rule.

4.2 Elements for Good - the Democracies

We have seen, by delving into the formation of WW2, how there was considerable knowledge around in the Western press that major crimes

Chapter 4 The Good's Response

against humanity were occurring in the Axis controlled regions. Who was seriously trying to stop this? How much better were the other great empires in their dealings with their citizens? One person had some advice to offer, see Fig. 4.3.

Fig. 4.3 Pavement street artist in London. 27 August 1939 (Green).

The problems of the citizens of the Axis controlled countries can be put down to them having few if any, personal rights. Their leaders decided what was good for them without asking if it suits them. Fine, if the leader knows what that is, otherwise it can be harsh and become very brutal: the right conditions, but only for the corrupted minds of men with absolute power!

Dictators are a mixed bunch. Some, not many, have been good for their country. However, you never know what you get until they seize power, then either showing their *Good* side or, too often, lapsing into egocentric madness using extreme *Evil* as a tool of achievement.

There is a simple joke of the time that illustrates dictatorship in action:

'Several rows of soldiers were being inspected by their new

Leader, an absolute power authoritarian in a theatrical uniform covered with braid, and gold bibs and bobs.

They stood firmly upright and precisely positioned. There existed a great hush; everyone was in fear of their lives living under the control of this person. What was he like?

The Dictator, who was having a bad day of not quite getting his way easily on all matters, heard someone sneeze in the back row.
He bellowed: "Stand forward the person who sneezed during my speech! If you don't, I will order the front row of soldiers be shot on the spot." No one stood forward. The Dictator turned to his aide: "Shoot everyone in the first row". Rat-a-tat: the first row of men fell dead. The rest were left shivering even more in their boots.

Again, he demanded, "Stand forward who sneezed". Again, no response ensued. Guess what? He gave orders to shoot the second row. Again rat-a-tat and they too fell. Not happy with this situation he issued the same order, with an even stronger voice, 'Stand forward who sneezed'. He had a terrifying imperative in his voice.

This time the diminutive voice of the culprit, somewhere in the back, and almost at whispering level, said. "It was I". The Dictator drew himself up, seemingly going red with rage.

After a long pause, he replied... "Gesundheit" being German for 'good health'.

He then asked the soldier "Why did you take so long to reply?"

An alternative to the various forms of autocratic dictatorship is called democracy: a system of government wherein citizen's rights are decided by the people through their elected representatives. These rights are recorded for all to see for they are used to govern the peoples. Although the Ancient Greeks are usually given as the founders of the concept, it also was developing independently in other nations of ancient times.

Chapter 4 The Good's Response

This form of government was first observed by the Ancient Greeks of Athens in 508 BC, Fig. 4.4, but then generally only for the privileged classes.

Fig. 4.4 Artist's impression of Athenian Greek democracy at work.

Alongside this kind of governance system is the need for codified laws. For example, possibly the oldest set of recorded laws is the *Code of Hammurabi* of Babylonia (today Iraq), carved into a block of stone around 1780BC.

The Ancient Romans were great with developing extensive bureaucracy having endless laws and regulations. There were even civil service duty statements recorded for the various levels of the occupation of *Torturer*!

Ancient Rome was, in the middle times of its power, ruled by a group of privileged senators who decided how to manage national affairs. However, this eventually gave way to dictatorial autocratic government wherein one man had the ultimate power; Caesars emerged thinking they were Gods!

Lack of flow-on for the records following the Greco-Roman period, and the resulting destruction of all but 15% of the written record in the 1st century AD, probably meant that the ideas of laws and the democratic government had to be reinvented and redeveloped.

Democracy has been slow to catch on. English historical development played a key part in its pathway to acceptance in a sound way. In Britain William the Conqueror, upon his conquest of England in 1066, did not institute a democratic government. He set up control of his new kingdom by giving power to Feudal Barons who ruled, as they saw fit, the serfs of their given lands. Laws were instituted with great variance, and seldom with insight into citizen's wishes.

A key British document, produced in 1086, was the *Domesday Book* that recorded the results of a national survey. The main purpose of this survey was for William the First to have a recorded account of his newly seized wealth for purposes of taxation and military support.

The book got its name from its certainty of judgements made. It clearly stated who had what, and which person was responsible for managing the collection of local taxes needed for the overall governance of the kingdom. Modern language versions of the Domesday Book are available today.

In 1215 another major English written work was created that set the pace of democracy. The *Magna Carta* (Great Charter), also called *The Great Charter of the Liberties of England* was compiled, not so much for truly democratic reasons, but because many of the powerful feudal barons wanted their rights to their wealth preserved in case King John of England decided to seize their assets. Those Barons had inherited wealth and many enrichment privileges from their descendants who had been granted assets after the Norman invasion. These estates had been variously improved by hard work, cunning and evil deeds, Collins (1988).

This document, its form did change over the centuries, has been described in modern times in Danziger and Gillingham (2004) as:

'The greatest constitutional document of all times – the foundation of the freedom of the individual against the arbitrary authority of the despot.'

It was not preferred reading by leaders of the Axis nations! A transcript of the document is available on the Internet. It is interesting reading for it covers many features of living harmoniously.

The charter was, most likely, sealed at Runnymede, on the bank of the River Thames by Windsor Castle, just west of London: that was the regular meeting place for the Anglo-Saxon kings - see Fig. 4.5.

Four copies of the original document exist, two being held in the British Library. It was reissued in the 13th Century, one copy being in Australia, another in the USA. Digital copies are now available for all to

Chapter 4 The Good's Response

see, showing their magnificent artwork.

Fig. 4.5 Memorial to the sealing of the Magna Carta in 1250.

The principle espoused was essentially that a defined group of Barons could decide if the King had gone too far with the breaking of the law, in so much as they could seize his assets. It started the ideas of democracy. One thing it did was to make the punishment of the serfs only permissible if they were tried according to the law of the land.

The Magna Carta was instrumental in providing the basis for many other governments in the English colonies of the 17th century, the Americas included.

Before the time of Caxton in the 1400s, one of the problems making it difficult to propagate ideas was that books were each handwritten and illustrated, being made as singular objects of high art. In England, they were compiled first in Latin and later, from 1066, in Normandy French. Few commoners could read them. So valuable were they, that they were often chained up to prevent theft.

A major development took place in 1440. Johannes Gutenberg, in Germany, began to use printing based upon the movable type, set up in a printing press. This allowed mass-replication at a reasonable cost; one set-up of the type blocks could be used rapidly to produce copies on paper. The result was a rise in the numbers of materials published, thus taking knowledge out to a much wider population.

William Caxton was the British hero of printing: he introduced the printing press to the English. In 1480 an epic book was published under his name called *'A Description of Britain'*. A rendering has been published, in modern language and with explanation, Collins (1988). This work gives an understanding of the situation existing in 15th Century England. Laws are briefly over-viewed, along with the division of the land and its rulers.

The Caxton account shows the many differences existing across the land. Midhurst, for example, was a market town established in the church See of Selsey, later to become Sussex. Its Market House was erected around 1551. It is reasonable to assume the Red Lion Inn in Red Lion Street, but now no longer an inn, was probably built at that time to service out-of-town visitors to the market that was held there each week, and to support business discussions and provide traveller accommodation. The Red Lion Inn building still exists and features in a later memoirs book. A brief history of that medieval era is found in *The Market Square* leaflet, Howard (2006).

In 1773 the British American colonies decided that the English law was not being applied to them following their home country's Westminster system of democracy. Their 'rights' were being ignored to make England richer. They had no representation of the colony in the British parliament yet they were expected to follow the Westminster Parliament laws, that had evolved over centuries.

The famous *Boston Tea Party* of 1773 occurred when the colonists refused to pay the tax to Britain for tea they imported. A band of revolutionaries demonstrated by dumping the incoming cargo of tea from its ship into the Boston harbour.

In 1775 the American Revolutionary War started, the outcome being that the distorted British rule of the American colonies was evicted. The British lost those colonies. By 1783 European countries recognised the sovereignty of the newly formed United States of America. It took a few years for democracy to be accepted in law, starting with the *Declaration of Independence* from Britain, in 1776, Fig. 4.6.

Chapter 4 The Good's Response

Fig. 4.6. Birth of Democracy in the new United States of America, 1776.

The infant US nation was set up with its democratic government using a system similar to, but not identical with, the Westminster one. It also has its famous *Bill of Rights* included; still not shared by all democratic countries as such.

In the 1930's decade, Canada, Australia, New Zealand, the West Indies countries, some states of Africa, and India all were using Westminster styles of government as the result of their British colonisation in their past. The French Revolution of the late 18th century eventuated because its people wanted a better way of government than they were receiving under an absolute Kingship Monarchy.

That revolution soon led to the three essential principles being enunciated - *Liberté, égalité, fraternit*é (liberty, equality and fraternity). The full application of democracy in France vacillated over many decades after the revolution, as Emperors and Kings took short term power intervals. By the 1930s, when war was seen to be coming, it was certainly governed by a sound version of democracy.

Thus, the Allied Nations of WW2 used recognisable democratic government; and that is where the differences lay in how human beings were being treated at the time, compared with Axis occupied countries.

It is important to realise that most of the citizens of the non-democratic Axis countries had never experienced democracy as a way of life. The 'common man' in those countries did not appreciate the virtues of democratic rule. Hitler's education system concentrated the lives and minds of people on his kind of socialism from their birth.

During the early 1930s decade, all of the dominant empire-building nations – both under the rule of the *Evil* or *Good* - were flexing their claims at much the same time. The British Empire was fading fast as a world-dominating entity; its colonised countries had started to push for their independence. There was, in the mid-30s, a significant threat that these evil Axis dictators would overrun Europe, Russia and Asia .... and soon Britain!

The main forces of *Good* comprised Britain, the United States, France, Belgium, Norway, Netherlands, Poland, Greece, some African states, Canada, Australia, and later in the 40s, Russia. Despite most of these them professing democratic principles of governance, it was slow to be applied to the people of their colonial possessions. All of these had, and needed to protect, their overseas interests in preserving their wealth incomes.

One by one, Hitler picked off the smaller countries close to Germany thereby expanding his available material and human asset base, He greatly enhanced his military machine experiences by improved technical design and more efficient manufacture than was had by the other nations; at least up to the late 30s.

My parents would have understood what was happening in the 30s to some degree, but there was still much talk about the proudly proclaimed, still powerful, British Empire. 'Britannia rules the waves' and the 'Land of Hope and Glory' all depicted this mood. Surely that would save Britain! British people did not get much education in political systems in the 1930s!

It needed action by the British Parliament to develop a much better war machine, and that meant more money and time that had almost both has run out of. The democratic process had to be used to this end but it

Chapter 4 The Good's Response

could be too slow.

Much has been said about the nature and use of democracy. Mankind is yet to establish the Utopian, ideal, form of government, but democracy has proven to be a good start.

Churchill, quoting someone before him, summed up the concept of the democracy:

> 'Many forms of Government have been tried and will be tried in this world of sin and woe. No one pretends that democracy is perfect or all-wise. Indeed, it has been said that democracy is the worst form of Government except for all those other forms that have been tried from time to time....'

The deleterious events occurring in the Axis nations were well known to the free world! What did these Allied nations do, through its League of Nations, to curb Hitler and Mussolini's ambitions?

They were slow to get started. Just lots of talk and passing of many resolutions; with little preventative action. The conservative governments of the Allies were unable to come to grips fast enough with the view that massive retaliatory military action was the only way to counteract developments by Hitler and Mussolini. Diplomacy was not going to work with Hitler!

Mussolini sought, and obtained, approval from the LN for some of Abyssinia's land to be passed into Italian control. Instead of sticking to that agreement he invaded the country, using poisonous gas and attacking Red Cross hospitals. Britain and France took no action to rectify the situation, Fig. 4.7. And his country was a member of the LN!

A key problem for the Allies was that their governments did not want a war and had felt, until Hitler appeared, that they could scale down their defence budgets. WW1 was supposed to have been the war to end all wars!

Democracies are not easily driven to join even small wars, let alone a world war. No peace abiding country wants to have to spend vast amounts of wealth waging war. Their governance methods require lots of time to negotiate their bureaucracy before agreeing to take action against those going astray. In the 1930s they also needed time to modernise their military force to meet a strong threat.

Fig. 4.7 Mussolini shows contempt for the League of Nations.

In contrast, the strong dictator can obtain faster results - at least in the beginning. Hitler could produce and install his Directives in a very short time.

The British Empire had considerable wealth, but it was not oriented to take a major war to another country. Its past colonisation had started to become an embarrassment. It needed to preserve what it had accumulated overseas and was still getting over the cost of its part in WW1. The smaller colonies of Britain were even less prepared for large scale war.

After WW1, Britain slowed its defence developments, concentrating on maintaining its colonial assets. Rearmament started cautiously in 1932. The Spanish Civil War soon showed that much improvement was needed in the British air and ground forces.

The USA had also been downsizing its military assets after WW1 and was not investing in modernisation of its war machine. It also had adopted an isolationist policy from the rest of the world, being neutral in its position toward a war.

Before the war broke out Prime Minister Chamberlain's government, whilst being remembered much for its appeasement policy with Germany, was already the driving force in military force improvements. They had started on the development of radar systems for aircraft

Chapter 4 The Good's Response

location detection. Boffins and factories were well on the way with manufacturing the new generation of the Hurricane and Spitfire fighter aircraft that became vital in turning back Hitler's attempt to decimate the Royal Air Force in the autumn of 1940.

Things were left until the situation was so dire that the Allies became compelled to take military action. The Allies (just Britain and France at that time) had a lot to catch up on so were badly caught out in thinking its two armies combined could hold back the highly modernised, crack German force that swept through Europe with lightning speed from September 1939 onward.

Fig. 4.8 Poster for H G Wells film, 1936.

Earlier, as has already been mentioned, H G Wells had a shot at predicting a solution to this deepening world situation in his 1933 book *Shape of Things to Come*; that begat a film in 1936, Fig. 4.8.

He wrote of a race of super pacifist people, *Wings over the World*, who would descend from the skies above to rebuild the world after 30 years of utter 'destruction, plagues and appearance of despots'.

No such super race exists; even today the strongest countries well understand the extreme difficulties associated with stepping into other country's conflicts.

Once he had started to implement their *Blitzkrieg* advances, stemming Hitler's rampage across Europe in 1939 was just not possible to stop. The speed of development of the Nazi war effort and its output of modernised, advanced technology, fighting machines and highly trained storm troopers could not be matched by any country of the world at that time. For British people, the similar aggression taking place across parts of Asia by the Japanese was low key in their thoughts.

It is now time to consider the *Good* side of the war to come; the formation and nature of the Allies.

Chapter 5. The Allies

5.1 Britain and Its Commonwealth.

Almost every country in the World, Wikipedia names some 120, were impacted by the hostilities. By the end of the war, most countries had formally declared war on the few *Evil* Axis powers - Germany, Italy and Japan.

This included Russia for a short period at the start of the war in 1939. Italy surrendered to the Allies in 1943 but was still occupied in part by the Nazis until the war ended in 1945.

The main Allies on the side of *Good* were Britain and its Commonwealth countries including Canada, Australia, New Zealand and India; the United States of America USA from late 1941, and some European countries including France, and Belgium and Norway as they were liberated by the Allies. Various other countries, mainly China, assisted in Asia.

Some declared they were *neutral*, hopefully, to avoid invasion. They were Afghanistan, Colombia, Iceland, Ireland, Malta, Portugal, Spain, Sweden, Switzerland, Tibet and Yemen.

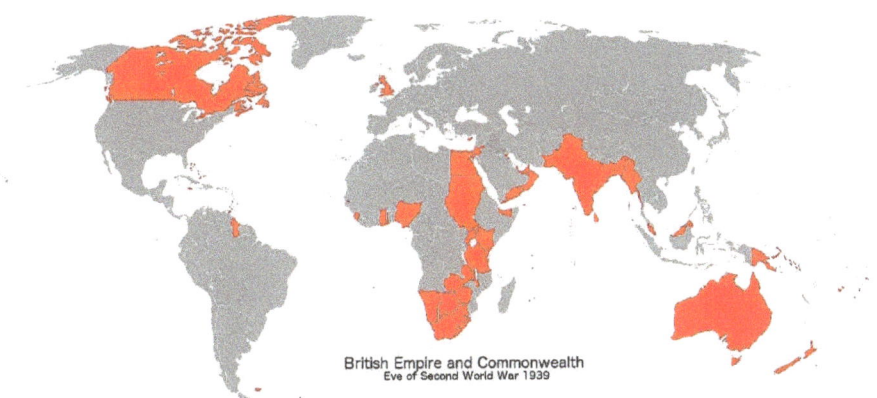

Fig. 5.1 British Empire and Commonwealth countries in 1939. (R Brukner)

Britain had a population of some 47 million people in 1935 and the

British Commonwealth then had 2 billion people, in 53 countries - about a third of the world's population. The extent of those countries that it could call upon to oppose Hitler in late 1939, is shown in Fig. 5.1. (Some smaller countries may be missing on the map; British Honduras being one.)

By selling off foreign assets, to finance its part in World War 1, Britain had done better than other European countries after the war; but that made it vulnerable in the 30s decade to diminishing world trade earnings.

The Royal Navy had a much-reduced fleet as the result of submarine successes by the Germans in WW1. With no apparent war looming in the early 30s, spending was diverted to assist correction of social issues and to industrialisation; not so much back to armaments.

Whilst this situation existed in Britain, the USA's Wall Street Crash of 1929 began the *Great Depression* in that country. Its impact on society was greatest in the USA, but it also made matters worse all around the world, including in Britain.

Not as dire as in the USA, from 1929-1934 unemployment in Britain rose significantly, peaking at almost 3.5 million in 1933. Its vitally important world trade halved. In the coal mining areas, unemployment reached 75%!

The consequence of these difficulties was that the government had to pay out massive amounts of 'dole' benefits to many more families. The cost to the nation of an unemployed person can be roughly valued as what they would have been contributing, plus the cost to support them with unemployment benefits. Their income reduced, passing on a significant impact on society due to reduced demand for goods and services. Productivity also dropped.

This depression greatly reduced the British government's ability to carry out improvements to the national state of affairs that was needed to advance its infrastructure and world position. Some suggest this period was a significant reason for the decline of the British Empire. Certainly, changing attitudes, both in the colonies and in Britain, were leading the colonies toward movements for independence in the early 1930s.

Another colonising Empire you say? How does this British one compare with the ambitions of the Third Reich?

Chapter 5. The Allies

Indeed, Britain had been building up overseas possessions since the 17th Century. It probably got this habit from the Romans and the Normans who invaded Britain, ruling there for many centuries.

In 1584, during the first Elizabethan reign, one push used to keep Spain under control in Europe, was by plundering its treasure ships that were bringing back immense wealth - gold and silver by the ton - from its *New World* possessions, being the bulk of the Americas. Britain also wanted to colonise some of the Americas.

Several naval captains had a charter from Queen Elizabeth that gave them her authority to act as warships, being hostile to Spanish ones. Whilst not having any natural rights at all, they were 'granted' royal assent to plunder and seize them. The notable *privateers* were Sir Walter Raleigh, Sir John Hawkins, Sir Humphrey Gilbert, Sir Richard Grenville and Sir Francis Drake, Fig. 5.2, who married one Elizabeth Sydenham. Not having any issue with her, Drake is not a bloodline ancestor of mine!

Fig. 5.2 Sir Francis Drake. A Privateer of Queen Elizabeth 1. (Linda Alchin)

England had no standing Navy at that time so these ships were a de-facto raider naval force. Elizabeth 1 eventually restarted a permanent navy; it having been neglected since Henry VIII founded it.

Drake is interesting for he was born a commoner and found it hard to break into the ruling-class structure. Significant wins against Spanish ships, and global circumnavigation wherein he claimed the California area, had earned him the dubbing of a knighthood, ordered by Elizabeth I. He also was second-in-command of the English naval fleet that faced the Spanish Armada.

With his grant of half of the bounty that he had plundered, he set himself up very well in Buckland Abbey, Devon.

Privateer ships were sent to colonise an area of North Americas, and call it 'Virginia' in honour as the Virgin Queen. That region had little population so the armed invasion was not necessary. Trading with the

New World natives was an easy way to exploiting their resources for the benefit of Britain. They were not conquered by bloodied war but were certainly taken short in the deals struck in return for their 'protection' by the Monarchs of England.

At that time England was also looking to the East for trade and its control; the private East India Company was licenced by Queen Elizabeth 1 in 1600. That eventually became British India. Again, it was an invasion by way of trade, not direct conquest under arms.

Around 1650 another target for British exploitation was the East Indies.

In 1660, under Charles 1, the British started to colonise the African continent with its Royal African Company. Trade had, again, opened the door; but here for a disgraceful commodity - the 'harvesting' of humans. That trade was mainly involved with slave trading for the productive sugar and tobacco plantations of the East Indies and the Americas.

The slave era was one of the greatest shames of humanity. It took place from the 16th to the 19th century with most colonising countries of Europe and Asia using slaves to create wealth as labour in the fields, or as house support in the homestead. Estimates of the number of slaves taken to these possessions range from 10-28millions! Men and boys had to carry out tough agricultural labouring tasks, Fig. 5.3; *holeing* and then planting being examples.

Fig. 5.3 *Planting the Sugar Cane,* 1823, by William Clark

Workers here are forming square boxes in the soil. Seen on the right side are cane cuttings being planted. These were needed each year, across numerous acres.

One particularly gruesome detailed description of the life and times of slaves is the 14,000-page *Diary of Thomas Thistlewood.* It is surprisingly candid, including gory details of the cruel and dehumanising

Chapter 5. The Allies

punishment regimes under which some slaves had to endure.

Slave ownership was too often a case of crimes against humanity being taken to the limit by many owners. (It is left to the reader to look up Thistlewood's crimes that were often too brutal and dehumanising to repeat here.) It is fascinating to me, to find that tyrannical regimes so often keep detailed records of how they ran things, and who they persecuted.

It was common for the number of slaves to outnumber their white owners by 9 to 1. They were regarded as a material asset that could be bought and sold.

Thomas Thistlewood was a successful plantation owner. He was born in Lincolnshire, UK, migrating to Jamaica in 1750 and living there until he died in 1786. He was not the richest of landed owners there, but he was incredibly rich by his home country terms.

He ran an authoritarian regime on his plantations. Being so far from his home base, and so wealthy, British law too often turned the deaf ear on his treatment of slaves.

Not all plantation owners were so cruel, but bonded human life as slaves was usually much worse for them than living under a serfdom regime.

Slavery gradually became unacceptable to the leaders of Britain (and other nations) when it became recognised that all citizens under British control had rights, enforceable by law.

The main pioneering campaigner behind the abolition of the slave trade was Thomas Clarkson. At the end of the late 18th century, he became deeply involved when he went to Bristol, a major shipping port, to investigate conditions of slave transports. He was appalled by what he found and begun his eventually successful campaign to abolish slavery conditions. By 1810 many actions were in force to prevent export and import of slaves.

In the Americas, President Abraham Lincoln declared that slaves should be given the state of *freemen*. This was made law there by the *Emancipation Proclamation* of 1863. Without this market trading availability, slaves no longer had relevance to landowners.

Another location for British colonisation was India. Trade was the way into new commercial opportunities. Traders there were not that well educated; they became the masters who ruled Indians with varying social and humanitarian consciences.

It started in India with wealthy London merchants forming a joint trading company to use better ways to import spices from the East. It grew from a small commercial group to become the foundation of Britain's control of the bulk of India. This group operated as though it was a separate country, with its own army.

Major General Robert Clive was a tear-away from the Shropshire town of Market Drayton, that behaviour stemming from serious, bi-polar like mental illness. He was drummed out of town.

He is, however, today, credited with establishing the East India Trading Company in Bengal around 1758. To do this he had to become supreme in both political and military aspects of the rule. He led several significant battles for this right: other European countries had the same ambition to become the major trading nation there.

He laid the foundation for the British presence in India that developed into it giving great wealth, and becoming a major part of the British Empire. Whilst this presence was achieved and held by a rule of force, it was given acceptable governance and social mores of some effectiveness for the following centuries. Clive died in 1777, sadly, by taking his own life!

The 'Kingdom of Great Britain' was formed from the collection of these many overseas possessions in 1707; the British Empire as a whole had its nucleus then. Its citizens were proclaimed to:

> 'have full freedom and intercourse of trade and navigation to and from any port or place within the said United Kingdom and the Dominions and Plantations thereunto belonging'.

Throughout WW2, India was still ruled by the British Raj, that is, the British Crown. India contributed more than 2.5 million volunteer soldiers to fight across the world for the Allies, Fig. 5.4. India also supported US troops on its soil.

Whilst WW2 raged, the battle for independence of India from British rule was not pursued with the same public vigour; but it was soon

Chapter 5. The Allies

Fig. 5.4 Recruitment poster for the British Indian Army in WW2.

strong again. Independence was secured in 1947.

This brief history tells of a past Britain that has had considerable baggage concerning how it treated the populations of its occupied countries.

The difference between 1930s Germany and the British Empire is clear. The Nazis were set upon making an empire of ideals by inhumane methods, that being some 200 years after much of the world had moved on from forced occupation.

The Allies each generally practised respect for humanity; doing that by improving the lot of people without the human sacrifice of many for the good of a few. They had evolved the better form of governance; democracy.

Whilst Britain in the 16th and 17th centuries did occupy many countries, they implemented the Westminster form of democracy and worked to improve life in those countries by similar methods of governance. That still stood well for the countries when they gained independence.

In sharp contrast, the ideals of democracy were quite distant in Axis countries, being virtually unknown to their peoples.

When WW2 came, the British Empire countries were loyal to Britain providing considerable support that helped it face off Hitler's intentions.

5.2 Canada

Canada's population was around 11 million people in 1935. It came into British hands as the outcome of late 15th century French and English expeditions to the eastern coast of the North America continent, that led to settlement and colonisation based more on trade than conquest. As a result of the 'Seven Years War', in 1763 the French colonies there became British.

In 1867 British North America, as it had become, federated into the four provinces of the Dominion of Canada. This gave Britain another possession to rule using its Westminster parliamentary experience.

In 1931 Canada gained the right to self-govern but stayed within the British Empire. This might have provided a reason to be less supportive in WW2 for it was less obliged to fight for Britain. It did not.

It was still an important part of the essence of the British Empire, but now as a member of the British Commonwealth of Nations; that had its naming time in 1921.

In 1926 Britain and its dominions had agreed these possessions were:

'equal in status, in no way subordinate one to another in any aspect of their domestic or external affairs, though united by a common allegiance to the Crown, and freely associated as members of the British Commonwealth of Nations'.

Fig. 5.5 *Let's Go Canada.* Poster (Henri Eveleigh)

Bearing in mind the large distance between Canada and Europe when war broke out, and there being no direct responsibility to fight for Britain, Canada exhibited a great willingness to joining the Allies and help defend Britain at the start of WW2, Fig. 5.5.

It was finally recognised that Germany, with its then evil kind of control and 'Old World' ambitions, had to be stopped, Fig. 5.6.

About 10% of the population joined the army voluntarily. Conscription into country *home service* supporting their war effort started in 1940, but the troops coming to Britain were volunteers. Conscription for *active overseas service* was made possible by law in Canada in 1942,

Chapter 5. The Allies

Fig. 5.6 Canada joins the Allies in September 1939

but not used until late 1944.

Canada's population was small compared to that of the major Allies players. Their role at the start of WW2 was largely to be a back-up army within Britain whilst British troops of the British Expeditionary Force BEF were committed in France from 1939.

On arrival, more than 330,000 Canadians went through the British Army base in Aldershot, 30m north of Midhurst. With such a large influx of Canadians posted to Britain, and most British soldiers overseas in France, their presence was very noticeable, especially in the South.

Midhurst and other local areas were overtaken with Canadian troops, as will be discussed in later books. In July 1941 large numbers of *Canucks*, as they were known as, moved into the south coast. As a leave destination many preferred to travel to the old quaintness of Midhurst. They were often seen training in the South Downs regions.

Becoming part of the population for several years, many made their presence known with lasting reminders:

'An estimated 30,000 Canadian War Children were born of unions between Canadian servicemen and unwed, single women in Britain and Europe during and immediately after the Second World War'
www.voicesoftheleftbehind.com.

Many of those offspring still seek to know of their roots in WW2 Britain. www.canadianrootsuk.org/historywarchildren.html

Canada supplied the Allies with munitions and war equipment from its homeland. Canadians served across the board; the army had 730,000 enlisted, the Navy had 115,000 personnel and the air force 260,000. Over 130,000 pilots received their flying training in Canada. Their Merchant Navy made 25,000 voyages across the most dangerous Atlantic route. About half of these people never left Canada for overseas deployment. They played a major part defending Atlantic supply convoys making their way to Britain.

Canadians, mainly army, started to arrive in Britain on 1 January 1940. Some were sent to France, only to return when Dunkirk fell.

Their strong presence in Midhurst is recorded in the Ruins Visitor Register book, many being in October and November 1941 entries; the register is held today by the Cowdray Visitors Centre.

There are few photographs of Canadian troops in the Midhurst Rural District. One is Fig. 5.7, where they are helping out on the land of the Henslow family in the Rogate area, 6 miles west of Midhurst. This rare photo is hanging in Alexandra's Kitchen cafe at Durleighmarsh Farm, Rogate.

Fig. 5.7. Canucks helping out with local farming in the early years of the war.

Chapter 5. The Allies

In late 1941, Canadian troops were posted to assist defend Hong Kong against Japanese occupation. Out-numbered 5 to 1, the Allied garrison force fought well until the surrender on 25 December, as the only reasonable option.

The saddest incident for Canadian troops took place on 1 July 1942. A Canadian force of 5,000 men, along with 1,000 British troops and 50 US Rangers, made the first trial invasion as *Operation Jubilee,* more usually called the *Dieppe Raid*, of France at Dieppe in 1942.

Their objective was to secure a port in France. A lot was learned, but many lost their lives in what turned out to be a disaster; almost no objectives were achieved. Even its rehearsal was a disaster. The fact was, there was a serious lack of appreciation about seaboard landings. There were serious shortcomings in air support, raid security and site intelligence; and the weather was consistently bad. On top of those factors, the Germans were ready!

However, the 1st Special Service Brigade, No 4 Commando, with its HQ based in Cowdray Park and led by Lord Lovat, was there along with three other commando units. Their assault made history regarding the way to successfully storm a major coastal gun fort; it became the manual model to follow. Midhurst had played its part!

Canuck soldiers in Britain were then not engaged with the enemy in a major way until August 1943, when they contributed to active service in the invasion of Sicily; they were itching to have a go. After that, they took a significant role in the invasion of France on D-Day in June 1944.

The Royal Canadian Air Force was busy operating from Canadian home bases, fighting the Nazi submarine menace that was seeking to stop supplies and troops from crossing the Atlantic to Irish and British ports. Many of those convoy ships were manned by Canadian merchant navy men.

Canada was a sound and valued partner of Britain. Their language, customs, way of living, approach to life, and democratic way of governance, were so similar to the British norm. Their French-speaking soldiers added spice to the situation.

Their presence throughout the war years was a major contribution that left a fine lasting impression. Being in Britain at its lowest time of the war, they greatly assisted the home-front to keep up hope and maintain the fight in its darkest hours.

Their presence is remembered in many memorials across Britain. The Canada Memorial was unveiled in 1994 by Queen Elizabeth. This water park is to be found in Green Park.

5.3 Australia

Australia's population was close to 7 million people in 1935. It was another loyal British Commonwealth country: situated a long way away from the initial war theatre, but already emerging by the 1930s as a good partner from its Boer War and WW1 participation alongside Britain. It took 6 weeks to travel back to Britain by ship. Flight was not up to the supply task needed at that time in history. An overland route had been well proven but it was a long and dangerous way to travel to Britain and it took many weeks needing to pass hostile country territory.

The usual reason given for Australia being colonised by Britain in 1788 was as the result of the need to put many hapless Brits, mostly driven to crime by the poverty of the times in Britain, in a 'prison' somewhere.

The newly explored continent of Australia seemed to be a fine place for that. Far away, it was also good to colonise for its flax to make the linen for sails. Both reasons seemed attractive and it would add another country to the reddish-pink areas of the older times world map showing the emergent British Empire.

As with Canada, that land was already occupied with small numbers of indigenous peoples, but that mattered little to the British settlers who had scant regard for them. Hundreds of small massacres occurred, each way, as the two completely different civilisations clashed.

Their cultures were so far apart. For example, the Australian Aborigines saw the crops grown by the settlers as being free to take as they needed them; that was their custom. Initially, the *Free Settler* pioneers, and freed convicts, struggled hard to make a long-term life there.

Living off the land needed much to be learned to get through a

Chapter 5. The Allies

season with a surplus of food and seed for the next growing season. Floods, fires and drought in an unknown land of extremes, in which wildly variable weather and the high temperatures ravaged crops as the seasons progressed. It was not like England!

The indigenous peoples had learned to just survive with what nature gave them. They had little know-how to offer the settlers in terms of agriculture and animal farming. They did not harmonise at all well!

After some prior passing-by visits, starting around 1515, by explorers from Portugal, Holland, Indonesia, Spain and France, the British decided to settle it in their name. Britain simply took over the land. It was the way things were done then: Hitler's way!

It was in 1770 that Captain James Cook took possession, on his third visit, by driving a British flag into the ground of Botany Bay in what is now part of Sydney. As we see in Fig. 5.8, Cook wrote in his journal:

'I now once more hoisted English Coulers and in the Name of His Majesty King George the Third, took possession of the whole Eastern Coast from the above Latitude 38°S down to this place by the name of New South Wales.'

Fig. 5.8. Artist's impression of Captain Cook taking possession of Australia, 1770. (E Phillips Fox)

There were no legal or founded negotiations; no dodgy purchase of rights; no piece of paper giving legal rights to do this. The colonists were told it was nobody's land (terra nullius) so was up to anyone to claim it!

That issue is still debated to this day.

The native aboriginal peoples were quite unable to fight for their land with their small numbers at any location and simple stone-age design spears, those alone pitted against muskets and the military discipline of the small, but very effective British force.

Whether it was an invasion, or not, is still being disputed. Some estimates suggest, at that time, there could have been as many as 750,000 indigenous people spread across Australia.

However, another historical rationale for the colonisation argues it resulted from Cook being commissioned by the Royal Society in London to observe an astronomical transit of Venus in the southern region in 1769.... and at the same time to look for sources of linen and flax with which to make sails for the Royal Navy's galleons.

Australia was originally called *Terra Australis*, that land that then was thought to balance the known landmass in the Northern hemisphere.

Colonisation of the whole of Australia followed the establishment of New South Wales by progressively taking in other land masses to form six self-governed colonies under British control.

In all cases, the native Aboriginal tribes were dismissed as being lesser humans than the British. Such was the evil side of the human disposition in that time of so-called European enlightenment.

In 1900 the six British colonies of the Australia continent, by then including Tasmania, were formed, by another paper record - the *Proclamation*, to be a Federation of States and Territories forming the *Commonwealth of Australia*. This action was permitted by Britain for Australia was also a member of the British Commonwealth and owed allegiance to Britain.

In the 1930s Australia was very close to the Mother Country in all spheres of life... sport, farm, foods eaten, motor cars, music, and family ties. Marriages of British women to Aussie soldiers, who then returned to Australian after WW1, shared the same love of life, with cars, planes and trains, steel, and prefabricated steel structures, largely being imported from Britain.

The Aussies were by then, well recognised as being wags that were easily irreverent to power and class, yet responsive to same. A *tall poppy syndrome* has always existed in the Aussie way of life. That is, anyone peaking above the crowd in any path of life has to be cut down to the

Chapter 5. The Allies

norm. No airs and graces there; an almost one-class society. This behaviour was carried into WW2 by the Australian forces.

Architecture, cityscape planning, and major building design and execution just had to have a major British contractor as the commissioning body: without it, investors did not feel safe with their investments. The bulk of the steel for the Sydney Harbour bridge came from Britain, but its 6 million rivets were made in Australia. Some concessions were made to assist increase local industrial capability.

Australia was then an extension, an outpost, of British life; but with plenty of sun and sea, and a more relaxed lifestyle. However, in the depth of the minds of the most British migrants, Britain was still home base. Migrants, like myself, would say "it is not done that way back home" to which highly annoyed, long term, residents would say "then go home, Pommie bastard".

The iconic Sydney Harbour, *coat hanger* bridge was opened in 1932. The poster of Fig, 5.9 shows the icons of the nation at the time.

Fig. 5.9. Sydney Harbour Bridge celebrations poster, 1932.

The Australian armed forces personnel served well over their weight in WW2. Initially, it was much about helping out the *old country,* the King, and in defeating Hitler for the sake of Britain.

By 1942 the Australian contributions had to swing over to being in Asia; fighting the Japanese. The statistics for Australians in this war are staggering!

Total army serving, in and outside, of Australia: 726,800.
Air Force RAAF: 216,000.
Navy RAN: 48,100.
Total who served, in and out: 990,900.
Killed in all service arms: 27,073.
Non-battle casualties are not included above, the highest number being in the RAAF.
POWs, mainly with the Japanese: 30,560.
Injured: 23,477.

It is obvious that Britain, in the 1930s, had many fingers in international pies for they governed an extensive part of the globe. Their possessions were so varied in climate, language, customs, and purpose for presence.

Australia had a lot to catch up on with its geographical isolation issues. Its first radiotelephone service was started in April 1930. Landline phones were then beginning to connect the capital cities. International broadcasting of the Australian Broadcast Commission ABC began in 1932. The ABC had its first permanent symphony orchestra by 1936.

Fig. 5.10. *The Japanese are coming.* Australian poster ca 1942.

Many families of the moneyed class, the aristocracy, the gentry and the privileged, had sons in the diplomatic corps, the military, or the civil service somewhere in the world.

Australia was a part of that scene, but almost the furthest from Britain and, unlike it, had its own threatening *Evil* coming down from Japan, Fig. 5.10. It was aware of that threat and in 1938 ceased exports of iron ore to Japan - they were 'seen as too militaristic'.

After the occupation of Singapore, by the Japanese in February 1942, Australia had no option but to redirect its resources to its own defence against the Japanese, who were then coming very close to Northern Australia.

Chapter 5. The Allies

The Asian theatre fighting by the Allies was greatly bolstered as the outcome of the Japanese raid on Hawaii just weeks before. It caused the USA to formally join the Allies and create an especially good relationship with Australia for strategic reasons.

As part of the British Commonwealth forces in combat, from 1941, the Australians contributed mainly in the Mediterranean, Middle East and North Africa campaigns; then moving to the countries north of Australia in the South-West Pacific Area. A small force of around 300 personnel with specialist skills participated in the D-Day landings; the others were needed to defend their homeland. They were also there to gain experience in amphibious landings, then becoming needed to fight the Japanese back, island by island, after mid-1944.

5.4 USA in the 30s.

The United States of America USA population in 1935 was approximately 127 million people. Refer to Figs. 5.11a and 5.11b. by Victor Gillam.

Following the formation of the United States of America in the late 18th century it had some skirmishes with other countries and was also once involved with carrying out some colonisation. These were not significantly large interventions to give the USA the name of an oppressive empire-building nation. It started to become significant in world terms when it began its own colonisation into the Wild West, the railways opening that up rapidly from the 1860s on.

Industrial development began in earnest in the mid-19th century when it began to think very big about exploiting its significant natural resources and national mood for things. Its progress was new, adventurous and spectacular. Having begun its life without experiencing a strong parent nation's influence, it did not follow all of the thoughts and the ways of life of other nations to the same extent, as did Australia and Canada.

Up to the start of the 20th century, the USA was more prone to having an inward-looking policy through which it mainly kept itself out the rising world disputes of the early to middle 30s. It was isolated by oceans on each side of it: that gave the impression of security that war

Midhurst WW2 Memoirs: 2. 'Evil' Rising: 'Good' Awakening

Fig. 5.11a. Early expansion of the USA - up to 1861.

Chapter 5. The Allies

Fig. 5.11b Expansion from 1861.

would not come onto their homeland. Also, at that time it did not have the power, technically, economically and politically, to take global dominance as a protector of democracy. It had yet to become a world power. It had a small part in the 18th century scientific revolutions, beginning its industrialisation in the 19th century. It did, however, practice modest accession expansion from its roots in 1783, Fig. 5.11a and 5.11b.

Woodrow Wilson, USA President in the 1920s, also made the case that democracy was precious to world stability and must be defended across the globe by the now more powerful US nation.

The best-known incidence of early international German aggression against the USA was the sinking of Cunard Ocean liner, the RMS Lusitania, on 7 May 1915. It fell foul of a German submarine working the Atlantic. It was sunk in a mere 18 minutes off the coast of Ireland. Killed were 1,198 passengers with 761 surviving the attack.

This was an attack on both the British and Americans for they jointly owned the ship. At the time the USA was neutral.
    Whilst the ship had been in the listed in *Jane's All the World Fighting Ships* as an auxiliary cruiser, the list the Germans used was that she was held back from a military role, being too easy a target. She continued to be used on the civilian trans-Atlantic route along with other ocean liners of note. She was painted white for civilian use; that was, without camouflage colouring. Her name was marked in gold lettering.
    The US people, through its democratic Congress, initially held back on participation in WW1. It was a string of German acts of hostility that rapidly changed public opinion to wishing to join that Allied Front. The sinking of the Lusitania ship enraged the nation across the world and certainly contributed to the USA joining WW1, Fig. 5.12. This event saw the end of that ideal; it was 'all-out' war from then on.

As part of an 'illegal' German strategy to blockade goods coming into Britain from the USA, they declared a sea zone encompassing the whole of the British Isles, to be hostile territory.
    On 22 April 1915 Germany issued a warning of its intentions in 50 American newspapers. It was known to the passengers on that voyage from New York to Liverpool.

Chapter 5. The Allies

Fig. 5.12. Sinking the RMS Lusitania increased resistance against the Germans in WW1.

'NOTICE!

TRAVELLERS intending to embark on the Atlantic voyage are reminded that a state of war exists between Germany and her allies and Great Britain and her allies; that the zone of war includes the waters adjacent to the British Isles; that, in accordance with formal notice given by the Imperial German Government, vessels flying the flag of Great Britain, or any of her allies, are liable to destruction in those waters and that travellers sailing in the war zone on the ships of Great Britain or her allies do so at their own risk.

                     IMPERIAL GERMAN EMBASSY
                     Washington, D.C. 22 April 1915'

There were 128 Americans on board, the rest being British and Canadian; some were responding to the call to go to Britain to take up active service. However, a large proportion of guests who died were civilians .... business people, socialites, millionaires, performers in the arts, scientists, other intellectuals – along with children and many babies.

The Captain of the liner took many precautions to try to prevent its position being known to the German submarine controllers, but they came to know of its location in the declared zone around Ireland.

The German U-boats used code in their radio messages and thought their whereabouts were not known to the British Admiralty. However, the British had broken the code used, so knew the general position when U-20 reported its location as being close to the Lusitania.

Due to unavoidable necessary reasons, the Captain had not stuck exactly to the Admiralty orders of sailing, resulting in the Captain being initially used as the scapegoat for its sinking. He was eventually exonerated in the enquiry.

After sinking other ships on its way to the Lusitania's position the German submarine U-20 torpedoed the Lusitania with just one torpedo. She was known to be a serious target but the Admiralty had made no special arrangements to send it protection. Surely the German U-boat commander would not wish to sink it?

The morality of its sinking came into major questioning. Blame, the rationale for the sinking it at all, and debate on if it had war material on board, all lent to a very confusing situation. Germany was breaking the rules of war in this kind of action... but was it? 'Was the British government secretly using a passenger ship to transport explosives? Had Winston Churchill sacrificed the ship to draw the United States into a war she had been reluctant to join?' Wikipedia.

The modern documentary film, *Sinking of the Lusitania: Terror at Sea,* of 2007, produced by a joint German-English team, provides the fuller

Chapter 5. The Allies

story, using facts now known: they, however, still did not resolve the situation.

The event was a great national embarrassment to the German leadership; to the point where the captain of U-20 was taken out of sight and not made into the public hero, he was expected to be.

Fig. 5.13. USA poster based on Lusitania sinking

It provided plenty of material for propaganda posters against the Germans, Fig. 5.13. This is but one of the milder posters designed to increase the level of disgust and hate of the Germans.

When the USA finally decided to enter WW1, their lack of readiness meant it took time to ramp up their output of military assets. They only started to be effective for the last few months of that First World War.

For that war, the country had, for the last year only, mobilised some 4.4 million people, half as many as the much larger British Empire had contributed. However, the USA lost a staggering 115,000 lives in less than 6 months: this was later to impact on the USA's initial reluctance to join WW2.

This loss rate, plus the lingering effect of their Great Depression, resulted in the USA people adopting, yet again, an *isolationist* policy during the 1930s. By around 1935 the impact of so many lost USA soldiers during WW1 had still not been forgotten.

The situation was not helped by their 17th-19th century, strong, supportive relationships with Germans that developed when a very large number of immigrants came to the States from Germany in former times. Furthermore, many then living Americans, had studied in Germany at its best universities.

In the 19th century 8 million people had immigrated from Germany. By 2010 those with close German ancestry in the USA had risen to over 50 million.

Germany, by 1880, had built up a massive navy and begun their strong imperialist expansion. They disputed, with the USA, the minor issue of who would colonise the Samoan Islands in the central Pacific Ocean; these were eventually divided between them in 1900.

Another friend-losing action was the secret plan the Germans proposed, whereby the Mexicans would invade America if the USA entered WW1. From that point on there was always a suspicion of any German action, but it did not entirely sever links until WW2, and even then, only after it became clear what Hitler was seeking to achieve.

Following WW1, the USA had not signed the Versailles Treaty of 1919 but had arranged another more advantageous arrangement with Germany.

The USA generously assisted Germany to begin to get back on its feet - until Hitler appeared in German politics. German intellectuals then came to appreciate what had become of the country and many abandoned it in haste, especially so if they were Jewish. Many, now famous, scientists, engineers, humanities scholars and intellectuals, left for the USA in the late 1930s.

By the 1920s *Isolationism* had returned, Fig. 5.14.

Fig. 5.14. USA isolationism in the late 1920s. (Seuss)

The American scene in the later 1930s was also influenced by a government seeking neutralism because Irish immigrants did not want to cooperate with Britain and by the growing power of its women citizens supporting pacifism.

Chapter 5. The Allies

To this end, Congress passed laws prohibiting the sales of arms to any foreign nations at war. By 1937 the law came into effect also prohibiting loans to other countries at war.

There was, in the USA, however, great sympathy with the victims of the democratic foreign countries. Initially, the national mood in the USA was to just feel bad, doing things more by private action, using the *wait and see* approach.

As in Britain, many lived on hope that the Nazis problem would go away. All of these factors meant the Americans had great sympathy for the German people but not at all for the Hitler regime; after 1941 they made it a top priority to defeat that tyrant's regime.

Looking back, the democratic countries involved in WW2, with their more peaceful ways, simply could not come to grips with these kinds of facts fast enough. When such conditions exist the only two recourses are to let the ill-founded person, or country, continue in the hope it might just stop before it affects too many; or to take up a serious major armed conflict requiring at least a similar level of preparedness and size of force as has the belligerent.

Thus, the United States, yet again, had an inward-looking non-intervention policy when the various *Evils* began to be recognised internationally. Over 1936 and 1937 several *Neutrality Acts* were passed by Congress. These, in law but not always in practice, prevented them from operating in any belligerent's (good or evil) ships and aircraft, or trading with them. This US stance remained until Britain and its commonwealth countries all declared war on Germany in September 1937.

The US had become the only major free-world power standing aside. Despite its overseas trade falling away, the mood was still to keep out of any conflict alongside the Allied powers. As we will see later, there were many illegal exceptions taking place before this, some right near to Midhurst on the RAF Tangmere airfield base. Initially, the USA was impotent to fight against non-observance of world peace: so many others wilfully chose to not work for it.

Other people's fights taking place far away, and with the protective rim of oceans around the USA, gave their public a sense of comfort that those overseas problems would not spill over to them.

Midhurst WW2 Memoirs: 2. 'Evil' Rising: 'Good' Awakening

Further, it has been argued that taking a neutral stand-point was beneficial for sales of materials - to both the early Allies but also to the Axis countries. Today that seems to be a weird situation but it needs to be remembered that the US was, in a manner of speaking, still coming out as a global nation of importance at that time.

The fact was that around 1935 when the all-out war was fast becoming the final and only option to counter Nazi oppression, no democracy was sufficiently armed and ready to take on Hitler.

His military might was so well prepared. The US held back until the Japanese raided Pearl Harbour on 7 December 1941: they no longer remained neutral. It was a rude awakening for them.

Despite being neutral before the USA declared war, it had become necessary for it to build a major presence in Ireland to support its role in protecting the Atlantic convoys from the USA that were supplying massive movements of *Lend-Lease* materials to Britain using the Merchant Navy, and other nation's ships.

This operation involved some 85,000 ship voyages, with 600 convoys each needing some 5 escort ships to combat the marauding and devastating Nazis submarine attacks in the duration of the long *Battle of the Atlantic*.

A significant early engagement of that long Atlantic sea war was the sinking of S. S. Athenia: its situation mirroring the sinking of the Lusitania at the start of WW1. The account Mearns (2017) gives a deep insight into this event after David Mearns reported there was a high probability that he had found the wreck in 2017. At the time of writing, it seems finance is still lacking for finally proving it is the Athenia by filming the wreck location that is only 200m deep, just off the Irish Coast. (Interestingly, David Mearn's company, *Blue Water Recoveries Ltd.*, is based in Midhurst's main street!)

Departing on 1 September 1939, TSS Athenia's Captain well knew that war would break out very soon. Her 1,103 passengers included some 500 Jewish refugees, 311 US, 72 UK, 469 Canadian passengers and 315 crew. Athenia left Glasgow for Montreal, via Liverpool.

She was soon seen, off the coast of Ireland, by the German

Chapter 5. The Allies

submarine U-30 on 3rd September. The German U-boat U-30, commanded by Oberleutnant Fritz Lemp, torpedoed her and she sank after 14 hours. Killed were 112 people; many of those deaths being from errors of the rescue that took place.

At the time Germany did not take responsibility for the error made by the submarine commander in torpedoing a merchant passenger ship: it was only admitted after the Nuremberg trials of 1945.

The event impacted on Canada and the US governments, who strengthened their resolve to keep sea traffic lanes as safe as possible.

Germany hushed it up. The Western press, however, had a field day of articles, increasing the disgust for Germany. One cartoon, Fig. 5.15, used the incident for effective propaganda. Truth is the first casualty of war: Hitler had given clear orders that a passenger ship could only be attacked with confirmation that it was performing an act of war.

Fig. 5.15. Caption: Hitler ordered to his macabre crew "Remember! Women and Children First"
(E. H. Shephard)

Britain was the major delivery and storage country for the Allies effort in WW2. Over a million tons of goods were needed each week to support the various Allied Forces campaigns of Europe. This massively exceeded the internal capability of Britain's resources. Churchill said:

'The Battle of the Atlantic was the dominating factor all through the war. Never for one moment could we forget that everything happening elsewhere, on land, at sea or in the air depended ultimately on its outcome'

In April 1941, whilst the USA was still not in the war formally, the Derry Naval base in Northern Ireland was begun as the first European base for the US, Canadian and the British Navies to support the Atlantic sea lanes. It was a while before it was formally commissioned as a US naval operating base in February 1942; soon after the US declared war on Germany, Fig. 5.16.

It was a major project involving accommodation for thousands of staff and service personnel, the building of a central administration building, lengthening of wharves, creation of storage sheds, setting up ship repair facilities, a hospital, radio station, ammunition depot, and refuelling berths.

An underground operations centre, with its control board, was also constructed there. A ship turn-around time was usually just 3-4days.

Fig. 5.16. US troops arriving in Derry, Ireland in 1942.

More than 1300 new buildings were involved, including numerous billets for the sea-going crew to get some quick R&R before leaving again.

'To prepare the young GIs (private rank soldiers - from their equipment stamped *Government Issue*) for what was, for most of them, their first trip away from the United States, a small booklet was written to help troops understand life in Northern Ireland. To begin with, they were given two cardinal rules that ring as true today as they did 70 years ago:

There are two excellent rules of conduct for Americans abroad. They are good rules anywhere but they are particularly important in

Chapter 5. The Allies

Ireland:

(1) Don't argue religion.
(2) Don't argue politics.

Perhaps most importantly they were warned to be careful with Irish women. Soldiers were also told not to boast about the power and might of the American military and instead urged to be humble among their new neighbours. However, inevitably a rivalry sprung up between the American army and the British army based in Northern Ireland.

> 'One day two American soldiers in Belfast heckled two passing British soldiers, "We don't need you here any longer; we'll win the war for you." The two British soldiers placed their hats firmly on their heads, doubled back and threw the two GIs in a water tank they had been casually leaning against. Then the four Allied soldiers went to a bar where they spent the rest of the day drinking together.'
>
> James Wilson 2017 on www.irishcentral.com

5.5 European and Nordic Countries - France, Belgium, Netherlands, Poland and Czechoslovakia; and Scandinavian Countries

In 1935 the salient countries that became involved with British forces had populations as follows: France 42 million; Belgium 8 million; Netherlands 8 million; Poland 35 million and Czechoslovakia 9 million. All of these countries had troops of which many escaped to Britain to join the Allies. Thousands of refugees also fled there.

France suffered much in WW1 for that war was fought on its land using up its resources and men. In the 30s, to hopefully protect itself from any more aggression by Germany, they built up major defences and a very large army.

The Germans would never invade them again; the defence obstacles would be too great for that to be attractive! Well at least that was the thinking, but it did not include fighting a highly modernised, rapidly, moving army and air force.

By the late 1930s, France had lost its territorial ambitions. Its army was solely for its defence, and it had many overseas possessions that drew off over 200,000 persons overseas leaving 360,000 soldiers at home. These all could be drawn on if war broke out. Britain and the USA saw them as the bastion of Europe. But their will was lacking.

Like many of the warlords of the West, French Generals still had not learned from WW1 that fixed defences were not the safe fortresses of yesteryear anymore. Those defences merely introduced a small delay against being overrun.

'Major resources, however, were still devoted to build the *Maginot Line* to the point that some declared it starved the army from being better strengthened. It stretched along the line from Switzerland to Luxembourg with an extension added on to the Strait of Dover when invasion by Hitler seemed likely after 1934. It was progressively built over the period 1930-1940. It was a massive construction using tunnels to connect forts, small and large. It had fire power all along it that covered all lines of attack.

There were over 500 major buildings, some being large forts with some 1000 men having a good range of artillery. In more detail there were 45 main forts at 15 kilometres intervals, 97 smaller forts and 352 case-mates between, with over 100 kilometres of tunnels.'

Fun Trivia, Question 104970.

Fig. 5.17 is a sketch showing the complexity of a French Maginot line fort of WW2. Like the iceberg, the parts above ground were a mere fraction of the whole.

It had two weaknesses against the German attack. First, the fast-moving modernised *Blitzkrieg* used new and devastatingly effective methods that the BEF and French forces could not stop. Second, gaps were left without defence walls where it was thought there was no need for defence assets to be built due to the terrain being impenetrable; as it was expected to be in the Ardennes region.

When the time came the German army simply went around the ends of the Maginot Line, and later through its gaps! Few guns were fired in anger. It was a monument to bad decision making. Despite the massive construction it was proven to be useless as a defence asset.

Chapter 5. The Allies

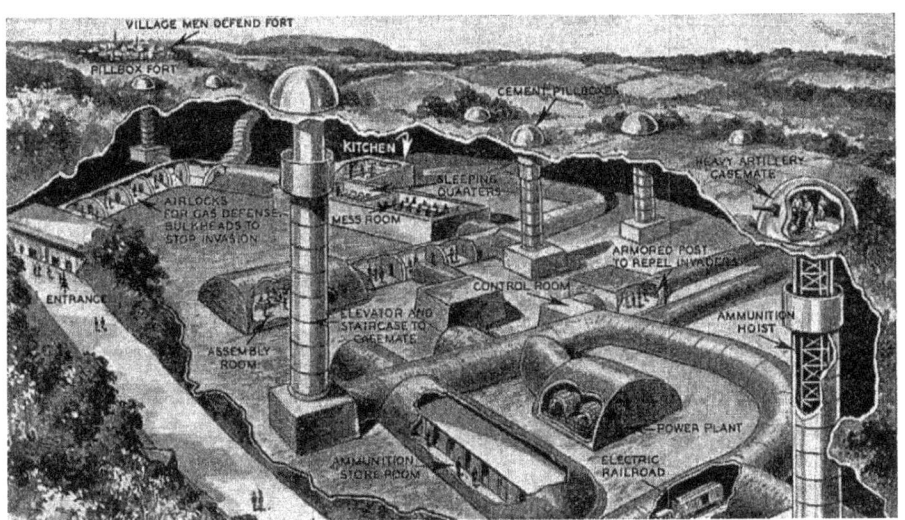

Fig. 5.17 Just one of the forts of the Maginot Line, 1934; the world's greatest underground fortification!

Perhaps a benefit was that the Germans were slowed a little before they could become a real threat to the British Expeditionary Force BEF, thereby giving the retreat at Dunkirk more chance of success. In reverse, when the Allies eventually returned to France the Maginot Line defences were quite an obstacle as the Germans used them effectively against the Allies.

The Germans had also constructed a WW1 defensive line along their western border. This Siegfried Line called the *West Wall* by the Germans, Fig. 5.18, was nowhere as strong at the Maginot line. However, with its 18,000 bunkers, tunnels and tank traps, it was also used against the Allied advance as they fought their way to Germany late in WW2. Around 140,000 casualties were reported then, with 100,000 US soldiers buried in close-by cemeteries!

In the end, French and British ability to stop the Blitzkrieg forces was insufficient. They, however, after occupation, kept up the fight with their renowned underground French Resistance. Some French soldiers and airmen were able to escape the Nazi occupation of France, then being able to contribute to the Allied Forces.

Fig. 5.18 *Siegfried* line along the Western Germany border.

Belgium and the Netherlands, being small countries, could not be expected to contribute major forces. Belgium had also followed the principle of a building a static line of defensive forts on the end of the Maginot Line, the design of locations having already been proved as effective in WW1.

However, they became the weakest point against the initial advance of the German forces in 1940; they provided little protection, allowing the Germans to pass around the northern end of the Maginot Line.

When war broke out in 1939, Belgium was able to mobilise some 460,000 men but they were not well equipped with tanks and artillery. In 1939 they instituted a crash programme to increase its war effort. But it was too late!

Far from helping matters, the Maginot line had acted as a deflector for the German army as they pushed around the Belgium end to get behind the line in neighbouring France. Belgium was a funnel point for Hitler's army: it was occupied within 18 days starting on 10 May 1940.

In the Netherlands, matters were no better. Their country's geography was very different from the others; it had water everywhere and was flat and small in area. There the Germans used a different

Chapter 5. The Allies

strategy to occupy them; paratrooper drops. They overcame the neutral country in just 17 days, also starting on 10 May 1940.

At the end of that success the Luftwaffe carried out a massive bombing raid on Rotterdam, killing many civilians. This raid was used to force the Dutch to capitulate, or have other cities so bombed. This showed how barbaric Hitler could be.

By mid-1940 Britain was then totally exposed to the German Wehrmacht, situated along the other side of the English Channel. They became extremely concerned for the US was still standing off; that will be covered in a later chapter.

To the east of Germany, Hitler rapidly occupied adjacent countries.

Poland, before it was invaded in 1939, had several large armies amounting to over 1 million men. They were near to being at the ready but as they did not expect invasion from Germany it was only half mobilised when attacked on 1 September 1939. Its war materiel was not up to that of the Germans. The small Polish navy mainly escaped, to fight with the Royal Navy. Its aircraft were of old designs and the horse-mounted Cavalry Brigades had only old design tanks, Fig. 5.19, that were no match for advanced design and proven German tanks and guns.

Fig. 5.19 Polish forces fight hard to defend the Hel Peninsular, October 1939.

Poland had signed a non-aggression pact with Germany in 1934. Hitler did this to keep Poland out of the way whilst he occupied other country areas around Germany; including Austria, the Sudetenland and Czechoslovakia.

Having taken over those regions, he broke his pact with Poland. It did not take long. Previous occupations had been easy with little hard fighting needed; this time was Hitler's first invasion by force. He was hesitant and was not ready to take on Poland: but it was a rout. They surrendered on 27 September 1939.

Whilst being invaded in part by the Nazis, Poland was also soon occupied in their western regions by the Russians. Britain and France had earlier agreed to support Poland if it was attacked but it stood back from joining the defence of Poland. This reneging by Britain was not well accepted: for Poland's far-off location, it would have been virtually impossible to help. This is still debated today.

When Britain declared war on Germany, on 3 September 1939, Hitler had well and truly commenced his occupation of lands destined by him to be part of his Third Reich. By this move, he had increased the supply of slave labour to further strengthen his war machine's supply of goods and his major civil defence structures. It also, in the Nazi minds, started to clear the world of the 'undesirables'.

The Germans soon started up Hitler's ethnic cleansing aims. Polish Jews were progressively concentrated into ghettos being used as slave labour by the 100,000s, or being murdered to fit his fantasy. Poland had become a significant part of German war materiel supply support.

For their part in decimating the Polish nation, the NKVD (Russian secret police), murdered an estimated 22,000 Polish officers in the Katyn massacre of April/May 1940.

Fig. 5.20 Hitler, victorious in Warsaw, 5 October 1939. (Bauer)

Chapter 5. The Allies

For Hitler, this invasion had been a gamble that went so well for his forces that his confidence as a war leader boosted his ego to consider which way next to move, Fig. 5.20. The American journalist William L Shirer reported on Hitler:

> 'when reviewing his victorious troops in Warsaw he made a speech of a conquering Caesar".

The Nordic Countries, sometimes described as the Scandinavian countries (population being a guesstimate 15 million in 1935) include Denmark, Finland, Norway, Sweden, Greenland, Iceland, Faroe Islands and the Aland Islands.

These are the main countries in this grouping, being in 1939, mostly independent sovereignties. Since 1952 they have had the official inter-parliamentary Nordic Council at which each country has elected members. At the start of WW2, they all suffered considerable, and different, hardships.

All of these locations were of strategic interest to the Axis for they had resources and seaboards that Germany badly needed. The Allies tried hard to keep the Germans out. However, Denmark and Norway were soon occupied by Germany. Sweden stayed neutral. Finland fought continuous small wars against German and Russian intrusion.

It was a carefully managed situation for Sweden; from time to time they gave Germany some assistance. On the other hand, it gave refuge to thousands of fleeing Jewish people. Its iron deposits were attractive to both the Allies and the Axis, so the Allies kept up a concerted effort to deny these to the Germans.

Whilst being somewhat peripheral to the main fight, those here under totalitarian occupation by the Axis troops, saw its peoples still contributing active service for the Allies. Many men and women of their land, air and sea forces escaped joining the Allies.

Heroic commando, and local resistance fighter, raids were carried out, many of which have been used as the bases of thriller films. Midhurst was significance in some commando raid planning.

Racial purity was a topic of widespread scientific interest before the 20th century. As soon as he came to absolute power in 1933, Hitler set in place policies that were intended to eventually create the master race of his Third Reich. (This reads like a sci-fi horror story - but it did happen!) The policies included sterilisation and extermination.

Those races he wanted as his core population had to be of Aryan descent; peoples of European and some of Western Asian heritage.

They were found in many countries. Germans, of high status and long descent, felt they were Aryan. Hitler, along with many of his top fanatical followers, wanted them to be the model person.

Fig. 5.21 was typical of the ideal, the Aryans - blonde hair, blue eyes, muscular figure, and tall.

One of the cruellest SS Nazis, Erich Koch, said in 1943:

'We are a master race, which must remember that the lowliest German worker is racially and biologically a thousand times more valuable than the population here'.

Erich Koch 5 March 1943

Fig. 5.21 German Calendar of *Racial Politics Office* Rally 1938.

In the top listing of who had Aryan blood were Germans, Germanic peoples, the Dutch, Scandinavians and, surprisingly, the English who were part-Scandinavian from intermixing with past Ancient Roman, Viking and French Normandy blood. Debated still, is that Hitler had a soft spot for the Brits and wanted them to be an occupied country by its acceptance of being a part of his Great new empire.

The Scandinavian countries were also caught up with Hitler's devious plans when it suited Germany's strategic needs.

Chapter 5. The Allies

Finland had a population of around 3.5 million in 1939; its people were sparsely located across a harsh landscape. It was attacked by both German and Russian forces at different times of the WW2 period and was thus, either with the Allies or being occupied by the Axis. Their situation and geographical location excluded them as being seen as a significant part of the Allied democracies forces.

Norway's population was around 8 million in 1939. They had not mobilised by 1940 so were easy prey for both strategic and racial interests pushed for by two of Hitler's Generals. They were quickly occupied by force in April 1940; they could put up little overt resistance but did operate effective underground resistance. Fig. 5.22 shows a group of Norwegians under-going training in Sweden. Norway was occupied by Germany for the rest of WW2.

Fig. 5.22 Norwegians being trained in Sweden for resistance service.

The Norwegian government had not allowed its border defences to be mobilised for fear of provoking Germany. It had had no option but capitulate and for this were given an easy occupation period under German rule. Part of its army was permitted to remain. Very few deaths resulted.

The majority of the Norwegian Army military units escaped into exile, joining other Allies. Many soldiers, by circumstance more than by choice, were part of the Axis forces during WW2.

British Army Commandos raided a Norwegian target in March 1941. They were led by Lord Lovat, who by then, ran his Commando brigade HQ from Cowdray House.

Denmark's population in 1939 was around 3.8 million. It was occupied in April 1940 by Germany, in one of the shortest campaigns; it took just 6 hours invading by air, sea, and land. Germany needed iron ore shipping ports.

Sweden, using careful realpolitik, remained neutral throughout WW2. At one stage they accepted over 8,000 Jews who had been deported from Danish concentration camps. They granted use of telephone lines to Germany but tapped the lines to give intelligence to the Allies. Being neutral was like skating on very thin ice. Fig. 5.23 shows their situation within Axis countries by 1942. They did so by cooperating in non-militaristic terms such as allowing rail access across its country and selling iron ore to the Nazis. For the Allies, they provided military intelligence and assisted in training soldiers who had become refugees.

Greenland, a population of just 18,000 people, was a tightly run Danish colony in 1940. It was not occupied by the Germans when Denmark fell to them so was then a likely target for Britain and Canada. The US stepped in to guarantee its safety - and to ensure Germans could not gather valuable weather information. A small armed force and a ship guarded its cryolite (used to form aluminium) mine, a major source of income during the war period.. Many minor skirmishes took place as all of these countries showed physical interest at different times. Constant patrolling was needed to detect and close down Germans attempting to set up weather stations, Fig. 5.24. When the US joined the war in late 1941, they took over the country using it as a major base; thousands of

Chapter 5. The Allies

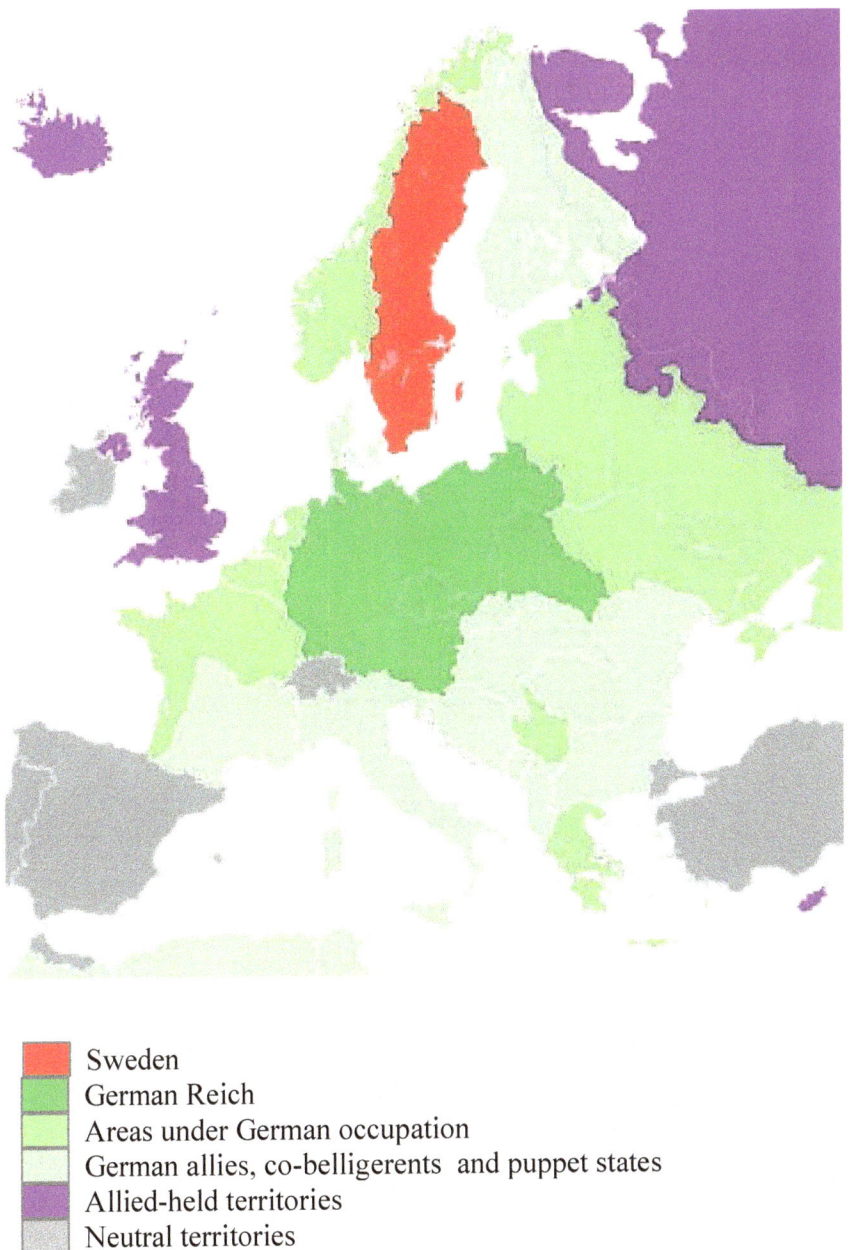

▪ Sweden
▪ German Reich
▪ Areas under German occupation
▪ German allies, co-belligerents and puppet states
▪ Allied-held territories
▪ Neutral territories

Fig. 5.23 Neutral Sweden was surrounded by Axis countries by 1942.

US servicemen poured in. They enjoyed close, harmonious, relations. Greenland supported North Atlantic air traffic control but it was not much use as an anti-submarine base due to the dreadful weather.

Fig. 5.24 US troops and Coast Guardsmen in patrol in Greenland. 1943. (Norman Thomas)

Iceland, a small nation of farmers and fishermen with no army or defence at all, had 120,000 people in 1939. It declared neutrality over the war period but that was ignored, soon being occupied by the Allies, first by a small British force in *Operation Fork*, Fig. 5.25, then Canada, and later by the US.

Despite its sovereignty being violated, it had to resign to its situation as the Allies needed to prevent it being occupied by the

Chapter 5. The Allies

Germans instead.

In 1944 it declared itself to be a republic after shedding its union with the Denmark nation in mid-1944. Its strategic importance was its position in the North Atlantic sea lanes, and good air and naval bases for US forces. It cooperated with the US and Britain. Around 230 Icelanders lost their lives on cargo and fishing vessels sunk by Nazi submarines. Many babies resulted from unions of local women and US men.

Fig. 5.25 Operation Fork in progress, 1940.

5.6 China

China had an estimated population of 514,313,000 people in 1938. It was, however, then a strongly divided country.

Midhurst WW2 Memoirs: 2. 'Evil' Rising: 'Good' Awakening

In 1931 Japan had annexed Manchuria. By 1937 this had become a full-scale war in that region of China, brought on by Japan. China was still at war with the Japanese when WW2 broke out! Inside China, two political parties were already locked in internal civil dispute; between the Chinese Nationalist Party and the Communist Party of China. The former became heavily involved with the opposition of the Japanese invasion. The Nationalists were aspiring to do what many Western countries had done: to overthrow the Chinese Monarchy. Its ideals suffered from internal intrigue that allowed Russian communism to blossom. Initially, Chiang Kai-shek was able to limit the power of war-lords. They tended towards dictatorship. In the end, democracy did not find a place in Chinese governance.

During WW2 China had little opportunity to assist the Allies in Europe but did send some troops to Burma. Their usefulness was that their armies kept 1.5 million Japanese troops in China away from American, Australian and New Zealand interests in the Pacific region.

China inflicted an estimated 1.5 million casualties on the Japanese but China paid for this dearly with 3.2 million Nationalist army casualties and 17 million civilians who died for just being there, at the hands of not only the Japanese but of the warring factions inside China.

When WW2 ended. China had earned a place internationally, but the internal fighting resumed! Eventually, the Communists, under the leadership of Mao Zedong, gained control on the Chinese mainland. In 1949 the Nationalists left mainland China, settling in Taiwan. That started the two Chinas situation, that still exists today.

Not well known, for it took place far from Europe and Britain, was the contribution made to the Allies war effort by 40,000 Chinese soldiers, sent to fight the Japanese alongside British and US in Burma, Fig. 5.26.
Inland the Chinese held the Japanese down with a loss of some 800,000 Japanese soldiers; the Chinese were ill-equipped but able to keep command because of their better use the rough terrain, and self determination applied to good effect.

Over the long period that China was fighting, it is estimated it suffered:

'14 million dead, 80 million refugees and the pulverising of its embryonic modernisation.

Chapter 5. The Allies

Fig. 5.26 Chinese army in WW2.

5.7 Russia

Russia's part in WW2 has already been discussed in Section 3.1. It was either on the *Good* or the *Evil* side during the period.

On the side of *Good,* there is a defendable argument that their extreme and heroic resistance to Hitler's *Operation Barbarossa* saved Britain.

Russia won the battle to keep squeezing the German Army by being prepared to lose millions of men and women soldiers; and having the capacity to find still more to keep up the fight, Fig. 5.27. Mind you, to get this response, with typical Stalinist *evil,* he had issued his Orders 270, and 227 that deemed:

'...any troops who surrendered or were captured by Germans would be executed as traitors. Almost a year later in July 1942, Stalin upped his threats with Order No. 227, which proclaimed that any cowards were to be "liquidated on the spot." He also personally intervened with generals, forbidding them from retreating even if loss and death were imminent.'

Fig. 5.27 *Pincers for Pincers*. Nazis meet Russia, 1941-45.

When the Nazis had reached the shores of France after the retreat at Dunkirk that was in June 1940, they could see, on a good day, the White Cliffs of Dover. It seemed to be only a matter of time when they would make a sea invasion of the South of England. The Nazis had already planned how to do it and had manufactured landing craft, maps, and guide books.

Goering positively advised Hitler that his Luftwaffe Air Force alone could make Britain submit; but he failed to win the, in the air, *Battle of Britain* that ended on 31 October 1940.

Seeing that invasion of Britain was not an easy, or risk-free venture after all, Hitler turned his attention to deploying much of his force to his other quest, the invasion of Russia.

In effect, that switch gave Britain time to rebuild its military strength with US aid, and also to see the US enter the war.

Thus, it can be seen that Russia, to a major extent, was both *Good* and *Evil* in the execution of WW2.

Chapter 5. The Allies

5.8 Other *Good* Contributors

The situation for the combatants is shown in Fig. 5.28; from Wikipedia's 'Allies of World War II' where more detail is available. As well as those Axis and Allies already covered before, numerous other states took part in the Allies union:

Africa; Algeria; Brazil; Bulgaria (from 1944); Ceylon; Costa Rica; El Salvador; Ethiopia; Finland (from 1944); India; Italy (from 1943); Mexico; New Zealand; Nicaragua; North Africa, Panama; Philippines; Romania (from 1944); South Africa; West Indies.

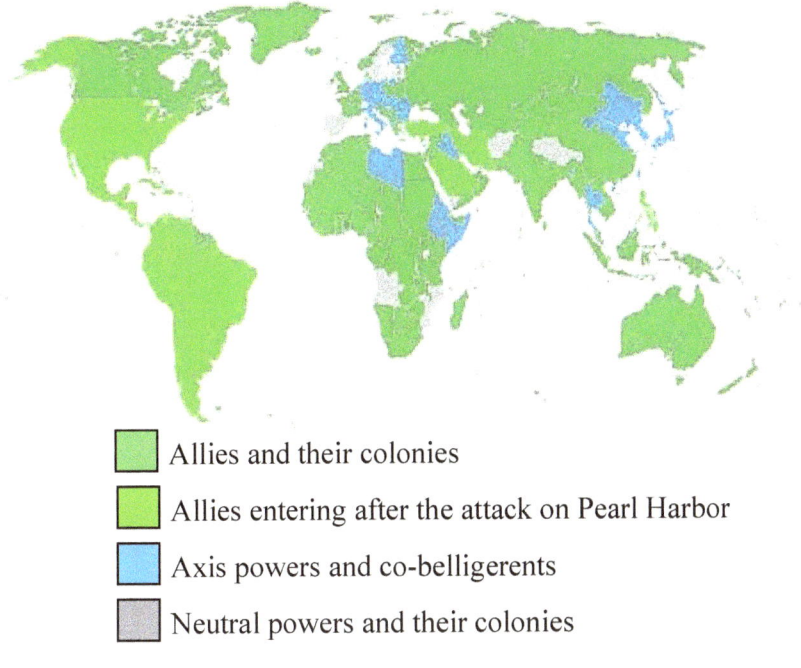

☐ Allies and their colonies
☐ Allies entering after the attack on Pearl Harbor
☐ Axis powers and co-belligerents
☐ Neutral powers and their colonies

Fig. 5.28 Combatants of WW2

From today's perspective, the Allies looked certain to be on a path to end the war, especially from the end of 1941 when the US entered it formally. However, whilst the Allies military might look positive, the fact was that the Nazis had embarked on a non-stoppable path needing major destruction by both sides to bring the war to an end in Europe.

Could the war have been stopped by diplomacy or an assassination? Not likely! Hitler wanted his people to fight to their end, as did Stalin; and there were some Allied generals who did not want those forces to be able to reappear.

A handful of top Nazis leaders saw the light well before the war ended but were not prepared to tell Hitler that his intentions would not work. Hitler was not a man to accept a diplomatic solution.

There were several dozen assassinations attempts on Hitler's life from the 1920s on. Remarkably, all failed.

The extremely cruel situation continued until all combatants fought to that point where overwhelming force existed, or the Germans and Japanese ran out of resources.

All this suggests on the surface, that removing Hitler would have ended it all. Not so, argued Duncan Anderson in BBC's *History - World Wars,* published in 2011. It is a lengthy explanation; here are its main points. The Special Operations Executive SOE created *Operation Foxley* in 1944. It was a detailed plan for a July application in Hitler's Berghof; it was never implemented. Its first paragraphs are given in Fig. 5.29.

```
                Operation.
                 FOXLEY.

INTRODUCTION.

    1. Object:    The elimination of HITLER and any high-ranking
                  Nazis or members of the Führer's entourage
                  who may be present at the attempt.

    2. Means:     Sniper's rifle, PIAT gun (with graze fuze) or
                  Bazooka, H.E. and splinter grenades; derailment
                  and destruction of the Führerzug by explosives;
                  clandestine means.

    3. Scene of   The most recent information available on Hitler
       operations: and his movements narrows down the field of
                  endeavour to two loci of action, viz. the
                  BERCHTESGADEN area and the Führerzug (Hitler's
                  train).
```

Fig. 5.29 First part of *Operation Foxley* document, SOE 1944 (NA UK)

Chapter 5. The Allies

The first idea had been to bomb his personal *Amerika* train, but they could not pin down any certain times of its appearance. Having learned of Hitler's habits at the Berghof, it was decided to use a sniper to kill him as he took his regular unprotected walk around to its Teehaus. Men and weapons were selected and the plan rehearsed.

However, more astute thinking was injected because it was not clear that his death would eliminate Nazism, as was needed; it was so entrenched that Hitler could well become a martyr of its cause.

Further, by that time in the war, Hitler had earned the title of being a poor, and grossly volatile, strategist. Many in the Nazi leadership might well make a better job of leading them: they would have been queueing up for the task.

No decision was made, and the plan began to fall apart as events changed the circumstances. Its implementation, if successful, would have 'thrown the system into chaos'.

Nearly all of Hitler's top generals had visions of grandeur and power. All had control of powerful sections of the German military complex. Only one or two wanted peace, for peace's sake. Some, like Himmler, and other leaders of the SS, had such guilt for crimes against humanity that they could not allow peace to come for fear of retribution.

As they saw it, the German people, due to long-time indoctrination and propaganda, were still largely in favour of Hitler's grand plan; his ills were directed at improving their nation. They did not see any guilt of Hitler as being theirs! Most also held the same evil aims he had promulgated.

With better leaders they might well have produced and used a, still better, war machine; so many new advanced, ideas and inventions had come from their leadership under Hitler Directives. They were the keepers of the know-how; not Hitler.

The Germans could well have given up their attack on Russia, releasing a huge force to commit elsewhere with devastating results on who was winning WW2. What Russia would have done if the Germans had left was then greatly feared by the West. They had solid major war production going and a huge battle-hardened army ready to make territorial gains at a rapid, possibly impossible to stop, rate. The war, dreadful as it was already, needed to be taken to its final devastating stages!

Midhurst WW2 Memoirs: 2. 'Evil' Rising: 'Good' Awakening

Whilst memories and detail of WW2 are still clear in many people's minds at the time of compiling this study, readers in the decades to come will not have that advantage. Hopefully, they will have no experience of the like of those of the WW2 era.

It has taken a while to get to this point in these memoirs. Now set in place is a suitable background to accompany our journey about life in the Midhurst Rural District in WW2.

As we progress you will see how, despite the District being small in size and population, its residents and 'visitors' - the military and evacuees - played their part in many of those countries.

Chapter 6. War Approaches

6.1 Unable to Comprehend

By 1937 a serious war against Germany was fast becoming a certainty. No doubt, for it was the national mood, most Midhurst District residents were unable to comprehend how this new war would impact their lives. It all would have seemed to be unreal and far away.

National newspapers ran short articles on how bad the Nazi regime was, or on the plight of some Jews in Germany but, somehow, war was not their problem. After all, Britain was the head of a mighty global Empire and had the world's largest and most advanced navy. Who would dare to make it a target? Indeed who?

The problem was that there were some countries around Germany that were readily persuaded to go under German rule, or that could be easily occupied by Hitler's Nazis forces. For many years *Pax Britannica* had rather stood silent, letting it happen.

Getting information on what local people felt about the situation is not easy for most folks just lived life then without recording its passage in some form or other. Before the war photographs were a modest luxury item for many; when war came, they were generally prohibited or unable to be taken for lack of availability of film.

Living in Worthing, on the South Coast, at the time was Mr Clare Fordham Harriss; not in the Midhurst District but not too far away; 26 miles by road. Each day, from 6th February 1938 to 15th August 1945, CF (as he entered himself), wrote up a diary giving most interesting information of the times. This has since been published in an extracted form with comments, Holden (2010).

He was in his late 50s when WWII broke out and so still had memories of WW1 well in his mind; he left us a mature precis on the affairs of the times that came to his way of thinking. Little was included about socialising; CF was intellectual in his interests so comments are on 'higher issues'. We can make use of his 1938 and 1939 reports to gauge one person's appreciation of the times as the war drew nearer - and nearer.

There was plenty on the news of a pending war by then.

Entry for Feb 25, 1938:

'The following noble and comfortable words were spoken in the House of Commons yesterday by Lord Halifax, who is Mr Eden's successor as Foreign Secretary. Having remarked that the conquest of Abyssinia (by Mussolini) could have been stopped by war, he continued: I am not afraid of Italy or any other power. I am not afraid of war in the sense that I fear defeat because I know the temper of this country. And I know that this country would never embark on war unless it thought it both right and inevitable. I also know that having embarked on war, it would not let go until, as usual, it had won. He and everybody else, however, detested war.'

March 12, 1938:

'Hitler has suddenly marched his troops into Austria and taken charge there. Yet to judge by the newspaper posters, the fight between the pugilists (strictly speaking, they were boxers with no gloves on) Baer and Farr is judged to be more attractive copy to the enlightened British reader. We preserve, indeed an admirable phlegm, but someday we will have to face up to this bully ourselves. I fear it is only too evident that Germany is once again making herself more and more intolerable, and that events are gradually moving to an inevitable course to war, just as they did before 1914.'

Throughout the year many entries report on Hitler's demands for territory by any foul means he thinks up. Chamberlain's September 1938 visit to Germany for a 'friendly talk' with Herr Hitler is an entry. The Sudetenland matter is still unresolved with its people clamouring to join Germany.

CF's diary aside for a moment, let's compare events in Germany and Britain at that time.
Hitler is well on his way to waging war as the key method of creating his glorious Third Reich through the use of a huge and progressive military system. His schemes for educating and

Chapter 6 War Approaches

indoctrinating the nation's youth to fight to the death for the Fuhrer are well established. He is already cleansing the German people of those who are not of close Aryan ascent. He had outwitted the peaceful nations on many an occasion by signing treaties he has no intention of keeping. He is about to 'feel the waters a little' by taking over Sudetenland.

Hitler has created a monster that is now going to be released to rampage, Fig. 6.1, over Europe and Russia before it took on more of the World.

Fig. 6.1 Hitler and Mussolini walk through Munich with some of the Nazi High Command in September 1938. (Bauer)

In Britain, these things are being seen to be happening but its Parliament is unwilling and unable to accept the events at a severe level of threat. The politicians are trying ways of delaying a war by insufficiently aggressive means.

The parliament processes delays, and delays; the policy of *appeasement* is continually being relied on. Democracy is showing its inability to make sound decisions with speed.

There are still numerous important people throughout Britain who see Hitler as a good leader, and who are prepared to sign national statements of their support. They think they would rather accept Fascist rule than go to war!

Hitler has a soft spot for Britain for it has Aryan roots, in his eyes. The British aristocracy honestly believes he will leave Britain's governance and class structure in place allowing the rich to carry on their lifestyles. They have their heads in the sand!

This leaves the people of Britain without adequate direction to counter the Nazis. However, behind the scenes government is making preparations for the defence of the country, relying much on sending an outdated British Expeditionary Force (BEF) to France to counter the invasion of France. Churchill still seems, to many, to be a war-monger with confronting, straight talk in Parliament on what the Nazis are up to. The British government is readying for war with the issue of gas masks all over the country; a gas bombing raid is on the cards, they up to. think.

In September an official called on CF's house to assess their family's ability to house evacuees. This was being done in areas deemed to be safe for them from any bombing.

On 28 September 1938, he writes in his record that he will not yet collect their gas masks because Hitler has summoned British and French leaders, and Mussolini, to a meeting to discuss the situation. It was, however, not to end the looming hostilities, but was merely a move to gain time for his army to reach a better state of preparedness to progress Hitler's country-grabbing intentions.

Later, for 21 October 1938, CF writes:

'Sir Samuel Hoare, Home Secretary, has been speaking of Hitler as a peaceable and honourable sort of statesman. On the other hand, Lord Hugh Cecil writes that to engage him in friendly wise is like stroking a crocodile's nose to see if it will purr.'

By 2nd December he writes that:

'the newspaper, as usual now, is full of alarm. Europe seems to be in ferment, and the Dictators grow so frantic that I fear a big war cannot long be postponed. When the German man-eater roars, the Italian jackal yaps - and we, and the French, run away. So it has been for the past five years. But someday we must stand at bay.'

Matters could only get worse - and they did. Entries for 1939 show that everyone would have known of the dreadful situation looming before their eyes, in more ways than by radio broadcasts or newspapers. However, messages along the appeasement line of thought kept coming right up to the line. The *Examiner* in Tasmania published this statement on 12 June 1939,

'SOME international observers are nervous about the speeches of the British Foreign Minister (Lord Halifax). and the Prime Minister (Mr Chamberlain) last week. They fear a return to an appeasement policy of the sort that led to the disappearance of Czechoslovakia

Chapter 6 War Approaches

from the map of Europe. Subsequent events have shown clearly that Britain's attitude at Munich was interpreted by Germany as one of weakness. There is an alarm that these latest speeches - particularly that of Lord Halifax - will be regarded as proof that no marked stiffening of British spirit has occurred in the meantime. There is no real reason, however, to believe that ground for such nervousness exists. Britain is daily becoming more qualified to talk to the aggressive nations from a position of strength. She is pledged to fight should the independence of certain European nations be menaced by force, and fight she undoubtedly will. Even Germany must now be convinced that Britain is not the senile and innocuous nation at which Herr Hitler so often directed contemptuous remarks.

But Britain's desire for peace is as strong as ever, and it is natural and wise that she should leave undone nothing that might lead Germany back into the comity of nations. It may be significant that an Italian newspaper hailed Lord Halifax's speech as "a return to common sense." Perhaps Signor Mussolini, the minor partner in the axis, is pressing Herr Hitler to move toward a way out of the explosive and impossible situation existing in Europe today. If such a way is to be found, and peace maintained, the formula will inevitably include trade arrangements that will enable Germany to transfer huge numbers of men from the army, and from the manufacture of war equipment to peacetime production, without the danger of an economic collapse that would be fatal to the prestige of the Nazi regime. Britain is anxious to persuade Germany that she is ready to make a genuine effort to assist her in this direction.'

Thankfully, some plans were actually in train if war came. Evacuees started appearing in the Worthing area by 1st September 1939. CF's family was told to take in 3 children but his 57 years could not cope with that so he compromised by taking in a lady school teacher who came there with her class of evacuees. Blackout was imposed. It was a very sad day from him and all others across the British Empire lands.

Territorial soldiers in uniform began to amass there on the South Coast. However, holidaymakers hardly gave them and some military aircraft much attention. Was it simply disbelief, or perhaps that British stoicism and conservatism were making that same old face of adversity - still upper lip and all that! In CF's diary entries we see that the British people knew the war was coming. Especially in the south where defence and troop mustering took place ready to send hundreds of thousands of men of the British Expeditionary Force BEF to France.

The local *Observer* newspaper had a remit to report the local news; fires, crimes, new local developments, traffic accidents, social events and, of course, the many advertisements for goods and services that made it all pay. In that paper was where you looked to find out what film was showing at the local cinema in North Street, but not to see what an upstart dictator was up to.

Starting in 1935, Hitler had been ignoring the conditions of the *Treaty of Versailles* in that Germany was not to rearm for aggression. But by all manner of shrewd politics and deals, plus fanatical determination, he was building up a force for 'the defence of Germany'. After all, France was amassing a very large force and they did not want to suffer as they did in WW1. The arms race was on again in Europe.

The *Western Argus* newspaper (Kalgoorlie, Western Australia) of 2 March 1937 ran a short summarising article on the arms race then in progress. Key points were that all the great powers were responsible for the escalation. Britain set an:

> 'amazingly quixotic example of disarmament ….. until its defences had reached a grave state of inadequacy which was beginning to be reflected by the amount of weight which her government exercised in international counsel'

Having suffered so much under the heel of Germany, up to and including WW1, France had built up a major defence system.

Russia also built up great strength for she was being told by half of Europe how she should govern herself.

It was suggested that Mussolini's war indiscretions be excused because he also nearly fell to the Central powers of Europe. Attempts by those powers, in the early 1930s, to end the arms race, were rendered fruitless by the poor decisions of France and Britain. It was, in hindsight,

Chapter 6 War Approaches

that they played into the hands of Hitler's opposing ideas for world domination by building up a crack military system under their noses. The arms race had indeed built up a stronger economy in Britain, but it is still being argued that it:

'is a sheer waste of money which could be better spent in countless different ways to the benefit of the people'.

By 1938 it was beginning to sink in; another world war with Britain heavily involved was a highly likely certainty.

Fig. 6.2 'Stepping stones to Glory'. (David Low)

That mad man Hitler had been building up Germany's military and industrial capability and had, by then, started his rampage to take over adjacent regions of the *Sudetenland*. Fig. 6.2 shows David Low's take. Hitler starts his rise toward being 'boss of the universe', by walking first on the backs of the Sudetenland areas. These were the many German-speaking peripheral regions of the current Czech Republic that had been taken from Germany as part of the WW1 land sharing agreements. They needed to be restored to Germany!

They seemed to want to be back as a part of Germany. He called it *annexation*, the first step in his plan to build a Third Reich by taking possession and then cleansing the peoples, not only those of the hapless nations but also of his own nation's population.

As a blind, Hitler's statement, made in May 1935, gave plenty of the sort of declared wisdom that Britain and France wanted to hear:

> 'The bloodshed on the European continent in the course of the last three hundred years bears no proportion to the national result of the events. In the end, France had remained France, Germany, Poland, and Italy. What dynastic egotism, political passion and patriotic blindness have attained in the way of apparently far-reaching political changes by shedding rivers of blood has, as regards national feeling, done no more than touched the skin of nations. It has not substantially altered their fundamental characters. If these states had applied merely a fraction of their sacrifices to wiser purposes the success would certainly have been greater and more permanent.'

Here appeared to be a sincere man who recognised the reality of war and who wanted peaceful development. He would be reasonable; at least so it appeared! It led to Chamberlain following the *appeasement* policy that allowed Hitler more time to move to his real intentions; that were far from his uttered words. He was the master of deceitful words that were the opposite of his intentions. Lies were tools in his toolbox of conquest. His real plans were revealed to his Army High Command in a secret meeting in November 1937. See one view of them at www.historyplace.com/worldwar2/triumph/tr-hossbach.htm

Enforced military recruitment commenced in Britain in October 1939, before that it had been voluntary. Then, the Home Guard was still not yet more than an idea to be set up when things got really bad. They could not be equipped properly until late in 1940. Their formalised existence was still being argued about in the mid-1940. They began training using broomsticks as rifle simulations.

The strangest, unexpected, need that showed up was how to treat dead dogs and cats; numerous owners saw the need to put them to sleep. Some 400,000 carcases had to be dealt within a short period.

An air raid with a poisonous gas start was expected, not a land invasion. Paratroopers were also expected. That apocalypse did not eventuate, at

Chapter 6 War Approaches

least when war was declared. Britain was then far away from Hitler's initial campaign intentions.

By the outbreak of war, shelter protection from bombing was being provided as open slit-trenches, blast proofed surface buildings, existing basements and tunnels, plus the ubiquitous corrugated sheet-steel Andersen shelters dug into the ground of back gardens.

Open fields had upstanding poles dug in to fend off paratroopers and deter aircraft from landing. This took place in Cowdray polo fields.

Sparsely placed, anti-aircraft guns were set up along the South Coast. Heavier guns were brought into action to defend ship attacks in the Thames estuary. Fig. 6.3 illustrates the point that the 1939 gun emplacements had little chance of staying active against incoming ship shells, or the dive bombings by German Air Force Stukas. Gallant crews with a short life expectancy indeed, but not much protection!

Fig 6.3 6-inch coastal defence gun at Sheerness, November 1939.

Barrage Balloons were set up to keep the enemy aircraft high, thereby making it easier to track them with searchlights in the defence of Central London, and at some other obvious targets.

The Royal Navy was brought into action, using aircraft carriers carrying a goodly fleet of carrier aircraft that, however, was not up to combat with 1939s German fighters. Their use was better applied to keep the supply lines open from the US and Canada by finding and destroying German submarines.

For all of these simple, quick to set up measures, defence of the South Coast was all rather last minute and minimal. When an invasion from the sea became all too likely in mid-1940, much more was done in terms of block construction for housing guns and beach defences.

From today's perspective that increased level of defence was also unlikely to have deterred, or defeated, the kind of military might that the Nazis soon showed they could bring to bear. Fortunately, Britain had a year's reprieve for Hitler was more interested in occupying European countries, leaving British occupation on hold, in what became known as the *phoney war* period.

MacDougall (2011) has lots to say about the parlous situation. Many government policy decisions made in 1938, and early 1937, led to decreased defence spending. It was, however, most unclear if Britain could even be defended! Too many decisions were based on defence provisions made for the two major prior threats of the Napoleonic War and World War 1. There was little to use as an exemplar model for defence in 1939: this war was then being conducted so differently to those of the past.

Fig. 6.4 Royal Artillery parading in Cowdray Park. 1937.

In 1937, Fig. 6.4, the 98th Surrey and Sussex Yeomanry, Queen Mary Field Brigade, Royal Artillery camped in Cowdray Park. They do not compare at all well with German artillery used to invade Poland, just 2 years later.

Midhurst was certainly an almost unknown town and very much off

Chapter 6 War Approaches

the beaten track. However, some top leaders of Hitler's regime, including Herr Hitler himself, are said to have already made plans for the future use of some places in the Midhurst Rural District; a suggestion needing more proof, as is discussed in the next section.

Britain was caught 'almost with its pants down'.

6.2 "Goering Stayed Here". Fact or Fiction?

Two key members of the German High Command were said then to be already familiar with the delights of West Sussex. They were fascinated with the British landscape; and so sure they would soon occupy Britain that they started to eye off which parts they would own. These two, namely Joachim von Ribbentrop and Hermann Goering, were the two highest Germans who supported Hitler in his quest to create a glorious Third Reich, Fig. 6.5.

Fig. 6.5 THE BANDIT'S FEAST "I've said it once, and I'll say it again, the British are starving Europe". LHS, Goering; centre, Hitler; RHS Ribbentrop. (Shephard)

This trio, at the post-war Nuremberg trials, was judged to have been the key people who took the whole world into a most horrific global war, in which the Nazis grossly violated humankind. Each had grand visions of their forthcoming ownership of countries and grand properties. To Hitler, it was the creation of even grander empire to rival the those of Greece, Rome and the like. To Goering, it was art treasures and the good life of excesses, and to Von Ribbentrop, it was to own his own country in Britain - with a castle and him as King of the Castle. Interestingly each had a high level of respect for the British way of life, but each did not think their way to achieve their goals was disagreeable to the democracies of the main western world.

Their likely association with Midhurst is a surprising tale, one that may never be fully proven, but one to keep the local historians engaged in the long search for truth.

According to local existing written records, they both had links to Midhurst. Much older readers may have seen them strutting down North Street, or dining in the Spread Eagle, perhaps in civvies for it was before war broke out. Hitler never visited Britain in the 1930s.

But first, on Joachim von Ribbentrop's ambitions. He first became Germany's Ambassador to Britain, and then its Foreign Minister. Just about a couple of years before war was declared, he openly spoke to a British person about his territorial intentions,

On one of his often-made visits to Britain, he spent a few days in the St Michael's Mount district of Cornwall, that being in the year of my birth, 1937. According to an article by Sam Greenhill, in the *Daily Mail* newspaper, Ribbentrop had spoken to Michael Lyne, a resident there. He was with his grandfather when they, by chance, both met Ribbentrop on his West Country visit. After the meeting, his grandfather told Michael:

> 'Ribbentrop has told me when they get world domination, he is going to live on St Michael's Mount as his holiday home - and Cornwall will belong to him.'
> www.dailymail.co.uk/news/article-1317511

Life has its highly satisfying compensations at times: Michael happened to meet up with this enormously arrogant man again when he guarding him during the Nuremberg trials in 1946.

Fig. 6.6 Ribbentrop (right) with his lawyer at the War trials in 1946.

Chapter 6 War Approaches

Ribbentrop was there under trial for his war crimes. This time the tables were well and truly turned. The guard and the prisoner exchanged words.

Michael said, "Your plans didn't work out as you planned, did they?" "No, they didn't, did they" replied the hapless Ribbentrop, Fig. 6.6. He was hanged for his war crimes on 16 October 1946,

That man may well have been fantasising on what he might gain from a successful invasion of Britain; it is recorded that he also was going to adopt Fernhurst as his 'away' home.

> 'After the war proof of a sort was found (but not given) to show that Fernhurst was the place chosen by von Ribbentrop for his adoption when Germany won the war. In fact, he had chosen *Ropes* for his residence, a very beautifully situated home......a charming country home with a perfect English garden'.
> Fernhurst Society oral memories.

Now named *Bollards*, Fig. 6.7, it is situated in Ropes Lane.

Fig. 6.7 *Bollards*.
Said to be what Ribbentrop would take when the Nazis took over Britain.
(Fernhurst Society)

Delving down into the Fernhurst Society website reveals this statement was taken from an oral history project carried out by the Fernhurst Women's Institute in 1958 - well before computers were freely available to form digital files of the audiotapes. It is unlikely that any more detail will be forthcoming unless the original audio was written up, and still exists. The statement was also republished, verbatim, in the compilation, WSFWI (1993).

That unknown Fernhurst historian also states another infamous pro-German person, James Joyce, had his honeymoon in Fernhurst and was often seen in the Spread Eagle Hotel in Midhurst. We look over this person's infamous story under his nick-name of *Lord Haw-Haw*, and his connection to the District in Chapter 9.3. Joyce married his second wife, Margaret, in the Kensington Registry Office on 8 February 1937. Perhaps this was the time when they stayed in Fernhurst?

Now to one fascinating, locally recorded story that reports that Goering and Ribbentrop had once stayed over in Midhurst, namely in the Spread Eagle Hotel.

I first read of this possibility on a visit to the *Spread.* Since the 60s, I often travelled to the UK from Australia on short visits for my academic career. Whenever possible I would fit in 25 minutes to do the *Midhurst Walk,* stopping here and there to recall events of my childhood during WW2. That walk still fascinates me today, despite changes to its paths.

I was on one of those pilgrimage visits to Midhurst in the late 80s. During that trip, I got some very good news on the successful outcome for an academic application I had made 2 years beforehand. A celebration of some significant kind was needed to mark the occasion.

Thinking about what would be good to do, I recalled my 1943 war year there, seeing the well-off people arrive at the Spread Eagle Hotel. I then lived in decaying digs in Red Lion Street, just by the hotel. I had always wanted to stay at the hotel to sample its atmosphere. With a sound reason to have a splurge, and to, perhaps, leave one of those traditional puddings hanging there, I checked in.

I registered and asked for a four-poster bed...as you do when playing the part of the well-off tourist. I cannot recall the actual detail of the room but it was a bit like that shown in Fig. 6.8.

Fig. 6.8 One-time example of a four-poster suite in the Spread Eagle Hotel.

After settling in, I explored the room's quaintness. On the wall was a small notice. I read it. I read it again. It seemed to be

Chapter 6 War Approaches

unbelievable; a joke.

In a nutshell, I think it recorded the sentiment, 'Goering slept here in 1938'. How could that be?

Surely a top Nazi would feel he would not at all be welcomed in England at that time, considering what dreadful things he had already helped to be done in Europe and especially Spain, against other human beings? The room shown here is not the one I slept in. The hotel seems to have reorganised the rooms since my night there. That particular notice seems to have gone.

Years later I messaged the then hotel manager, Edward James, to confirm this. He provided a copy of the small booklet they published, Balfour (2007). It tells the history of the Hotel. Section 4 is titled, 'So They Say':

'Probably the most infamous visitors the hotel has received are Hermann Goering [added here: Founder of the dreaded Gestapo and later Commander-In-Chief of the Luftwaffe Air Force] and [Joachim] Von Ribbentrop, Hitler's Ambassador in London just before the Second World War. Perhaps the hotel's name alone attracted them! They dined at The Spread Eagle Hotel one evening in July 1939, after attending the 'Glorious Goodwood' race meeting. Apparently, Goering had previously been to see the Leonardslee Estate, near Horsham, having selected it as his future headquarters in the presumption that a German invasion of Britain would be successful (perhaps they backed losers at Goodwood too!).'

Edward James later added to the story:

'Hitler wanted to base himself in the South East of England and he was keen on Leonardslee House/Gardens [now a private house again] for his Head Office, but others in his party were very keen on the Spread Eagle. Goering and Von Ribbentrop, the German Ambassador staying at the Spread were reputedly overheard at dinner suggesting this would be a perfect base. They both stayed and Von Ribbentrop was a regular as he and many of the German Cabinet were keen racegoers to Goodwood. But it is only hearsay.'

James' message was quick to point out 'This is only hearsay'. The caption given with the register extract states the 'actual date of the entry is unclear'.

The last sentence was my trigger to spend time researching this issue of them being there at all. What is the truth of this statement? The following study consulted Bloch (1994), Manvell and Fraenkel (2011), Ribbentrop (1953), Schwarz (1943), Snyder (1998), Urquhart (1987), and several newspapers reports to try to verify this unexpected Midhurst event with non-local records.

At this time of writing (early 2019), on display in the hotel is a page said to have been taken out of the hotel's Aliens Register. It includes a signature that looks to be written by, or for, 'Ribbentrop'. The entries include the days 5 and 11 July, of an unrecorded year. Could deeper examination of the only records - the Spread Eagle booklet and the page from their Aliens Register - lead to the truth of this situation?

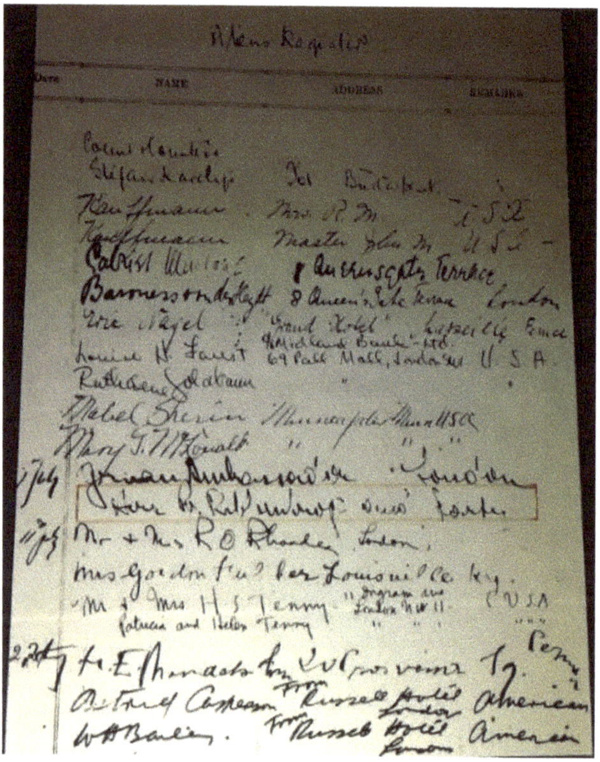

Fig. 6.9 Portion of Aliens Register page of Spread Eagle, including a Ribbentrop signature.

Serious doubt is soon apparent. Under the Aliens page in the display frame is a caption, presumably written by a hotel staff member at the

Chapter 6 War Approaches

time the framed page was assembled.

It states:

'This signature of Von Ribbentrop was made when he was Hitler's Ambassador to England. He and Hermann Goering, together with four other officers dined at the Spread Eagle in July 1939 (date?) when attending Goodwood Races. Lieut. E.G. Hollist, who still (in 1978) lives near Midhurst, remembers the occasion well as he was also dining at the hotel that evening.
It seems to have subsequently transpired that Goering had been to Leonardslee near Horsham, then the home of Lady Muriel Loder. He had selected this beautiful estate as his Headquarters after the invasion of England (Operation "Sea Lion", the German invasion plan 1940 refers to this.)'

Here is another line of enquiry seeking to establish a reliable truth. Lieut. Hollist was seated near to the Nazi group and overheard them talk about these intentions. Research, however, has not yet uncovered what he heard, or what is the independent evidence for Goering being there at all.

The elements of Hollist's words may have been more myth than reality and needed deeper research. It had to be treated as a detective hunt by calling in more local investigators.

The Ribbentrop signature in the register is another starting point. Associated with other German political positions given with his name, it seems reasonable to first assume that it was indeed Ribbentrop that signed in.

The first issue is, however, that the registered signature is quite different from many examples of his signature found elsewhere. It does have the same thick robustness in its verticals but, most importantly, that in the Spread Eagle Aliens Register has a slight slope to the left.

All of the many examples of reliable Ribbentrop's signatures, seen in books and on the Internet, slope strongly to the right, with closed-up letter spacings. Two are compared in Fig. 6.10. The reliable signature used here is taken from a photo-plate in Schwarz (1943), as it is in a family photo used in the 1943 book.

Fig. 6.10 Ribbentrop signatures.

(a) With family photo in 1937, from Schwarz (1943).

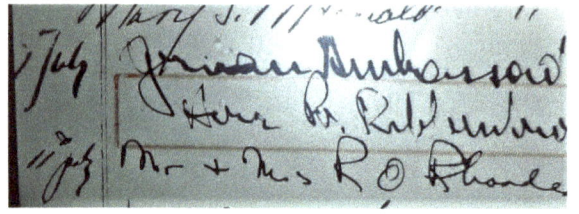

(b) On Spread Eagle Hotel register page.

That in the Register entry does not compare at all well with his verified signature. It does not have the same ruggedly bullish appearance and close up letters. Also, the first name does not seem to have the first letter of 'Joachim'. It also uses 'Herr'. Joachim was hardly that humble to use the common name for Mr.

Whereas that seems to make our chase as 'case closed and a fake', the entry may have been written by one of the supposed party who was present according to the Hollist account. Alternatively, it could have been added by a hotel person to clarify, by name, who the Ambassador was. Also, it could simply be another Ribbentrop person! To look into this first needs to settle what the year of the visit could it have been.

We need to probe more deeply to establish if that date is reasonable. July is the recorded month of the entry. The caption record states they had attended the Goodwood races at that time.

A local authority on Goodwood events, Ian Wegg, studied the dates for that event and established the regular pattern of the four-day meeting that was always held in the last week of July:

> 1936: Tues 28th July - Fri 31 July
> 1937: Tues 27th July - Fri 30 July
> 1938: Tues 26th July - Fri 29 July
> 1939: Tues 25th July - Fri 28 July

Importantly, the date of the entry as being in 1937, was independently confirmed with strong evidence. Tania Pons, another local historian,

Chapter 6 War Approaches

looked into the presence on that page of the two lady's names just above the Ribbentrop entry. She found that Mabel Sherin of Minneapolis left the UK on 20th August 1937 aboard the *SS Hamburg*; Louise Faust left the UK on 7th July 1937, aboard the *RMS Aquitania*. That pins down the year of the page entries to 1937- a point of truth at last!

Ribbentrop regularly was in Britain carrying out his appointed roles. At that time in 1939, it is recorded that he was deeply engaged in odious discussions in Germany, mostly with the British Ambassador to Germany, Sir Nevile Henderson.

By 1939 it was common knowledge that the Nazis were evil, and by then most unwanted in Britain. Joachim Von Ribbentrop was in the thick of diplomatic games and surely would not have been taking it easy in Midhurst then. It was just all too close to war with Poland, and then Britain, to have happened this way.

Additionally, in that year Goodwood races were from 27 July onward, that is, many days after the apparent presence of Ribbentrop and party in the Spread Eagle. That does not fit the Spread Eagle manager's statement given above.

There might, however, have been a more likely reason for some Nazis being there at that early July 1937 date. The Fascist Party, under the name of the British Union of Fascists BUF, then in 1937 known as the British Union BU, had its *Munich of the South Coast* base in Worthing.

Their summer camps were organised in the South of England, at Pagham and Selsey. The Chichester Observer reported that 700 members of the BU had arrived at the Selsey camp as the first contingency. It is also confirmed that Joachim Ribbentrop attended those camps.

The Nazi party in the Spread Eagle hotel that day, might well have been British *Black Shirts* hosted by, possibly, Joachim Ribbentrop. They might have been wearing their threatening military uniforms. Paramilitary uniforms were, however, banned in 1937 at political events in Britain from 1 January of that year. Notwithstanding that order, a film of the 1937 camp shows that whilst the participants wore ordinary day Oswald Mosley, their political leader in Britain, was still in that black uniform at that camp.

Again, no real lead to put the story to bed. Where next to investigate? We already have newspaper evidence that Ribbentrop visited Cornwall that year - see above - but how likely is it that he was in Britain in 1937?

Ribbentrop became the German Ambassador in London on 11 August 1936. He was promoted to be the German Foreign Minister on 11 March 1938. That confirms that Ribbentrop was an Ambassador at the time of the Spread Eagle meeting; if it had been in July 1937. From the newspaper story above, about his expected kingship of Cornwall, he was at this time in his best arrogant presence of mind, so confident and overbearing. Also, as we will see a little later, his son was in school in London.

Using newspaper reports of the time, Tania Pons followed Ribbentrop's UK movements during July 1937. Her tentative reply stated:

'We already know that Ribbentrop was at Buckingham Palace on 1st July. The following day, Friday 2nd July, he was at the meeting of the "Non-Intervention Sub Committee" (regarding other nations entering the Spanish Civil War) held at the Foreign Office in London.

According to the *Portsmouth News*: "he arrived in a car carrying a red and black Nazi flag and a swastika, accompanied by Dr Woermann who had brought latest instructions from Hitler".

I think it unlikely that he would have left Buckingham Palace on Thursday, checked into the Spread Eagle for the evening and returned to London the next morning, no matter how well adorned his Mercedes.

Meetings of the Non-Intervention Committee, of which Ribbentrop was one of the most prominent members, continued the following week and Friday 9th July followed an almost identical pattern, with Ribbentrop and Woermann arriving in the morning and the committee adjourning (with no agreement) at 4.30 pm.

Therefore, Ribbentrop could have been in Midhurst mid-week on the 7th, or gone thereafter to the meeting at the Foreign Office on Friday 9th, which I think more likely.'

There is still the matter of verifying any presence of Goering at the the Spread Eagle. Working backwards in time, the facts show he was most unlikely to have been there in 1939.

Chapter 6 War Approaches

The first date set for the military Invasion of Poland was 26 August 1939. However, Hitler postponed it several times. This was to be his first real all-out war; not what he intended, for it had the risk of pulling in several Allies countries who had treaties to that effect. Hitler's highly armed, aggressive might was expected to see Poland simply capitulate, as had been his territorial conquests to that time: Poland, however, was increasingly defiant and fought on hard.

Hitler had called the second meeting of the Reich Defence Council on June 23; Goering presided. Later in July, more meetings were called.

Goering was the person who, by then, had proposed using forced Czech labour to make up the numbers of people needed to take on that level of war. Furthermore, Goering was quite ill in this period from his long-standing health problems caused by drug-taking.

I, also, cannot see Goering being readily allowed into Britain in 1939 for, by then, the horrors and lies of Hitler were well publicised all over the Western world.

So perhaps Goering was in Midhurst in an earlier year; throughout the Summer of 1938, especially in June and July. Then, however, he was involved in Germany with negotiations over Germany's attack on Czechoslovakia. Goering also then had numerous high-level guests, including the French Air Force head at *Carinhall* in Germany; his favourite place of abode. This was a very anxious time for the Nazi leadership, as they debated attacking Czechoslovakia.

Goering, on 8 July 1938, made a speech to aircraft makers in *Carinhall.*

In that month Goering had made unofficial enquiries in Britain to see if an official visit to Britain would be welcomed. According to Manvell and Fraenkel (2011), it had not happened by November. As expected, Ribbentrop was furious at this overture; he alone was the diplomatic channel for such overtures!

Goering and Ribbentrop despised each other by this time; hardly up to be being dinner companions. That rules him out for the year 1938.

Going back another year to that perhaps looking more promising, on 12 May 1937, King George V1 of Britain had his coronation. Goering was not present. He had just made a major diplomatic faux pas and had been expressly told by the Nazi hierarchy not attend because they still were trying to get Britain on-side with their plans to take over some

European countries.

However, disregarding his given orders, Goering flew over to Croydon Airport near the time of the coronation. Ribbentrop got wind of this and met him at the plane, escorting him to the German Embassy in London. Goering flew back the next day without attending the coronation. It seems unlikely that he was socialising with Ribbentrop in England that year.

So many unexplained leads need to be followed up here to see if more truthful flesh can be put on these bones. What can we find out about Lieut. E.G. Hollist?

Edward Gerald Hollist was born in Maidenhead in 1909 and was commissioned as a Second Lieutenant in the Land Forces (The Royal West Sussex Regiment) in August 1929.

In the Imperial War Museum (no 938 on the *Interwar Period*) are 5 reels of oral history spoken by him. He tells us, from his 21st year of life onward, how he spent time in India as his first wish in military life. He was impressed with the lifestyle and contributions he could enjoy, and make, in that country. No photograph could be found of him.

He was still there in 1935 when political agitation for self-rule became apparent to the military - as they began to see and feel the physical reactions of the Indian people. The Army was being kept well away from the latest political realities going on behind the scenes; their job was not to be involved in such matters.

Hollist lived, at the end of his life, in *Henchers*, Bepton; where he died, age 57, in February 1986.

Tania Pons had worked in the Spread Eagle from 1983 when the registry page was on display with its caption mentioning Hollist's memory. It is, therefore, to be deduced that he had not objected to the wording being publicised, thus giving it some credence.

As this whole incident looks increasingly suspicious, an obvious idea is that the registry page frame might have been devised for reasons of gaining publicity for the hotel, especially with the American Forces brass who came there from 1943.

After the war unidentified Americans donated to the hotel, an eagle statue purported to be Goering's own. A wall-mounted caption about this

Chapter 6 War Approaches

Eagle reads:

'It is rumoured that American GIs liberated this eagle from Hermann Goering's office in Berlin - donating it to the hotel as a thank you for happy times spent here during the Second World War.'

Fig. 6.11 The Eagle purported to have been Goering's.

Facing you as one enters the door today, from the rear car park of the hotel, is that grand eagle carving sitting over an aged, well-polished, brass plaque. It reads:

THE SPREAD EAGLE HOTEL
A.D. 1430
THIS EAGLE ADORNED THE CHAIR OF HERMANN GORING
IN THE REICHSTAG OF THE GERMAN THIRD REICH
DURING THE SECOND WORLD WAR 1939-1945

Again, no proof of veracity seems to exist! The hotel had been in the local courts during the war. The local newspaper reported on 4 December 1943 that the hotel chain owners had been fined for buying 398lbs of fish, instead of its given ration for the 8 weeks of 270lbs. This

Midhurst WW2 Memoirs: 2. 'Evil' Rising: 'Good' Awakening

came about when their refrigerator had broken down losing stock. Records were poorly kept, even altered, the blame being placed on a temporary person then in control.

'The framing of the register page and the publication of the booklet – and therefore, the genesis of this story - would have been done when the hotel was under the stewardship of a man called Brian Tonks. My memory of him is that he was something of a curious character, somewhat unpredictable in his attitude to his patrons. My feeling is he may have had more of an eye for publicity than historical accuracy'. Source unknown.

Desperate to find more truth for any aspect of this incident, another line of enquiry was taken that might verify if Ribbentrop had visited Midhurst in the late 1930s.

Marked on the winding wall of the circular staircase of the tower of the Cowdray Ruins is a large collection of graffiti made as visitors left their names and other marks to record their presence during the 1930s and 40s. Fig. 6.12 shows the 'Wot No, Mr Chad' doodle, a rage of the time mentioning here the lack of Watney's beer brew that was at its demand peak in the 30s.

Fig. 6.12 Graffiti drawing on Cowdray Ruins wall.

Allied to these scratchings is the existence of related Visitor Books from that period, held at the time of writing this account in the Visitor Centre of the Cowdray ruins.

Tania Pons had pointed out that entries in those books might well have a signature of Von Ribbentrop there, that being a long-held locally held verbal myth. Neve (2011) also states the possibility that Ribbentrop visited the ruins and may have signed the visitor log, but these statements

Chapter 6 War Approaches

are likely to have come about from a single source of the rumour. The date of such an entry would, indeed, be a clincher that he was there.

To follow this up, in May 2018, Tania and myself were hosted by Sally Guile of the Cowdray Heritage Trust. Hoping to find his obvious signature and German address, a quick eyeball scan of the book entries and a large amount of graffiti on the walls, did not reveal any Ribbentrop-like entry. A more thorough study is needed to confirm this lack of evidence, but it does not yet support his visit.

Consulted was one volume, Fig. 6.13, starting on 1 September 1932 and going beyond 1943. That list is most useful for its large amount of visitor information - from numerous countries, including Germany, as the war was approaching! There are to be found there many soldier's names and regiments, including evacuees and Canadian troops.

Fig. 6.13 The Cowdray Ruins register book consulted in May 2018.

To open this detection story along yet another thread, Ian Wegg surmised that it may have been another Ribbentrop who signed in? The signature certainly looks more like an R than a J.

Joachim's son, Rudolph was born in May 1921. During 1937 he had been, unconfirmed, in Midhurst.

'When his father was German Ambassador to the Court of St. James in London in 1936, Britisher Sir Robert Vansittart tried to get Rudi into "Eton for the coming half," according to von Ribbentrop's biographer, Michael Bloch: "Ribbentrop was particularly keen on this idea since he believed…that Eton would show Rudolf 'how English boys live, and he will be able to teach the Hitler Youth.' …The Eton authorities rejected Rudolf on the grounds that he was too old and had been put down far too late, which Ribbentrop naturally interpreted as a snub by the British establishment.' Blaine Taylor's variation from Bloch (1994).

See ihffilm.com/rudolf-von-ribbentrop-commander-fronts-east-west-essay-by-blaine-taylor.html

'Ribbentrop spent a year at Westminster School, London while his father was Ambassador to Britain, that being from the British diplomat Brian Urquhart, a student at the same school during Ribbentrop's time there, his autobiography "A Life in Peace and War (1987)" describes the latter person as being "doltish, surly and arrogant". Urquhart recalls that Rudi Ribbentrop, much to the dismay of his schoolmates, "arrived each morning in one of two plum-coloured Mercedes-Benz limousines". Urquhart further recalls, "On arrival in Dean's Yard, both chauffeurs would spring out, give the National socialist salute, and shout "Heil Hitler!'
Wikipedia.'

Brian recalled that a growing crowd of students at the Westminster School would gather; all laughing loudly when the 'Heil Hitler' salutes were made. In response, the German Embassy lodged a strong complaint 'for insults to a friendly power'. Brian Urquhart was matted by the Headmaster as the leader of that game.

The Headmaster was not at all sympathetic with Brian's predicament until he pointed out plum coloured motor vehicles were reserved for use by the British Royal family only. That was the last straw to the Headmaster; that was just not done! The outcome was that Rudi then walked to school!

Urquhart (1987) also tells us:

Chapter 6 War Approaches

'In 1937, the Nazis were not be any means generally unpopular in England. Many conservatives positively admired them for their discipline, for their harsh treatment of communists, for making the trains run on time, and so on.'

There was then much support for them, especially by the gentry classes that believed Hitler's ways would suit them; they expected he would let them carry on enjoying their privileges, as they had for centuries before.

Rudolph's obituary in the New York Times, of 10 June 2019, tells us that at school in 1937 he wore a class uniform of morning coat and top hat. He was then proud of his Germanness, prominently showing the Nazi party youth badge – swastika and eagle – on his lapel.

Rudolph was the exemplary young man that Hitler's education system was grooming to fight to the death for the Third Reich. He joined the Hitler Youth before going into the Waffen SS, the paramilitary armed wing of the Nazi Party's SS organisation.

Figure 6.14 shows Rudolph as a young man in his London school time. A photo elsewhere of him, when 15 years old, shows he could easily be taken as an adult.

His following military career was as a hard and close-up fighter. He was in the thick of close-up combat from 1942, receiving bullet and fragment wounds on five separate engagements, many being in tank regiments.

His bravery and wounds earned him many German war

Fig. 6.14 Rudolph von Ribbentrop in London, 1937.

medals, including the Iron Cross. He survived the war to die on 6 June 2019 at the age of 98.

Returning to Rudolph's signature, perhaps being that on the Spread Eagle Alien Register. Googled images reveal some examples. However, Rudolph's photograph is well sought after, as are many signed pictures of decorated heroes from both sides of the war. If they have a signature the value to a buyer is considerably greater then without it. There exist unscrupulous people who add a counterfeit signature for this reason.

Given this fact, those found were far from consistent. One set for sale is reported to be faked as they look all too much like the very distinctive Joachim signature. There has not yet been found one that could be reliably used in this study as proof of Rudolph's real signature. The one that is on the Web is not like his father's and not like that in the Spread Eagle Register. That line of research is still open for further enquiry. It does, however, seem more promising that he was there in Midhurst.

We now turn to the statement that says Lieut. E.G. Hollist overheard the conversation by a Nazis group in the Spread Eagle.

He certainly existed, being from a long-standing local family. He had been in the British army in India and had returned to Midhurst just before 1937. But, was he able to recognise that it was Goering and Ribbentrop he heard or saw, or was it in reality, Rudolph with a party of fascists down south for the summer camps?

From strong evidence, Goering was not there. Ribbentrop's photo was in the main British press a lot but would a soldier just back from India have seen it enough to remember it?

As already stated, at the start of 1937 para-political parties in Britain were not permitted to wear uniforms at functions. But assuming these black-shirt fascists were prepared to break the new law, would they have paraded as a 'gang' of Nazis in their all so recognisable black outfits, with those highly polished, black, jackboots and a red swastika on their armband?

So, where does all that research verification leave us? Sadly, we get to this point still realising that a Ribbentrop may have been there after all! But not Goering.

Chapter 6 War Approaches

What do you think? Was it really a story concocted by the hotel management of the day to attract interest in the hotel by Yanks staying and drinking there in the later years of WW2? It worked. They sent artefacts to the hotel that were claimed to be Goering's.

This visit to Midhurst story has some way to go to prove it is true, or false. There is not much truly proven about it; a few true solid facts keep the door open to an answer that is still tantalisingly ajar.

With all that evidence and suggested locations over the period 1937-1939, the best conclusion to this point is that Goering never had dinner at the Spread Eagle and that Ribbentrop may have had it there in 1937, his only British summer as the German Ambassador; his son Rudi being present with local BU members.

Before leaving Goering and Ribbentrop it is interesting to have a snapshot of these two partners in crime with Hitler; who were recorded at the Nuremberg trials as the evilest persons who pursued taking WW2 into its devastating existence.

6.3 Goering and Ribbentrop Unravelled.

Goering and Ribbentrop were judged to be the two people that led Hitler to War in one way or the other, not for their personally carried out actions against the actual peoples the Nazis oppressed, but for the top-level support and guidance of the political ambitions of Hitler's thrust to create his glorious Third Reich - by any means.

Goering

Goering was useful to Hitler in the early 30s for his high society connections, for which Hitler had virtually none. He was able to influence the leadership of the decimated Germany democracy to support Hitler into power as the supposed saviour of their country and its honour. Goering supported many of Hitler's ambitious ideas with highly exaggerated promises of success.

Hermann Wilhelm Goering was born in 1893, as was Joachim Ribbentrop. His father was a poorly paid diplomat and not high born.

Hermann was interested in the military from his teens and was sent to boarding school, an experience so tough for him that he escaped back to his home.

He continued his military career starting in the infantry when WW1 began. By forging his transfer document, he made his way into the Air Force with a commanding rank. There he was considered to be arrogant and often totally disobeyed official orders to do with his squadron. When a fighter ace in WW1 he was known as *Blue Max* having inherited the place of the *Red Baron* after that German Ace was shot down.

During the 1923 disastrous *Beer Hall Putsch* attempt to seize power using paramilitary tactics, he was shot in the leg. As a result of hospitalisation in 1923, with heavy doses of pain killers, he became a heroin addict for the rest of his life. Early in that period, he was confined to a mental asylum in a straitjacket during detox rehabilitation.

Later, politics carried him on to become a leading member of the Nazis Party in which he soon founded the dreaded Gestapo, supporting the implementation of the holocaust solution. Ironically his godfather was Jewish.

From 1935 to the end of the war Goering was the Commander-in-Chief of the Luftwaffe (Air Force). He just loved collecting high standing posts: they included being President of the Reichstag, Minister President of Prussia, and the Federal Hunt Master, the last matching his passion for hunting. It is said he had no conscience when exercising those duties.

He had favour with Hitler; until they fell out in early 1943. When it became clear that Hitler was going to commit suicide in April 1945, Goering sent a private message to him seeking confirmation that he should assume overall control. This action was in keeping with an earlier Hitler decree that he would take over if Hitler was not capable of leading. Goering's worst enemy within, Martin Bormann, intercepted the message and made Hitler see otherwise; Hitler, regarded this as treason, ordering Goering's arrest.

Goering avoided being executed by his staff by resigning from the party under the order of Hitler. He escaped house arrest to surrender himself to the Americans, there being too much risk in going to the Russians. That, however, did not help his situation for he was the first person tried and convicted in the Nuremberg trials. He was proven to have been being a leader, in many capacities, of inhuman actions - as second-in-line in the Nazi movement and thus a war maker, for directing the slave labour programme, and for leading the oppression of the Jewish people. The day before he was due to be hanged, he took cyanide poison that had been smuggled into his cell; thereby dying before his execution order could be carried out.

He came from humble roots with little money. At the end of WW1, the German air force aircraft were broken up to be scrap wood and metal, destroying jobs for airmen. He went to Sweden to keep flying. Despite the hardships he made the most of his talents, being very wealthy by the time war broke out with Britain.

He loved outlandish and very extravagant things. For the pre-wedding night of his second wedding in 1935, he held a lavish reception in the Berlin Opera House, over which flew fighter aircraft.

Goering had managed to become a very wealthy man when WW2 broke out, Manvell and Fraenkel (2011). This was because he had to pay little for his enormous lavish entertainment receipts and likewise for the upkeep of his mansion *Carinhall* - all were listed as being for official business. He also had large incomes from books he, and others, published about himself.

He inherited considerable land and property and had many gifts of art. His art acquisitions were kept apart from Hitler's purchases that were made for the intended national Reich museum.

That was the situation before the war broke out. From then on, he had other ways to get prized art possessions!

Apart from having no humanity he was very interested in everyone else's valuable art treasures - these came from a spin-off from his day job; stolen from persecuted Jews to be displayed in dedicated buildings he built. Over 26,000 railway cars of stolen treasures were taken to France by the Nazis. Much remains to be found!

Nazi leaders rapidly became the subject of numerous unflattering, ridiculing, depictions drawn by leading cartoonists across the democracies. Goering had a penchant for flashy uniforms and dress that dominated his presence.

He once attended an important meeting with Mussolini's brother-in-law, Gian Ciano. He wore:

'A flashy gray suit, an old-fashioned tie passing through a ruby ring, with more rubies in the rings on his fingers, and he had a large Nazi eagle set with diamonds in his button hole. Ciano thought he looked like Al Capone.' Manvell and Fraenkel (2011)

Fig. 6.15 is a cartoon, drawn by Artur Szyk, a Polish Jew artist who fled to the West in 1937; he settled in the USA in 1940. It, as did many, 'played on Goering's weight and flamboyance'.

Fig. 6.15 Goering is easily recognised in caricatures. (Artur Szyk)

Chapter 6 War Approaches

Was Goering *Evil*, or *Good*?

> 'Descendants of the leaders of the Nazi regime have spoken on camera for the first time about the feelings of pain and revulsion they have for their ancestors. They include Bettina Goering, great niece of Adolf Hitler's second in command Hermann Goering, who says she has had herself sterilised so she would 'not pass on the blood of a monster'.
> MailOnLine, 21 Jan 2010, by reporter Allan Hall.

The rise and fall of Goering are covered in several *YouTube* films. He got the dishonour of being WW2's *Evil Worst Enemy Number 2* and was the first to be tried at the War Crimes trials. He had no conscience!

Ribbentrop

Joachim von Ribbentrop was the second person essential for Hitler, again for his circle of international contacts with the wealthy that he had developed through wine trading and lavish socialising. But he also was the *errand boy* for Adolf; a lap dog that agreed with anything Hitler said. He was the one who carried the diplomatic will of Hitler to the various negotiating tables of surrounding countries. He played his cards appropriately and very dirty at times, using many ruses to stay physically close to Hitler; to ensure others did not take over his place in Hitler's ambitions. He preferred solutions to Hitler's needs to be implemented by war, not peace. He also was very inept in diplomacy and he often read situations completely incorrectly.

So, who was SS-Obergruppenführer Ulrich Friedrich Wilhelm Joachim von Ribbentrop? Born in 1893, he was 46 years old when war broke out.

From his youth, he was a person who did not fit in well with the 'normal' society, Snyder (1998). His 'vain, domineering and self-important' persona had many, very denigrating, personality characteristics. They said he got his Iron Cross by his petition.

He was poor until he married into money and thus moved to a much more distinguished class. Using a distant cousin, he got himself titled as 'von', implying he was a noble. He seems to have been disliked by almost everyone; however, he gained Hitler's patronage for being subservient to him. His emphasis on manners earned him the name of *Von Ribbensnob*. Goebbels said of him:

> 'Von Ribbentrop bought his name, he married his money, and he swindled his way into office'.

He was a regular visitor to England who had built up a good network of VIPs there. This made him useful in the political post as a German Ambassador taking up that post 11 August 1936, actually arriving in London in October 1936, a month before Crystal Palace burned down.

He came to be Hitler's Foreign Minister in March 1938. Then, Ribbentrop's role for Hitler was to negotiate an Anglo-German alliance; yet another Hitler feint to gain more time and avoid war with Britain.

Or did war break out in September 1939 because Von Ribbentrop gave Hitler the wrong information that the British were on the brink of civil war and so would be too involved with that to oppose Hitler's invasion of France?

From several reports, he was not seen as a man with much cleverness. Many reports about the man record that he was an arrogant person who often fell into a rage and did irrational things. In the cartoon of Fig. 6.16, Ribbentrop is out of control, symbolically earning Hitler's favour.

Fig. 6.16 Ribbentrop forcing a politician to sign. (1939?) (NA INF/1390)

Chapter 6 War Approaches

Wikipedia provides a long account of the man: it is not favourable. It says of him:

'His time in London was marked by an endless series of social gaffes and blunders that worsened his already poor relations with the British Foreign Office'.

In his defence, his wife, Anna Elisabeth "Annelies" Henkell, added her notes to his autobiography that he hurriedly compiled whilst in prison during the Nuremberg trials; the notes explained away some of these with reasonable explanations, Ribbentrop (1954).

For example; in 1937, Ribbentrop was at a British Court reception. As he met the King, up went his stiff arm to make a *Heil Hitler* salute - at the same time as the King stepped forward to shake hands! Some say it was a gaffe. His wife wrote that he had been ordered to do this by Herr Hitler!

'Ribbentrop did not understand the King's limited role in government; he thought King Edward VIII could dictate British foreign policy. He convinced Hitler that he had Edward's support; but this, like his belief that he had impressed British society, was a tragic delusion. Ribbentrop often woefully misunderstood both British politics and society.'
[…as did most Germans of that time who had no idea what, and how, democracy operated. Being indoctrinated from their childhood education in a socialist regime, they were not given much opportunity to learn of alternatives.]

'Ribbentrop reported to Berlin that the reason the crisis (he perceived to exist in Britain) had occurred as an anti-German Jewish-Masonic-reactionary conspiracy to depose Edward (whom Ribbentrop represented as a staunch friend of Germany) and that civil war would soon break out in Britain between the King's supporters and those of Prime Minister Stanley Baldwin's. Ribbentrop's civil-war statements were greeted with incredulity by those British people who heard them'

And later in Wikipedia:

> 'Ribbentrop's habit of summoning tailors from the best British firms, making them wait for hours and then sending them away without seeing him with instructions to return the next day, only to repeat the process, did immense damage to his reputation in British high society.
>
> London's tailors retaliated for this abuse by telling all their well-off clients that Ribbentrop was impossible to deal with. In an interview, his secretary Reinhard Spitzy stated: "He [Ribbentrop] behaved very stupidly and very pompously and the British don't like pompous people". In the same interview, Spitzy called Ribbentrop "pompous, conceited and not too intelligent", and stated he was an utterly insufferable man to work for. In addition, the fact that Ribbentrop chose to spend as little time as possible in London, so as to stay close to Hitler, irritated the British Foreign Office immensely, as Ribbentrop's frequent absences prevented the handling of many routine diplomatic matters. (The Magazine *Punch* referred to him the "Wandering Aryan" for his frequent trips home.)
>
> As Ribbentrop alienated more and more people in Britain, Göring warned Hitler that Ribbentrop was a "stupid ass". Hitler dismissed Göring's concerns: "[but] after all, he knows quite a lot of important people in England", leading Göring to reply "Mein Führer, that may be right, but the bad thing is, they know him".'

As the result of the findings of the war criminal Nuremberg trials, Von Ribbentrop was hanged, in October 1946, as a war criminal for his part in assisting the war to begin and his part in enabling the Holocaust. He was the first politically appointed person to be executed from the trials. How such a man got to assist the evil aims of Hitler seems to be beyond belief!

The rise and rapid fall of Joachim von Ribbentrop are given in a YouTube, *Hitler's Henchmen II: Diplomat of Evil Joachim von Ribbentrop*. This 58-minute film explains how WW2 came about through poor diplomacy, much led by his disastrous management of diplomatic affairs.

He got the dishonour of being WW2's *Evil Enemy Number 3*.

Chapter 6 War Approaches

Finally, on this evil trio's possible presence in Britain, there is no evidence that Hitler ever visited England following WW1; he surely would not have chanced a trip in the 1933-38 period for his notoriety was well known across the world by then, and he had already had several assassination attempts on his life in his home countries.

There are, however, reports of him visiting his half-brother in Liverpool for a short period when he left Germany to avoid being called into army service just before WW1.

The severe change of lifestyle brought about by the totalitarian German Reich regime on the peoples of its own, and the occupied countries, created all manner of difficult relationships. The vast majority just accepted what was happening, not believing they could do anything to get back to a peaceful state of living. When Hitler came to Dictatorship in 1933 the German people felt a move for good, for they were promised a return of the dignity they had lost at the end of WW1.

Some individuals and groups, however, found themselves driven to resist Nazi rule. They saw the Third Reich might suit Hitler's idea of a utopia but that they were being made to fight to the death as pawns in his game; not as participants with a democratic voice. What their Fuhrer said was to be obeyed!

The next section is of a love story that endured through the lives of a German Jewess and a German soldier. The relationship began as Nazism was erupting in Germany, and lasted into the war. Its record is significant for the home movies it left for us as a remarkable record of private life in Germany during the 30 and 40s.

6.4 Pre-war Life in Germany - Love Story Extraordinaire

From time to time here I have chosen real-life stories of people and their circumstances that have no known direct link to the Midhurst Rural District. These are included to illustrate what was going on elsewhere whilst the Midhurst district residents were enjoying an almost laid-back lifestyle, albeit with some concern for their future and a few inconveniences, such as rationing, shop queues, blackouts and numerous soldiers in town.

All of these chosen stories have fuller explanations available on the

Internet, in a book, or be from local memory records. Many have films made of them so are usually available as a YouTube film, a DVD or other digital sources. Where they are fictional (rarely) that is made clear.

We have already seen (in Chapter 1 of this book) how German citizen Joachim Liebschner, and the German Jewish Feuchtwanger family, were experiencing life in pre-war German locations.

This following account gives us insight into the times in pre-war Germany from another angle. It is about two young German teenagers, Helmuth Cords and Jutta Sorge who came to be in dangerous love. It illustrates how there were many in Germany who lived through most of the war in their normal lifestyle. Some of these assisted this couple in-love.

It is a remarkable love and resistance story that ran all through the war years with both, remarkably, surviving to finally marry in post-war Berlin. Through those years they were often in dire situations with little chance of escape. It shows the noble, courageous and brave actions that humans are capable of doing when pressed hard; as they were so often were doing under the Nazis, and also how many did not align with Hitler's maniacal ideas.

This brief account is condensed from a 2010 film, *Surviving Hitler: A Love Story,* directed by John-Keith Wasson and from a newspaper article in the *Litchfield County Times*, Connecticut of February 25, 2011, by Kathryn Boughton.

There must have been many instances of such situations but this story was very different; Helmut took home movies that visually recorded what daily life in the Nazi period was like for them. A pre-war picture of Jutta and Helmuth is shown in Fig. 6.17. Earlier pictures of them are to be seen in the film.

At the time Hitler came to power in 1933, Jutta was 13. She met Helmut at a dancing school in Berlin; she was 14, he was 15. She was wearing a stunning French dress and had enchanted Helmut so much that they danced for hours; until a girl came up to them and told Helmut they should stop or she would not kiss him again. It was love, or perhaps just a 'crush', at first sight.

From this encounter Jutta was suspicious of his intentions; he was good looking and had many girl-friends. They had to part and did not

Chapter 6 War Approaches

meet again until some years later - in quite different circumstances. Both were then enjoying a good life in well-to-do German families.

Fig. 6.17 Jutta Sorge and Helmut Cords, pre-war.

Her uncle was a well-respected citizen who had been Chancellor in the former government and had received a Noble Peace Prize for his reconciliation work between France and Germany after the Treaty of Versailles.

They both were apparently of the right stock - Aryan - so were given the best chances by the Nazi regime. Helmut would become a soldier of the Third Reich and Jutta would have babies just as Hitler wanted. They both would assist, whether they wanted to or not, his idea of forming the 'perfect' society of people with Nordic origins.

One day at school the teacher handed out forms that asked students for the names of their parent's family history information. From this Jutta was amazed to find she was not pure Aryan, despite her blonde hair and slim litheness.

Her maternal grandparents had originally been Jewish until they converted out of being that. That was a major problem for her and her family. At that stage in Hitler's diabolical plans, she almost certainly could not progress in the German society with education, or to a marriage with a true Aryan such as Helmut.

The rules of the Aryan Law were promulgated in a 54-page booklet; available on-line at https://research.calvin.edu. It made the case for its need; it said Jews were over-represented and their arrogance could not be tolerated. The family link went back two generations of Jewish heritage. It was virtually impossible for her not to fill in the proforma as it would have to be verified by the Gestapo staff.

The family was devastated; it was unimaginable but it was the case; those were the latest rules against Jewish people. Extermination had not started then, but these rules made life in Germany intolerable to Jews! Even Jews with centuries of German citizenship were targeted.

For a brief period, Jewish people were permitted to leave Germany. Fig. 6.18 shows an unidentified group leaving in that pre-war period - stripped of their possessions apart from a little case. They faced a hard time getting re-established if they did not speak English, and had no support.

Fig. 6.18 Once well-to-do, German Jews leaving Germany without their possessions. (*Times*, Israel)

To make matters worse very few places were available for Jewish refugees in safe western countries.

These severe German anti-Jewish laws commenced in 1933. Some of the restrictions put into place during the 1935-6 period, and listed by the British Library in *Learning: Voices of the Holocaust* were:
- Jews no longer allowed to vote and lose German citizenship
- Benefit payments to large Jewish families stopped
- Jews banned from parks, restaurants and swimming pools
- Jews were forbidden to use the German greeting 'Heil Hitler'
- Jews no longer allowed electrical/optical equipment, bicycles,

Chapter 6 War Approaches

typewriters or records
- Passports for Jews to travel abroad restricted
- Many Jewish students removed from German schools and universities

Jutta's mother was born into Protestantism so technically Jutta was not a Jewish person. Hitler, however, was starting to cleanse the German peoples of all with genes of Jewish origin. At that stage, Jutta's family could leave Germany but her father refused to leave for that would have been worse in his mind, as things were at that time for them.

They stayed and chose to test the system. Jutta was allowed to stay at her school as long as she made the *Heil Hitler* salute for 30 minutes each school day. She chose to plaster her arm with a fake bone break to avoid that. Her indomitable courage was already shining through. They managed to survive by staying under cover of the father's religion.

When Jutta was 19 years old that option of leaving was shut securely by Hitler. She was, however, able to use her father's heritage that allowed her to flee to England, and then onto Switzerland. However, she soon felt the need to return to Germany to care for her parents.

To those with close contact with Jewish families, by this time it was becoming clear how their lives were being impacted by the anti-Semitic actions that were being ramped up by the Nazis.

As we have seen earlier how the boys were *educated for death.* Helmut did his duty and was indoctrinated, then joining the army. He was first sent to the Western Front having little idea of those anti-Semitic laws or the ongoing plight of Jutta. It was not for some time yet that Helmut and Jutta would meet again.

Lives like this were typical of so many people caught up in the plans of Hitler working to purify the race who would form the Third Reich. Every story is a little different, but many are about resistance to the Nazis taking away human dignity for hundreds of thousands of his citizens; making life intolerable on so many ways and too often extinguishing life itself.

To place the rest of their extraordinary story in its proper wartime context I will continue it in the next book. It gets very involved with significant events involving the Gestapo, and against Hitler himself. For those impatient to read it all now, do view the YouTube film *Surviving Hitler: A Love Story.*

Midhurst WW2 Memoirs: 2. 'Evil' Rising: 'Good' Awakening

We have now looked into the lives of the key German leaders and some ordinary German citizens, portraying life as it was in Germany before the war.

The next chapter covers the stories of two Jewish lads who, as members of those Jewish refugees before the war with Britain was declared, managed to escape Nazi clutches. Around 1938 they escaped to England to take up their lives in Midhurst starting their new Western democratic way of life.

Chapter 7. Persons Without Essentials

7.1 Kinder Transport to Midhurst

As the persecution of the Jews in Germany began to close in on them, they were initially given incentives to become refugees in other countries. Already there existed some organisations that would assist them to make a new life. However, they were not always welcomed because of the centuries-old distrust of them for being Jewish, and especially for those of German birth. Anti-Semitism was not just a Nazi thing!

The Nazi process was extreme. Being pushed out at such speed often stripped the children of all of their heritage history; all of the names of their parents and siblings; their birthplace, religion and past connections. It was a harrowing situation in which some, later, managed to salvage identities by relentless research, and lots of luck over decades. The Jews from European countries have recorded thousands of accounts of what that time was like for them.

Following the legitimisation of the *British Mandate of Palestine* in 1922, the need arose for a charitable organisation to fund and administer the movement of Jewish people from Germany who were being assisted to resettle in Palestine. This led, in 1933, to the formation of the World Jewish Relief (WJR), originally called the Central British Fund for German Jewry (CBF).

Later, in 1936, the British CBF coordinated with the American Jewish Joint Distribution Committee (JDC) to create the Council for German Jewry, which carried out much of the pre-war operations to emigrate German Jews. Before the declaration of war on Germany in September 1939, some 68,000 Jews had registered to move to Britain.

The *Kindertransport* programme was a notable, heart-warming, movement carried out with the authority of the British Parliament. It was also called the Refugee Children Movement or (RCM). This rescue mission took place just before the outbreak of the Second World War over the years 1938 and 1939, Guske (2009).

In this project, some 10,000, predominantly Jewish, children from Germany along with some of the soon to be occupied Eastern countries, went into foster care in places throughout Britain, and other free world countries. Many of these children were of families that died in the Holocaust starting around 1933. They often became the last living survivor of their family line.

Just after 1938, the British government allowed this to happen on a 'fast track' basis, with little paperwork, for these children who came unaccompanied. It was a significant step for Britain as it formally recognised what was taking place in Germany under Nazi rule. Fig, 7.1 shows one of the three magnificent memorials to this scheme that was placed by Liverpool Station in 2006.

Fig. 7.1 *Kindertransport - the Arrival* memorial outside Liverpool railway station, by Frank Meisler.

All manner of accommodation arrangements was set up to cope with these arrivals. One way used hostels, and the seaside Dovercourt Holiday Camp, near Harwich in the South Eastern region. Until the holiday season arrived in the summer months, it was used as holding accommodation whilst places were found for the children.

Fig. 7.2 Kindertransport arrivals at the Warner's Dovercourt Holiday Camp in Essex.

At that time the British authorities believed the war would soon be over and the Nazis removed from power. The children were expected to then return to their families at the end of the hostilities. However, many could not; no one expected so many of their parents to lose their possessions, and their lives under German persecution. Some children lost not only their country but almost completely, their heritage and personal identity.

Midhurst played its part by hosting two boys from this programme;

Chapter 7. Persons Without Essentials

their story is given later in this section. First though, we need to learn of the plight these children might have to endure for, despite being safe from Nazi intentions, they were still at the mercy of a confusing country, this happening as Britain hurriedly ramped up its plans for war.

The plight of *Kindertransport* children was varied. One family account has been published by Josephs and Bechhofer (1996), later being made into a TV film. It well illustrates the life faced by them after transport to a strange, different and foreign land. (This true version is not to be confused with that by W.G. Sebald that follows the same story quite closely, but with variations that place it in the truth-fiction genre.)

The Bechhofer account is a good entry point into appreciating the lot of many *Kindertransport* lives. This following precis is written to follow the events in the Josephs book, and the YouTube version of the BBC TV film made of the experience.

It began when Rosa Bechhofer, with seven generations of Aryan blood in her direct paternal ancestry, failed to be accepted for German citizenship according to the *Law for the Protection of German Blood and German Honour*.

Rosa was born Jewish from her parents and that was enough to close many doors in Nazi Germany; they said she would taint any German union. Getting employment became a real problem. She moved to Munich where she met Joseph Otto Hald, an Aryan German soldier with too much charm; a lady's man who may, or may not, have had some honour in mind.

The outcome was that in 1935 Rosa became pregnant by him, with twin girls. During February 1936, Otto did not marry her and abandoned her during the pregnancy. Her twin babies, Lotte and Susi, were born in May 1936.

It was not a good time for her; her application to the German authorities to move to the USA was declined. She, to make matters worse, had too much-inherited baggage to accept her as Aryan under the newly created rules.

At that time the *Nazi Final Solution* to 'eliminate' all Jews from Germany and her then occupied territories, was not yet in force. Jews could survive in Germany by careful choices and hardship.

Being a Jew greatly restricted her income. She found live-in domestic employment with Jewish families. That, however, did not provide her with accommodation for her twins to live with her. They had to remain in the, then still operational, Jewish hospital.

Late in the summer of 1936, when the twins had just turned three years old, a matron from Munich's Jewish orphanage, Fig.7.3, came and took them from Rosa to look after them for her in that institution.

Fig.7.3. Munich Jewish orphanage c.1936. Josephs and Bechhofer (1996)

Rosa came to see the twins each week but was quite unable to care for them herself. It was remarked:

'It was the same story every week when it came to saying goodbye to the twins. She could hardly bring herself to look at them because she used to get upset. That's why she was always to be seen rushing away from the building'.

The children were mostly looked after by the other children. Food was short, with many a meal being missed. More laws, and tighter persecution, saw the orphanage come under physical attack from the authorities.

Things came to a head for her after the *Kristallnacht* on 9 November 1938. On that night, hundreds of Jewish properties were destroyed by fire and vandalism. The Nazi authorities had incited this action and took no part in trying to stop it. Over 300 synagogues were set on fire. Killed were 300 Jews, with 30,000 arrested.

Many women were raped. That was breaking of the law of fraternisation for the Germans who did it, them being overlooked by the authorities. To add to their woes the Jewish people again were heavily squeezed of their assets. The result of a meeting, at which Goering told of

Chapter 7. Persons Without Essentials

a letter he had received from Hitler, was:

'A fine of 1 billion marks was levied for the slaying of Ernst Vom Rath, and the 6 million Marks paid by insurance companies for broken windows was to be given to the State coffers', Snyder (1989).

An explanation is needed here. Ernest Vom Rath, RHS of Fig. 7.4, a Nazi Third Secretary in the German Embassy in Paris, was assassinated by a Polish-German 17-year-old lad, Herschel Grynszapan, on 7 November 1938. Herschel was a much-aggrieved person over wrongs being done to the Jews. He simply walked into the office of vom Rath and shot him five times. This was the only successful assassination attempt on any high-ranking Nazi during the build-up and the war period.

Fig. 7.4. The Jews were increasingly sent to camps after Ernest Vom Rath was assassinated. (Slide Share)

Hitler used this circumstance, saying they 'fired the first shot' in the war on Germany. That resulted in the event called *Kristallnacht* (Night of the Broken Glass), because of the shattered store windowpanes that carpeted German streets. It was a key turning point to the very worst, in Nazi Germany's persecution of the Jews.

Returning to the life of Rosa, there was then, in 1938, great tension in Munich. She could not escape herself, but she might be able to send her twins to the USA. It was not known to her if that would work.

However, behind the scenes that was already being tested by others.

One person did not wait around during that state of affairs. Whilst Rosa was elsewhere, a helper came and took the twins away on 16 May 1939. She was not able to be told where they went for their escorts had also left the country. A few weeks later their orphanage was burned to the ground, along with its records.

The twins, Lotte and Susi, arrived on 18 May 1939 at the Liverpool Street station in London, along with many other Jewish children, Fig.7.5. German was the only language they knew. They had endured a long journey with no idea of what was happening to them. They had only just turned three years old and at that young age would not have been able to properly understand, or perhaps even remember the situation.

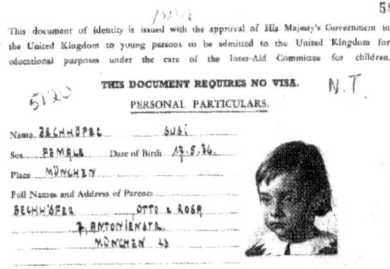

Fig. 7.5 Susi Bechhofer's British entry card of May 1939. Josephs and Bechhofer (1996)

Through the *German Jewish Aid Committee*, a Welsh Baptist minister, Rev. Mann and his wife volunteered to foster the twins. On arrival, they were very undernourished. 'Lotte was warm and outgoing. Susi was timid and withdrawn.' They were provided with clothes having the 'British look' to make their heritage less obvious; they were given new English names. Lotte became Eunice Mary Mann, and Susi became Grace Elizabeth Mann, Fig. 7.6.

Fig. 7.6 Fred and Audrey Mann, foster parents with Susi and Lotte, age 8.

War was declared in their first year in safety, but things were looking good for them. However, whilst they had escaped Nazi oppression, their German nationality was still a problem because people

Chapter 7. Persons Without Essentials

in Britain had begun to develop deep animosity toward anything Germanic. Every effort was made by Rev. Mann to hide that in their life; mainly by obliterating their past identity and keeping them out of contact with others. That included not telling them who they were.

To that end, the Reverend gave it out that they were his biological children, a curious thing to expect others to believe. Would they fall for that? How does one suddenly acquire children when they are already seven years old? Children at school asked why they could speak German. Even they were not that sure!

Their new foster parents genuinely believed it was the best for them to have their previous life completely obliterated.

Then followed a long, often tragic, period in both of their lives; a time studded with the sadness of many kinds. By being sent to Britain they had escaped the horrors of Nazi persecution with imprisonment as slave labourers, or to end their lives in an extermination camp. However, they had gone from one kind of bad place to another kind, to be imprisoned in equally unbearable circumstances that would last for decades. Luck had run out for both of them.

Eunice, that is Grace, suffered operation after operation in a heroic effort to beat her original cancerous brain tumour that made its presence known when she was but nine years old. Despite her suffering from that, she was also affected by her new parent's difficulty in coping with her condition. Punctuated with some happiness and notable achievements she passed away from this illness when she was 35 years old.

Grace, that is Lotte, had to suffer a dreadful trauma of another kind; an even worse way of life, some would say. From early in the time with the Mann family, her new father had slowly wheedled his way into her psyche that she should often 'comfort him'…..in bed, in ways that will be left to the imagination.

Susi had little experience of the outer world; her parents kept all that back, where they could. She went along with this sexual abuse for years until in her early womanhood, when she began to ask was this normal. Why did she have to perform things for him in bed? She often thought about reporting him, but a strange sense of love and loyalty held her back.

She finally escaped his hold over her when she was married; against the persuasive talk of her obsessive father. The wedding, in

December 1966, was to a decent man who supported her journey from that time. She bore them a son 10 months later. That might be thought to be the start of a good life from then on.

Having her child, however, triggered her past childhood experiences; her spirits often lowered into depression. Susi's response to that was to enter the nursing profession into which she buried herself in order to cope with her demons.

A hysterectomy operation in 1985, plus a bout of inevitable post-operative depression, led to her thinking about her past. She just had to know the details of her heritage!

We here, now know of that story but she only had an inkling of it via her early childhood memories – of her first name and some other hints along the way. Children remember little before 2-3 years old. Little incidents gradually opened doors, previously shut. She realised she was not a Mann and, therefore, wanted to know who her real parents were, and what had happened to them. The family name was eventually seen to be Bechhofer. She felt the need to get away from it all for a while. She said:

> "Not knowing who are your real parents are, means you have nothing at all to hang on to. It is like being on a raft on the middle of the ocean - you are drifting, where there is no anchor, you just do not know where you have come from. I always knew I would have to face up to this."

After having put off tracing her parents for so long she began this journey of discovery in Munich in 1985. The first obvious step was to see if there were any Bechhofers in that city's telephone directory. There were none, presumably because of the Nazi 'cleansing' actions of WW2.

Two years later things began to become clearer when she joined a creative writing class in Rugby, England. There a friend, Hazel, started to draw out Susi's history suggesting this was material for a great story.

As it does when clues are scarce and often distorted, and where false starts are many, it took many more years of searching to establish her parent's identities.

Changes to adoption data laws of that time suggested the adoption papers of the Mann's would be a good start - but who had them? That led

Chapter 7. Persons Without Essentials

to the help of a social worker, a person required to be involved as you carry out the search process.

The twins had been formally adopted by the Manns when they were 9 years old so a search back into court papers of that time was tried. But the court had no birth certificates: the detective work had to continue elsewhere.

Her husband saw how this seemingly futile chase was not helping Susi, who by then had buried herself in their study, working on the issue. He gave her lowered support for a fear that helping too much would not help her mental situation. From her determination she had, however, become obsessed with finding out who her parents were.

In the summer of 1988, she received a reply to an enquiry she had lodged, from the German Consulate in London. They had found a copy of Susi's birth certificate. Both parent's names were on that document; that they had different surnames implied they were not married. It told her where she was born. All this was not known to her before.

What was the next move to find some more answers? What had become of their parents, Rosa and Otto? From more clues about her timings of events, she began to suspect she was, in fact, a *Kindertransport* child and that there may be records of their transport to Britain. She found an ally in a person who was named as the contact in a *Woman's Hour* radio programme in which her story was featured.

Together they worked on this line of reasoning that suggested she make contact with the Central British Fund for World Jewish Relief, CBF.

Agonising on the decision to find out - or not - she applied to see the papers that had been located of her transport event. It then became a real possibility that she was Jewish for that was the main aim of the transports; to move Jewish children to safety. Here was a major issue for her to absorb; she did not feel or appreciate Judaism in any way. That experience was only present before she started to take in events into her baby mind; she had been brought up in the Christian religion by a priest, her adopted father. Rather than release the papers to her immediately, the CBF counsellor told her she should learn about Jewish ways before they could be accessed.

Grace decided it was the time to revert to the name Susi. Changing religion, from that in which she had been brought up in, was a difficult issue to face for Jewish life is very much a lifetime of encompassing family activities in which you have to be more involved than the Christian church expects.

More searching led to learning her mother, Rosa, may have also come to Britain at a later time; hence there was a possible path to her mother's visa application. That was, however, an unproductive path for no visa seemed to have been issued.

Progress in her quest came as the result of the 50th anniversary of the *Kindertransport* held in 1988. For a reunion event, an Israel national radio programme told of her case briefly as a call for information.

Within days a Bechhofer family member in New York wrote to her. The letter showed the writer was a first cousin of hers. Her mother's name had been Tante Rosel. Susi began to learn that many of the people who had helped her had perished in concentration camps.

Later, Susi said the letter was one of the earthmoving experiences of her life. She now had learned who was her mother, and that she was one on a very large family of Bechhofers that had branches all over the world.

Susi then went on to learn of others in her life who had escaped the Holocaust. Photographs, including one of her mother, came forth. She also learned that she had a half-sister from a brief marriage of her father, Otto, to another woman.

It has been mentioned in the research that Rosa also escaped to Britain but this was not so, as Susi later learned. Rosa had no opportunity to leave. She survived for a couple of years in domestic service, moving from Jewish family to family of well-off, or well-connected Jews who had managed to avoid problems with the Nazis.

Most departure routes had closed by the mid-30s but some Jewish people still were trying to go to the USA, it then not being at war with Germany and having long-standing friendly associations.

It was the Gestapo police records that finally told of the end of Rosa's life. One record showed that she had been deported to Piaski in Poland in April 1942, as one of a group of 343 Jews. None had survived: 'she was possibly shot'. But the agony of her mother's true fate was still actually in transit.

A later letter, from a former friend of Rosa, contradicted that

Chapter 7. Persons Without Essentials

account; the real truth came out. A pile of German WW2 police records was found including a sack of 50 passports of people sent to the most notorious death camp, Auschwitz; that implying their death. That had happened after the expected, but not carried out, deportation mentioned above. Rosa's document was in that sack. Receiving that passport was the closest she got to escape the death camp; was the issue of a passport just a cruel way by the Nazi Regime to locate Jews for that camp?

Fig. 7.7 Susi Bechhofer, celebrating 70 years of the Holocaust c.2007. (Redditch Advertiser)

Susi Bechhofer died in 2018 age 82. Karen Pollock of the British *Holocaust Educational Trust* said of her work:

> "Susi dedicated the later years of her life to uncovering the truth of her past and understanding what happened to her family during the Holocaust. She spent many years sharing her most painful memories with young people across the country."

With these experiences and difficulties in mind we can move on to a Midhurst perspective of, and participation in, the *Kindertransport* operation.

As names of children in that scheme were often not known and because, no doubt, the authorities felt their real names were likely to get them hostile reactions, they were allotted dehumanising identification numbers for public use; it assisted record keeping.

When the Midhurst Grammar School MGS held a reunion, before it became a part of the Midhurst Rother College in 2009, former MGS members Janet Newman, Colin Crouch, Edward Fischer and John

Midhurst WW2 Memoirs: 2. 'Evil' Rising: 'Good' Awakening

Newman produced, Newman et al (2010), a souvenir booklet *Midhurst Grammar School Remembered*.

Two stories of Kindertransport boys No 348 and 393 are included there. Being short, they are repeated here in full:

> 'Kinder Transport was the escape route that enabled hundreds of Jewish children to survive the Nazi holocaust. The Association of Jewish Refugees keeps an archive of those who came to England. Two, out of over 1,000 listed [actually some 10,000], came to Midhurst Grammar School.
>
> The archive does not reveal names, and of Number 393 we know only that he left Vienna in December 1938 at the age of 15,
>
> and was with us till July 1940, his mother dying in the Auschwitz concentration camp.
>
> The other, number 348, his mother already dead and his father to die in the camp at Theresienstadt, fled from Essen's *Goethe Gymnasium* school at the age of 14 and took a train to the Hook of Holland.
>
> On the 25th May 1939, he arrived at Liverpool Street Station and spent time with nine other Jewish children in the Sion Hill refugee hostel in Ramsgate. In January 1940 he came as an MGS boarder to Midhurst, and left three years later, in July 1943, to serve with the infantry in India for four years. He was to publish books, to marry, and to have four children.
>
> It is only because of No 348's published books, (that give him considerable Internet exposure and were used to write this account), that we know more of him.

Fig. 7.8 He came to Midhurst as Karl Hartland but left as Charles Hannam.

After being in the army in India, where he experienced the British class

Chapter 7. Persons Without Essentials

system and the army's virulent racism, he entered the academic world, first teaching at a 'posh' prep school then studying at Corpus Christi, Cambridge.

His first books were about teaching and children. In 1977 *A Boy in Your Situation* (Hannam, 1977) appeared, the first volume of what was to become known as *The Hartland Trilogy*. Praised by C.P. Snow as "one of the most exact accounts of early adolescence yet written", it was followed in 1979 by *Almost an Englishman*, (Hannam, 1979): then later, a study entitled *Refugees* (Hannam, 1988).

We shall never know how these two teenagers remembered their early days in Midhurst, at the MGS, but it is good to think that, lonely and frightened, they once found refuge with us'

The boys and girls of that transport scheme would have all have suffered difficulties, in one way or another, when coming to cope with their lack of identity...an issue explored at depth in Guske (2009):

'It sheds light on the lifelong influence which early attachment has on coping with massive cumulative trauma'

Leaflets explaining the terms of government support, including support payments made for taking in a *Kindertransport* child, were issued by the Billeting Officer for the various regions. That, for nearby Littlehampton, is shown in Fig. 7.9.

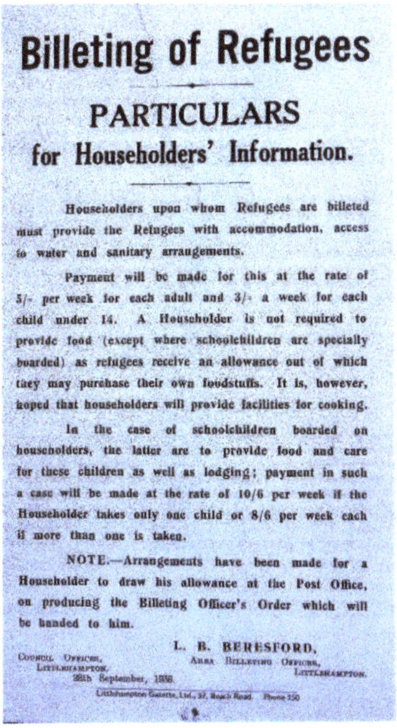

Fig. 7.9 1938 leaflet on hosting refugees before the war was declared.

The life story of lad No 393 is yet to be revealed; all that is known about him is his number!

223

Other accounts on Kindertransport children are available on the Internet. The Imperial War Museum has several poignant artefacts of some of these children.

One is the hand puppet, Fig. 7.10, Stephie Leyser was given to her as she left for Britain. She had a less harrowing experience than Rosa, and her parents managed to survive the war and come to Britain to live:

> 'Stephie Carola Leyser (later Stephanie Kester) volunteered for the Kindertransport and left Germany for Britain in February 1939. This Siamese cat puppet was given to Stephie by her favourite uncle and accompanied her on her journey. It was one of the few items that she was allowed to select and pack for herself before leaving Chemnitz. Stephanie's parents eventually immigrated to the UK, where her father was initially detained as a foreign national and sent to a civilian internment camp on the Isle of Man. He was eventually released and reunited with his wife and daughter but died shortly after. Her mother lived until 1993.'

IWM.

Fig. 7.10 Hand puppet given to Stephie Leyser, as she left Germany in 1939. (IWM)

Charles Hannam, the Kindertransport boy with the identity of No 384, searched for his place in the world; such is the upheaval to body and mind when one moves irrevocably from one's country of birth to another. This situation is covered in the next section.

7.2 On Being a Recognised Citizen

In a lesser way, I can personally associate with the change of culture, country, climate and, at first for me but not all immigrants, that kind of rejection given by local children at school as soon as they found out you were not 'one of them'.

My experience had nowhere the level of trauma suffered by those from Nazi Germany. Mine was all for the good and I went with loving parents in a time of joy and with a chance to make something of the situation. Charles Hannam's choice of the book title, *Almost an Englishman,* can be rephrased to be, in my adult circumstances, '*Almost an Australian',* a common situation with migrants.

Migrating to Australia when I was 14 years old did not immediately make me an Australian. In my own eyes, I was still a *pom*. It took decades to feel that I had added to myself another nationality.

Still today, the 'Englishman' in me remains, thanks in a large way to my formative time in Midhurst.

Charles and Boy 393 came to Midhurst via the *Kindertransport;* they had much more to contend with for they had lack of the right language, reduced living conditions, culture shock and severe loss of family to contend with. They had escaped the death camps and other living horrors, but in Britain, they then had to pass through a lifetime of change to come to grips with the facts of their experiences. Many of the *Kindertransport* children must still wonder about such issues.

I arrived in Adelaide, from London in October 1951 as half of a *ten-pound pom.* That was the cost to get there by ship for an adult; just why they bothered to make such a little charge still mystifies me. It, however, did need modest saving by a family as it was at least a week's salary then. It may well have been a way for the government of Australia to sort out the more serious applicants.

On arrival for me, the most common and very irritating to locals, Pommie phrase heard too much, in striking English accents, was "*back home* it was different" implying it was better there. The retort to that was simply "go home Pommie". That feeling was with me for decades.

Some *New Australians,* as we migrants were correctly but derogatorily called then, never really got over it. It did not help when fellow Aussie school kids would shout at me around a school building's corner, "go home pommie".

When I started work, in 1952, I became a *pommie bastard.* Surprisingly most of those uttering such unkind rhetoric, themselves had a migrant background a generation or two before.

Those migrants from the UK who were dissatisfied often returned home: a good proportion of them then realising it was not so bad after all, using assisted passage migration to get back to Australia again - some even yet again! They were known as *whingeing poms.*

You may be surprised to learn that being called a Pommie today is today a term of endearment in Australia. It is less heard now. The same kind of treatment has been passed to each of the successive groups of immigrants that have come since. As a group, they too easily became named with an unkind phrase and blamed for many of the societal ills of the day.

Jewish boys, Nos 348 and 393, would have had to learn to live with similar, but far worse anti-Semitic statements for some time to come. They also would have found they were *almost an Englishman* for years to come after arrival there.

For me, as an experience of relevance, officially becoming an Aussie was not helped by the fact that for many years people from Britain there was no call to take the *oath of allegiance* to Australia; and there seemed little need to do it. A British person could enter Britain and get back into Australia with a British passport. That changed in the 1970s; a Labour government gained power and passed a requirement to have a visa, or Australian citizenship, to get back into the country. Not surprisingly, there was an increase in Citizenship ceremonies.

At a civic ceremony held on 27 November 1975, usually but not always so, performed on Australia Day, 26 January each year, I became an Australian. Unlike those born in Australia, we *New Australians* received a very special certificate. Figs. 7.11 and 7.12, of the document, say so. My Australian born wife never got a grand document like this!

That change still permitted people to retain their UK citizenship. Despite the new rules, I felt I was always in a middle land until January 2012. I was then awarded the local Civic award for contributions to our resident's association.

Sitting in the audience, hearing some Citizenship oaths being taken, and waiting for my time to mount the podium for the award, it suddenly dawned on me,

'At last, I had become an Aussie. They had said so!.

Chapter 7. Persons Without Essentials

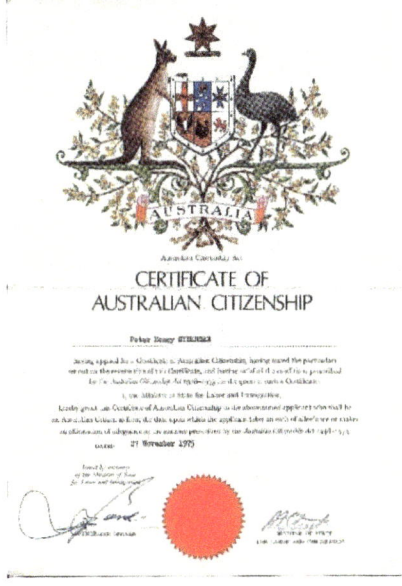

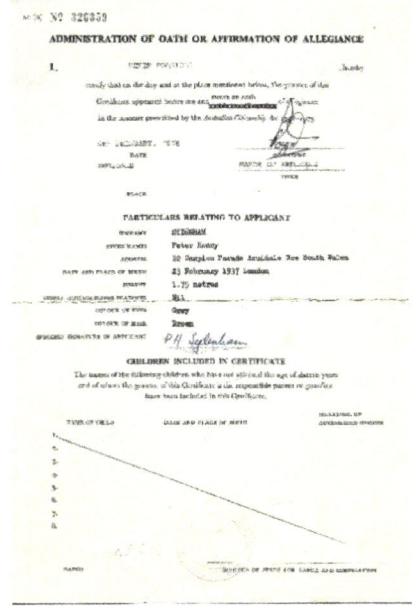

Fig. 7.11 Australian Citizenship Certificate for the author, 27 November 1975 (front side).

Fig. 7.12 Record of Oath of Allegiance for Author, 6 February 1976 (rear side).

Mind you, this citizenship issue can be complex. An Australian Member of Parliament cannot have citizenship of another country thereby ruling out dual citizens. But! Many migrants to Australia do not know they have second citizenship for in some countries it is automatically conferred without formal notice.

Making the change for me was easy with little downside. I had moved to a variation of an English country with the similar ways of thinking, and with deep harmony and sameness. I was speaking much the same form of the English language. Overall, it was like taking a perpetual holiday. To me, it was another England, but with a different climate and a massive sense of openness, blue skies and more freedom of action.

For Karl, who became Charles on arrival in England, things were far worse. He had moved from a Nazis Socialist society that had become a dictatorship that was brutal in its aims and practices.

There was much to adapt to in England, but the changes were not brutal. He states he was initially led to believe that to fit in he had to learn the English language, be conservative toward others, not to be too forthright, not be 'posh', and to not expect rights of any kind: he was still a refugee with citizenship from the enemy, Germany.

It was not all kind and straightforward. When he joined the British Army that introduced him to harsh rituals and bullying. Serving in India also opened his eyes to the English style of racism.

His upbringing in Germany, as a less than orthodox Jew, was in an ordered society having good manners, respect for others and good family virtues. Too often he was disappointed by what he then had to live with. As his English language skills developed, he was disappointed with the sloppiness in its use by those born into it. It took him a long time to become English in his own eyes; he had to think and act like them. 'He had to become tough to survive.'

So, when did people of the British Isles began to feel 'Englishness'; having part of them being a subject of a particular land? Historians tell us it happened in the Middle Ages when the *Kingdom of England* came into being. By the 19th century, the words 'English' and 'British' were often interchangeable by those peoples of England; as they are still somewhat today. The debate continues! Germanness, in contrast, can be traced back only to the late 19th century.

Many other Jewish refugee *Kindertransport* stories have been written up. The search for acceptance of these children in their new country may well have produced the internal drive that made many of them famous for their achievements. They must have recognised their salvation from Nazi rule by the *Kindertransport* programme.

One person of note that came to England this way, also via the South of England, is Alfred Robert Bader (1924 - 2018). He was born in Vienna, being of Czech descent. His family had highly acknowledged members of

Chapter 7. Persons Without Essentials

society, one being knighted for contributions to civil engineering on the Suez Canal.

Alfred, Fig. 7.13, started to feel Nazi oppression when he had to leave school in 1938 at 14 years old. Jews could not progress their schooling further under Nazi rule.

Soon after that, his family made the timely decision to send him away from them on the *Kindertransport* scheme. His adoptive mother died in 1942 in a concentration camp. His father had died just after he was born.

On arrival in England, he attended the East Hove Senior School for Boys, and then Brighton Technical College.

Fig. 7.13 Alfred Bader, much-acclaimed scientist and philanthropist, was a *Kindertransport* child.

That was interrupted when, in 1940, he was sent to a Canadian internment camp that 'assisted his academic and social education'. After passing entry exams into University level he suffered anti-Semitism discrimination when his application was rejected at McGill University. Limits were in place there for the number of Jewish students accepted. This policy came into being earlier in the 1930s when Jewish migrant entrants began to exceed locals.

He, fortunately, found a sponsor and mentor that supported him into a solid footing in academic Engineering Chemistry. He finally got entrance to Queen's University in Ontario graduating first in Chemistry, and then History. From then on, his place in Canada became firm as his work found great acclaim; he graduated, by programme, into 6 degrees in the Chemistry field. These he applied well: he was not a 'perpetual' student! Over his lifetime of work, he was awarded no less than 9 honorary degrees, many being from England and Scotland.

Alfred had a serious romance in Bexhill-on-Sea in the late 1940s but that did not endure at the time, rekindling in the 1980s. Alfred spent the rest of his life in Canada.

A private side of his life was being an 'inveterate collector' of stamps, and then paintings. He was much interested in Art History. Fortunately, he published several books, one covering his life from his Nazi oppressed early life, to becoming an Arts connoisseur as well as being a Worthy in Chemistry. He was also a philanthropist to many institutions. In one generous gifting situation he bought Herstmonceux Castle in East Sussex, (once the Royal Greenwich Observatory until The 1988) passing it over to Queens University which opened there the *Bader International Study Centre* in 1994.

Fig. 7.14 Herstmonceux Castle, now the Bader International Study Centre in Hailsham, East Sussex.

Alfred Bader passed way in 2018; he surely must have felt he was a Canadian and even more, an International citizen. He has lost his parents but found new acceptance by many in his new country.

The Midhurst District is not only a beautiful rural place, but also has been host to many quite unexpected skills and contributions to international matters.

The next chapter is concerned with global resources and methods of mankind management of the same.

Chapter 8. Money Makes the World Go Around

8.1 Currency Guidance; from Midhurst

Richard Cobden was born in a farmhouse *Dunford*, near Heyshott, in 1804; his story was also partially covered in Book 1.

He strongly campaigned to change the Corn Laws; that made corn dearer by not permitting imports. That resulted in local produce being more expensive than it needed to be, thus lining the pockets of the wealthy who controlled the corn markets. Corn and wheat were the staple food of rural workers and this cost was a large proportion of their outgoings.

This task set the scene for the concept of *free trade* by nations to be much in debate. There are many reasons to defend free world trade for its place in helping keep world peace; but whilst it did make bread cheaper for the poor at that time, it also has strong reasons for not always being practised.

David Ley, see Book 1, Chapter 12.1, suggested that Canadian over-production grain being dumped in Britain was one factor in the level of rural poverty still existing in the early 20th century in the Midhurst District. Local production lost commercially viability as general national wages became too high; that occurring whilst the agricultural wage was being driven down, the net effect being to increase rural poverty. That in turn, forced many to leave the District to chase better paid industrial employment and the perceived availability of housing elsewhere.

The Law was eventually abolished in 1846. In 1847 Cobden bought back his childhood family home, that being Dunford farm; he extended it greatly. Fig. 8.1 shows how it was in the 1860s.

Fig. 8.1 Dunford House: 1860s.

The *Cobden Club* had its humble beginnings in a little Heyshott cottage situated across the road from the Church. It was:

> 'Presented by Jane Cobden to the village in 1880 which she had converted to form a club with a library, common room and kitchen, with a field for croquet, behind. It was a temperance club, known at the time as The Coffee Tavern, to which members paid one penny a week. Inside the cottage, on the massive tie-beam, is carved the inscription:
>
> **This Cobden Club and Village Room**
>
> **The Gift of Jane Cobden to Heyshott 1880 Trust**
>
> An emblem of corn sheaves and sickles commemorates her father's achievements. The club has now moved to the former village school nearby and the cottage is a private house.' Howard (2004).

Dunford House became a memorial to his contributions in 1866; with its aim to promote:

> 'Peace, Free Trade and Goodwill among Nations'.

Publications on matters of international interest, were still being released by the Cobden Club during WW2, Barbara Ward, later the Baroness of Lodsworth, was also contributing to the global economic arena; see next section.

The Cobden Club enjoyed an extensive network of member countries. *Google Free E-books* makes available the full record of their Annual Dinner held in Greenwich on 24 June 1871, the membership then including Britain, US America, Australia, Austro-Hungarian Empire, Belgium, Brazil, Denmark, Egypt, France, Germany, Holland, Italy, Mexico, Norway, Portugal, Russia, Spain, Sweden, and Switzerland. Numerous papers and reports were presented that made much mention of free trade and peace.

It began as a Gentleman's club; that meant it was then used by men who could live on their wealth and thus had time to think about the world

Chapter 8 Money Makes the World Go Around

as *Natural Philosophers* (today we call them scientists), and to do good works for the society where they felt the call. Its main interest was free trade and its influence on peace; it had a publishing arm of its own, Fig. 8.2.

Fig. 8.2 Publishing logo of the Cobden Club, used from 1881.

In the early 20th century interest in the club fell away. Being aligned with Liberal thinking, the decline in support for free trade, the take-over of professionally practised science by university staff, and the growing availability of learned journals collectively meant its purpose and influence was less in demand. The London Club building changed hands; the club presence in Heyshott was, however, still operational during WW2. Its history is available, Cobden Club (1939).

Richard Cobden completed the resurrection of Dunford House in 1856. After he died in 1865 the house was tenanted many times, including by the London School of Economics in 1920. In 1928 it was gifted to the *Cobden Memorial Association* for educational and international uses.

After 1952 it became the national training centre of the YMCA. It cares for many Cobden artefacts.

According to the publication place credit given in Hirst (1943) it was still the home of the Cobden Club during WW2.

Fig. 8.3 Dunford House today.

Francis Hirst, Fig. 8.4, born in Huddersfield in 1873, spent much of his working life contributing in the field of political economics as a journalist and writer, and Editor of the *Economist* magazine. He was much published. In 1903 he married Richard Cobden's grand-niece, Helena, in St. James Church, Heyshott. Dunford became their home away from various London addresses.

Fig. 8.4 Francis Hirst.

The Hurley-Skidmore family history, on the Internet, fills in the details. Francis had close affection for the Cobden Club. Francis and Helena were the last family members to keep up the Cobden cause.

His family lived in Dunford House where he organised the Dunford House Conferences. They left the house in 1952: he died at age 79, of influenza early in 1953. Helena moved to London. In 1951, they had decided it was better to transfer ownership of the house to the National Council of the YMCA. Helena died when she was 97.

Helena had become very involved with the suffragette movement working to gain the vote for women. Francis was not at all in agreement with the views held by his wife:

"Despite having two intelligent sisters and an intelligent wife, Francis Hirst believed that women were fundamentally irrational and therefore should be denied the vote. His wife disagreed, but they had a pact that neither would take a public stand on the issue. But in private the disagreement sometimes boiled to the surface."
Charles Burlington.

To contemplate and prepare his publications, Francis would sit in the very room that was once Cobden's study. One document written during the war was Hirst (1943), on the problem of currency exchange. He worked on currency and the problems caused by depreciation. He had there, for his research reference, seventeen bound volumes of *The Bullion Report* from 1810. His paper debated the issues of the use of gold and silver as monetary standards concerning the use of paper money. It deals with a definition of money; difficulties of a metal currency compared

Chapter 8 Money Makes the World Go Around

with paper money that is more easily counterfeited; prices and wages; Churchill's speeches on same; international exchange and control; and the mid-19th century Walter Bagehot's ideas for an *International Coin*.

One issue being discussed in that paper is the potential overpowering application of bureaucracy (defined as an "excessively complicated administrative procedure" or "the unnecessary bureaucracy in local government"), see Fig. 8.5 for a realistic view of it at work:

'Refer to Committee 3, Investigation Subcommittee 6. Section 8B, for consideration" - government response to the news report that 100,000 Jews were being killed monthly by the Nazis.' Eric Godal, Cartoonist. Oct 1943.

Fig. 8.5 Bureaucracy at work.

Professor R V Jones, a publishing colleague of mine in the 1960s, once spoke to me of its problems. When he worked from his WW2 Air Force Intelligence office, his messages too often suffered from 'bureaucratic attenuation'.

In the Parliament, sometime in 1943, it was reported that the Board of Trade had taken over its bureaucratic role in unsatisfactory ways, virtually killing off free markets across the country. An example was reported in the 3 April 1943 Daily Mail newspaper.

I leave to you to decide if the article is the real truth or just an indicator of what might happen if they got full control. It might well be an exaggeration, but it does illustrate the kind of issues that every city, town and village person had come to live with after war was declared:

'TRADERS QUEUE AT DAWN
For a Month's Supply of Razor Blades.
By Daily Mail Reporter.

SEVEN hundred shopkeepers from all parts of the country queued up from 5.30 a.m. yesterday outside the Wholesale Trading Supplies depot at Mitre House, London Road, S.E.

They had travelled from all parts of England to get their month's quota of "utility" razor blades which were being released. And the maximum any of them was allowed to buy was 18s. 3d. worth.

Some of the shopkeepers spent at least twice that amount in travelling. Others got up at dawn to drive long distances to collect their share of the precious blades which they will have to ration to their customers. Most of them went away with their April supply in their pockets, but some in the line of cars outside the depot were also replenishing their stocks of cosmetics and similar supplies.

Mr J. Barnett, who had driven from Dagenham, waited hours for his monthly "ration" of blades. "Even by selling only one or two to each customer, the monthly supply will not last more than a week," he said. Such was the rush that the firm's 80 assistants were almost over-whelmed when the doors opened at 8.30 a.m.

The principal of the firm, Mr Lionel Schneiderman, and the manager, regulated the queue. They scrutinised their clients to ensure that only their regular customers were served.

So, the 700 shopkeepers will be able to supply their customers with a few blades for at least another week. After that, there may be no further supply from the wholesaler during April.

The Board of Trade gave in 2 months later and dropped the use of quotas to restrict supply levels.'

We can now look into the work of another local person who also made an international difference from the Midhurst area in pre-war and war times,

Chapter 8 Money Makes the World Go Around

namely, Barbara Ward.

8.2 Barbara Ward: Voice in the Wilderness

International issues were much in mind for some in the 30s. So many countries were on conflict paths at the time. The West was recovering from the effects of WW1, but the doors had been opened for harsh dictatorships to emerge that took advantage of the parlous state of their people.

It also was becoming clear that colonised countries, particularly India, were gaining the strength, courage and commitment needed to wrestle themselves out of the control of another country.

Social conditions in Britain were under still more reform - there was plenty more to take on. The division of wealth between the gentry and the workers was relentlessly being worked upon by the Parliament in Britain. Privileged estates were being broken down by heavy death duties. Social justice was biting hard in the rich man's land.

All of these issues were collectively a huge problem, that needed the attention of the best of minds to see how to work on such issues for the good of the peoples.

A key base to start from was how to consider management of the scarcity of global resources whilst preserving the global environment. Yes! That was an issue that far back.

The need for critical resources, like oil, coal and a range of minerals, has long been a reason for countries to invade the sovereignty of others. The soon-to-be Axis powers of Germany, Italy and Japan all had this in mind as they endeavoured to develop their, by then out-dated, ideas of resurrecting glorious empires.

The Midhurst District has a claim to a key leader of these global contributions for the *Good*, a person who stated:

'Our visionary perspective is true realism - and that is what we must pursue'
By Barbara Ward, later to become *Baroness Jackson of Lodsworth*.

Edward heath said of her:

'She was the first to see problems in global terms and to recognise that they required global solutions. This was no superficial approach, urging simplified solutions through glorified government operations. If ever a mind had a detailed grasp of the variety and suitability of all measures possible in overseas development, backed by practical experience, it was her's.'

Fortunately, her life-story has been recorded in Gartlan (2010), and in numerous places on the Internet; those accounts allowing me to provide a short review of her life.

Barbara Mary Ward, buried in Lodsworth, was born in York on 23 May 1914, moving soon to Felixstowe. She was raised as a Catholic, her mother's faith; and was also much influenced by her father's following as a Quaker. She was schooled in a Catholic Convent in Felixstowe.

Her father believed in his children experiencing the world. Her older brother, John, was sent to school in Germany, a country then known for its excellence in intellectual and technical areas. Barbara went to Paris in 1929, and then on to Germany to study German not long after.

In 1932 she went back to Germany for a short period to also take tuition in singing. Barbara was soon back in England, this time to the Sommerville College, Oxford University reading philosophy, politics and economics - with drama and singing as extracurricular recreations.

Here she began her political activities; she was 'deeply affected by the degree of massive unemployment', that being in the perspective of events elsewhere in Europe. She, Fig, 8.6, graduated with 1st Class Honours in 1935 as the only women to have done so in her speciality.

Fig. 8.6 Barbara Ward, in her 20s, later to become Baroness of Lodsworth.

She then spent the next three years in Austria and Italy studying their social problems. By the summer of 1937, whilst I was just a tot,

Chapter 8 Money Makes the World Go Around

presumably giving my mum and dad sleepless nights, Barbara, now ready to act at 23 years old, was starting to make her mark in the heights of international politics and economics with early publications resulting as her PhD studies proceeded at London University.

Here was a young woman right ready to help redirect international thinking on many global tasks, such as serving on committees for Catholic assistance of refugees escaping from Nazi policies.

She saw the link between the persecution of Catholics during British Reformation times (see Book 1. Chapters 4, 5 and 6) and then in 1930s Europe, and how freedom of thought and speech was her privilege in Britain. Her family hosted a refugee boy, Heinz, possibly from the *Kindertransport* scheme.

Amid her prodigious contributions, she wrote her first book, published in 1938. Called *The International Share-Out* it was a critical study of colonialism and how it led to conflict. This work was used to form the basis of an important parliamentary address; it made Barbara's presence known in the highest political circles.

It was a penetrating book, exploring the situation of those countries possessing the wealth generated by others for Britain. It debated whether Hitler and Mussolini's demands for more territory should be accepted. The huge crimes against humanity by them, by then, were not yet that clear in the 1937 period of her committing pen to paper.

She wrote numerous articles for all manner of outlets. Papers and presentations covered the issues of *Democracy Versus Dictatorship; The rise of Fascism; Europe on the Verge;* and the internal workings of the European States.

Defence of the West was published in 1942; it examined the role of Christian virtues in WW2.

By the start of WW2, she was a regular staff member for the *Economist;* as its foreign editor. During the war, she continued to make addresses to a wide range of audience including the Lords and Ladies, and politicians of Britain and statesmen of other countries. These were carried out despite air raids, of which one destroyed *The Economist's* offices.

In 1942 Barbara was sent to the USA to speak on behalf of the war effort.

Her contacts were at the highest level - the White House.

Discussions included issues regarding international affairs after the war had ended. Presence in numerous countries provided her with considerable on-site research opportunities and relationships with many national leaders.

Barbara met her husband to be, Robert Jackson, in London in 1943. He was born in Melbourne, Australia and by then had held posts in Robert soon became the Director of the Middle East Supply Company, MESC. His role there was to assist the supply and feeding of peoples in the British parts of the Middle East that were being isolated by the Axis blockades. His career complemented Barbara's ambitions. He worked on some to the world's greatest civil engineering projects.

They saw each other from time to time when their international travels coincided; eventually falling in love when on a romantic interlude in Rome in 1946. Marriage was on their minds, but that was complicated for Robert was separated from his then wife in Australia and needed an annulment. The path to marriage was not easy. Robert converted to Catholicism. After a very long and unhappy period, Robert was finally granted an annulment by the Catholic church, freeing them to marry.

On 30 September 1950, their engagement was notified in the *London Times.* It attracted many messages of congratulations, including one from the French Ambassador. Her influence was strong indeed. They were married on 16 November 1950.

They left for Australia soon after, going into a rather barren intellectual area; as it was seen then. One travelled to there by a slow going, but luxurious, ocean liner; the minimum time then needed was 4 weeks or so, but often as long as 6 weeks. No jet planes, taking only 25 hours to travel from Australia to Britain, were available then.

Australia was still coming of age. Any major project had to have British or, perhaps but less so, USA leadership! Today in the reverse, it is often found that an Australian company will be senior on creating and managing major works programmes elsewhere, such has been the change over the past half-century of Australia's place in world affairs.

It was a time when many go-ahead Australians left for 'better places' in London and New York. There was more opportunity in larger cities with internally focussed audiences. Barbara had become pregnant

Chapter 8 Money Makes the World Go Around

when on a well-earned holiday in Australia. She returned to London to be ready for the birth of her only son Robert (or Robin), Fig. 8.7, who joined the world prematurely on 25 February 1956.

Fig. 8.7 Barbara Ward with son Robert, c1958.

For a few years, the relationship with her husband Robert was a happy one but they often had to be apart for considerable periods as each had commitments across the globe. They did not lead a stable family life.

After Australia, it was off to India, then onto the Gold Coast of Africa to live in Accra, the capital of Ghana. It had just achieved self-government and Robert was there to lead the Volta River dam and a hydroelectric project that was built between 1961-1965; see Fig. 8.8. It stretches upland from its location for some 250 miles and generates 1020MWe.

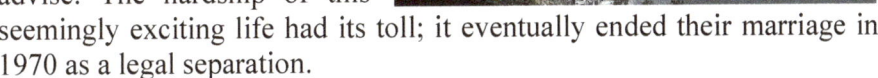

Fig. 8.8 The rock-filled, Volta River, *Akosombo* dam is one of the largest man-made reservoirs on the globe.

Many journeys were made by Barbara to take up invitations to speak and advise. The hardship of this seemingly exciting life had its toll; it eventually ended their marriage in 1970 as a legal separation.

The midwife, Joanne English (later called Anna) who tended her child in a hospital, subsequently joined the family as their nanny for the next 17 years. Her presence in that role certainly allowed more freedom for Barbara to work on her numerous projects.

Throughout her journey of life, she suffered from cancer of the oesophagus, that had first appeared way before in the 1940s, and had gone into seemingly permanent remission by 1957. However, it reappeared in 1968 and she was operated on it in London. At that time, she was living in Jersey.

The year 1970 was a significant one for her. It was the year in which she moved into her first and only ever, permanent home - in Lodsworth. It overlooked the Sussex Downs and provided a haven of peace for her, from her past and hectic life. But not so for Robert; their relationship was no more loving, as it had started. This was the year they agreed to a separation. Anna came with her, living in her self-contained flat attached to the house.

That house in Lodsworth was called *Pound House*: it is still there - but it has had a chequered history!

The Lodsworth history of Pounds states it is in Manor Farm Lane and was:

> 'Previously called 'Domus' and later 'The Thatched House'. The original Domus was constructed of horizontal wooden rough-edged boards and probably built in the late 1800s. That house was burnt down in the early 1900s. A brick or stucco house was built in its place and this burnt down in 1933 or 1934. A third house was built shortly after. This had a thatched roof which caught fire and burned off in the 1950s. http://lodsworthheritage.org.uk/

It was surely a great place for early retirement, but Barbara was still full of fire and interest in assisting where the need was apparent. She became the President of the International Institute for Environment and Development, IIED. There she provided 'a clear voice for our planet', the apt title of the last chapter of Gartlan (2010). This institute was a think-tank set up in London. It looked at global sized issues, such as, how to create a sufficiently large buffer stock of grain to feed the world.

Just after she had a stay on the ranch of Lady Bird Johnson in 1974, her illness started to show itself again. In December of that year, she was released from a hospital in London to receive her insignia of

Chapter 8 Money Makes the World Go Around

Dame Commander of the British Empire DBE. She was then 60 years old. Soon after, on 18 October 1976, she was elevated to be the life-time, Baroness Jackson of Lodsworth.

In 1978 she began, with others, her last book *Progress for a Small Planet*. She was still communicating with world leaders but her health was failing. She had to slow down and so resigned her Presidency of the IIED in 1979 – to 'smell and tend the roses' in her country garden, and receive distinguished guests.

Baroness Jackson died on May 31, 1981; 67 years old. Her funeral mass was held at the modern Midhurst Catholic church, *The Divine Motherhood and St Francis of Assisi*. As her wish, she was buried in the lower graveyard of the Anglican St. Peter's churchyard in her favourite village, Lodsworth, Fig. 8.9.

Fig. 8.9 St Peter's church in Lodsworth, where Barbara Ward is buried.

Such was her standing, that a Memorial Mass was held in Westminster Cathedral in London. At the time of the homily by Bishop Mahon, the congregation was:

'Referred to the Gospel story of the Good Samaritan, so often quoted by Barbara herself, saying that she had been the eloquent voice of millions of voiceless poor symbolised by the wounded figure lying abandoned on the Jerusalem to Jericho road.'

She left an extensive archive of personal papers that have allowed her biography to be written up, recording her magnificent life's story of great and continuous contribution when under great personal stress.

She was not forgotten: a Royal Mail postage stamp, Fig. 8.10, was issued with a picture taken late in her life.

Fig. 8.10 Barbara Ward, Baroness Jackson of Lodsworth postage stamp, 2014.

War was coming in mid-1939. The Nazis were the enemy who might just invade Britain. The Fascist BU movement was present in the UK, possibly being already an undercover spy network. So, what was that movement doing in Sussex? Was it something to be afraid of?

The next chapter delves into Nazi happenings that were taking place, so openly until the war was declared. One of these developed a very close connection with Midhurst town and local villages!

Chapter 9. Glimpses of a then Possible Future.

9.1 Fascists in West Sussex

Suspicion and dread came to those ruled under Nazi occupation. There, one had to be looking over your shoulder; even the most innocent person could suddenly be taken off and shot, or killed in some dreadful manner, as we shall see in later Books.

It was not like that in Midhurst; democracy was worth defending; the authoritarian Fascist rule was a return to a life of being a slave where people's lives are a just a commodity to the rulers. It got close to happening! Life would have been a whole lot different if Hitler had had his way.

In the early 1930s, many influential people in Britain seriously felt that Hitler was a man of stature and sound leadership, who was pulling his German people out of the disgrace of WW1 the led to the people, of that time, to suffer greatly for sins they had not committed.

His politics was based on fascism applied with strongly applied socialism and added evil aspects of humanity as a Dictator. What that could mean to British future lives, under his 'protection' as an occupier or on a close-by land constantly there as a threat, was not appreciated by many leaders of Britain.

Thanks to the collected comments of people with pre-war Germany circumstances by Julia Boyd (2018), we are pulled right in to see and feel the attitudes of foreigners as the Nazis rose to power.

Just after Hitler obtained complete power in 1933, Owen Tweedy and Jim Turcan, forty-year-old friends from their Cambridge University days, were on a driving holiday through Germany; their comments are interesting to read:

'Tweedy expressed astonishment at the breathtaking change taking place in so short a time. The election [that gave Hitler power] has completely altered Germany both outwardly and inwardly so much that it is hard to realise that we are in the same country that we entered a month ago. The Nazis are out-fascisming Fascismo.' Boyd (2018).

Elsewhere in the country, 22-year-old Geoffrey Cox was in Berlin during that election. He was visiting the popular destination of Heidelberg to learn German. His description of life then is sobering indeed. Geoffrey lists public meetings being banned; armed police everywhere; police cars with police holding rifles with bayonets fixed. He wrote:

> 'I give Germany six months more before she either goes communist or [in her determination to expand east] has warred with Poland. The great danger I feel it that the Dictator party will make war as soon as they have the German Army up to strength to counter the forces of Communism. It is a hell of a shame as the German people are such splendid people. Among the younger people, there is a sort of eager desperation as they realise, they are going to be the cannon fodder.'

Churchill was telling the British Parliament of this threat but few wanted to know at that stage.

As the 30s matured it all came into better focus. The trauma and brutality being wrought by the Fascists in Spain, Italy and Germany were then becoming apparent from the incidents described in earlier chapters; they had been revealing their extreme methods since the 1920s.

The cartoon, Fig. 9.1, shows Hitler, Mussolini and Franco hearing the statement "Excellency, the Moorish troops are disturbed - they say our conduct of the war is unchristian".

Fig. 9.1 The Fascist way was brutal.

In Britain, fascism took root in the early 1920s as small groups joined up

Chapter 9 Glimpses of a then Possible Future

in 1932 to become the British Union of Fascists BUF. This political push arose out of much the same reasons as its model had, that of Italy - unemployment, low wages, poor health care, and poor working conditions existed and new wealth became concentrated increasingly in the purses of the upper classes and nobility - see Fig, 9.2 for a chart of fascism development in Britain.

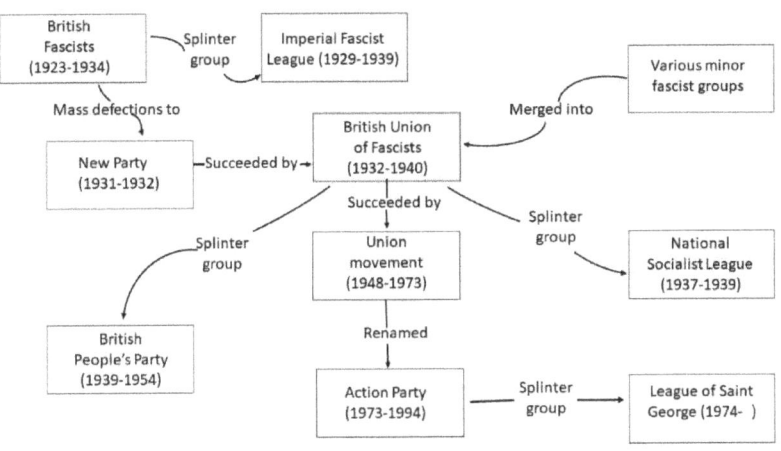

Fig. 9.2 Development of Fascism in Britain.

The BUF policy, proclaimed in a 1933 *Blackshirt* issue, was convincing to many and worthy of a second look, Kenny (2003).

'All shall serve the State and none the faction. All shall work and thus enrich their Country and themselves. Opportunity shall open to all, but privilege to none. Great position shall be accorded only to service. Poverty shall be abolished by the power of modern science released within the organised State. The barriers of Class shall be destroyed and the energies of every citizen devoted to the service of the British Nation.'

In practice, it is the manner of how it is done that mattered more than basic aspirations. Here, however, all the ills of a nation would seemingly be repaired by a government that did everything according to the will and directive of a very strong leader having little regard for humanity.

It seems it had to act always in the extreme, with the application of violence, military force, government censorship and control, far-right rampant nationalism, and enforced discipline; all this being determined by the God-head figure, the all-powerful Dictator.

I say it goes like this:

'I, your all-knowing Dictator, will tell you what you need to do to be better off. I will provide it for you and you MUST do and act as I say. If not, you will be punished most severely. You must follow my plan for national greatness, and oh, we will need to take what we need from you wherever it is to be found; that may need you to give your life for it. You WILL follow my dictates wherever they take you. That's it; no ifs, no buts. And you WILL glorify me for doing all this for you!'

The core unit of interest here was the British Union of Fascists BUF. Its influence and disruptive nature in the British all-allowing democracy was not to be ignored.

As seems to be the case with many on-the-fringe politicians, they have some good causes that are badly tainted by their well-off-the-side activities that are often strongly racial. Racialism, too often allied with physical force, sidelines them.

Such was it with Hitler at the start of his rise to power – initially he gave his nation better and more stable living conditions for the people; the autobahn network; the Volkswagen (people's car) car for everyone; and numerous civil infrastructure works. To begin with, he even cared for the individual sick! Mussolini, also, introduced major civil projects, and other socially responsible public programmes in Italy, to start his climb to Dictatorship.

So it was with the BUF movement, founded by the then youngest elected conservative parliamentary member, Oswald Mosley MP, who later moved into the Independent Labour Party from 1930. He was born in 1896 in Mayfair, London being schooled at the Royal Military College, Sandhurst.

During WW1 he served in the cavalry, then the Royal Flying

Chapter 9 Glimpses of a then Possible Future

Corps, as an observer. A crash from his recklessness in an aircraft ended with him having a permanent limp. He left the battlefield for an office job with the Ministry of Munitions and the Foreign Office. He inherited his Baronetcy in 1928.

His interest in politics began in 1918. He was good orator, but fell foul as time passed, because of the strong words that lost him mainline parliamentary support. Becoming impatient with the main parties he formed his own New Party in 1931. That was his start with fascism policy and its way of operating, Fig. 9.3.

Fig. 9.3 Sir Oswald Mosley, with men and women Black-shirts in London, 1936.

The BUF found interest in its campaigning for a range of worthily sounding issues. In the south, the main centres of all this activity were in the towns of Chichester, Selsey, Bognor, Littlehampton, Worthing, Midhurst, Petworth, Horsham, Cuckfield, East Grinstead and, biggest of all, Brighton.

Leaders desperately wanted to avoid war, but somehow on the back of their minds they must have known being allied with Hitler would most certainly take them there.

The very apt cartoon by David Low, in a March 1936 *Evening Standard*, Fig. 9.4, conveys that well.

Fig. 9.4. "How much will you give me not to kick your pants for, say, twenty-five years" (David Low)

It changed the name in 1937 to the British Union BU, which existed until 1940 when it was *proscribed,* that is, was publicly identified and condemned as an 'enemy of the state'. When the BUF was founded in Britain many members of the party then were accepted citizens of high standing. These people were not the skin-head followers that today we rightly, or wrongly, associate with the BUF's successor. They were often respectable men and women, knights of the realm, top military men, politicians, scientists and an aviator, many having become disaffected with the Conservative Party and seen that social adjustments, unwanted by them, were needed to get Britain out of its diminished state on world affairs.

The Remains of the Day is a 1993 film, adapted from a novel by Kazuo Ishiguro. It is truth-fiction and borrows heavily from real situations that prevailed in the mid to late 1930s Britain.

The storyline is about a classical Butler, Mr Stevens, of the fictitious Darlington Hall, who is trapped in the time when the upstairs and downstairs attitudes were blurring. Many people, in both classes, were not able to move with the times in which the aristocrats were rapidly becoming uncomfortable as their long-held wealth declined.

It is the main back story that is of interest to us here for it well illustrates the secret intrigues going on then; by 'Hitler's British admirers' in the aristocracy. They were pushing for 'appeasement' with Hitler's ambitions. Their expectation was, join up with him and that will save their estates and keep their positions in society, with their well out-dated privileges.

The film script gets onto the issue that many of the 'my good fellow' aristocratic personages still truly held that their centuries-long held talent and right to rule from the heart, came from their 'past culture and honour'; that being contrasted with the emerging class of 'professionals' who were experts in their fields and often not well connected to the aristocracy.

This attitude, and those who sided with the Nazis in the later 30s, are dealt with in James (2009.) Some dominant names picked out for their stupidity, by Paul Callan in the *Sunday Express*, of 12 September 2009, included Lady Nancy Astor, Lord Redesdale, the Duke of Westminster, the Fifth Duke of Wellington, Lord London and many

Chapter 9 Glimpses of a then Possible Future

others, including Lord Oswald Mosley, see back to Fig. 9.3, is the link to Fascism in Sussex, to a family in the Midhurst District, and to the so-called *Lord Haw-Haw*.

By 1936 the Black-shirts had become very active in London's East End events; too often degenerating into violent confrontations. The *Cable Street Battle* of 4 October 1936 was the main reason why para-military uniforms were soon banned in political gatherings.

As conditions between the participants of a BUF march began to turn nasty, the march was forbidden. Some 2000 communists and others, being mainly Labourites, opposed a similar number of BUF supporters; with the police also acting to bring order.

A truck was overturned, timber, glass and bricks were thrown as the three-way battle took place. This event rings of the Hitler's *Beer Hall Putsch* of 1923. It was a case of 'If you can't get what you want, take it by force!' Here, however, it was mainly Jews and their supporters who stood up to the Black-shirts and came out victorious.

James asserts the strong initial support garnered by the Fascists in London was connected to their fear of communism being allied to the Jewish People:

> 'A knot of peers adrift in an uncongenial world, united by paranoia, pessimism and panic'

Hitler, and his terrier dog ally Mussolini, seemingly offered them a safe world if Fascist Germany and Britain aligned by some treaty, or other. By 1935 the downside facts of Nazism were well known in Britain and the US; if only they could believe them!

Such an arrangement got close to being a reality as Chamberlain visited Hitler offering 'appeasement'. Goering is said to have visited Britain to set up a secret deal like this. His idea was suggested to be such that he would be elevated to the throne of England.

As mentioned earlier in Chapter 6.3, Von Ribbentrop, the eventual Foreign Minister of Hitler, was swanning his way around Cornwall in 1937 telling how he would take over Cornwall and live in the Mount St Michael castle as his home. I provide a scenario in a later book on what the Midhurst District might have been like under Nazi based rule!

The Wikipedia entry on the British Union of Fascists BUF provides a long list of senior British followers. At the time they were not acting without honour or being disloyal to Britain. They were members of a valid and, at first, acceptable political party; many of those signed-up members eventually went on to vehemently oppose Nazi policies.

One such person of great reputation was Lloyd George, past Chancellor of the Exchequer and the spearhead person of many of the reforms that were implemented in Britain.

He visited Hitler at least twice. Fig. 9.5 shows him on the left of Hitler when at the Obersalzburg where Hitler had his *Berghof* mountain residence. Joachim Von Ribbentrop stands in the centre behind them.

Fig. 9.5 Lloyd George visiting Hitler at the *Berghof.* (US Holocaust Museum)

The Wikipedia entry for 'Lloyd George' provides some incidents of his experience with the mid-30s Nazi regime. He supported German demands for territorial concessions and recognition of its 'great power' status. The Germans welcomed him as a friend in the highest circles of British politics.

In September 1936 he went to Germany to talk with the Hitler, who said he was pleased to have met 'the man who won the war'; to which Lloyd George was moved to call Hitler 'the greatest living German'. Whilst there, he visited Germany's public works programmes and was greatly impressed.

He later wrote an article for *The Daily Express* praising Hitler. He wrote:

Chapter 9 Glimpses of a then Possible Future

'The Germans have definitely made up their minds never to quarrel with us again.'

He believed Hitler was 'the George Washington of Germany'; that he was rearming Germany for defence and not for offensive war; that a war between Germany and Russia would not happen for at least ten years, and that Hitler admired the British and wanted their friendship. However, there was no British leadership wanting to exploit this.

It may come as a surprise to learn that regularly visiting, or living in the local Midhurst District, were some Nazi high command persons and sympathisers. They were able to come and go freely up to the declaration of war in late September 1939.

The British Union of Fascists BUF started as fascism had done in many of the defeated European countries of WW1. The prevailing conditions provided the opportunity for single-minded leaders to tell the voting public that they would bring about prosperity for their State. Indeed, they usually did - to begin with.

BUF meetings so often erupted into violence. The party members were known across the world for their ruthless way of campaigning and physically manhandling people at rallies, and in the streets at election times. Two examples were a rally in London in 1934, and a later one in New York in 1939.

One super-disastrous BUF rally was that held in the exhibition centre Olympia, London in June 1934.

'Oswald Mosley and the British Union of Fascists had held their huge staged rally at Olympia for which the Daily Mail had offered free tickets to readers who sent in letters explaining "Why I like the Black-shirts".'

Fig. 9.6 BUF rally in Olympia, 1934.

The rally, Fig. 9.6, with 2,000 Black-shirts there to keep the 12,000 strong attendees on order, had been designed to attract more recruits but also to impress the invited audience of politicians and journalists of their good intentions for Britain.

However, the anti-fascists were also there in force; the scene was set for violent confrontation. Mosley, their leader arrived on stage an hour late: he soon launched into an anti-Semitic speech shouting about the:

'European ghettos pouring their dregs into this country.'

It wasn't long before some 500 anti-fascists at the meeting started shouting abuse. Mosley paused whilst the hecklers were picked out by roving spotlights and ferociously attacked by black-shirted stewards who used physical contact methods. The female stewards had been trained to deal with the women hecklers by 'slapping, instead of punching'. www.nickelinthemachine.com/2013/07.

The retaliatory violence of the anti-fascists, mainly communists party members, led to much bad press. The organisers had the right to eject those it wanted to from the meeting using reasonable force on both sides. From reports of doctors patching up the wounded, it was obvious that weapons had been brought in!

Across the Atlantic the same kind of events took place, Fig. 9.7, as the US nation began to see and feel, the hatred being peddled by its Fascists taken up much by 'patriotic Americans of German stock'. That Bund (league) also had children involved, as had the Nazis.

Fig. 9.7 New Jersey, US. March past by fascists of the America-Germany Bund on 18 July 1937.

Chapter 9 Glimpses of a then Possible Future

Moseley was still at it on 16 July 1939 when he organised a rally at Earls Court in London, advertised in posters as the 'World's Largest Indoor Rally' and the 'Colossal Britain First Rally'. America was still neutral when Britain declared war on Germany in 1939. Many Americans had considerable leanings toward Germany because of their German heritage and admiration of its pre-war intellectual and technical standing. Small fascist organisations amalgamated to form the American Nazi organisation in 1933, being the *Friends of New Germany*.

They originally used much of the imagery kind of the German Nazi party; white shirt and black trousers for men with a black hat festooned with a red symbol; and the women members in a white blouse and a black skirt. To begin they adopted the signs, symbols, banners and the *Heil Hitler* salute but, with time, the US government eventually became less tolerant by 1938, resulting in some toning down by them to be less Nazi-like.

In February 1939 some 22,000 Nazi supporters attended a huge rally at New York's Madison Square Garden, Fig. 9.8.

Fig. 9.8 German-American Bund rally; Madison Square Garden, New York, 1939.

Demonstrators protested against this event; a police guard was in place.

'Aside from its admiration for Adolf Hitler and the achievements of Nazi Germany, the German American Bund program included antisemitism, strong anti-Communist sentiments, and the demand that the United States remain neutral in the approaching European conflict.'

This can be evidenced in a banner hanging at the rally: 'Stop Jewish Domination of Christian Americans'. A huge portrait of George Washington is to be seen. The organisers depicted him as the kind of model hero that all brave and virtuous American Aryans should follow. It also was there to appease the US government.

In the rally, the name of the then-current US President, Franklin D. Roosevelt, was continuously spoken as 'Frank D. Rosenfeld' signifying him as being a Jew.

In the 1930s British fascism had its headquarters and training camps in and around West Sussex. Some people of the Midhurst Rural District took important parts of that movement; one becoming a daily name across the whole of the British Isles.

9.2 Creation of Lord Haw-Haw

A very well-known nickname during WW2 was *Lord Haw-Haw*. His real name was William Joyce. During the war years, British people would listen to radio messages broadcast by this man from Germany.

His broadcasts would start with "Germany calling - Germany calling - Germany calling". His voice was highly suited to radio broadcasting: he had the x-factor needed for that job. People felt compelled to listen to him, initially for the apparent content of his messages, but very soon as a source of great amusement.

He rapidly became much despised in Britain. Journalist and novelist Cecil Roberts described a speech given by Joyce as:

'Thin, pale, intense, he had not been speaking many minutes before we were electrified by this man ... so terrifying in its dynamic force, so vituperative, so vitriolic'.

'He speaks English of the haw-haw, damn-it get-out-of-my-way variety, and his strong suit is gentlemanly indignation'.

His scripts would pour on, as Over-The-Top propaganda messages that derided, belittled, distorted and criticised a recent event, or one to come. It was done with an overly posh, 'plum in the mouth' accent from which, upon hearing it, almost any Britisher would cringe.

Chapter 9 Glimpses of a then Possible Future

His broadcasts:

> 'urged the British people to surrender, and were well known for their jeering, sarcastic and menacing tone'.

This sounds like '*Evil* talking - *Evil* talking - *Evil* talking'.

In 1940 Joyce had about six million regulars, and 18 million occasional listeners in Britain, Fig. 9.9. Because of extensive internal censorship of British transmissions by the war department, his broadcasts often supplied breaking news, but with an all too familiar slant meant to purposefully demoralise the British nation!

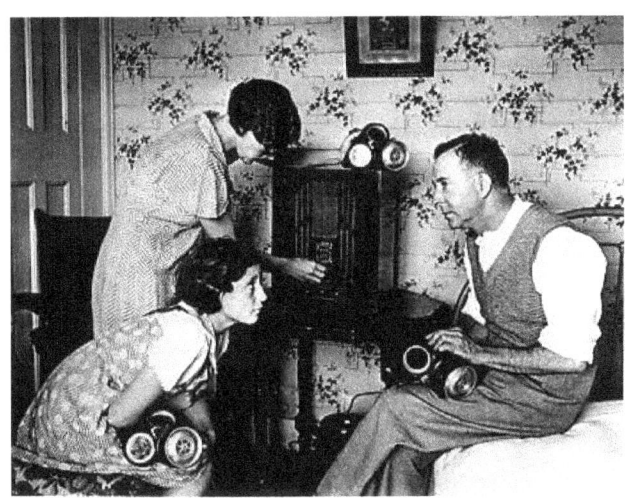

Fig. 9.9 A family listening to Lord Haw-Haw during the early war years. Note the gas masks at the ready.

Whilst these broadcasts were intended to take psychological misery to the British people, he was much listened too for his entertaining comedy. Few ever really believed what he said:

> 'Besides broadcasting, Joyce's duties included writing propaganda for distribution among British prisoners of war, whom he tried to recruit into the British Free Corps (covered in a later book of these memoirs). He wrote a book *Twilight Over England* that was promoted by the German Ministry of Propaganda, which unfavourably compared the evils of allegedly Jewish-dominated capitalist Britain with the alleged wonders of National Socialist

Germany. Adolf Hitler awarded Joyce the *War Merit Cross* (First and Second Class) for his broadcasts, although they never met.'
www.nickelinthemachine.com.

His programmes ran from 18 September 1939, until 30 April 1945. Some original soundtracks of these broadcasts are available today in several YouTube films about him. One was centred on the intended invasion of Britain by Germany in mid-1940, following the collapse of the Allied forces in France.

His final talk was broadcast in May 1945. It discussed the reasons for the war and why it did not work out as Hitler intended. In it, he was blaming Britain for not joining forces with the Third Reich.

So, how did he get that nickname?

On 1st September 1939 Jonah Barrington, Fig, 9.10, a journalist and radio critic of considerable standing, had been sent to *Radio Towers*, Lord Beaverbrook's private short-wave radio receiving station in a back-garden hut, Barrington (1948).

Fig. 9.10 Jonah Barrington, ca 1945.

It was situated near to Leatherhead, about 50 miles northeast of Midhurst. He was there to pick up international news that was hoped to be more direct and complete than that edited by the British War Department's censors.

To begin with Life in the hut was hectic as he had to find and provide accommodation for several translators who would listen to many radio receivers for useful news. That hut had only been built for use by one or two people, who would want a 'cuppa' during the day!

As it turned out there was no gain from this venture for other

Chapter 9 Glimpses of a then Possible Future

sources were flooding the news lines with right up-to-date news.

To break his boredom and to justify the use of the radio hut he set about to generate his form of propaganda by ridiculing those who sent false-truths over the airs from Germany:

'When some pert and prim Nazi Miss came to the Breslau microphone to tell British women that their lipstick was poisoned or some similar drivel, I wrote her up in the comedy vein under the name of Winnie the Whopper and the paper, welcoming light relief in a dull life, printed it. Mopey the Baby, Auntie Gush and Mr Smarmy, and Uncle Boo-Boo (of Moscow) followed'

This sort of childlike humour is so typical of the British; not everyone's cuppa tea! In this theme of titling put-down, he agreed that Winnie the Whopper had to have a romantic lover.

'Searching round among the propagandists. I pitched on the owner of an oily, hectoring, nasal voice who spoke in English at regular intervals, from Hamburg. His signature tune was his opening announcement: "Germany Calling! Germany Calling!"

This 'nasty piece of work' man was the one to be Winnie's lover. After 'communing with a cow', outside in the field around the hut, Jonah hit on the name *Lord Haw-Haw.*

The next day, on 18 September 1938, that nick-name was unwittingly set in stone when it appeared in a London newspaper article Jonah had submitted.

That name took off, being used without credit, in all manner of publications. Today we would say it had 'gone feral'. A Parisian newspaper announced they had discovered a new radio traitor to Germany calling him, incorrectly, as:

'Lord Ah! Oh!'- whose real name was Jonah Barringstone'

Songs were written that used it. Variety shows mentioned it. The Lambeth Walk was often sung as 'doin' the Haw-Haw walk'.

Lord Haw-Haw's listeners rapidly rose in number to 50 per cent of all Britons. The actual Lord Haw-Haw came to see a book Jonah wrote about this character, Barrington (1939). He was not amused and could not resist calling it a 'cheap five-shilling satire'. He learned over time that his traitorous mischief had only resulted in 'hearty British Laughter'.

Jonah had become rather too famous; but not for something done of intellectual excellence, but in an idle moment of brain relief. Henceforth he was introduced to audiences, of high literature and journalism, for his naming episode. He saw that 'as a curse'.

There is a quite unexpected link here to the Midhurst Rural District. We start with the English music composer and critic, Cyril Carr Dalmaine. who studied at Eastbourne College. By the late 30s, he had become a household name for his composing talent with chamber music, transcribed cantatas of J.S. Bach for the piano, and many other musical achievements, including being a music critic.

A few years before war broke out, he felt the calling to be a journalist. Even as he was being interviewed for a 'journo' post he realised it would not work out well if he worked under his birth name; he was just too well known for his musicology contributions.

He first adopted the pen-name, 'Hector Hamilton'; his editor at the paper was not in agreement. Together they used a list of old diarists, as was the custom for nicknaming, coming up with 'Jonah Barrington' - a late 18th-century judge and memoirist's name.

Jonah was a modest and humble person. Later in his life, he felt that his many contributions had been so diverse and scattered. He told a close friend that:

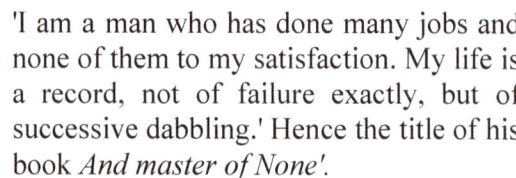

'I am a man who has done many jobs and none of them to my satisfaction. My life is a record, not of failure exactly, but of successive dabbling.' Hence the title of his book *And master of None'*.

Fig. 9.11 Cyril Dalmaine's gravestone in the Midhurst Cemetery - also using his pen-name of Jonah Barrington.

Chapter 9 Glimpses of a then Possible Future

Cyril, aka Jonah, died on 21st September 1986, having the last address of 2 Heatherwood House, Heatherwood, Midhurst - a home that is still there, just out on the Petersfield Road.

He had spent his earlier life in Eastbourne. Just how he came to be buried in plot 1880 was not revealed; but there he is, to be remembered in the Midhurst Cemetery by the Midhurst Common, Fig. 9.11.

Now follow me, looking into what went on in Joyce's formative years. What were his links to the Midhurst area?

9.3 William Joyce's Story

Joyce was born in Brooklyn, New York in 1894 to an Irish Roman Catholic father and an Anglican mother. They returned to Ireland soon after. His political associations led to what he claimed was an assassination attempt on his school-time life. He moved to England, with his parents following soon after.

When 17 years old, in 1924, whilst running a Conservative Party meeting in Battersea, he was razored (a popular weapon of thugs in the 20s) resulting in a dreadful, disfiguring, facial scar. Fig. 9.12. Joyce was convinced that his attackers were 'Jewish communists'. That incident became a massive influence on the rest of his life.

Fig, 9.12 Joyce was easily identified from his facial scar.

In Britain he took up several lines of interest, starting with attempts to join, and stay in, the British Army. He was, however, discharged for lying about his age.

Fascism then interested him; showing his colours in many ways got him much noticed. In 1932 he joined the British Union of Fascists, BUF, then under the leadership of Sir Oswald Mosley. He quickly became a leading and much-praised speaker.

Joyce became much influenced by Hitler's party views but they deviated greatly from those of the BUF. Mosley sacked Joyce in 1937, denouncing him as a traitor. He condemned him for his extreme anti-Semitism.

Along with other British Nazis sympathisers Joyce, in 1937, started the short-lived political party, the Nationalist Socialist League: it floundered when most members were interned.

In 1939, the war was getting very close; he and his wife Margaret fled to Germany where he became a naturalised German in 1940, Fig. 9.13.

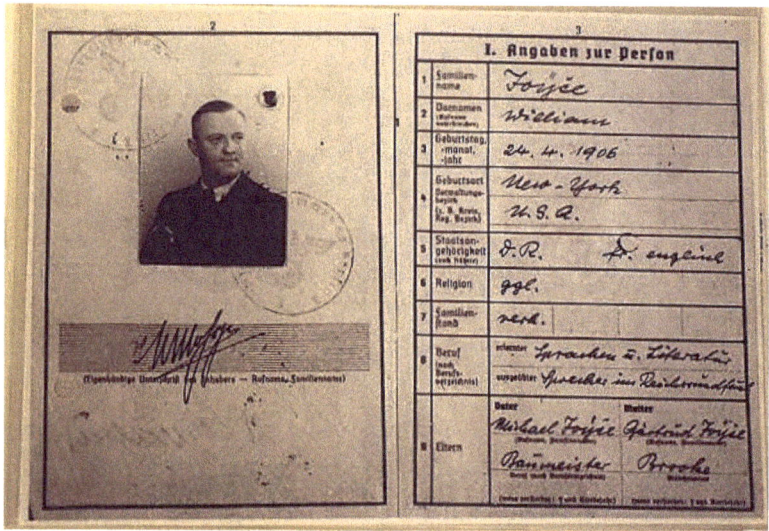

Fig 9.13 Joyce's German ID. (Country Squire)

In an email to me, Paul Baxter the local historian researching the fascists in Sussex stated:

> 'I also heard the story about Joyce fleeing via the Wispers airfield – in my case from a Redford resident when I was trying to find Ethel's house. The fact that Wispers [see Chapter 11.3] was built for the Scrimgeour family I suppose gives the story some credibility, but it no longer belonged to them at the time of Joyce's departure for Germany.'

Chapter 9 Glimpses of a then Possible Future

However, as happens in oral history, this was not how he left Britain. In Joyce's biography, Kenny (2003), it is clearly stated that he left England, boarding the boat train from Victoria station on Saturday morning 26 August 1939 being bound for Berlin, via Ostend. As he made his way from English shores, he lounged on the boat smoking a cigarette: he recorded in his autobiography that:

'We kept our eyes fixed upon the Dover Cliffs until the haze drew over them that impenetrable veil which for us, was the ending of the old life and the beginning of the new. When we could see no more of the land which we had loved and tried to serve, I said to me wife, curtly enough, "Let's go to lunch" and so we did.'

He was in luck; he missed being arrested by just a few days because of the need for the authorities to follow democratic legal processes. The security people had a plan to arrest him on 3 September 1939, but to do so this they first needed the *Special Defence Regulations* to pass into law, and that came too late.

Joyce was a man of great conviction and top oratory skill, but it was wasted by his brutal actions and venomous tongue. He called anyone he wanted to, by the evilest of names and intimations.

His daughter, Francis Beckett, said of him in her most honest biography of him, said:

'My father had a cruel tongue' and 'but the only person he never said a bad word about was William Joyce'.

Joyce was loved by the upper echelons of the Nazi party. At first, he was desperate for a job in Germany but he was soon 'discovered' by former Mosley links from Britain. He soon worked in the German Radio's English Service as that person to be nick-named *Lord Haw-Haw* by Jonah Barrington; see above section. To begin with, Joyce was not named in his broadcasts but he eventually announced his name. In the winter of 1941/2, he gave lectures to SS members on 'English fascism and acute questions on the British Empire'.

His last broadcast was composed as Berlin was falling, being signed off with 'Heil Hitler and farewell.' That was certainly recorded but may not have been broadcast.

He wrote much propaganda literature, including some for distribution to recruit members for the *British Free Corps* set up by Hitler using sympathetic POWs; see a later Memoirs book.

Joyce was the subject of much cartooning, Fig. 9.14. He was

arguably never an Englishman as he was not eligible for a British passport, but he did create a false one. In Ireland, he was able to get an Irish identity, but not a British one.

Fig. 9.14 Cartoon of Lord Haw-Haw. (Disney)

On 28 May 1945, Joyce was captured, Fig. 9.15, he was seen, very much for the worse, collecting firewood. He was challenged by intelligence soldiers, whereupon he was asked, "Was he, Joyce?".

He reached into his pocket for ID papers; the soldiers thought he was armed and shot him through his buttocks, giving

Fig. 9.15 Joyce's freedom ends; no more Lord Haw-Haw hilarious broadcasts!

Chapter 9 Glimpses of a then Possible Future

him four wounds. He was handed in at a border post and taken for trial at the Old Bailey courthouse in London on three counts of high treason:

1. Traitorously adhering to the Enemy, broadcasting propaganda.

2. Being a person owing allegiance to the King of England who did adhere to the King's enemies.

3. As in 1, but for a different period being defined.

He appealed because being in 'possession of a passport did not entitle him to the protection of the Crown'. The appeal failed on 13 December 1945.

Despite never having been granted true British citizenship he was, nevertheless, tried and found guilty of treason against Britain in 1945.

He, at age 39, was the next to last person to be executed in Britain for any offence other than murder. It took place at Wandsworth Prison on 3 January 1946.

He died unrepentantly:

'In death as in life, I defy the Jews who caused this last war, and I defy the power of darkness which they represent. I warn the British people against the crushing imperialism of the Soviet Union. May Britain be great once again and in the hour of the greatest danger in the West may the standard be raised from the dust, crowned with the words – "You have conquered nevertheless". I am proud to die for my ideals and I am sorry for the sons of Britain who have died without knowing why.'

and

'may the Swastika be raised from the dust'.

His remains were, in 1976, finally interred in a Protestant cemetery in Ireland with a Roman Catholic Latin mass being celebrated for him at the time. A detailed biography of him is Kenny (2003).

9.4 Midhurst Connection with Fascism

These Memoirs began to take root as the result of a lecture I gave to the Midhurst Society in 2014, Sydenham (2018). Paul Baxter came up from near Chichester to join the audience. It was held in the Cowdray Hall.

Fig. 9.16 The lecture that started these memoirs.

Afterwards, we spoke of his work exploring the Fascist presence in Sussex in the 1930s. His published newspaper articles, and personal communications, have greatly helped me bring together the following accounts. Sadly, Paul died, too early, around 2016.

This account is based much on his communications, and the three short articles he published in the local Observer newspapers in the period 2013-5. They are reproduced here with the permission of his wife.

[Additional detail, that has come to light since then, has been provided within and following these articles. Pictures have also been added by me to further enhance the imagery.]

Article 1 by Paul Baxter, Observer of 3rd January 2013

Fascism, Lord Haw-Haw and West Sussex

Paul Baxter reveals the notorious broadcaster's local links.

'The 1930s witnessed the rise of a number of groups on the political far-right, the largest being Sir Oswald Mosley's British Union of Fascists (BUF). Skirmishes frequently broke out between Mosley's *Blackshirts* and their left-wing adversaries, notably at Cable Street in 1936, when demonstrators tried to prevent the BUF marching through an area of East London with a large Jewish

Chapter 9 Glimpses of a then Possible Future

population. Mosley and his followers eventually retreated after the Commissioner of Police had banned the march.

An intriguing fact is that Mosley's movement was not confined to large cities like London but drew a strong following in some rural and coastal areas, including West Sussex. It attracted support across a wide spectrum - from disaffected working-class people worried about rising unemployment to right-wing Conservatives who feared the advance of Bolshevism. In its attacks on the City of London and its championing of the farmer and the small businessman, the BUF also tried to appeal to typical voters in small towns and the countryside. West Sussex was fertile ground for its campaigning.

Fig. 9.17 Sir Oswald Mosley inspecting followers at a Sussex summer camp. (The Telegraph)

The county was the location of national *Blackshirt* summer camps, held at West Wittering, Pagham and Selsey. These have been thoroughly documented in J A Booker's *Blackshirts-on-Sea* book. Campers, young and old, were able to take part in sea bathing, dances and in a range of sporting activities to leaven the diet of far-right politics, Fig. 9.17.

Several leading BUF members had other connections with Chichester and places nearby. The best known was William Joyce, who became notorious as 'Lord Haw-Haw' when he moved to Germany just before the start of World War 2 and began broadcasting for the German radio service. Joyce's link with this part of the country seems to date back to when he worked at Warblington House, near Havant, as secretary to the Marquess of Tavistock (the then future 12th Duke of Bedford). My wife's late great aunt, who grew up in Havant and was friendly with the Marchioness of Tavistock, recalled that Joyce taught her to play cricket!

    Joyce's biographers describe a man who presented an unusual combination of brain and brawn. On the one hand, he was a gifted linguist, who obtained a first-class honours degree in English from London University. On the other, despite his small stature, he was a tough street-fighter who bore a scar on his face after a razor attack by what he termed 'Jewish communists'. Joyce joined the BUF in 1933. A virulent anti-Semite, he was, according to contemporary accounts, a mesmerising orator and was soon appointed the movement's Director of Propaganda.

He was a regular speaker in Bognor, Chichester and other West Sussex towns. The Bognor Regis Post (28th April 1934) records a packed gathering in the Chichester Assembly Room. With a Blackshirt stationed either side of him, Joyce spoke for two hours without notes, praising Hitler and Mussolini for raising their people 'from despair to hope.' Later that year he, Mosley and two others were arrested and charged with riotous assembly after fighting broke out in Worthing between BUF supporters and a contingent of anti-fascists. Sent for trial at Lewes Assizes, the BUF men were able to claim victory after their defence counsel argued that there was no case to answer and they were discharged.

    Joyce was also friendly with the Scrimgeours - retired stockbroker Alexander, who lived at Honer Farm, South Mundham and his sister Ethel, whose cottage was at Pigeon Hill

Chapter 9 Glimpses of a then Possible Future

near Midhurst. A frequent visitor to their homes, Joyce apparently loved the wooded Sussex countryside as a contrast to his London base. Perhaps more importantly, the Scrimgeours contributed substantial cash for the BUF coffers.

In 1937, Joyce broke with Mosley and, with a small group who looked to Hitler rather than Mussolini for inspiration, formed the National Socialist League. The rest of his story is well-known. In 1940 many British fascists, including Mosley, were interned as a perceived threat to national security. Joyce avoided this fate as he and his wife, Margaret, had already fled the country.

Joyce's wartime propaganda broadcasts began with the now-notorious words 'Germany calling, Germany calling...' They inspired a mixture of fear and ridicule amongst his listeners. As the war progressed there was increasing ridicule and less fear but calls for retribution were inevitable when, in 1945, he and Margaret were captured by British soldiers near the German-Danish border. Despite doubts about his nationality and the legality of a treason charge, Joyce was damned by having (wrongfully) obtained a British passport in 1933 (he was a US citizen by birth). Found guilty and after the rejection of two appeals, he was hanged on 3rd January 1946.

Even in his final days, when he had become a national pariah, Joyce had some reason to be grateful for his past connections with Chichester and its environs. After the death sentence was pronounced, one of several pleas for clemency from prominent people was sent by his former employer the Duke of Bedford. Another long-standing ally, Ethel Scrimgeour, visited him in prison and attended each day of his appeal hearing by the House of Lords.

As well as the connections documented above, I came across one other possible Joyce link with the area. The late Michael Alford's book *The Paradise Rocks* states that Joyce was a 'one-time resident of the [Aldwick] Bay Estate'. I was not able to confirm this.

I would like to thank Ralph Cousins, Len Ruffell, the staff of Hampshire and West Sussex Libraries and the Archivist of the Bedford Estates for their help with research for this article.'

Midhurst WW2 Memoirs: 2. 'Evil' Rising: 'Good' Awakening

Article 2 by Paul Baxter, Observer of 10th January 2013

The Blackshirts of West Sussex

Paul Baxter uncovers more about the county's pre-war fascists.

'Hurrah for the Blackshirts!' ran a headline in the Daily Mail in January 1934. A few months later, Lord Rothermere, the newspaper's owner, withdrew his support from Sir Oswald Mosley's movement, alarmed by the violent scenes at some of its meetings, notably during a rally at London's Olympia. However, the quotation reminds us that, particularly in its early days, Mosley's British Union of Fascists (BUF) enjoyed a degree of political respectability. Indeed, Rothermere's change of heart may have been partly due to pressure from major Jewish-owned firms threatening to withdraw advertising from the paper.

The headline must have drawn an approving nod or two in West Sussex. As I noted in the previous article, William Joyce, the future 'Lord Haw-Haw', was one of several leading fascists to address well-attended meetings in the county. Nor were these gatherings always marred by the brutal treatment of hecklers which gave the movement a bad name elsewhere.

Violent incidents were not unknown on the south coast. The previous article referred to the arrest and subsequent acquittal of Mosley, Joyce and two others following fighting in Worthing in October 1934. However, it appears that some anti-fascists on that occasion had descended on the town, seeking a confrontation. In doing so they brought a glimpse of the kind of street fights often seen in London between far left and far right. Generally, local opposition seems to have been more muted and many events passed off peacefully. The Bognor Regis Post (20th July 1935) reported that a 'large and orderly crowd' had attended the Bognor Theatre Royal to hear Mosley himself speak.

Although these meetings no doubt drew the curious as well as the committed, the movement had a strong local base, including branches in Chichester, Bognor Regis, Worthing and Littlehampton. In Worthing, there was even a rare electoral success

Chapter 9 Glimpses of a then Possible Future

with the return of Charles Bentinck Budd, for both Worthing Town Council and the County Council. In those days, most local councillors stood as independents but Budd's fascist sympathies must have been well-known. He, Fig. 9.18, came from a wealthy family.

Fig. 9.18 Charles Bentinck Budd c1930.

Charles Budd was severely brain-damaged when fighting in WW1. He was described, according to many people, by his biographer Michael Payne, as being:

"dislikeable, vain, excitable, prone to wild talk, unstable and with a mental outlook bordering on the pathological. All agreed, however, that his military bearing, coupled with his general appearance - he stood at six feet, with dark brown hair and moustache, and piercing blue eyes - belied his psychological problems and endowed him with charismatic force."

Not everyone was enamoured. *Worthing under Attack*, Chris Hare's excellent account of the town in the '30s and '40s, documents how the Worthing Journal mocked the men and women of the far right. For instance, it ridiculed the BUF's lightning symbol (the equivalent of the Nazis' swastika) as a 'magic circle' and a 'childish device'. Some BUF luminaries were easy targets for mockery. Sir Archibald Hamilton, who lived at Selsey, was in the habit of marching around accompanied by an escort of bagpipers.

Some opponents hinted at the darker side of fascism. In the Bognor Regis Post (7th July 1934) a letter signed by 'Centurion' complained of fascist paper-sellers in Chichester. Centurion considered them to be 'a blot upon the landscape', objecting particularly to their wearing military medal ribbons on their

Blackshirt uniforms. Hinting at the real or imagined threat of violence, he added that he was not signing his real name 'lest I might be "Hitlerized" in my bed!'

The roll-call of leading West Sussex fascists included some nationally important figures in the movement. Near the top of the list was Norah Elam, who lived at Northchapel and was County Women's Organiser. She travelled an unusual route from militant suffragette to fascist, serving time in Holloway Prison as one of Mrs Pankhurst's lieutenants and later as a Mosleyite. Also highly ranked was Jorian Jenks, Fig. 9.19, the BUF's adviser on agriculture, who was a farmer at Angmering and an early advocate of organic cultivation.

Fig. 9.19 Jorian Jenks 1938 booklet. Food imports were undermining home agriculture.

Although opponents accused the BUF of anti-Semitism and thuggery, the crucial issue after the outbreak of war was that of loyalty to Britain. BUF members considered themselves to be patriots and it has to be acknowledged that some joined the armed forces and fought against Nazism.

However, the movement's admiration for European fascist leaders inevitably attracted the attention of MI5. In 1940 the authorities across the country controversially rounded up about 800 fascists, including Elam, Jenks and Budd. A revealing statistic is that more detainees came from West Sussex than from any other county.'

The link between Midhurst and Joyce has been further researched by Paul Baxter in a third article.

Chapter 9 Glimpses of a then Possible Future

Article 3 by Paul Baxter, Observer of 23rd June 2013

Ethel Scrimgeour: A friend to Midhurst's sick children and to 'Lord Haw-Haw'

'To discover that a fascist sympathiser spent much of her life caring for sick children at her home may surprise modern readers. Still more shocking is to learn she was the confidante of a notorious traitor. But before the second world war, fascism was a more 'respectable' creed than it is today, and in all ages, personal loyalties may transcend political or national ones.

Researching a previous article [that given above] on the West Sussex connections of William Joyce, the future 'Lord Haw-Haw', I found references to his friends Ethel Scrimgeour and her brother Alexander. Joyce regularly visited Ethel's home at Pigeon Hill, Redford, near Midhurst, and Alexander's at Honer Farm, South Mundham. His friendship with the Scrimgeours even aroused jealousy in some fellow members of the British Union of Fascists, who suggested (almost certainly falsely) he was not handing over all the money which Alexander and Ethel had donated to the movement.

Alexander Scrimgeour died in 1937, but Ethel's friendship with Joyce and his second wife Margaret survived all the later events – the Joyce's' escape to Germany, their propaganda broadcasts to wartime Britain and William's trial and imprisonment, culminating in his execution.

Just before they left for Berlin in 1939, Margaret took some belongings to Miss Scrimgeour's home, including William's pistol, which she buried under a tree close to the house. One of the couple's first acts on reaching the German capital was to send Ethel a postcard confirming their safe arrival. When Special Branch officers called on her looking for Joyce, they were too late.

After the war, Ethel travelled up to London every day to attend Joyce's appeal hearing by the House of Lords. Rebecca West, Fig. 9.20, describes her vividly in the book *The Meaning of Treason* – 'a tall and handsome maiden lady... whose appearance was made remarkable by an immense knot of hair twisted on the nape of her neck in a mid-Victorian way'.

Fig. 9.20 Dame Rebecca West DBE b.1892: d.1983. (Madame Yevonde)

Age had turned Ethel into 'an apocalyptic figure... bowed', her hair 'shining snow-white'. She appears to have been a kind of second mother to Joyce, who wrote some of his last letters to her. He thanked Ethel for her friendship which, with that of her late brother, 'did so much to contribute to my happiness during my stay on earth'.

Joyce's biographers touch on another side of this Miss Scrimgeour's life. A trained nurse, she cared for children with tuberculosis and other illnesses at her home, running a kind of small-scale sanatorium.

Some of the children were orphans from London. In our modern age of vaccinations and effective drugs, it is easy to forget the scourge that TB once was. In the early 1930s, it accounted for almost half of UK deaths for people between the ages of 25 and 35. TB affected all classes but was particularly prevalent where there were poverty and overcrowding. With no drug treatment possible, the medical profession's main response was to remove sufferers to special hospitals – sanatoria – where there was a regime of fresh air, graduated exercise and a healthy diet.

The King Edward VII Sanatorium, Midhurst was close to Miss Scrimgeour's home and opened in 1906, soon after she started her

Chapter 9 Glimpses of a then Possible Future

work at Pigeon Hill.

I have not been able to establish any direct connection. The nearness may have been a coincidence, except in the sense that sanatoria tended to be in isolated south-facing locations so that patients received as much sunshine and fresh air as possible.

Ethel was born in 1865, the daughter of Alexander Scrimgeour, a London stockbroker. The Scrimgeours made West Sussex their rural base and an outlet for their wealth. Ethel's father had the large house 'Wispers' built near Stedham in the 1870s (now St Cuthman's; it has lately become the focus of a row about a proposed new school for London children). John, another of Ethel's brothers, acquired Stedham Hall in 1910 and he and his wife Jessie were notably generous to the village.

For this family, financial security was no excuse for idleness. The Scrimgeours also bred some strong, independent women.

Elizabeth, one of Ethel's sisters, reared horses and owned a riding school at Selsey. 'Good works' are a recurring theme there also: other Scrimgeour ladies ran an orphanage, at Myrtle Cottage, Stedham and a school at Elsted. [Fig. 9.21. During the war the local fire engine was kept in its garage.]

Fig. 9.21 Myrtle Cottage, on the left, was an orphanage run by a member of the Scrimgeour family. (Gravel Roots)

Nursing was another option for women from privileged backgrounds wanting to do something worthwhile. By the late 19th century, reforms by Florence Nightingale and others had transformed the profession – it no longer recruited only from the humbler ranks of society.

Ethel trained at St Bartholomew's Hospital, London where she came top in the examination results in 1897 and won the gold medal funded by the Clothworker's livery company. Glowing reports on her progress from ward sisters during her training describe her as 'punctual... most kind and attentive... always obedient... clean and neat... tactful and capable...devoted to the children'.

The 1911 census lists 14 'invalids' (nine girls and five boys), resident at Pigeon Hill, ranging in age from 5 to 17. All were from London or the home counties, although, perhaps confirming their orphan status, some have question marks against their birthplaces. Patients would sometimes find work as cooks or other helpers at the home after treatment.

Interviewed in about 2008 at the age of 94, Midhurst resident Marjorie Bishop recalled being treated at 'Scrimmages' for tuberculosis of the bones. At Pigeon Hill, there was fresh air, good food and, less appealingly, cod liver oil. Mrs Bishop lost a finger from the illness but otherwise recovered her health, as her longevity indicates.

Ethel's work with sick and crippled children at Redford lasted for nearly 50 years. She died in Midhurst Cottage Hospital in 1953 at the age of 87. Curiously for someone who believed diet was important in treating illness, her death certificate shows that scurvy (due to Vitamin C deficiency) contributed to her demise.

An interesting footnote is that in the next generation, another Scrimgeour descendant also devoted her life to the care of sick children. Ethel's niece, Isabella Forshall, carried out pioneering work as a paediatric surgeon at Royal Liverpool and Alder Hey Children's Hospitals.

Chapter 9 Glimpses of a then Possible Future

Acknowledgements: Archives staff of St Bartholomew's Hospital; Christine Dicks and Sanchia Elsdon, authors (with Colin Dunne) of *Stedham and Iping Remembered;* Phil Dixon of www.gravelroots.net'

Additionally, to Paul Baxter's contribution, I follow on about those fascists. The BU was strong and determined to win over the people of Britain. Blackshirt's vans would visit the towns and cities to give public meetings and hand out literature. Fig. 9.22 is the publicity for a proposed road-show itinerary from their *Action* newspaper of 10 September 1936.

Fig. 9.22 Great British Union Countryside Campaign, September 1936. (BU Newspaper *Action*)

FASCISM AND FARMING
Great British Union Countryside Campaign

Page Six—September 10, 1936

The British Union commence a concentrated campaign in the rural areas on Saturday, September 12. Posters explaining Sir Oswald Mosley's agricultural policy are being exhibited in all parts, advertising space has been taken in farmers' papers, and a number of vans, equipped with literature and experienced Blackshirt speakers, are touring the country. Here is a list of the towns to be visited in the near future and the date on which the visits may be expected. Readers of *Action* living in these vicinities should look out for the Blackshirt van.

IN THE SOUTH

Sept.	Sept.	Sept.
12—SWAFFHAM HEREFORD ANDOVER	CHICHESTER 21—NEWMARKET SOUTH MOLTON HASLEMERE	28—MARKET HARBOROUGH BLANDFORD FAVERSHAM
14—EAST DEREHAM GLOUCESTER BASINGSTOKE	22—SUDBURY TIVERTON GODALMING	29—LOUGHBOROUGH SALISBURY CHISLEHURST
15—KING'S LYNN STROUD ALTON	23—SAFFRON WALDEN TAVISTOCK EAST GRINSTEAD	30—MELTON MOWBRAY DEVIZES MAIDSTONE
16—WISBECH CHIPPENHAM WINCHESTER	24—BRAINTREE NEWTON ABBOT HORSMONDEN	Oct. 1—PETERBOROUGH MELKSHAM BATTLE
17—WYMONDHAM BATH PETERSFIELD	25—MALDON HONITON TONBRIDGE	2—DOWNHAM MARKET HUNGERFORD HAYWARDS HEATH
18—THETFORD YEOVIL MIDHURST	26—BIGGLESWADE DORCHESTER ASHFORD	
19—BURY ST. EDMUNDS CREWKERNE		

IN THE NORTH

There they were scheduled to visit Petersfield on 17 September, Midhurst on 18 September, Chichester on 19 September and Haslemere on the 21 September. Whether it took place is yet to be determined. One thing was to be sure of happening if it did take place; most fascist events

277

degenerated into physical violence, Hare (2011). This source has considerable material on the Sussex fascists and what the local people felt, as reported by newspapers.

To end this chapter on the Fascists in Sussex I just have to include comment on the Midhurst Community plays of Bob Ratcliffe; one of those plays dealt with this topic.

Around 1991, the date could not be verified, Bob authored and directed a Midhurst Community Play, *Sweet Bessy*, based on the visit of Queen Elizabeth 1 to Midhurst. The only physical record that appears to exist of that event is the programme booklet, Ratcliffe (1991). I contacted Bob for a score but he confirmed that none was ever printed so I am unable to report on its detail; only cryptic scene names exist.

This must have been a magnificent event for it had a cast of over 70 townsfolk actors, many who had never acted before. It took weeks to prepare using the good services of dozens of townsfolk, businesses and government departments. If only it had been videoed for us to enjoy today! It took some time to establish the reason for this play; the anniversary of the formal visit to Cowdray by Queen Elizabeth II in 1591.

Bob Radcliffe went on to write and produce another Community Play around 1995, *A Patriotic Duty*, Radcliffe (1995). This time it was about aspects of the Midhurst District during WW2 and especially the fascists. It seems he got his inspiration for part of that play's theme from the time that he had lived in the isolated cottage where William Joyce, "Lord Haw-Haw" visited, that is, at Pigeon Hill.

For this play, Bob carried out a serious research study into the lives of many of the people discussed in this chapter - the Scrimgeours, Johan Barrington, William Joyce, and the local fascist movement. He also covered the *Kindertransport* children, all of those being at the time when "Caps of all nations were piled on the tables of the Spread Eagle".

Again, there is only a programme booklet available for us to see today; it also is not dated anywhere; here one can surmise it was in 1995, that being the 50th anniversary of the end of WW2. It seems to have been presented to the public in late September.

The booklet does, however, state that a word processor was used

Chapter 9 Glimpses of a then Possible Future

suggesting that copies of play scripts were issued. By that date, the use of Microsoft *Word* was in common use so there might just be a digital computer file of it somewhere on a mini or floppy disk?

There were, again, a huge cast of actors and helpers involved. Despite me now knowing numerous Midhurst District residents of today, I do not recognise a single name that is mentioned in those two lists. For this reason, I have been unable to delve deeper into this study carried out Bob Radcliffe.

[If any reader of these memoirs can improve the knowledge of these plays do please contact the author. The books are to be updated over time.]

At the start of the 1930s-decade, interest in fascist politics was becoming strong in many countries, especially where the effects on the economy and people's lives had been impacted in very negative ways, by the trials of WW1 and the Great Depression.

By wartime, however, those same people were coming to understand that whilst fascist policies seemed to be beneficial on the surface, they always led to dire circumstances in lifestyle. Fig. 9.23 sums it all up. It shows a skeleton removing a mask, behind which alludes to the eventual fall of the Nazi regime.

Fig. 9.23 1942 US poster. 'The world now knows that Fascists have nothing to offer the youth but death' Franklin D. Roosevelt.

Midhurst WW2 Memoirs: 2. 'Evil' Rising: 'Good' Awakening

With the presence in Sussex of the fascists as war developed now covered, we can move on to look into how the people of the Midhurst District were coping as war drew nearer.

Chapter 10 Midhurst Life with War Imminent

10.1 The 30s -Time of Changes for the Worst

When WW1 ended in 1918 it might be thought the general public would be ecstatic with joy at the end of so much needless and unconscionable killing and destruction of badly needed assets. That mood did not last long!

Almost all families, organisations, grand estates, shops, civil service groups and so on, had lost not one, but many members. They were mainly menfolk who died or were injured for life. Many women died in war service, but they have been somewhat overlooked in war records unless they made an impressionable contribution that led to a lasting place in history. Of course, with much fewer women than men in service, they are less seen in memorials to those who gave their lives. For example, at RAF Kidbrooke one service woman died in the V1 flying bomb attack that nearly took my own father's life.

The net result was great loss of manpower to maintain farms, to staff factories and civil services, and to generally hold the society together as they did before that war. On the home front, it was now up the women to carry things on in the family, and often the farm.

That issue alone would have been enough to depress society for so many people had pictures on display at home, or names on the local market square memorial, to remind them of their lost loved ones.

The Midhurst town WW1 memorial, Fig. 10.1, was dedicated on 6 May 1923 by Major the Hon. Harold Pearson. The memorial had added later, to the names of the 71 people who had served in WW1, names of 11 local servicemen who died in WW2. Many more would have been celebrated in individual village memorials of the District.

Nations were settling down in recovery mode with some, however, adopting radically different political systems that were bearing fruit at the start of that decade. There were, however, other issues that added to the sharp upturn in gloom for people of Britain over the 1930s decade

First, immediately came the Spanish flu, [Book 1, Chapter 11]. It killed even greater numbers of people than died in the First World War.

Then there occurred the 1929 US Wall Street stock market crash with its economic flow-on to other allied countries. British people were not as affected by it, as were those in the US. Britain had far fewer investments in that market.

Fig. 10.1 Midhurst Town's WW1 memorial erected in 1923.
Looking South side.

Fig. 10.1 Looking North side.

Chapter 10 Midhurst Life with War Imminent

As there existed no massive economic boom in Britain there was no major bust. The downturn in Britain was more a matter of which currency was being used as it's standard. Britain had abandoned its idea of getting back to using the Pound Sterling as its base and left it to use the gold standard linked to the US Dollar.

That meant exports were falling in Britain causing wages to rise, that giving relief because of the higher consumption that came with it. On the surface it looked good; but there still existed high unemployment; around 3 million. That situation had been in existence since the end of WW1. The value of the huge British coal and steel market had plummeted!

Many British families, Fig. 10.2, were in dire need of enough food:

'Annie Weaver, a 37-year-old mother of 7, collapsed and died while bathing her six-month-old twins. She was unable to support the family of 9 on her husband's unemployment benefit of 48 shillings per week (£2.40).' Daily Mail, 2010 report.

Fig.10.2 1930s. One very poor family trying to cope with unemployment in South Wales. (Daily Mail)

The government was not that sympathetic! One large group of barely employed men undertook a protest march for higher benefits. They thought that might work; instead, they were docked some benefit for not being available to work! Soup kitchens were well visited, Fig. 10.3.

Fig. 10.3. Soup kitchens existed in Britain. (Science Museum)

In the US the crash led to the highest unemployment levels seen that century - some 14 million men were out of work there. With no paid work, they needed charity to keep alive.

This situation lasted for many of the 1930s years, only improving as the nation started to ramp up its war expenditure from around 1936.

Against that depressing background arose numerous wars between, and within, foreign nations:

Columbia - Peru 1932-33
Bolivia - Paraguay 1932-35
Saudi Arabia - Yemen 1934
Italy – Abyssinian 1935
China-Japan 1937-45
WW2 - 1939-45
Chinese Civil war 1927-49
Spanish Civil war 1936-1939
Italian Mafia - US Mafia 1930-31 (Castellammarese war)

This 'mother of all national failures' brought to the fore the need for major changes to the implemented national political systems. The main methodologies for a national rule in use were Democracy, Communism, Fascism, and many forms authoritarian Dictatorship.

Almost gone from those countries that had had colonies for centuries, was the concept of colonisation as a way to obtain wealth by

Chapter 10 Midhurst Life with War Imminent

taking it from others. It was, however, at that time resurrected by Italy, Japan and Germany in the 30s, each recreating their national systems on the concept of building glorious empires; see earlier chapters.

Political dogma set up by authoritarian rule was usually crudely implemented, and done with lack of planning and prediction of outcomes based on rigorous thinking; these often led to national disasters. Mathematical modelling of the likely effect of changes at a national scale was still in its infancy then. For example, the Russian people suffered greatly from agricultural collectivisation imposed upon them over the 1928-40 period. Starvation killed millions!

Those countries with colonies, formed before the 19th century, began to see their control of those countries slip away. A major loser was the British Empire, in which India was its greatest possession - and income generator. Canada's formalised allegiance to the British Empire was reduced considerably.

The idea of possessing colonies had run its course for the older colonist nations. The colonial peoples wanted independence and payback from its occupier. They were resisting occupier rule, using both violence and political methods of protest.

Assassinations were rife: French President Paul Doumer in 1932: Englebert Dollfuss, Chancellor of Austria, in 1934 by the Nazis: US Presidential candidate Huey Long in 1935: Alexander 1 of Yugoslavia in 1934: and the numerous unsuccessful attempts on Hitler's life before 1939.

Dollfuss was Federal Chancellor of Austria in 1932. He manoeuvred his position becoming a Dictator. In a crisis he shut down parliament, and banned the Austrian Nazi Party, imposing *austrofascism* in 1934 to suppress the socialists. Ten Austrian Nazi agents assassinated him in that year.

To gain a deeper feeling of what it was like under 1930 Nazi rule in Germany do view the film *13 Minutes,* made in 2015 with some screenwriter's licence about the private life of Georg Elser. Georg was a young, timid German man living in a small village in rural Germany.

In 1939 he attempted to assassinate many senior leaders of the Nazi Party, who were all attending an indoor meeting of the faithful in

Munich. He missed killing any Nazis by 13 just minutes! They had left when his self-designed and self-made, ingenious time-delay bomb exploded just a little late.

His journey from a carefree sensitive lad, to the point where he felt compelled to try and stop the Nazis, is told from the time when he began to impacted by the arrival of Nazis in his village.

He was not successful in his attempt to 'decapitate the Nazi Party' but he did come the closest of such attempts at that goal. One can't help wondering what the world would have been like if he had managed to kill Hitler. Would another similar person step up to carry on the work of the German Wehrmacht and still try to conquer Europe, Russia and Britain?

I will leave it up to you to learn his remarkable story; one of a single man fervently doing it all alone to try to stop the Nazis rampage across humanity. The factual story has also been published, Ferry (2016).

For the middle classes, the standard of living was rising over the 30s. They were beginning, again, to have fun in their leisure times. These people were enjoying the rising standards of a good life, Fig.10.4. This postcard is marked 'Mrs Elliott, The Crown Inn, Edinburgh, Midhurst, Sussex 1924.'

Fig.10.4 Postcard marked 'Mrs Elliot, Crown Hotel, Edinburgh Square.'

This, however, came more slowly for the rural community for they lived in houses that were rented or tied

Chapter 10 Midhurst Life with War Imminent

to their job. Landlords were quick to improve their own housing but were less speedy to spend out on their rented properties.

'Friday night was bath night in the Stringer household. Fires were stoked to heat water for the big tin bath in the wash house in the garden and the children took their turns running back and forth from the house. It was not until the late 30's that the Estate started to 'modernise' the cottages and install hot water, indoor bathrooms and toilets.'
John Stringer, Litchfield (2011)

'[In 1940] a Cowdray cottage in Heyshott was requisitioned for them. Elsie said it was quite a shock coming to the country. Their flat in London had running water, gas and electricity, and an indoor loo. Their cottage had none of these luxuries. But it did have a nice big garden. There was a great big black cooking stove in the kitchen that did not cook properly, so they complained to the Cowdray estate office. Two men called round, and Elsie's mum, not being one to mince her words, declared, "I shouldn't think Lord Cowdray would have such a stove in his kitchen." Little did her mum know at the time that the two men from the estate were none other than Lord Cowdray himself and his agent. Shortly thereafter, they were given a new cooker.'
Elsie Pack, Litchfield (2011)

The 30s also experienced the possibly greatest changes yet seen to that time, in the use of advancing technologies of communications, motor vehicles, ships, aircraft, factories and agricultural methods. Things could be done easier, faster, cheaper and better than before.

Women had entered the workforce during WW1 and that factor gave them more confidence to press for their rights. In Britain, they first got limited voting rights in 1918, but it took until 1928 to obtain the same terms as men had at the ballot box.

Britain, however, was having to pay back the huge loans given to it to fund its participation in WW1; this being at a time when its massive Empire incomes were diminishing.

There were many natural and man-made disasters of epic dimension during the 1930s:

1935 US Labour Day hurricane killed 408 people with massive destruction of assets.
1930-36 US Dust Bowl was caused by major agricultural damage practices and extreme drought. It coined the name *Dirty Thirties*.
1937 German Hindenburg airship, Fig.10.5, exploded in the air in New Jersey, the US killing 36, including VIPs.
1938 New England hurricane killed some 800 people and destroyed over 57,000 homes.
1938 500,000 lives lost when the Yellow River region in China was inundated for over 21,000 sq miles (54,000 sq km.)

Fig 10.5 Hindenburg's last trip ended in disaster in May 1937.

And on top of those, there were numerous earthquakes, volcanic eruptions, floods, heat and cold waves, tornadoes, hurricanes, typhoons,

Chapter 10 Midhurst Life with War Imminent

tsunamis, fogs, wildfires, and even a rare meteorite impact in Curuçá River, South America that left a 1km diameter crater. Geomagnetic storms set off alarms and disrupted radio services.

During the 30s international communications improved greatly. They became faster, cheaper, more available and of better quality as the art and craft of electronics were developed in the service of men and women. The 30s was a bad decade to live through. But it was to get worse. Some were simply philosophic about the situation, Fig. 10.6.

Fig.10.6 Girls out for lunch in a London park.
Green (1989)

In architecture, the tall skyscrapers of that era in the US would have been hard to imagine: the famous Empire State building was built in 1931.

There had not been built such a density of tall buildings as then came to New York. The Golden Gate Bridge was built in 1937. It was a time when everything the US did was larger than large!

In Britain, there was less to show off in the gigantic size class, but progress was still made with such things as Whittle's jet engine (in 1930), Baird's TV (in 1926), the economic theory of Keynes (in 1936), and TV broadcasts (in 1936).

It was not all bad; good achievements gave confidence to leaders in society to take bigger and bolder risks in developments for civilian betterment of life. But that human skill also was applied to the worse; in the execution of massive war-making and human oppression.

Music and film entertainment were cheap ways to have fun and feel inwardly good. They allowed people to stop thinking about the depressing issues.

New music styles that came were Swing style, Delta Blues and Gypsy jazz. Black men were gaining acceptance for their forms of music. The electric guitar was invented.

As the decade progressed, all of the world 'news' would appear to have continuously become more depressing, finally reaching a dark place as the crescendo of major war arrived again.

To those with wealth, the situation was also very worrying. Their concerns were not about getting food on the table, but on whether their centuries-long lifestyle would remain for much longer.

This time one extra fear, barely experienced on British soil during WW1, was added; that Britain could be bombed with explosives and poison gas at an annihilation level not seen before; and for which there seemed to be little chance of stopping it happening.

Invasion of Britain might also happen, something that had not been successful before since 1066!

10.2 The Rich Play On

Whilst many people were driven into dire poverty when the Great Depression spread its wings over Britain from the 1930s, much of the upper classes retained their wealth and were able to cling onto their too often lavish, self-centred and selfish, lifestyle habits. They did not see their practices as decadent. After all, it was their choice of how they used their wealth. Such matters have been explored, see James (2009) and McKibbin (2000).

Many of the ruling class were large estate owners enjoying a stable, good life. They were led to think Hitler might not occupy Britain, but allow them to carry on in the manner to which they were accustomed. It was from the titled class that the House of Lords membership was drawn.

It was an automatic birthright.

Fig. 10.7 shows them in session in the former House, rebuilt as we see it today over 1840 to 1870, following a fire in 1834. Also, Women, through inheritance of their father's life title, were allowed membership in 1958. More categories followed in 1963.

Fig. 10.7 House of Lords sitting c1810.

Chapter 10 Midhurst Life with War Imminent

Change in the status of title is seen by the view, Fig.10.7, where it was no longer an automatic right to sit, but only to be eligible for selection for membership of the Lords.

Fig. 10.8 Today, membership of the House of Lords is more democratic.

That came about in 1997 when Tony Blair got the first stage of his campaign in place; he was after the banishment of life peerage, but did not get all then. By 1999 membership the House of Lords became a competitive appointment process, Fig. 10.8. Today, most sessions are in plain day attire; robes being used on special occasions, like the opening of Parliament.

Many, centuries-old, aristocratic traditions, such as inherited titles and honours, were still retained within Britain by the end of the 1930s. However, in most of the one-time British Commonwealth colonies these, British style life honours for service, are not seen as appropriate anymore for them to align with. There, instead, individuals can be awarded an honour and title for life only. Universities still award life honours with titles but they are hard won with higher degrees, being titles of proven attainment.

Titles by birthright have much reduced standing today, and they certainly do not automatically imply a high level of private wealth and useful influence. The capitalist world respects people who can create or use wealth, more than them having a title.

Since the mid-19th century, the lot of titled persons has changed from being aloof and superior to the common man, into such ways as now needing to host commoners as paying guests to dinner and overnight stays in their magnificent mansions – to get first-hand experiences of how the past once was.

Long-standing privileges, practices and entitlements were sliding away fast once WW1 came. By 1939 they were again reduced in relevance still further, for they did not compare in importance with the matters of life or death that needed to be faced up to, and lived with.

Some past practices have been retained for they provide what the middle classes like to see occur.

Fox hunt participants still assemble on Boxing Day to enjoy, first, that glass of mulled wine before heading off to the sound of the hunting horn. This custom has endured today, but mostly now without a fox to hunt down.

The spectacle is as great to see, as it would to be part of. The event always makes local news. Fig. 10.9 shows an aspect of the spectacle for the now combined Chiddingfold, Leconfield and Cowdray Hunt in 2012. The Hunt may have once been about catching a fox, but the spectacle itself of horses, riders and hounds carrying out the range of things they can do, will always captivate the general public:

Fig. 10.9 The local Hunt and Hounds in action. (CLC)

'Dozens of people turned out on [2015] New Year's Day to support the

Chapter 10 Midhurst Life with War Imminent

Chiddingfold, Leconfield and Cowdray (CLC), Hunt. Some 45 mounted followers met in the car park of the Spread Eagle Hotel in Midhurst. This was significantly more than last year due to the improved weather. Last year it was torrential.

As with Boxing Day, the hunt was well supported by foot followers of all ages. People enjoyed being able to get up close to the hounds and wandered among the mounted followers. The followers enjoyed mulled wine and sausage rolls kindly supplied by our hosts.

After the field master called for hounds, the field made their way to Ambersham/Heyshott Common. The Huntsman blew for home at 3 pm with all followers having enjoyed their day. The Chiddingfold, Leconfield and Cowdray's huntsman is known as 'Sage'. He is supported by the first whip and four amateur whips. The responsibility for managing the hunt lies with the Mastership, made up of four riders.

The New Year's Day meet follows on from a successful Christmas turn-out when the hunt had 88 mounted for its Boxing Day meet, and 77 at Coombelands on Christmas Eve. The CLC Hunt will again hold its 'pub of the month' meeting in The Cricketer's at Wisborough Green that being followed by a Burns supper at Petworth House.'

Condensed from the Midhurst Observer, January 2015

Hunts still have a following but retaining them in all their former level of effort has diminished as a result of the social changes that became very obvious by wartime. The cost of keeping hounds, horses, clothing, pastures, etc. has become a luxury not everyone wants to keep up.

After the Hunt season, there would invariably be held a grand ball in the estate's grand mansion. This was a lavish affair, that then being by invitation only. Clothing styles were usually dictated by the best French fashion. Mounted members of the Hunt were invited to attend in their long-tailed scarlet coats.

'Hunt balls were traditionally held in the grandest houses around, but nowadays that is incredibly rare. Mostly, guests are bidden to

> a marquee in the middle of nowhere, so that the party can go on into the wee hours while limiting the risk of causing offence or damage. If you enter a private house, you are at a SERIOUSLY smart party'

It might have to hand:

> 'chillout rooms, hairdressers stationed by the loos to resurrect flagging hairstyles… Some balls even have make-up artists on site to redo any make-up that was hastily applied in the car en route to the party'
>
> From *Rules for Attending a Hunt Ball.* Netia Walker, Tatler 3 November 2017.

The war years changed much of that; today Hunt to make ends meet Ball tickets are often sold to whoever wants them. Auctions are used to raise cash to assist the upkeep of the hounds. But not all are in that situation; some still have as many as 850 guests for the sit-down dinner.

Cowdray made its international presence in this high life of luxury by becoming a world centre for polo events, and as the 'home of British polo'.

Harold Pearson, the son of the first Viscount Cowdray, had formed the local club in 1910. Two polo grounds were laid out in the Cowdray estate. It was first called the Cowdray Park Polo Club, later named the Cowdray Park club.

Players, stable hands and horses would come from America and India to do combat with the local teams, Russell-Stoneham and Chatterton-Newman (1992). In the 1930s as many as 5000 spectators attended these events in the Park. There were held social events and tea parties. However, it had to come to an end when war arrived:

> 'Polo came to an abrupt halt at the start of World War II. The majority of players were called up and ponies were put out to grass. The grounds at Hurlingham and Roehampton were ploughed up to assist the war effort to grow home-produced food.

Chapter 10 Midhurst Life with War Imminent

Cowdray Parks polo pitches were used for agriculture and the House was used by the Royal Army Service Corps'.
www.sussexlife.co.uk

The age-old spectacle at Cowdray was restarted after the war, but it took considerable effort to restore the grounds, raise teams, breed up horses and transport them there from all over the world for events.

Archery was another social sport carried on by the guests to Cowdray, often done in their best finery.

It revived the military skill from earlier times. In 1591 Queen Elizabeth I visited Cowdray for a week. She is said to have hunted in the park. The so-called, '500-year-old' oak tree in the park was a spot where she reputedly rested her bow. It is also recorded that she stood on a stand by an enclosure in which 30 deer were herded. From there she killed four with a crossbow.

She was serenaded by singers in the park as this took place! In the evening she witnessed sixteen bucks being killed by greyhounds! – see Roundell (1884), Guy (2003) and Neve (2011).

Archery was an often-seen event at Cowdray gatherings in the late 1920s and early 30s, Fig. 10.10.

Fig. 10.10 Archery underway for guests to Cowdray.

It was taken seriously by sportsmen and women of that time. Christopher Campling, Dean Emeritus of Ripon Cathedral, recalls in his memoirs, Campling (2005), visiting Cowdray for archery competitions in the late 1930s. As a young schoolboy, he competed in an adult archery club with a member, Mrs Petronella De Wharton Burr, who later twice became the *Archery International* winner.

Today Michael Chevis, Midhurst's photographer and a trained archery instructor, is reviving interest in archery with his *Leaping Hart Archery* club that holds courses for all ages in local woods, fields and indoor places.

Life in a country seat was not complete enough for many; it was quite isolated from the madding socialite scene if you resided in a country house away from the London set. Guests could be invited home to gain more connection with the aristocracy and the gentrified society but to really be part of that scene one needed opulent presence amid the high society of the annual *London Season*.

It took place from May to July. If you did not own your own house in a suitable location in London you would rent one for the season in London's Mayfair and Belgravia.

> 'This tradition began centuries before for many reasons - being 'up' for parliamentary duties originally, but later for attendance at horse racing, gala balls, debutante's coming outs, finding a wife or a husband, or finding a way into the King's court to garner favours from the monarch - or give them!'
> Dawn Aiello in www.thehistorybox.com

In the 19th century, this custom was at its height. When not 'up' for the Season your fine furniture and other possessions, needed to furnish the rental house, would be stored in a London furniture depository for safekeeping.

One famous depository was the *Pantechnicon* in Belgravia. It was from this place that large removal vans got their name; initially being horse-drawn wagons with rear loading ramps driven by certified *carters*.

These premises, built in Belgrave Square, originally as a shopping centre for art, had been converted into a fire-proof establishment by providing rooms lined with water-filled walls made of cast iron plates. They were advertised as 'fireproof.'

It was THE place to store your magnificent housing treasures during the period when they were not needed for the London Season.

However, it turned out that the items stored there were far from

Chapter 10 Midhurst Life with War Imminent

being fireproofed! In 1876 the Pantechnicon went up in a tremendous, catastrophic fire.

It was so significant that its story ran for over a week in the leading London newspapers. The hugely valuable antique furniture, carpets, Manchester etc., of the rich, along with storage materials, burned so strongly that the solid-silver flatware and plate services, bronze works of art, furniture, clock ormolus, glass chandeliers and mirrors dripped onto the floors as molten masses.

In there was stored some of the 18th and 19th-century French furniture owned by the collectors of what today is known as the Wallace Collection. Much was lost, but just what, will never be known.

The retained staff of the great houses and tenants on the estate did get some flow-down benefits from these major occasions - presents given out on Boxing Day, passing down of leftover food after banquets and balls, the supply of housing, and in many cases a genuine interest existed by the estate owners in assisting those not so well off to keep up a basic level of living comfort.

Downstairs staff thought themselves privileged to get special invitations to join events, such as participation in a grouse and partridge shoots.

But those offerings sometimes went with a rider. Professor Reginald V Jones, Assistant Director of Intelligence (Science) during WW2, told me in the 1970s that he was invited by a Scottish landowner friend to fish for trout in his trout run. The condition was that he could take the fish at a reduced price!

Somehow, reading the little there is published about the pre-war Cowdray Pearson family's lives, it seems most unlikely that they made these annual trips to a London address for the season; they had responsible posts and jobs to fulfil. They were more likely to have been content with their circle of friends and work colleagues and did not need to attend the 'London set' in search for gaiety, or a husband.

On 18th January 1939, Lady Beryl Cowdray's' son, the 3rd Viscount John Cowdray, became engaged to Lady Anne Bridgeman. They married in July 1939. Three children came in quick order, Mary (b1940), Liza (b1942) and Michael (b1944).

Fig. 10.11 shows Lady Beryl Cowdray, of the Spencer-Churchill family and wife of the 2nd Viscount Cowdray, enjoying tea during the Goodwood week of July 1939. In their time the railways and private motor cars made it far easier and quicker to get to London from Cowdray.

Fig. 10.11 Lady Beryl Cowdray (centre) serving tea in July 1939. (Russel-Stoneham and Chatterton-Newman 1992)

Perhaps the war, with its heightened likelihood of the death of the 3rd Viscount had a bearing on the situation; the Viscount went into active service in France, needing in the eventuality of his death, an heir. As luck would have it in such matters, along came two girls until Michael arrived to take his inheritance place, ready for future ownership and responsibility.

I wonder what these people felt as they thought about their life during the war to come. Most likely, more concerning for them personally was the possibility of Hitler being England's ruler! They had less worry than most about getting their bread on the table, but they also had far more to lose.

When war came all of this style of living no longer seemed appropriate. The war, and its aftermath, made it very hard for the wealthy to keep up their lavish lifestyle. Many of their copious numbers of downstairs staff went into war service and on return wanted more in their life than the tied, almost totally closed, the existence of being 'in-service'.

Taxes and changing fortunes of agricultural derived incomes much diminished their wealth.

After WW2 ended the government provided retraining for returned service people. My father, Henry, changed from being a glorified message carrier to a skilled structural steel draughtsman, who assisted build major buildings in Adelaide in the 50s.

The working classes had become very aware of their previous exploitation. The *Gilded Age* had passed on in America, Britain and Europe. Having an inherited title no longer meant wealth to splurge.

Until war came, old ways persisted until the first shot was fired; suddenly British society was levelled.

10.3. Life with War Imminent

With that decaying situation in Germany described, and the nature of the countries at war on the *Good* and *Evil* sides outlined, we can now get closer to local history.

Just what did local people think, feel and do for the looming war? The local memories books - Midhurst, Elsdon (2010): Fernhurst, Fernhurst Society (2006): and Easebourne, Litchfield (2011) - have only a little to contribute to the topic.

Searching through the around 100 interviews recorded in the MILM transcripts, Elsdon (2010), also reveals very little on the concerns about a possibility of war that residents, of adolescence age, had had.

They were far more talkative about matters of everyday life - baths, food, work, enjoyments. We might then conclude that such dire thoughts were just not on their minds. They lived a relatively uncomplicated life with the external world being rather isolated.

Those residing in the mansions would have been more concerned. The 'it will be over by Christmas' was not so likely as realism prevailed. Being in farming jobs, many of age and eligible sons of the district would most certainly have been classed as being in a *reserved occupation.* The number who went into active service, and did not return to the Midhurst District from WW1 were relatively few. That was the same pattern for WW2 where the town war memorial only lists 11 servicemen who died in service. However, these may not all be from the town. Also, some may have not been listed there, instead being named on other District memorials.

Midhurst in the early 30s was relatively out of the way, small rural town. It is situated roughly in the centre of the north to the south line across the South Downs. Road connections from the north to the south were as now, the A3 on the West and the A24 to the East. Neither of these main road routes came close to the Town so it was largely by-passed. There are no trains in Midhurst today.

Trains then connected the area via three branch lines, with a medley of three Midhurst stations for which their rail tracks did not allow the obvious east-west journeys to be made without changing trains at the central station. The eastern link connected to Pulborough and went on to London's mainline Victoria Station. The western link took passengers to Petersfield, and then on to Waterloo Station in central London.

A magnificent, now historic, system map for the LBSCR (the line branching down south) was erected in Victoria Station, London, Fig. 10.12. Being made in glazed tiles, it is still as sharp today as it was on the day it was made in the latter part of the 19th century.

Fig. 10.12 Historic map of the Brighton railway system; still in Victoria Station, London.

Fig. 10.13 shows a D1 class, no 34 Balham train on the LBSCR line around wartime. These locomotives and rolling stock were made locally at the Brighton Railway Works from around 1874 and only left service in British Rail in 1951. Trains were made much over-tough and long-lasting then. Maintenance of rolling stock and boiler tube cleans were demanding recurrent expenditures.

Chapter 10 Midhurst Life with War Imminent

Fig 10.13 Regular train on the LBSCR line to Brighton.

During the war several sets of rolling stock were loaned to other lines; some were converted into fire engine trains being deployed at key London locations ready to fight any incendiary bomb attacks. The routes are shown in Book 1, Fig. 8.11 and Fig. 8.12.

Bus services were good during the war years and serviced people reasonably well. I well recall, as a young boy, making many short trips with my mother to see someone now forgotten. Once a route left the town streets, residences were sparse and miles apart on dark winding, narrow, unlit country lanes. The bus then, as has now started to happen again on some routes, would take a passenger to the actual house needed, stopping right at the door.

However, not all services and timings were coordinated with people's life events. Several contributors to the *Midhurst in Living Memory,* Elsdon (2010) project well remembered that they could not always see a film to the end in the, then called Town Hall Cinema.

It was indeed a rural town. Milk was taken to the train by horse and cart. Cattle were often seen being herded down main roads; cars were sparse then and were not driven that fast.

John Holland, Elsdon (2010), recalls a nice little earner for enterprising lads. Something not seen today was the delivery of coke for household fires and stoves, that came from the smelly Gas Works down at the Wharf.

Trucks were available to deliver it, but local lads would carry on their own small business. They made a box-cart with pram wheels and took this to the Gas Works to buy a box-full for 'tuppence', carrying it to people's homes where they sold it for fourpence. They made a good profit for their effort.

In 1936 John left school but found it hard to get an apprenticeship in the grocery trade. Another secure job was offered to him but it only paid five bob a week; he could not live on that. He told of how these old ways all changed due to the war.

'Cattle for the Easebourne Soutar, Belling and Gosden farms were moved around the country on the train. To get to the train carriages they were herded from the station in the east (that being on the Chichester Road and going to Pulborough), through and down the main North Street to get to Easebourne in the north. Can you imagine that; the smell, the noise and uncertainty of their behaviour. Stand aside and pop into a shop until they passed!'

Robert Bridger recorded, Litchfield (2011), how the beef cattle from their farm were being herded up Rumbold's Hill at the top of North Street. On one occasion a bullock broke away, straying into narrow Wool Lane. It wandered into Mrs Waller's china shop, now *Expressions* the hairdresser. This was a 'bull in the china shop' moment for sure. Fortunately, no vase or plate was broken; and it did not leave a contribution on the floor.

The parents of Andy Robertson, a current and WW2 resident of Midhurst in the 1930s, had a large shop in North Street, Fig. 10.14. Andy lived in the town as one of the more grown-up children during the war years.

This shop had one of the hi-tech things available at that time; a labour saving, overhead trolley wire cash carrier system used to take payments. This kind of machine was fascinating to my young

Chapter 10 Midhurst Life with War Imminent

mechanically-tuned mind. I just loved to watch the container launch and swish off to the back-office somewhere as the shop assistant pulled back the cord.

Fig. 10.14 Robertson's Shop in North Street. (Andy Robertson)

These systems came in many styles and were seen everywhere, such as in Dawson's (a department store), City Road, London:

"Probably the thing I remember most about Dawson's was the procedure for paying. Having given the assistant your money it was put into a metal tube and hooked into a contraption above the assistant's head. The assistant then pulled on a string or lever, I cannot recall which, and the tube was propelled along a metal line to a mystery department where the tube was removed and its contents checked. Once the sale was recorded, the tube was filled with the change and a receipt and shot back to the assistant. I always found this process fascinating and imagined a little world away from the rest of the store where people spent their days emptying and filling these tubes.'

Charles Jenkins. East End Memories website.

You can see a Lamson system in action at the Beamish Open-Air Museum in County Durham, Buxton (2004), Fig. 10.15.

Another version of this, also used commonly, was the vacuum pipe. In this kind, a small cylinder was used, but this time it was placed into a long pipe system. As soon as the cover flap was shut the vacuum inside the pipe worked to whisk it away to the cashier.

Life in Midhurst before war broke out probably seemed too normal, too

humdrum, to be worthy of writing up.

Fig. 10.15 Cash carrier in a 1930s restored shop.

Fortunately, a great, highly readable, autobiographical account of the life of a person, born of poor parents there in 1924, has been compiled by Ronald Boxall; some of his story has been given in Book 1, Chapter 9.3. He wrote his childhood memoirs in 1983, with its dedication being to his mother and friend Charles Bowyer, Boxall (2003), 'who both instilled in me the urge to write my tale'.

He thanked them for their encouragement, as do I for his effort; long accounts dealing with everyday life in the Midhurst District are rare.

It covers his life from birth in Duck Lane, then not one of the spots of local beauty, to his first set of long trousers worn for his first day at work in late 1938, at almost 14 years of age. He took us up to the time when war was soon to be declared. He recorded no more notes on how it was in the wartime, or what took place in his later life.

As a young man still with a lot to learn about the deeper affairs of society, Ronnie reported on how it was being seen that the Germans, in 1937 were being very aggressive, and how not all people listened to Churchill's call for action in readiness for war with Hitler's regime.

He recalled how social conditions were improving with new housing estate start-ups, and better medical advice and follow-ups. He saw war preparations and social improvements taking hold, needing considerably more paid labour.

Newsreels of the aerial bombardment during the Spanish Civil war front were shown in the local cinema in North Street; no doubt those he

Chapter 10 Midhurst Life with War Imminent

saw were the illegal raids being prosecuted by screeching and wailing German Stuka dive-bombers gaining work-experience in readiness for invading Poland.

In 1939 bomb blast shelters were being built throughout Britain; Ronnie's local gang of boys just had to have one of their own. They built theirs in June Lane, a then undeveloped road opposite Duck Lane, where he lived.

In their play, their medieval bows and arrows became guns! They took prisoners. They enjoyed playing war games - but of their own choice, not by a regime deliberately training them for death as a soldier.

Their life models were Cubs, Scouts, Brownies and Girl Guides that taught honour, loyalty, comradeship, and peaceful pursuits: not like the youth's education and upbringing that took place in Hitler's Germany, just a few hundred miles away, as are covered in Chapter 2.1.

Photos, or images of any kind, giving reality to daily life in the District for this pre-war period, are as 'rare as hen's teeth'. To overcome this deficiency Ronald's book was copiously illustrated with humorous style line sketches by Mike Avery: they bring it to life.

Ronnie's experiences had so much in common with my own, a decade later in Midhurst during the war period. It is as though he was running a dress rehearsal for my time there. His adventures so often became mine. This is, of course, to be expected for the things boys get up to seem to be built into their genes.

He had a visit to see the grand Crystal Palace. He recalls how he was overwhelmed by its size and grandeur but was somewhat disappointed; he felt a palace has to have turrets, which it did not. That was before its demise in 1936.

It should have been possible for him, from a high vantage spot in the District, to just make out the glinting of sunlight reflecting from the silver-coated barrage balloons raised around London in 1939.

The worsening situation was felt in all manner of ways. Stuart Baldwin was evacuated to Eynsham, west of London:

'A job he had, around 1937, was to put dust covers on new copies

of *Mien Kampf* printed by Hutchinson's Anchor Press. Doing this evoked some mixed feelings - "this can be defined as what a young man feels when he sees his mother-in-law drive over a cliff in his new car""
The Evacuee, issue 205, 2017.

As the 30s advanced, so did the availability of life-enhancing and task saving, technology. The dash-dot Morse code signal telegraph gave way to teletype and radio communication. Television was around by 1939 but not many had it, and it wasn't that good to watch as its coarse black and white lines on a tiny screen provided very poor definition.

To have a phone was an accomplishment; first to be able to afford it, and second to have it available where you wanted it. The call numbers were short and used names of the manually operated exchanges, where sat the ever-waiting switchboard girl who would organise the call for you, ringing back to tell you it was ready.

Not all living conditions in rural areas were rosy. The local authority for Midhurst during WW2 was then the Midhurst Rural District Council MRDC. To improve health sanitation a Rural Sanitary Authority had been formed for the Midhurst Union in 1872. This happened sometime before nearby Worthing, due to poor sanitation, had its typhoid epidemic in 1893. Human waste disposal conditions were very bad at that time. It is said that it was still commonly done, even during WW2, to empty the overnight bed pot in some streets!

In medicine, improvements were happening slowly but often to great effect; that discipline is conservative because negative effects are not easily accepted, and it can take months to years to show up side effects.

Penicillin was discovered by Alexander Fleming in 1928 and needed time to be thoroughly tested and put into production. Its first mass application was during the 1944 D-Day invasion for field dressing of wounds.

Heart complaints were the main cause of deaths then. If you survived one heart attack then, for sure, another would soon come to take you off in a few months. The vitally useful *electrocardiograph* recorder for determining heart function defects was in existence by 1920, but the

Chapter 10 Midhurst Life with War Imminent

first machines were so large as to require the patient to go to the machine.

Portable units became available from 1932. Fig. 10.16 shows the world's first direct recorder for instant diagnosis by providing an ECG trace. It was just about portable, weighing in at 30 lbs (14kg).

Fig. 10.16 Both Bros. portable ECG machine 1932. (Harry Daly Museum)

Improvements were being made all over the many facets of living in Britain. Effects of the Great Depression were fading fast. Widespread health reforms were under serious parliamentary debate. New housing estates were being built, and slums were being cleared.

Peace had its rewards for those living under the democratic way of life. Those countries had realised that empire building and colonisation were not the way anymore to develop a country's own economy and standard of living anymore.

For all that experience gained, the dictators in Germany, Italy and Japan had started on a course to rebuild ancient empires that they were to rule by harsh authoritarian methods. They were so sure that their visions were the ultimate way to exist; provided any means of using humans was acceptable to them to reach that goal.

They were to learn that they were out of step with multi-millions of people, whose past had already traversed that mind-set.

10.4 The World is Invaded

It is painfully clear that everyone, who reads a newspaper, looked at publicly displayed posters, listened to the radio, went to the cinema, or talked it all over in the local pub, knew a lot about the *Evil* side of this *storm clouds* period.

War was coming without a doubt. The last war had taken place some 20 years before so most families were still smarting from the accounts they had seen, or perhaps suffered, in the trenches of the Great War. They could easily see that it was not going to be *Good* ahead. The prospects strongly suggested the totalitarian way of Nazism was something to contend with.

We normally associate Dr Seuss (real name being Theodor Seuss Geisel) with entertaining children's books containing his unique cartoon-like sketches. During WW2 he also published poignant political propaganda cartoons in the US. They have been reviewed, along with a political explanation of each, Minear (1999). Fig. 10.17 is one that has relevance to the situation in 1939 but was drawn in 1942. By then the US had come to see that the *Evil* forces of the Axis Powers were out to drag them into war again.

Fig. 10.17 Totalitarianism was fast becoming a prospect for Britain and the US under Nazi rule. (Seuss)

People had become so sensitive in the post-WW1 years to hearing of disaster, depression, bad economic news, bad unemployment figures and falling fortunes of many kinds, that they easily took a fictional event as a real one – a nation could be panicked, thinking they were in fear of their very existence!

Broadcast radio, as a wide-spread business, was born commercially in the early 1920s. It had been developing for two decades before that but the technology had to mature to be cost-effective, reliable and have sufficient range and channel selectivity.

Manufacture of affordable radio sets needed time to design using

Chapter 10 Midhurst Life with War Imminent

the latest 'valves', to set up production lines, and then to take them to market. Sales of radio sets were slow in the 1920s but eventually took off as the 30s progressed.

Early radios were hungry for electrical power. Their thermionic tubes, also called 'vacuum tubes' but most commonly known as 'valves' because they acted like that for electrical flow, each used a red-hot filament that glowed in the dark. A good radio needed at least four of these valves so the overall electrical demand rose above 100W or so; that is, were only able to operate for only a few hours on a freshly charged lead-acid battery.

Mains electricity was usually needed to periodically recharge the direct current accumulator; a large heavy wet cell battery working just like those in most cars today - but not made for portable use. Eventually, the right kind of electrical power was available without the battery by running off the mains electricity supply.

Supporting their use in rural situations had the difficulty of supply of electricity. Many people living in the countryside of the Midhurst Rural District did not get mains power until after WW2.

For example, my cottage home at the top of Easebourne Street had none in 1943, nor did the gate lodge into Fitz Hall. Peggy Guggenheim's Yew Tree Cottage in the Hartings, that I cover later, was connected to mains supply around 1938.

Houses on main road routes started to receive electrical mains wiring from the early 1930s, but those in the rural countryside were without unless they had a petrol or oil-fuelled electrical generator.

Today we take having a radio of some sort as a given, but imagine a world without any of the broadcast services, radio, television and modern extensions of that for getting messages around; the mobile (cell) phone, email and Internet communications.

As a kid of 9 years old I constructed a little crystal set and spent many hours tickling the 'cat's whisker' on the surface of a little black galena crystal to find a strong enough signal that I could then tune into a station by adjustment of the position of an electric coil connection. Great fun; they did not need a battery to operate, but they were far inferior to radio set of the 1930s.

The technology of basic electricity in the 1930s can be seen in Newing and Bowood (1962) where its content about electricity is exactly as I grew with up in 1940's books.

In the mid-20s the radio set was still an expensive luxury item of good living. Not everyone had one, by far. A radio set cost a couple of pounds in the early 1930s. That was a week's wage for a rural worker in the Midhurst District. The wealthy in town, or with large estates, had them.

Numerous models were available, an early one being shown in Fig. 10.18.

Fig. 10.18 British made Philco radio model 70, ca1933.
Left: Front view of controls and loudspeaker vent.
Right: Inside view of electronic parts; the glass envelopes are the electronic valves.

By the later 30s almost everyone in Britain had access to listen to a radio, be it new, second-hand, home built, a neighbour's, or listened to in a radio shop in town. The programmes, as well as bringing music into the drawing-room also gave other styles of entertainment: a variety show of singing, jokes, talks; a regular news presentation and, what was looked forward to each week - the Sunday night play. The British *Radio Times*, a weekly programme and information guide, hit the streets in 1923.

Radio was soon seen by governments as an excellent medium for controlling a population's habits, and its general thinking. In the UK that was done by the British Broadcasting Corporation, just BBC for short, Beaven (2016).

The Germans then, in sharp contrast, had an approved, 'you are allowed listen to', list of stations; but their authoritarian use was blatantly

Chapter 10 Midhurst Life with War Imminent

obvious. It was controlled by:

'The *Reichsministerium für Volksaufklärung und Propaganda* (Ministry of People's Information and Propaganda). The ministry stated that all stations not listed are foreign stations not to be listened to. The German radio listener would thus only tune into transmitters of this list! According to the Act of 1 September 1939, anyone caught listening to the foreign stations will be detained.'
Radioheritage.net

Television became a regular broadcast service in Britain in 1936 but its coverage was very limited; by modern standards, it was of very poor fidelity. TV made very little contribution during the war, moving-film then being the image medium that was then based on wet-processed chemical film technology. Wire-based, field-portable, sound recorders came into use by German war correspondents toward the end of WW2.

As radio broadcasts became a routine part of daily life, listeners became used to the subtle prompts often given within a programme. This practice, however, is dangerous if programme material is not managed carefully.

Listeners tend to believe what they hear; all too easily at times. As an exemplar situation, let's look into two instances using the same line of thought.

Way before these electronic devices became common, the following two examples of fright invoking experiences were set up making using of a novel by H. G. Wells, *The War of the Worlds,* that was first published in late 1897.

As time passed there grew a large following of the many science fiction stories published in magazines, like *Amazing Stories*, *Flash Gordon, Strange Adventure* and *Marvel Science Stories*.

H. G. Wells stories were highly popularized in the 20s and 30s. In August 1927 *War of Worlds* was featured in *Amazing Stories* Vol 2 No 5. Elaborate image portrayals of that fictional future-history event were added to these publications.

Other ideas of what the technical future might hold were given elsewhere in that issue in an article by E D Skinner *Electro-Episoded in AD2025*. He envisioned how we would be able to locate people anywhere across the globe using his *Electric Spark-screen Broadcaster* machine.

He includes, Fig. 10.19, his vision of finding and communicating with a person in AD 2025. The caption reads:

> 'Inserting a needle-point barely beyond and to the left of the higher of the two mountain peaks, he took a delicate copper wire and connected this with "Local". Throwing the clutch back to "Local" the faint of the Parker Pass replaced it with…..
> [Continuing] he was not able to find his beloved, but as she had her *Electric Spark-Screen Broadcaster* turned on at the time her image gradually appeared on his screen.

Fig. 10.19 Finding the location of a person; idea of the 1920s. (Amazing Stories)

He was also able to change its function to get photographs from anywhere in the world using his *Radioelectro-dictaphonotypograph.*

With such imagination and futuristic fantasy, based on a few real truths, let's step back a few years to a 1927 incident in far-away Adelaide. It may well have been the spur for a similar one in 1938 - that got millions of Americans very scared.

We can now join the first example. In Australia, radio broadcasting commenced in 1924. In 1927 the 5CL broadcasting station of Adelaide, South Australia, was already well known for its stunts performed on listeners. They made use of the way people have grown used to hearing news broadcasts and bulletins to fool them. This time it was a little too

Chapter 10 Midhurst Life with War Imminent

successful.

It took the form of a one-act play about an invasion taking place into the seaport of Adelaide. Fig. 10.20 was one vision around at the time of how the world might be invaded. It was drawn for a magazine cover in the late 20s, being representative of the *War of the Worlds* book by H G Wells.

Fig. 10.20 How people could have thought about an invasion from outer space in the 30s!

An announcement at the start of the play stated that it was only a stunt! The short programme was, however, so well delivered that listeners who joined into the programme after it had started, and had not heard any of the preamble, really thought they were being invaded.

A programme had begun with orchestral music, as it did every week. It kept being interrupted with a reporter talking against a background of worrying noises:

'Listeners-in were keyed up to a high nervous tension by repeated announcements that there was trouble at the Port, but for lack of confirmation of the rumours they were unable to give any definite information. Following that, a soprano singer was unable to finish her song, and the explanation given was that she had become terrified at the news of the happenings at the Port. Still, we were left in suspense, and some minutes later the awful news of the enemy invasion in all its sickening detail was given us. So realistic was it that the statement of the speaker, "Be calm, listeners-in, as long as I am spared to stand here, I will tell you what is going on" was just the breaking point for many overwrought nerves.'

2 July 1924 Adelaide Register

This particular event took place well before any clear threat of WW2 starting. When the event died down a press release was issued.

> 'I cannot understand in these days of wireless and cable communication throughout the world, when there are newspapers every day, and when there has not for years been any suspicion of war between the Empire and any foreign countries, how people could be sufficiently upset as to think it was real. ... If we caused distress to anybody, we are sorry, but our action was taken solely with the object of adding to the interest of the programme prepared for the listening-in public.'
>
> William Smallacombe, Station 5CL 2 July 1927
> Adelaide Register.

It is not as though listeners had not had an advanced warning for it had been announced several times that a special programme would be run in a 'few nights time'.

They played listeners along, starting with the usual introduction to the programme slot; orchestral music backing a women singer. The singer's song was interrupted with the sound of a bomb exploding. She screamed and the 'sounds of the invasion' were introduced. Something was going on in the Port Adelaide area. A long pause; and then a detailed account was given of the invasion

It was all done with simple, studio generated, sounds - coconut shells, tin sheets, drums, rushing water, fans…. It was just too effective.

> 'Hundreds of people ... telephoned to the newspaper offices, the police, harbours, and telephone departments, and the fire brigades for confirmation of the invasion.'

All evening the station kept announcing it was just a play. A week later, 5CL ran another magnificent hoax wherein a journey in a car to Mars was followed in noisy detail as it was attacked by Martians. A rocket was also fired from the station!

In 2013, an in-depth study of these Adelaide hoax events, and the public reaction recorded in the local, national and international newspapers, was assembled by R R King of the *Metropolitan Washington*

Chapter 10 Midhurst Life with War Imminent

Old Time Radio Club, at www.Mwotrc.com. These hoaxes had been run in times of peace, with little idea that a Hitler would set the world at war a decade later.

Whether, in 1937, Orson Welles in the USA had heard of this event or not, matters little but he did much the same thing during a radio broadcast under his direction. The difference was that it was, this time, set against a truly desperate global background – and that scared many, many, Americans.

On 30 October 1937 the Columbia Broadcasting System radio network put to air an adaptation of the same *The War of the Worlds*, H G Wells', 1898 novel. That was, perhaps, not a good time to do it for war in Europe was on everyone's mind.

It was one play in a series *Mercury Theatre on the Air*; this one ran on the Halloween evening. That should have been a clue that it was not real.

Orson Welles reset the 62minute play as a then-modern adaption from the 19th-century setting used by H G Wells. Fig. 10.21 shows the young Orson at his studio job.

Fig. 10.21 Orson Welles broadcasting in 1938.

Many names of real places and services were altered just a little to make them all fictional, but sounding rather like real places and organisations.

It was not so much the almost real places named, but how it was presented. It used much of the front-end time as News Bulletins of the detail of events. Long pauses were used as if the presenter or the

Midhurst WW2 Memoirs: 2. 'Evil' Rising: 'Good' Awakening

broadcast had been interrupted in flight.

Normally presented advertisements were held off, also adding realism to the listener, especially those who had tuned to the station after it had begun. By chance, a more popular show on another channel had run over time, meaning many listeners were late in joining the play; they did not hear of the warnings given. Repercussions of the Welles 1937 broadcast were in people's minds for several years, Fig. 10.22.

Fig. 10.22 Hitler's invasions were a joke, but the *War of the Worlds* radio programme instilled the deepest fear in millions of listeners. (Toronto Star)

The caption of this editorial cartoon by Les Callan reads:

'From time to time some quirk of fate, some state of mind, or

Chapter 10 Midhurst Life with War Imminent

some brilliance of thought makes a broadcast memorable. As such it deserves to be preserved, for after it passes from the news it becomes part of the colour and woof of our history. As history and as a commentary on the nervous state of our nation (Canada here) after the Pact of Munich, we present this recent none-the-less celebrated broadcast.'

Toronto Star, February 1939

The Toronto Star newspaper used this cartoon in an editorial to show the similarities after the Munich Pact had been signed in 1939. Reaction to the fake *War of the Worlds* play on 30 October 1937 scared the 'world', as had the rise of Hitler's *Evil* that was then always in the news; and was too horrific to believe.

Radio Digest reprinted the script of *The War of the Worlds* play:

'as a commentary on the nervous state of our nation after the Pact of Munich'

How did this apparent realism come about? Normally radio stations have censorship controls in place to ensure this sort of thing does not make listeners angry?

When the play was first rehearsed by Orson Welles it seemed to him to be too tame to capture an audience's attention. Fearing a poor rating, and being on Halloween night, the script was radically changed in haste the night before. One section ends:

'A news reporter, broadcasting from atop the CBS building, describes the Martian invasion of New York City – "five great machines" wading across the Hudson River, poison smoke drifting over the city, people running and diving into the East River "like rats", others "falling like flies" – until he, too, succumbs to the poison gas. Finally, a despairing ham radio operator is heard calling, "2X2L calling CQ. Isn't there anyone on the air? Isn't there anyone on the air? Isn't there anyone on the air? Isn't there anyone on the air? Isn't there anyone.....?"'

The reaction of the public went so much further than had been expected from this kind of show. It hit the international news services.

One later summary of it was that by Frank Brady, in his biography of Welles, Brady (1989):

'The shadow of war was constantly in and on the air. People were on edge….. For the entire month before *The War of the Worlds*, radio had kept the American public alert to the ominous happenings throughout the world. The Munich crisis was at its height. Adolf Hitler, in his address to the annual Nazi party congress at Nuremberg in September, called for the autonomy of the Sudetenland, an area on the Czech border regions populated by three million Sudeten Germans, as they were called. Hitler ranted and lied over German radio … For the first time in history, the public could tune into their radios every night and hear, boot by boot, accusation by accusation, threat by threat, the rumblings that seemed to be inevitably leading to a world war.'

Radio can be used as an effective way to deliver propaganda. People too easily accept what they hear! The press was told, in October 1938, that the broadcasters had no idea it would get this level of panic response for its 60minute programme, Fig. 10.23.

Fig. 10.23 Reporters being told that the radio station did not think the play would cause so much panic.

Chapter 10 Midhurst Life with War Imminent

Fig. 10.24 Who would have thought the radio hoax would be so frightening?

This event proved the power of radio broadcasting, Fig. 10.24, as a message carrier that could portray false-truth so well, especially when it hit the spots of existing anxieties?

Parts of the play, like this following example, kept up the state of alarm:

> 'There again the audience is stunned by this news. But the situation portrayed soon gets worse. Listeners are told that the state militia is mobilising, with seven thousand men, and surrounding the metal object. They, too, are soon obliterated by the 'heat ray.' The 'Secretary of the Interior,' who sounds like President Franklin Roosevelt (purposely), addresses the nation.'

"Citizens of the nation: I shall not try to conceal the gravity of the situation that confronts the country, nor the concern of your government in protecting the lives and property of its people. . . . we must continue the performance of our duties each and every one of us, so that we may confront this destructive adversary with a nation united, courageous, and consecrated to the preservation of human supremacy on this earth."

The radio reports that the U.S. Army is engaged. The announcer declared that New York City is being evacuated. The program continues, but many radio listeners are already panicked.

Overall, the public reaction, in this case, seems to have been overstated by the press, but the play did get many people ringing public authorities for confirmation. The many individual reactions are interesting to read about… if they can be believed!

The 30s were a time of ever-intensifying fear; to the point where most people in Britain were ready, by 1939, to take it to the conclusion that the *Evil* had to be overcome by force; not appeased by words alone.

I came into the world in 1937. The fires of Crystal Palace that my mother had witnessed a few months before that, were but as nothing compared with what was soon to come to Britain, and later to Germany. From that time on, for the next 8 years, the threat of death, injury and occupation was always near.

Chapter 11 Where the 'Other Half' lived.

11.1 Cowdray Estate

We have seen how the working and agricultural classes and the very poor lived in the 1903s. We now need to see a little of the homes and estates of the wealthy that were significant to WW2 Midhurst District memoirs.

These, usually land-estate owning, families enjoyed useful connections in the national political system, with the aristocracy and with the new-rich, in general. After the middle to late 19th century, new industrial wealth incomes allowed many of these long-standing, caretaker-guardian, families to revitalise their estates: or to sell them on to the *new-money* wealthy who largely carried on enjoying life as it was by those that went before them in those landed estates .. for a while, that is.

For years of the late 19th century up to the mid-1930s, the financially ailing English aristocrats, still with their titles and large attractive properties, were often wooed by American Heiresses who had large fortunes but lacked the connections they desired to have in British high-society.

In effect, they bought their way into the British establishment and in doing so brought about many changes to how the aristocrats behaved. Fascinating 'cash for coronets' stories are presented in De Courcy (2018). The history of the British aristocracy has been discussed in depth in James (2009). Lawrence James says:

'The word aristocracy appeared late in our language, arriving via France in the mid-sixteenth century. It was a compound of the Greek 'aristo' (the best) and 'kratos' (government) and defined Aristotelian notions on the distribution of political power in an ideal State. Aristotle's aristocrats were men of learning and wisdom whose wealth gave them the leisure to devote their lives to government and the general welfare of the rest of society.'

Following on from that:

'The Aristotelian notion of aristocrat reinforced an already deeply rooted sense of superiority and public responsibility which justified power and privilege.'

Just why it lasted in force for several centuries is covered by James (2009). Simply put they, as a class of self-promoted wise and capable men and women, were able to generally convince the wider populace that they were in good hands. However, their power was gradually weakened by democratic rule that allowed the common man and woman to challenge and modify that power - often after much struggle being needed to overcome the self-indulgent ways of the powerful.

By the mid-1930s this change was becoming very clear. War-Lords, diplomats, and other leaders of the British nation, previously appointed by their position in the aristocracy, gave way to people judged to be competent, rather than by merely having birthright.

Some landed, and otherwise old-money wealthy, families had been losing their overall wealth over the centuries and were feeling the pinch of severe wealth-sharing government reforms. Much belt-tightening took place. The Cowdray estate has roots going back to Norman times, but had changed family lines several times over its, at least 5 centuries of history. There existed no centuries-old, single, family line at Cowdray.

The current Pearson family line began in Cowdray when Weetman Dickinson Pearson, 1st Viscount Cowdray, Fig. 11.1, bought the estate in 1909 for a bargain price.

Fig. 11.1 1st Viscount Cowdray, c1917.

Before that, it had been owned by Charles Perceval, 7th Earl of Egmont, who succeeded to the peerage in 1874.

This local example of the new money wealth situation arriving in the Midhurst District was described in a report in the *Argus* newspaper of Melbourne, 15 July 1927.

When the 1st Viscount Cowdray died in 1927 his estate was valued at

Chapter 11 Where the 'Other Half' lived.

£4,000,000 for which death duties of £1,000,000 were then due. (Taking off the duties and converting that to today's purchasing value that is around £1,000,000,000!). By 1939 this then amount of monetary value had inflated to around then, £5,000,000. This, however, was not all ready cash, but assets that could be used to create recurrent income, or be sold off in part, or whole.

That ownership had originated not by inheritance, but was paid for by the 1st Viscount Cowdray who purchased the Cowdray Estate with income from his highly successful civil engineering company. It was based on rail and oil enterprises in Mexico and Britain. The 2nd Viscount, as his starting point, then inherited the life title and that wealth from his father.

These huge levels of wealth came about from the leading industrialists having close and useful connections to national leaders of many countries! Fig. 11.2 shows the extent of oil well-heads, on the Californian coast in the 1890s.

Fig. 11.2 Sheer Wealth! The appearance of oil-rich development in Southern California in the late 1800s.

Little is reported about the lifestyle of the current Cowdray dynasty. All of the Viscounts are known for their shyness in public and reticence to talk about their family businesses and private life. Interviews were rare.

This immense wealth was not squandered, as many other heirs and heiresses had done. There is no evidence that their new wealth was poured into hugely extravagant, lavish lifestyles as were seen at that time in Gilded Age buildings, such as are seen today, largely now in trust, on the Eastern seaboard of the USA in places like those at Newport, Rhode Island, Cheek and Gannon (2008).

The inherited titles were first earned for original contributions made to society in many different ways. All generations of Cowdray made notable contributions to the life of those who served them on their estates. There is no evidence of harsh treatment or overpowering control of their workers and tied staff.

Today it maintains its situation by use of careful and inventive enterprises that maintain the estate's state of beauty and great care of the environment in the long term, Edwards (2017).

In terms of land ownership in Britain, the Midhurst Rural District (MRD) was not that large an area, just 66,700 acres or 194 square miles. Of this, the Cowdray Estate has about 16,500-acres (26 square miles), give or take a lot.

Other land ownership in the 30s MRD was predominantly held as private ownership of properties on which sat more than 15 grand houses that had been built over the preceding centuries.

Allowing for Crown land ownership, some very guestimate averaging suggests these had around 1500 acres each on average, some much smaller, some much larger.

The families of these houses were very influential in local and national matters - and were quite wealthy, as will be seen when war fundraising events in the area during WW2 are discussed in a later volume. These leaders countered Cowdray families from taking too large a measure of control, as Cowdray owners had done in earlier times; such as when parliamentary seats could be easily bought by control of local property owners.

With this background, it is now time to look into the local mansion estates. These houses are now shown and their part contributed to WW2 is given in brief, where it is known. Unfortunately, it has been an almost fruitless task at finding any substantial records of the part played by most of these families during WW2; a topic for others to research.

Let us start this account of WW2 use of the houses of the grand properties within the District, with that of the dominating estate; Cowdray. These will point up the range of lifestyles and contributions, and the management of wealth by the landed gentry of the Midhurst District before, and sometimes, during the war. Their life stories are often fascinating.

Chapter 11 Where the 'Other Half' lived.

Fig. 11.3 Cowdray House in the 1930s.

The Cowdray estate is the largest single-family land ownership across the boundaries of the former Midhurst Rural District.

Its recorded history has considerable coverage of its early times, but diminishes to very little being available since the late 1930s, the start of WW2. What is recorded up to then is held in an archive of the WSRO. One key early account, Hope (1919), gives detailed explanations of ascendancy and ownership starting in Norman times. The handsomely produced, large format, original of this book is rare but it has now been poorly reproduced as a small facsimile version, that being useful for research purposes.

More detail will be given about Cowdray history in a later book when my time living in Easebourne is the topic.

The Cowdray Estate once had its magnificent grand Tudor mansion, of such standing that Queen Elizabeth 1 'stayed over' on several occasions. However, it was burned to the ground in the 19th century and was never rebuilt.

Midhurst WW2 Memoirs: 2. 'Evil' Rising: 'Good' Awakening

The ruins, seen today from Midhurst, are the remains of that Great Tudor house that burned down in September 1893. It was too damaged to make complete restoration attractive, and by that date, the practical need for such large properties was passing. Unliveable, it was left fenced off for a century as decaying, dangerous, ruins.

The then insignificant, far smaller, Cowdray Lodge, situated a mile away, became the Poyntz family home, displacing the keeper who lived there then. In 1843 Cowdray estate was sold to the 6th Earl of Egmont for £300,000 (roughly £30,000,000 today). The bulk of that value is the land.

At some time before 1897, the 7th Earl of Egmont pulled down much of the Lodge and rebuilt it, much larger, to be a 'jolly and un-pompous Victorian' residence.

The current Pearson dynasty began when the soon to be 1st Viscount Cowdray (then Sir Weetman Dickinson Pearson), purchased it in 1909 for much the same price as it had been sold earlier.

After also deciding not to build a replacement Cowdray House, he added a North Wing and modernised the rest of the existing building complex.

Between 1909 and 1914 he engaged Sir Aston Webb to organise preservation of the ruins; Webb had then just designed the main building of the Victoria and Albert Museum, and soon after that he redesigned the principal facade of Buckingham Palace. He left his mark!

The changing needs of the current Pearson generation have made Cowdray House too large for today's family needs; that story will be taken up in a later book.

During its early life under the Pearsons, Cowdray House was furnished with a good stock of treasures; as was the thing to do at that time when that 'new great wealth' flowed to a few who felt the need to own art treasures. This was at the time of the 'Gilded Age' of the USA.

Buck Hall in Cowdray House still shows some of that art treasure as a spectacular backdrop for special intimate wedding receptions with its single-piece dining table for over 25 people and 11 bedrooms. It can host up to 150 guests for a sit-down event. Much of the pre-fire era of the Tudor house was lost to the fire! Cowdray House is no longer the family home; they now live elsewhere in the District.

Of interest to these WW2 memoirs is that in 1933, it passed on to the

Chapter 11 Where the 'Other Half' lived.

3rd Viscount Cowdray (Weetman John Churchill Pearson, 1910-1995), father of the current 4th Viscount Michael Pearson.

Just before the war was declared he married Lady Anne Bridgman in 1939, the ceremony, Fig. 11.4, being held in St Margaret's Church, Westminster, London.

Fig. 11.4. Wedding of 3rd Viscount Cowdray to Lady Anne Bridgman in July 1939.

At the start of WW2, the 3rd Viscount went across to France, presumably with the British Expeditionary Force. There he had his arm amputated in the retreat to Dunkirk. This disability did not stop him following his favourite 'at home' pastimes; game bird shooting and polo. He revived polo there after the war to it being known as the home of polo in Britain. All levels of society can enjoy playing, or watching the game; sometimes with Queen Elizabeth in the prestige audience, or with a royal playing in a team.

Unfit for active service after the Dunkirk retreat, but still needing to serve, Viscount John Cowdray, became a Lieutenant-Colonel from 1940 to 1941 in the local Home Guard. He then served as Parliamentary Private Secretary to the Under Secretary of State for Air from 1941 - 1942.

The Family have long had senior links to the Royal Air Force, the 1st Viscount being, in 1917, the President of the Air Board created in May 1916 to improve cooperation between the then-fledgling Army and the Navy air services.

An Army link also developed; the 3rd Viscount John Pearson formed a troop of the Sussex Yeomanry in 1932, Russell-Stoneham and Chatterton-Newman (1992). Cowdray Hall, in Easebourne, was the Section Head Quarters. Several 18 pounder field guns were stored there.

It was 1937 when the 98th Surrey & Sussex Yeomanry, Queen Mary Field Brigade, Royal Artillery camped in Cowdray Park, see back to Fig. 6.4.

When WW2 broke out, areas of the estate were requisitioned by the War Department to build a small 'secret airfield' establishment at Selham. It was used for storing and modifying aircraft of the Royal Naval Air Service RNAS that attacked enemy ships with air-dropped torpedoes, for downed aircrew sea rescue, and sea mine watches. The detailed history of this small camouflaged airfield has been written up in Pons (2017); more about its part in WW2 active service will be included in a later book.

Lord Cowdray went off to France. The Royal Army Service Corps RASC took over most of the space of Cowdray House, the stables buildings and parked many vehicles there - trucks, VIP cars, coaches to take troops to exercises and more.

A year or so later, Lord Lovat, Fig. 11.5, set up the Head Quarters of his army commando group in the House, billeting troops in the stables.

There, the commando explored operational ideas to be used in upcoming raids and field-tested facets of those operations in the fields and river around.

Fig. 11.5 Lord Lovat at work in Newhaven, 1942.

The wartime use of the Cowdray estate needs researching for although at least three books have been published on the exploits of No 4 Commando, details of its daily life at home are rarely recorded in their war diaries. Records of the use of the Cowdray estate in WW2 have not yet been located. What I have gleaned on them will be – maybe - included in a later book. Additionally, as the war progressed, the estate lands were used for troop camps and training, and public events such as fundraising fetes and exhibitions. Polo took a break during the war!

Chapter 11 Where the 'Other Half' lived.

As was the general disposition of all owners over the centuries of Cowdray, Viscount Cowdray John was generous toward the estate worker's needs during WW2, for instance, once allowing Cocking residents to take wood for their home heating.

During his life, he took interest in the work on his estates often doing his 'rounds' on horseback, stopping to offer advice or issue an invite to this or that event. However, he seems to have not been that interested in growing, or even maintaining, the level of wealth of the estate.

As the effects of vibrant new technology changed the estate, farm practices and markets needed updating. Published reports hint at him not keeping up with the income generation aspect. That task was inherited by the current 4th Viscount Michael Cowdray to sort out.

George Nugent, in his obituary of Weetman John Churchill Pearson, published in the *Independent* newspaper, on 21 January 1995, said it was tempting to see:

'his lack of immediate interest was not in disparagement of a famous part of the Cowdray empire but reflected a rather patrician attitude to life, in which business properly serves the ends of family and country, and can be effectively managed through prudent delegation, leaving one free for estate management, and polo.'

And later, on his apparent disregard for daily issues:

'A shy reclusive man with his passion for property and polo, as an exemplar of the decline of Britain's entrepreneurial class. He would not have cared for, nor much cared about, this aspersion and it misses the point that he possessed a sense of business and family pride that sustained and expanded the Cowdray empire.'

With Cowdray covered we can now look into the many mansions that are dotted over the Midhurst District. They are not ordered here in any special way.

It was pointed out to me by resident Dawn Ades, Professor Emeritus of Art History at Essex University, that these wealthy estates were built around the western curve of the uprising southern Weald (*wooded land* in Saxon terms).

Being in somewhat isolated rural situations, those locations afforded owners much sought-after seclusion from the 'madding crowd' of London and other urban areas.

11.2 Stedham Hall

Fig. 11.6 Stedham Hall on the Rother.

Stedham Hall, Fig. 11.6, a large impressive house, is in Stedham, just 2 miles to the West of Midhurst. Stedham and Iping have been conjoined as one place since their ecclesiastical parishes were combined. The Hall has origins back in the 16th century but has been much altered over time. It was described in Pevsner's *'Buildings of England'* as having:

'a formidable fairy castle effect from the riverside'

The Hall was remodelled in Victorian times to look as it does now. In the 1970s it was converted into apartments.

How it was architecturally, just after the war, has been recorded in Salzman (1953). Its long history can be obtained from its website www.stedhamwithiping-pc.gov.uk. Memories of its history have been compiled in the book, Dicks et. al. (2012).

Chapter 11 Where the 'Other Half' lived.

Early in the 20th century John and Jessie Scrimgeour arrived to become the Lord and Lady of the Manor; that then meaning they owned the whole village. Previously they had lived in *Wispers,* see later, at Stedham.

They lived at Stedham Hall and altered and enlarged it to be much like that seen today. His family were great benefactors to the villagers of Stedham.

Whilst those living in the mansions generally enjoyed well-appointed facilities, conditions for the villagers were quite tough in the 1940s for, as was the case elsewhere out of towns, reticulated public utilities had not come to the village, Dicks et. al. (2012):

'My Mum had a copper that she lit a fire under in the scullery. A big black thing and she used to polish the brass on it every week. That's how we had to have a bath, in front of the fire. We did have a bathroom but it only had a cold tap in it so in winter it was in front of the fire when we were little, but when we were bigger the water was carried down to the bathroom at the end of the passage'.
Sally Page.

This Scrimgeour family were public-minded and cognisant of their duties for they provided an improved level of services to as good a level as was possible in the isolated location.

They gave Stedham its first pumped water supply and installed a bath-house with hot baths available to villagers in the Collins Club building, which was originally a barn.

'We had electricity which came from Stedham Hall where the Scrimgeours had a generator. There was no main drainage or sewers or anything. We had running water which came from Ash House down by Meadowhills. There was a little reservoir, and there used to be booster reservoirs on the way down. It came down underneath the river to the front of Stedham Hall and the farm. Our end of Stedham was very privileged.'
Geoff West.

John Scrimgeour died in 1925, and his widow Jessi in 1943. Their daughter, Mrs Esther Chatterton, had to break-up the estate - but not before every tenant was given the chance to buy his home on favourable terms. That was in 1950.

Esther's husband was the celebrated Brigadier George Chatterton, Fig. 11.7, well known in WW2 history as the Commander of the British Glider Pilots Regiment; more is explained about these brave men in a later memoirs book, Chatterton (1982).

Fig. 11.7 George Chatterton D.S.O, O.B.E., Brigadier, British Glider Pilot Regiment, British Army; in WW2.

At the end of the war their actual regimental flag was placed in the local Stedham church of St James; it has since been relocated. A permanent memorial to the WW2 British glider pilots has replaced the flag in the church.

Nothing has yet been found on the use of Stedham Hall toward the war effort, but it surely would have been used as billets; accommodation space was at a premium as troops, and evacuees and relatives escaping the London bombings, filled the District to overflowing.

As has been covered in Chapter 9, another close branch of the Stedham Scrimgeour family during WW2 supported the pre-war British fascist movement. These were Ethel and her brother Alexander. Ethel's father was the, above mentioned, John Scrimgeour of Wispers and then Stedham Hall.

Chapter 11 Where the 'Other Half' lived.

11.3 Wispers/St Cuthman's School

Fig. 11.8 Wispers/St Cuthman's School, converted to student accommodation in 2006.

Wispers, Fig. 11.8, is a Grade II listed British country house; also situated in the parish of Stedham with Iping, near Midhurst.

It has had a chequered history. The house was built in 1874-1876 by architect Richard Norman Shaw, in the Tudor Revival style, more commonly known as *Mock Tudor*. It was built for the stockbroker, Alexander Scrimgeour, who is discussed in Chapter 9.

The house was sold in 1928 into the Bedford estate of Dame Mary Russell (the wife of the 11th Duke of Bedford) as a weekend retreat, to which she added the huge eastern wing and a light air-plane hangar in the 1930s. Her flying experiences are covered in Book 1, Chapter 8.

Born Mary du Caurroy Tribe in 1865, she only became interested in flying at 63 years of age, that is, in 1928 when Wispers became hers.

With such little flying experience, she, amazingly, just after she bought *Wispers*, made a record-breaking return flight to India in just 8 days, carrying it out in her single-engine *Fokker F.V11*. Fig. 11.9 shows her with her pilot, Captain Barnard, on their return to Croydon Airport in August 1929. Her mechanic, Bob Little, also was on that flight with the plane.

Wispers was a private house from its construction until 1939. From then it has housed several schools and became accommodation for leisure

Fig. 11.9 Duchess Russell and personal pilot Captain C D Barnard back from India, 1929.

and weekly boarding of secondary school students. In 2009 it was sold again, but at a price for less than it was bought. Due to commercial forces, many houses were converted into apartments; large houses had become less in demand as single-family residences.

'Most of the Canadian troops were up at Wispers, just at the top of Redford, and that's a very big old house, in fact I think it was originally owned by a titled lady who was called the Flying Duchess - who some years before the war flew off in a private plane and was never seen again.'
Michael Gates. Elsdon (2010).

Following her death, the house was sold in 1939 but the 'Military Authorities' requisitioned it to house Canadian soldiers. After the war, it became a school known as St Cuthman's, before the West Sussex council bought it as a special-needs facility. http://thecountryseat.org.uk

Since 2010 Wispers was a part of the Durand Academy, a state-funded Boarding school for children from Lambeth in London. Teaching standards not being up to requirements, the State withdrew funding and the parent-school decided it must close the boarding school in Stedham. A transfer to another school was recorded to be on the cards in 2017. In June 2018 its new ownership was still in doubt for the school and its debt was considered to be 'too risky' to take on. Will Wispers become another upmarket housing development as had been proposed well before?

Students were being bussed down from their London homes to board there for the teaching week. I find an easy affinity with this use, for the Midhurst District environment would still be giving children much of

Chapter 11 Where the 'Other Half' lived.

the experience I and other evacuees from a large city, enjoyed during WW2.

11.4 Fitz Hall

Fig. 11.10 Fitz Hall main house, with extensions.

Just 3 miles out of Midhurst, to the west on Elsted Road, is Fitz Hall, a somewhat smaller mansion property, Fig. 11.10.

Fitz Hall was built by Christopher Bettesworth in Elizabethan times. In 1793 it was passed on to the Piggot family that lived there until 1931 when it was purchased by J H Hollingsworth.

In 1824, however, the newly wedded husband of Jane Piggott took the Piggott name and arms by Royal Permission - see *Gentleman's Magazine*, vol 94, pt 2. pp 368, 1824. In the mid-1800s this family was listed in the Aristocracy of the County Families of the United Kingdom, 1892.

According to District resident John Hills, in Dicks et al, (2012), after the war years, it was taken over from the Hollingsworth's by the Bridger family for use as a nursing home.

The buildings have been completely rebuilt in the 19th century and have English Heritage Grade 11 listing since 1959.

Additions made in 1932, a porch and a south wing range, indicate it was still being kept up and was still lived in. In the 90s it was owned by two lovely ladies who did afternoon tea's - sometimes.

The web site www.wildehobbs.plus.com/teashops/teatable.htm lists Fitzhall in its Teashop list, but the date of that list is not given.

It is included here for this estate has significance to my time as an evacuee there in the District during WW2. What is relevant there is the entry gatehouse.

In the late 30s it was still a primitive home; water from a well in the back garden, no central heating, no electricity, and with a long drop 'dunny' situated way down the garden - more details are to be found in the Fitzhall part of my visit there in 1944, given in a later book.

Fig. 11.11 is the gatehouse in 2014. It is now called *Fitzhall Lodge*. At the time it did not appear to be that big a house; perhaps extensions have taken place since then?

Fig. 11.11 Gatehouse at Fitz Hall, today.

During the war, my cousins Marjorie and Arthur, also evacuees from London, lived in the gatehouse with their mother, my aunt Lizzie.

The surrounding plantation of pines and the sandpit quarry area were well used by the military during WW2. There was a hut there somewhere that was used by the Home Guard.

Chapter 11 Where the 'Other Half' lived.

It was so silent there at night. One could hear the calming drone of an aeroplane high up on the sky. We always thought it was friendly... but was it?

11.5 Bignor Manor House

Fig. 11.12 Bignor Manor, 1933.

The West Sussex website tells us that Bignor is the site of magnificent ca 200AD mosaics of a Roman villa.

Not so well known is the role in WW2 of one of the significant houses in the Midhurst District; Bignor Manor, Fig. 11.12; just 10miles SE of Midhurst. It would have looked like this picture when the war began; then, however, it was all too 'secret' to talk about.

It is situated in a very secluded place way off the main roads; just the place for its special kind of use during WW2.

This, a modest Elizabethan farmhouse, was rented by Major Anthony Bertram when he and Barbara were married in the early 1930s. They enjoyed a good start to their married life at Bignor Manor, not knowing what they would soon do for the war effort.

Its utilities were basic but it had just been connected with electricity and had installed a new bathroom and washbasins in three of the four bedrooms. Water was pumped up from a river. Fig.11.13 is a photo of the Bertrams at that time.

Fig. 11.13 Barbara and Anthony Bertram, 1930s, Wake-Walker (2011).

In late 1940 Tony was summoned by the War Office to attend a meeting at the Minimax Fire Extinguishing Company in London. To his surprise, it was the office of the Secret Intelligence Service, SIS.

At the meeting, he volunteered the use of their house as a secret forward base for members of the French Resistance who were waiting to be flown into, and back from, France via the nearby Tangmere Air Force base.

At the time Barbara was not relishing her role as a foster mother to the rather rough evacuees she had been allocated and easily took to the idea of looking after secret agents as a better option. In her favour was that she was on familiar terms with the local landed gentry families.

From 1941-1944 she provided boarding for the agents, also checking that their clothing and equipment was consistent with being French before they left on a mission. Returning agents would be taken there for food, rest and their initial debriefing. Fig. 11.14 is of the

Chapter 11 Where the 'Other Half' lived.

drawing-room, as it was used at that time. Barbara had to feed the agents; there were often a house full of as many as 9 guests, plus drivers and others. When at a full house situation, the drawing-room had to sleep agents on the chairs and sofa.

Fig. 11.14 Bignor Manor drawing-room during wartime, Wake-Walker (2011).

Even being in a secluded place did not keep its presence secret so it was put around that is was for convalescing French officers. They even had men with make believe broken legs in plaster there. In this guise, the agents could make good use of the White Horse pub half a mile away, in nearby Sutton.

What it was like for agents dropped into Belgium, and similarly so for France, can be viewed in the 96minute film *Against the Wind* from the Ealing Studios, February 1948. Films made during, or just after the war, were realistic in the props and ways of the people who then still vividly remembered their own experiences, or more likely, that of the sacrifices of others.

This film covers all stages from being recruited, trained, and inserted, taking action, being retrieved by light plane, along with their emotional thoughts on their colleagues and their own countries.

It is not so surprising that returning agents were so stressed when back in England after time behind enemy lines. Many lost their lives, even simply at the result of their parachute jump going wrong. Some were saved. A long account of the SIS being at Bignor Manor is available, Wake-Walker (2011).

Midhurst WW2 Memoirs: 2. 'Evil' Rising: 'Good' Awakening

The war-time airfield, so close by in Selham, appears to have had no connection with what took place in Bignor. That airfield's purpose was to hold small aircraft used at sea by the Royal Navy, them being taken there to have modifications and maintenance needs carried out.

11.6 Bohunt Manor

Fig. 11.15. Bohunt Manor.

British History On Line tells us that Bohunt Manor, as a place, has roots back in the 1100s. By 1158 it was known as the Rogate-Bohunt Manor. It was rebuilt in 1770, retaining its walled garden.

Situated 8 miles to NW of Midhurst, it is in Hampshire on the boundary of the Midhurst Rural District. The current Manor was built over a previous building in 1928; it used stone from that. Fig. 11.15 is of Bohunt Manor, as it is today.

Its magnificent gardens, with the large open land spaces, were begun in 1953 when the property was bought by Sir Adrian Holman. He sought the advice of George Brown, Assistant Curator at Kew. Sir Adrian Holman and Lady Holman lived there following his retirement from the Foreign Service in 1954.

Adjacent is the magnificent course of the Bohunt Manor Golf Club that was formed in 1923. In 1974 Sir Adrian bequeathed it to the *World*

Chapter 11 Where the 'Other Half' lived.

Wild Life Fund (WWF UK). Lady Holman continued to live there until 2004. After she died in 2005 the WWF sold the manor.

The Manor house estate has now been sold in parts and is gradually losing much of its originality. It went, in 2007, to IML Ltd who specialised in interactive communication technology. It was sold on again and was the subject of a housing estate proposal; then refused.

During the WW2 years, it was used as a service hospital.

11.7 Uppark House

Fig. 11.16 Uppark House, from the front.

The history of Uppark house, Fig. 11.16, started when it was built around 1690. What you see architecturally today is still much as it was then.

After being bought by Sir Matthew Fetherstonhaugh in 1747, it was redecorated extensively being filled with household items; many still there today were obtained on their personal Grand Tour. Additional items and building extensions were added later. As happened with so many stately homes that could not be kept due to the costs involved, long term family owners were often forced to quit. In 1954 this house was passed over to the National Trust.

The house has had many fascinating ownership changes over its long history, see Rowell and Robinson (1996), including a marriage to a dairy-maid in 1825 who was 50 years younger than the owner Sir Harry Fetherstonhaugh, and a voluntary name change by Col. Turnover to carry on the Fetherstonhaugh family name.

At the end of the 19th century, the house was the home of two aged ladies, Miss Fetherstonhaugh and her companion. She was the last of that line. In 1931 she bequeathed the house to a son of a neighbour; Admiral Herbert Meade-Fetherstonhaugh, Fig. 11.7, who, with his wife Lady Meade, spent 35years restoring it. They were the occupants during WW2 who contributed much to the war effort with their bare hands.

Fig. 11.17 Sir Herbert in full ceremony dress with Lady Meade-Fetherstonhaugh. (National Trust)

Passed on by gift, the house went into the care of the National Trust in 1954; the Admiral and his son Robin continued to live there as tenants.

In 1989 most of all that preservation work and expenditure, went up in smoke. According to Peter Pearce, who was the National Trust's Managing Land Agent responsible for the restoration taking place at that time, it was a properly thought out safety requirement that was ignored:

> 'I had drawn up and signed the contract with the builders who caused the fire (which started from lead workers ignoring carefully drafted "hot work" rules against precisely this risk)'
> on the West Dean website.

Chapter 11 Where the 'Other Half' lived.

A blow torch being used by a plumber repairing the lead flashing in the roof set off a devastating fire.

Fig. 11.18 Uppark House was gutted in a matter of hours. (National Trust)

Peter was not blamed for this and was appointed that very day to lead the large restoration team over the next 6 years. It was the largest restoration undertaken by the National Trust.

At the time of the fire Featherstone family members carried out many of the treasures, but the building was badly damaged.

The way insurance worked best for them led to it being restored, rather than be paid out as a total loss. The insurance battle went right up the House of Lords and generated 4 tons of paperwork!

Restoration, done under pressure of the insurers, took many years but needs to be seen to be believed for its artistic interior decorations are now, maybe, better than new! It was fortunate to have the West Dean College nearby; its staff and students specialise in fine art restoration. The house reopened to the public in 1995. The restoration has been recorded in great detail in Rowell and Robinson, (1996).

H G Wells had a close association with the house in his youth. See Chapter 7, of Book 1, where his early life is covered including his time there at Uppark with his mother.

What is of interest to these memoirs is the part played by the family during WW2. As well as being a staging care-post for evacuees on arrival, they also produced much-needed goods for war use.

Its large parklands garden grew copious amounts of herbs for medical use. Lady Meade-Fetherstonhaugh recorded in Harting Residents (1995):

'Uppark was, before the last war, in a position to Harvest annually, between 2-4 tons of Belladonna (Atropa) which grows freely in the park and it was sent to manufacturing chemists for herbal use every summer. In 1940, several offices and warehouses were destroyed and the need for gathering and drying of herbs intensified. I, accordingly, organised a regular industry, not only of Belladonna but also of many other herbs. Help in collecting was given by Women's Institutes, Schools and other groups, until in 1944, over 70 varieties of medicinal and culinary herbs were dried in quantities totalling hundreds of pounds or even tons.'

Belladonna is extracted from the highly poisonous weed, *Deadly Nightshade,* Fig. 11.19. Its hallucinogenic effects have been long been known and were documented in-depth, as Atropa, in the free Google e-book, Encyclopaedia *Londinensis,* of 1810. It is now used in the treatment of numerous body complaints, including some heart conditions, and bone and muscle aches and tremors.

Fig. 11.19 *Deadly Nightshade* is a poisonous, commonly found, weed.

The area in which Uppark House situated, the *Hardings,* also had a significant cottage industry making grommets used to protect wiring passing through metal frames of radios, and aircraft, tanks and ships. That aspect is covered in a later book where local District industries are discussed.

Chapter 11 Where the 'Other Half' lived.

11.8 Stansted Park

Fig. 11.20 Standsted House.

Stansted House, with origins 800 years ago, sits 15 miles south-west of Midhurst on 1750 acres in the South Downs National Park.

The grand house seen today was originally built in 1688 as a hunting lodge but it burned down in 1900. In 1903 it was rebuilt with the same footprint; it is again mainly as it was. Its chapel, consecrated in 1819, was damaged by a bomb in November 1940, but that has also been restored.

It was purchased in 1781 by Richard Barwell, an influential Bengal civil servant. He gained one of the largest fortunes in early British India. He lived at Stansted Park until he died in 1804. His life was not without hints of corruption.

The estates were then sold out of his family by his trustees to Lewis Way, and hence on through several ownerships each of which carried on the development of the house and gardens.

In 1924 it was bought by the 9th Earl of Bessborough, Vere Ponsonby, born in London in 1880, Fig. 11.21. He was described in the Canadian Encyclopedia thus:

'The handsome, rich, well-fed and impeccably dressed aristocrat must have been an incongruous sight at the height of the Great Depression, but he showed his sympathy with the plight of Canadians in small ways, and was granted his wish for a 10% cut in salary.

Fig. 11.21 Vere Ponsonby, 9th Earl of Bessborough and his wife Roberte.

From 1931-35 he was the Governor-General of Canada. He did many things of note. He and his wife made a good name for themselves there; they set up the *Dominion Drama Festival* that promoted amateur theatre in Canada from 1932 - 1978.

He was on the Staff of the League of Nations LN High Commission for Refugees from Germany between 1936 and 1939. During the Second World War, he served in France and Africa, achieving the rank of Captain in the 98th (Surrey and Sussex Yeomanry) Field Brigade of the Royal Artillery (TAReserve). This was probably the same unit that had camped in Cowdray park in 1937.

He enjoyed a distinguished career involving much overseas travel and so was rarely 'at home' during the 30s and 40s.

Since 1983 the House and Estate have been administered by the Stansted Park Foundation, an independent charitable trust set up by Frederick [Eric] Ponsonby, the 10th Earl. He was most concerned for the longevity of the estate.

Chapter 11 Where the 'Other Half' lived.

During WW2, Vere Ponsonby helped establish a department in the British Foreign Office dedicated to the welfare of the French refugees in the United Kingdom.

Being where the massive invasion force swept through into the Portsmouth area for the D-Day invasion in 1944, the Stansted estate was used to good effect,

> 'I was 8 years old when I was moved out of my home in Holland Road, Southsea to Redhill in Rowlands Castle, (right next to Standsted Park) This was to avoid the German bombs falling on Portsmouth.
> As I was at an impressionable age the build-up to D-Day was very exciting as the village had British and Canadian troops milling around.
> I can recall the build-up to the invasion and how I became the first casualty. My uncle Bill had a dairy at Links Lane near *The Green* and I used to love playing all over the area. The soldiers, British and Canadian were everywhere, in the woods, in tents on The Green and Stansted Park.
> I remember my uncle complaining about the Canadians, whom he described as 'great big fellas' because they used to come to the dairy and drink all his milk.
> ....
> I would go in and out of the soldiers' camp with my little mate and pick up .303 bullets and put them in my truck.
> ....
> My next encounter with the Army was when I climbed over the wall at Stansted Park near the railway bridge and I fell on the other side. I cut my arm on some sharp flints and cried. The soldiers picked me up and took me to a first-aid post. I was bandaged up and still have the scar now, making me the first casualty before they suddenly moved out'.
>
>   Brian Stallard, BBC people's stories.

On 7 May 1944, Royal Canadian Air force Flying Officer Justin Clermont, Fig. 11.22, died when his Typhoon aircraft, from nearby Tangmere airfield, crashed in the park after it had burst into flames.

Fig. 11.22 Flying Officer Justin Clermont died when his aircraft crashed in Stansted Park. (Petersfield Post)

The *Petersfield Post* reported the rebuilt wooden memorial, being dedicated in 2016. The original simple, evocative, wooden cross and an engraved table had been put up in May 1944, by 14-year-old Graham Alderson, who saw it happen.

As will be seen all through these Midhurst District memoirs, the Canadians greatly supported their commonwealth kinship in Britain. The memorial plaque reads:

'Let all know who read this epitaph know that he died helping to ensure our freedom'

With the long military connections of the 9th Earl, it is to be expected that the house also was put to good use toward the war effort.

11.9 Parham House

Sixteen miles to the east of Midhurst, Parham House – in 3733 acres - is not quite within the Midhurst Rural District. It has already been mentioned in Book 1 for its Roman cistern that is seemingly proof of early Christianity in Roman Sussex; and for its priest hole.

Following the dissolution, Henry VIII granted this manor to Robert Palmer. Its foundation stone was laid in 1577. He sold the house in 1601 to Sir Thomas Bysshopp. For 320 years their descendants lived at Parham.

In 1922 the 17th Baroness Zouche sold the estate to the Hon. Clive and Alicia Pearson, Fig. 11.24. Clive was the second son of Weetman Dickinson Pearson, the 1st Viscount Cowdray.

Chapter 11 Where the 'Other Half' lived.

Fig. 11.23 Parham House.

When they took over the House it had no electricity or drains, and the roof leaked. The estate's website provides insight into the use of this mansion during WW2 and what has been done there.

Fig. 11.24 Clive and Alicia Pearson in 1956. (West Sussex Gazette)

Over the years they, and then their daughter Veronica Tritton, restored both the garden and the house, furnishing the latter with some original pieces and in a style sensitive to how it was in the past: see Kirk (2009), for a scholarly, comprehensive account of the house restoration.

'With the outbreak of war in 1939, Parham became home to 30 evacuee children from Peckham in south-east London. Most had never been to the country before, and Clive Pearson built them a small wooden house in which to play. To persuade them to eat vegetables, he divided a section of the walled garden into vegetable plots and gave the children tools and lots of seeds. The resulting competition to produce the best crops was a great success, and meant that everyone finished everything on their plates!'
Parham House website.

As soon as the war was declared, rooms were cleared of art-works and furniture to make space for the evacuees, with their two teachers from Peckham. Sisters of many of these boys also came later.

It was a major new experience for them to live in the country. They were lucky to be away from Peckham when 49 High Explosive bombs and other ordnances were dropped there during the German bombing Blitz of 1940-41. It was a harsh first winter there for the evacuees but they had plenty of snow on which to toboggan, to make snowmen, or to throw snowballs at each other. They each were given dressing gowns. In the summer of 1942, they moved on to nearby Storrington. No doubt this move would have been welcomed by the Pearson family owners!

The reason for moving them on could have been the need to clear the area for the influx of Canadian troops into the South Downs Training Area in readiness for the D-Day landing and advance through France. Soldiers were stationed all over the park, with the Head Quarters and staff billeting being set up in the Great Hall and western end of Parham House.

Evacuees billeted in the large house were tantamount to being boarders but without enough pastoral house support. It was usually better for children to be with a family; however, as we will see in the next book, not all evacuee experiences were good!

Extended family and friends of the Pearsons, gathered up from

Chapter 11 Where the 'Other Half' lived.

various locations, lived in the other part for the duration of the war:
> 'the lack of regular maintenance and the use of the house by the army, and as a home for the evacuees from London, did positive harm'. Kirk (2009).

Londoner kids are often reported as being rough and loutish to varying degrees: they were not all like that! Some people, however, in the district positively loathed them being there and let them know in no uncertain terms! *Goodnight Mr Tom,* Magorian (1981) tells a nicer story of an imaginary London lad. Also, let's not forget that 'boys will be boys' and have been much the same over the centuries; ask any parent of today!

Kirk's account tells a little about troop use at Parham for 4 years during WW2. They requisitioned the Great Hall and the West Wing, the family stayed on in the east end. A hardcore of resident knitters supplied the troops with socks and balaclavas.

The swimming pool, built-in 1930 in the grounds, came in handy for training Canadian soldiers how to repair bridges. In 1942, they built concrete roads on the eastern end of the estate that remain today.

It could take years for places like this to be de-requisitioned. The War Department had many post-war needs to cover, such as readying German POWS to return home after they learned about democracy - and also had somewhere to return to in their shattered country.

The Pearson's got their beloved house and estate back in July 1946. When the military left the House it was far from a desirable living place. Several years of soldier inhabitancy without enough strict control of cleanliness and decoration work, left it smelling of an army. It required much repair and restoration. Nissen huts used for troop accommodation were removed at the end of 1946.

To repair the house needed £2000 (£100,000 today). After a great family effort, the house started to have limited openings to the public in July 1948; revenue was again coming in to help the recovery of the house and gardens.

As was the case for many estates then, post-war building regulations restricted work to a mere £25 p.a., that being £1000 per year in present value. The wealthy were not going to recover their estates to the former asset value in a hurry. Also, building materials were in very high demand, with low availability.

Relevant to these memoirs is a collection of 1922 - 1948 photographs, covering local events of those times. These are on display in the Long Room, Fig. 11.25.

Fig. 11.25 Long Room of Parham House, where some records of WW2 events are on display. (Parham House)

The Pearson's two eldest daughters both married soldiers soon after war broke out. Lavinia' husband became a POW for most of the war. Veronica's husband died of wounds in Libya in 1941.

Whereas Parham suffered from 6 years of low maintenance it can be said of soldiers of the 1st, 2nd and 3rd Canadian Infantry Divisions, who were stationed in hurriedly erected Nissen huts in the grounds, that they kept it in good order.

Soldiers of all nationalities in Britain were instructed, under threat of high penalties including imprisonment, to care for what they found and used. View the sweet children's film *The Canterville Ghost,* to see pre-D-Day US invasion forces being instructed on this issue as they took up residence in a large country mansion. History has shown that the Canadian and other soldiers left the south of England very much as they found it. Few signs of them ever having been there are to be found today.

A charitable trust now looks after the house, opening it to the public since 1948. Lady Emma Barnard, from the Guinness family line, has lived there as the chatelaine with her husband and children. Since 1993 she has been keeping up the tradition; that she is just the current keeper on a long

Chapter 11 Where the 'Other Half' lived.

line of minders:

'..... like her relations before her, Lady Emma remains humble about her role at Parham House. "I'm just a tiny link in a very long chain of people that have lived here and loved it and looked after it. It's been here for centuries and it will outlast us all"

www.britain-magazine.com

Fig. 11.26 Memorial stone for Clive and Alicia Pearson in Parham village. (Find a Grave)

Clive Pearson died in 1965, aged 77 years. He is buried in St Peter's Churchyard, Parham, Fig. 11.25.

Everyday, flowers from the estate are refreshed in every room, a custom having been started by Alicia Pearson in 1948:

'Garden flowers throughout the house are a family tradition,' Lady Emma Barnard

11.10 Leonardslee Estate

Another place of wealthy ownership, 27 miles to the NE of Midhurst, and just out of the Midhurst Rural District, is Leonardslee. After many years the estate is now open again to visitors.

An existing, Grade II listed, elegant Italianate house was finished in 1855; the gardens were started in 1801. The 240 acres of gardens were established by Baron Sir Edmund Loder.

This house is of interest to these memoirs because, if an overheard conversation was heard correctly, it might well have become the Occupied British HQ of the German Luftwaffe - that has been covered in Chapter 6.2.

Fig. 11.27 Leonardslee Estate.

Sir Edmond bought the property, Fig. 11.27, from his in-laws in 1889. He was a 'dedicated plantsman', having a rhododendron variety named after him.

Fig. 11.28 Sir Edmund Giles Loder in 1947.

His career record as a Justice of the Peace for Sussex and Northamptonshire seems to have been more a case of fulfilling a necessary public duty, than as an income-driven path of his life. He was a *gentleman philosopher* in terms of his day. He was gifted with the ability to see massive amounts of information, instantly retaining it in his photographic memory.

Edmund was trained to be a professional engineer but was interested in so many more subjects. On completion of his undergraduate period at Cambridge University, his first strong interest led him to study a love of astronomy. He published a significant book on astronomy, Loder (1880).

His path through life aligned with interests that he found success in doing. He must have had independent means of support, for this book

Chapter 11 Where the 'Other Half' lived.

was the result of a world tour of famous astronomical observatories. The now sought-after image plates in it were made using the albumen silver print photography method.

His greatest interest, however, was creating 'the finest woodland garden in England'. He needed the Leonardslee site to satisfy a passion for plants, and the many kinds of garden setting to show them off; in the main, the plant's species are rhododendrons, azaleas, camellias, magnolias, bluebells and exotic trees. Fig. 11.29.

Fig.11.29 Leonardslee gardens in full bloom.

In 1981 he passed the property over to his younger son, Robin. Sir Edmund died in 1920, possibly as one of the last renaissance *gentlemen scientists.*

At his memorial service his daughter, Patience, fittingly eulogised:

"Father had a peculiar grasp of any subject in which he was interested. . . from astronomy and colour photography and from collecting conifers to jade. . . I wonder whether the Garden he now walks in is much fairer than the beloved one here [Leonardslee] which he made so beautiful, and I like to think of him gardening still – privileged to add even to the glories of Paradise"
Cowan's Rare Books Auctions website.

He also travelled through many countries following an interest in wildlife, large animals. The result was a living zoo, still maintained at Leonardslee, of gazelles, beavers, kangaroos and a colony of wallabies.

According to a description in the listing of the gardens, they entered a period of neglect during the 1930s. Its history from that time does not appear to have been recorded.

In 2008 it was put up for sale, selling in 2010 to a virtually anonymous private buyer who then closed the gardens to the public for several years. There are, however, several magnificent YouTube videos of its beauty, all made around 2009 - 2013.

In April 2013, plans in support of reopening the garden went to the Horsham District Council planning committee who approved them with great interest.

> 'Considerable investment is planned for the long-term development of the estate, including Leonardslee House, to provide a sustainable strategy to maintain and enhance the gardens and buildings and to provide a range of visitor attractions and services.'
>
> www.wscountytimes.co.uk

There has long been an air of mystery about the reopening of these magnificent gardens. When will the gardens again be open to the public? There was even a rumour on the Web that the new owner had been kidnapped abroad and when released he bought the gardens.

What is true is that in 2017, Penny Streeter OBE acquired the estate taking it through the many hoops of eco approvals needed to be open to the public. In July 2018 the house was used for its inaugural wedding reception. The restored gardens opened again in April 2019.

Returning to the first remarks on how it seems to have been saying it would become the HQ of the Luftwaffe. It is good to see that it did not - imagine sieg heiling Nazis in their resplendent but threatening uniforms being entertained in the house, and marching around the garden paths. Worse still, would have been to see Nazi swastikas everywhere, including flying from the house flagpole and at the entrance gate.

Chapter 11 Where the 'Other Half' lived.

11.11 Woolbeding House

Fig. 11.30 Woolbeding House.

The large country residence, Woolbeding House, Fig. 11.30, is 1-mile north-west of Midhurst. It was originally owned by the Lascelles family.

Between 1791 to 1831 it was occupied by the son of the 3rd Duke of Marlborough, who entertained many famous guests there, Walker (2006).

In the 1920s it was owned by Mr and Mrs Henry Lascelles. During WW2 it was owned by Mrs and Mrs Edward Lascelles; by 1947 it had passed to Mr Edward Lascelles.

The 1,102acre estate, with its 26 acres of garden, was gifted to the National Trust in 1956 but needed a tenant because of the lack of any associated funding with the handover.

In 1972 it was leased by the timid philanthropist, Sir Simon Sainsbury (who died in 2006) of the Sainsbury supermarket family, and his partner in life, Stewart Grimshaw. They, with the assistance of American garden designer Lanning Roper, implemented sweeping changes.

In this garden is a replica of a great treasure, the fountain that once stood in the middle of the Great Court of the Tudor Cowdray house; the Ruins today. It was, Fig. 11.31, given to Woolbeding after the fire that destroyed the Tudor house. Being so significant a work of art, the original is in the V&A Museum; what you see at Woolbeding is a faithful copy.

Fig. 11.31 Grimm's 1782 record of the Fountain when in the Tudor Cowdray House.

The property is still in the hands of Simon who uses it as a weekender home for which he helps upgrade the gardens and is happy to see the public in attendance once it opened for visits in 2011.

Just what its WW2 contribution was, is not covered in its detailed history, Walker (2006). As billets for the military officers were in very short supply in Midhurst the most logical use was for that purpose.

11.12 Petworth House and Estate

Another estate of significance to the Midhurst District is the Petworth House, just 6 miles away to the east, Fig. 11.32.

Fig. 11.32 Petworth Park and House. (Artist: Jean Courtauld).

Chapter 11 Where the 'Other Half' lived.

Petworth and Midhurst have long been linked in many ways. The local newspaper was founded in 1882 as *The Midhurst Times*. It underwent a series of name changes in the 1930s: first it became the *Midhurst and Petworth Times* (1935), then the *Midhurst, Petworth, Haslemere and District Times* (1936), then the *Midhurst, Petworth and District Times* (New Year 1940). It briefly became the *Midhurst and Petworth Times* once more in 1962 before relaunching under its present title of the *Midhurst and Petworth Observer* in 1964. Some of its material also appears in the *Observer* Series of newspapers covering Chichester and Bognor Regis. Beginning in August 2007, an archive of over 20,000 articles is available at www.highbeam.com.

The local district Courts combine the two areas. The Catholic Churches of each are today administered together from Petworth. The landed Lords of these manors have often worked together over the past centuries on issues of common interest.

Petworth is less interested in rural matters than is Midhurst. Petworth, on the other hand, is focussed as 'a Centre for Arts and Culture'.

Petworth has been voted the 'Best Antiques Town'. Known as the 'Antiques Centre of the South', its Petworth Art and Antique Dealers Association (PAADA) boasts having over 30 dealers within a mile radius whereas Midhurst has almost nothing in that line to offer.

This major difference in outlook may have come about because the dominant Cowdray Estate is still a privately-owned commercial business working in rural products. It has its international focus on polo. The Petworth grand house is now owned by the people and is a cultural place to visit for its art treasures and cultural events. Some lesser hung artworks are to be seen in the Midhurst Gallery, an independent retail shop for artists materials and works.

Petworth and Midhurst have quite different street-scapes. Both suffer from inadequate car parking availability in peak visiting times!

Petworth seems to be smaller than Midhurst town but has one-star attraction - its original stately Petworth House in a park of some 700 acres.

The estate, Maxse (1972), came into the Percy family as a royal gift in the 12th century. The current house is the manor house of Petworth Manor, being built in 1688.

When just 2 years old, Lady Elizabeth Percy inherited the estate in 1668. By the time she was 16, she had been widowed twice! She then married the 6th Duke of Somerset combining their considerable wealth, thereby seeding the turbulent situation that was to follow.

The history of the estate is worthy of an engaging television series period drama; it was so full of intrigue and manoeuvring by the inheritors and those who felt sorely aggrieved by not benefiting as they expected and took actions at the Royal level. Since 1750 the house and estate have been in the Wyndham family.

Successive death duties led to the Petworth House and deer park being passed over to the nation in 1947 by Charles Henry Wyndham, 3rd Lord Leconfield (1872-1952). These aristocratic titles and family names can be confusing at times! He lived and died in the 'big house'.

Charles had a long military career beginning in the Boer War, and as Commanding Officer of the newly reformed Sussex Yeomanry originally raised by the 3rd Earl of Egremont. He continued to serve in the 98th Sussex Yeomanry and was Lord Lieutenant of Sussex between 1917 and 1949. His military involvement in WW2 is unclear. From his picture, Fig, 11.33, his interest in aristocratic pastimes is clear.

Fig. 11.33 Charles Wyndham in 1908, owner of the Petworth Estate in WW2.

His daughter, Elizabeth Wyndham, accomplished in many languages, worked in the code-breaking department at Bletchley Park during the war.

Today Lord Egremont, (John Max Henry Scawen Wyndham, 2nd Baron Leconfield. 2nd Baron Egremont), and Lady Caroline Nelson Egremont live in a third of the house. This Lord Egremont has lived there since his childhood, being born just after WW2 in 1948. His 'career'

Chapter 11 Where the 'Other Half' lived.

is as an acclaimed novelist and biographer. Their family tree is available from the National Trust.

> 'One of the things I like about the Trust is its determination not to turn the house into a great showplace with all sorts of attractions that aren't suited to it',
> Current Lord Egremont in 2011.

His story is presented in an article by Angela Wintle, *Sussex Life*, 25 May 2011.

During the WW2 hostilities, the grounds were used as troop camps. For the D-Day invasion, it was a battle tank holding area. Interesting accounts about its use in wartime are included in later books of these memoirs.

11.13 West Dean House

Just 7 miles to the south of Midhurst is the civil parish of West Dean. It is on the boundary of the Midhurst Rural District being midway between Chichester and Midhurst town.

Fig. 11.34 West Dean House before WW2.

Before WW2 the estate covered some 8000 acres. It has a grand house, Fig. 11.34, now the West Dean College, that is devoted to the conservation of the national and international cultural heritage. That theme grew from the heartfelt wish of its last private owner, Edward James.

The imposing grand house was built in 1804 for Baron Selsey;

much remodelling took place around 1892. It was purchased in 1893 by William Dodge James.

Edward W. F. James reached his age of 25 in 1912, taking control of his inherited West Dean estate in 1932 as Lord of the Manor. He inherited considerable wealth as the result of American railroad business generated by his father, William. He married Tilly Losch in the early 30s but was divorced in 1934. Fig. 11.35 shows him as a sensitive young man with his wife.

Fig. 11.35 Young Edward W F James and wife, Tilly Losch.

During his short, married period there was much going on in the house:

'Mrs James led a life typical of the super-rich in the late Victorian and Edwardian periods. The colossal house parties, complete with private orchestra, which she gave at her enormous property in Sussex were often attended by Edward VII, both as Prince of Wales and later as King. She appeared to have no fear of convention, and, in 1896, was reported to have bicycled through the night with twenty-three of her house guests to watch the sunrise over the Downs. One of the male guests had to offer his jacket to stop her from freezing, as, it was noted, she was wearing "next to no clothes." '

Anon (2011).

Edward was best known as a poet, and for his support of the surrealist art movement. He was, however, a man of many artistic talents; the kind of person who makes a difference in the thinking aspects of life. You may not agree with all of his actions for they were 'way out' at times. The meaningful biography, Anon (2011), shows his slant on a life that

Chapter 11 Where the 'Other Half' lived.

made a great difference to the lives of many, not only whilst he lived but lasting to this day; as will be explained below.

Some insights to his life from his biography Anon (2011) are:

'James was an eccentric, hugely wealthy Englishman in search of something, and somewhere: the truth is, probably he didn't even know what it was he wanted to find.'

'James's life illustrates many things, but one of them is that social connections and great wealth do not necessarily augur great happiness, and may instead condemn a man of promise to a restless life, blighted by uncertainty both in himself and in those around him. James was also homosexual, and early marriage to the ballerina Tilly Losch only served to confuse and complicate an already tortured existence.'

It was not uncommon for wealthy young persons to suffer this kind of mental struggle. Their freedom gave them too much time to ponder on the meaning of life and how it should be conducted, all that being without close contact with others who were 'run of the mill' and 'down to earth'.

How we turn out largely depends on our surroundings and the opportunities that beset us. Some wealthy young men or women dissipate the wealth; others end up using it to great purpose, as did Edward - even if that purpose earned him the name of 'another amazing rich freak' on *Mondo-blogo* BlogSpot.

His anonymous biography states his miserable marriage was probably the reason he decided to be 'out of town' during WW2. It might be thought he did it to avoid having to fight for his country but his marriage ended in 1934 well before the realisation that war was going to happen.

If he ever returned to West Dean during the war period is not discussed in his biography. Whilst away he had become deeply entangled with love relationships, and with work on his passions for travelling, the pursuit of orchid growing, and that of designing surrealistic concrete garden sculptures and *follies* that he made in Xilitia, Mexico, Fig. 11.36.

It is often for a simple error we have made somewhere that we get remembered for. Edward had one early in life:

Fig.11.36 Edward James in Xilitia in later life.

'After Oxford, James had a brief career as a trainee diplomat at the embassy in Rome. He was asked to send a coded message to London that the Italians had laid the keels for three destroyers, but got the code wrong; the message said "300 destroyers". Shortly after this, he was sent "on indefinite leave".'
Wikipedia

Major house redesigns took place at West Dean during the 30s. Edward gained a lasting name for work in preserving his estate for a well-deserving, long term use by the people.

In 1939, as war broke out, he expressed his fear that after the war the techniques of the craftsmen would be lost. He then suggested the estate be set up as an educational community to preserve, restore and create artworks.

It is to be expected that West Dean house and grounds were put to good use for the war effort. His war service, if any, is not mentioned anywhere.

In 1964 he passed over his family mansion, art collection, and estate with its gardens, to *The Edward James Foundation*, a charitable educational trust. It became West Dean College in 1971.

Chapter 11 Where the 'Other Half' lived.

He died in 1984 leaving no heir. He, however, had realised his dream with the College in place. He is buried on the estate. The monumental stone, Fig.11.37, declares he was a poet - but he was much more than that.

Fig.11.37 Edward James is buried in a modest grave in the grounds of the estate he left to the nation for a useful purpose.

On-line cataloguing of his archive began early in 2018. From this resource so much more will come forth about his contributions to the creative arts - visual art, literature, music and ballet, and on his life as a patron, collaborator in projects, publishing and modern art collecting.

One cannot help thinking that he might have got on well with Peggy Guggenheim, a famous Modern Art collector, when she lived in the District in the late 1930s; see Chapter 12.3. However, her time there was just after Edward left for overseas. His life has been compared with that of Peggy:

> 'Peggy's life as a collector is based on two short, intense periods of acquisition: from about 1938 to 1940 in England and principally France, from about 1941 - 1946 in the United States. She was not the only collector of her day: and there were more women than men among her peers. She only took to the art world at someone else's instigation, and she scarcely ever made a move within it without someone else's advice. Eight year's collecting in a lifetime of eighty years (if one discounts the relatively desultory activity after she moved to Venice) is not much, especially when one looks at the careers of Edward James, or Walter Arensberg, or the Cone sisters, of Katherine Dreier.'
>
> Gill (2002).

Peggy may have met him, for she asked a friend to call Edward:

> 'an extremely big fish in the surrealist world who had recently commissioned Dali's lobster telephone, and someone Peggy would have wanted to win over - and bring him to her gallery so that Peggy could have sold him a Tanguy.'   Dearborn (2004)

That phone call was made, but it is not given that the meeting resulted. There is so much still to be discovered about Edward James' life!

11.14 Goodwood House and Estate

Fig. 11.38 Goodwood House.

Goodwood, Fig. 11.38, in West Sussex, is an estate at West Hampnett, 9 miles south of Midhurst; it is just outside the Midhurst Rural District. As it is easy to drive from Midhurst to there, many visiting people choose to stay in quiet Midhurst when attending the nationally significant events held in the estate of that name. The Spread Eagle hotel has had many famous persons stay over for Goodwood events.

Chapter 11 Where the 'Other Half' lived.

The Goodwood house and estate have been the home of the Dukes of Richmond and Lennox for over 300 years; since the time of Charles II. It started life as a hunting lodge, being enlarged many times. Today it covers 11,500 acres, being a little smaller than the Cowdray Estate of 16,500 acres.

The present Lord Charles March, (correctly speaking, the Duke of Richmond since 2017) took over the estate from his father Charles Henry Gordon-Lennox in 1994. He shares Goodwood House with his wife, Janet and their four children, and Lord March's daughter by his previous marriage.

Their home is in a self-contained wing that has been the family's living quarters since the end of the 18th century - See 'Goodwood House is glorious again', Matthew Dennison, The Telegraph, 15 September 2011. This 'great English Country house' is open for visits by the public.

During WW2 it was the turn of Frederick, 9th Duke of Richmond, Fig. 11.39, to care for the estate having inherited it with its famous racecourse in 1935.

Fig. 11.39 Frederick Gordon-Lennox, 9th Duke of Richmond. (Goodwood)

Upon his father's death, their Scottish Estates were sold in 1935 to settle the death duties; they moved to Goodwood to live. This way he was able to retain the long-standing family ownership, but then needed to find ways to fund its future. He married Elizabeth, daughter of the Reverend Thomas Hudson, and was succeeded by his eldest son, Charles, the present Duke.

During World War II Frederick served in the Royal Air Force. To assist the war effort, Goodwood Aerodrome was created on the land of the Estate. It was known as RAF Westhampnett, this being a satellite landing station of Tangmere RAF station. It was active from July 1940 to May 1946 as a Battle of Britain airfield. Many RAF squadrons used it, as did Belgian and New Zealand squadrons, a USA fighter group, and several support units. Flying training began there in 1940, Fig. 11.40, when young pilots were taught operational flying techniques in Hurricanes and Spitfires.

Fig. 11.40 Young pilots under training in 1940. (Goodwood)

After the war Lord March, having retained the land's title, converted the wartime Westhampnett airfield's perimeter track into the Goodwood Motor Circuit. It was Britain's most prestigious circuit for eighteen years from 1948-1966.

Many world-leading sporting events are now held there on the estate. 'An idiots guide to Goodwood' covers these on the Goodwood website. Frederick was passionate about cars and planes; he trained as a motor mechanic on the shop floor of Bentley and became a racing driver, winning the Brooklands Double 12 Race in 1931. He created many major events centred on car racing, and themes of such. The principal events are:

> **Motorsport** with the 'Goodwood Revival' meeting. Its 'spiritual home of British motoring' race track opened in 1939 making up for the loss of the Brooklands motor racing circuit. The event is for road racing cars and motorcycles that would have competed in the original race track period of 1948-1966.

A sister motoring event is the 'Festival of Speed', a motor hill climb and cultural event celebrating historic vehicles. That takes place within Lord

Chapter 11 Where the 'Other Half' lived.

March's grounds, being coupled with many other motoring events of a varied nature. It began in 1993. Today it draws such huge crowds that tickets sales are now limited to 100,000.

> 'On the manicured lawns of an English stately home, the tranquil sophistication of a summer garden party is shattered by a piercing wail as a Formula One car screeches up the front drive, wreathed in tyre smoke. It's an unforgettable experience: a visceral assault on the senses; an intoxicating display of speed and power; a unique joining of the past, present and future of automotive.'
> FOS website.

Horse racing at the Goodwood racecourse is with Royalty and high fashions present in the 'Qatar Goodwood Festival'. This track began in 1802. It is affectionately called 'Glorious Goodwood', and has 19 unique race days. During WW2 races were suspended but did run in 1939 just before war was declared. The track, with its many additionally attractions and facilities, is NW of the aerodrome and the motor circuit within the Goodwood estate.

There is also there a flying school; golfing; shooting, cricket and still more.

Turning to other uses of the Estate during WW2, the description of the Goodwood Estate Archives collection held in the WSRO, states that during WW2 the Goodwood home was at the disposal of the 1st London Hospital.

Goodwood House was used extensively as a hospital facility. Lucy Shier in Harting Residents (1995), recalls going there during the war for it had been taken over by the army who organised dances.

With D-Day approaching in June 1944, there was need to develop nursing groups in anticipation of considerable casualties arising from the invasion into Normandy.

Wikipedia states that for 'nursing', emergency commissions and a rank structure were created in 1941. It followed the ranking structure used in the rest of the British Army. Nurses were given rank badges and were then able to be promoted to ranks from Lieutenant through to

Brigadier.

A unit, of some 40 nurses, of the Queen Alexandra's Imperial Military Nursing Service (the QA's) of the 23rd British General Hospital (BGH), was stationed there in early 1944, Fig. 11.41. They left in late June for France to set up a tented advance field hospital in Bayeux. Many men injured in that invasion back into France would come to thank these lasses in due time.

Fig. 11.41 The QA Nursing unit stationed at Goodwood during the early part of June 1944. (Gereig)

Nurses and Hospital Research, including that for WW2, by Sue Light, has been made available on the Scarlet Finders website where data are shown for some 122 field hospitals near to the front lines of the Allies. Times of nurses being at Goodwood during WW2 are here extracted from the copious records she collected.

BGH Number	Arrived Goodwood	Departed Goodwood
5	8/40	11/42
9	4/44	6/44

Chapter 11 Where the 'Other Half' lived.

23	Early 44	7/44
27	1/40	7/40
29	11/44	1/45
33	5/45	7/45
36	6/40	6/41
43	7/41	8/41
44	6/41	8/41
47	9/41	6/42
94	5/42	11/42
98	10/42	3/43
121	7/43	4/44

An interesting local incident took place on 12 September 1940, when 'two German airmen, who parachuted from a Heinkel bomber that was shot down in the Battle of Britain, are marched off by the Home Guard near Goodwood', Fig. 11.42.

Fig. 11.42 German pilots marched off to Goodwood.

Clearly, during WW2 Goodwood House and Estate were places of considerable activity.

11.15 Other Country Houses

As well as the grander country mansions, the Midhurst District has many more modest, but still large, country homes. These also would have been used for billeting troops and refugees. However, little seems to be recorded for their use during WW2. Some are listed here to assist historians of the Midhurst District locate places that are occasionally named in records. Again, they are given in random order.

South Downs Hotel - on 10acres in Bepton; originally a 19th-century country house, Fig.11.43.

Fig. 11.43 South Downs Hotel.

Park house - Bepton Road

Fig. 11.44 Park House Hotel.

Around 1900 the original cottage and timber-framed barn of this estate were bought, along with extensive additional land. The 9-acre site was then developed over 2 years to become Park House, in Bepton.

During WW2, by acquisition, it was used as a nursing home, the

Chapter 11 Where the 'Other Half' lived.

owner then being Lady Manners. After the war, it became quite derelict. 'Pop' Edmunds, just back from many years in India making his fortune, wanted to buy a place to live, literally finding this estate in Midhurst by chance. He bought it to live in just one room and died there in 1947. It was left to his daughter, Ione.

Not being able to then sell the property Ione, and her husband Michael O'Brien, decided to turn it into a country house hotel that opened on 1st May 1948. Patronage by international polo players coming to Cowdray events greatly helped it along.

Ione ran the hotel until 1991, dying there in 1997. Refurbishment started in February 2001, opening again as upmarket accommodations in May 2002, Fig. 11.44.

Brigadier John Hardy, a family friend who lived opposite the hotel, wrote up this story around 2002, from which this account is condensed. Hardy (2019).

Ariabelle Manor - Built 1850, in Stedham. On the estate of 40acres was built a large house that could have accommodated at least 20 people, Fig. 11.45.

Fig. 11.45 Ariabelle Manor today.

Aldworth House - is in Lurgashall 10 miles from Midhurst, near Haslemere: it is just out of West Sussex. It, see Fig. 11.46, was originally the home of the poet, Tennyson. He bought 60 acres of land on which to build this seven-bedroom house. It has also been discussed elsewhere in Book 1. Fig. 14.2. Aldworth House was Tennyson's 'escape' during the summer months. The view from his large estate looks out at

Midhurst WW2 Memoirs: 2. 'Evil' Rising: 'Good' Awakening

the Sussex Weald and Downs and, on good weather days even to the English Channel, 40 miles away.

In his poem *Green Sussex*, Tennyson wrote:

> You came, and looked and loved the view
> Long-known and loved by me,
> Green Sussex fading into blue,
> With one gray glimpse of sea.

Fig. 11.46 Aldworth House today. (Flickr Clive.s)

The grand house, built for Lord Tennyson in 1869 by designer Sir John Knowles, is on the site of an old smugglers' inn. Aldworth House is a Grade 1 listed French-style Gothic house, made from sandstone.

When it was built, the house included the latest modern luxury of piped hot water; Tennyson used to enjoy at least three baths a day. The private setting, and being clear of the local inhabitants, enticed him to invite literary friends such as George Eliot (real name, Mary Ann Evans) and Henry James to stay when he desired company.

Tennyson died at Aldworth in 1892 and was found holding a book of Shakespeare in his hand.

The house passed onto his son Hallam, who sold it in 1921 to an Indian Maharajah, His Highness Sir Sayaji Rao Gaekwar of Baroda.

During the Second World War, the house was taken over by the Admiralty and used at one point as a convalescent home. It was used by Canadian troops as billets.

Chapter 11 Where the 'Other Half' lived.

It returned to private ownership in 1993, the new owners restoring the property in its then reduced 12 acres. It seems it is possible to take tea in Aldworth by arrangement with the owners, Mr and Mrs Keeley.

Dunford House - was built in 1847. It was the home of Richard Cobden [see Book 1, Chapter 7 for his personal history]. It is situated on the site of the very farmhouse in which he was born in 1809. He died there in 1865.

Cobden's daughter Jane, and her husband T Fisher Cobden, then gave the house to the Cobden Memorial Association to form an institute in his name. In January 1952, the National Council of YMCA's accepted the endowment of Dunford House for general educational purposes.

Nothing has come to light about its use in WW2 but a photograph shows volunteers, Fig. 11.47, clearing the ailing property as the start of restoration.

Fig. 11.47 Dunford House being resurrected in 1952.

Over the next decade, Dunford House became a recognised centre for critical thinking, new ideas and action. By the 1970's it was used by commercial groups for training Senior Managers. This kind of use continued until today. At the time of writing, however, it has become the subject of land reuse for housing; Cobden's descendants are pushing for it to be kept as a memorial due to its historic associations.

During WW2 Francis and Helena Hirst remained in the house. Then being quite elderly in their 70s, they would not have taken in evacuees. They may, however, have provided billets for a few soldiers.

They left the house in 1952, it by then, having been quite neglected with regards to the upkeep of its fabric and grounds.

We have seen that the quite small area of the Midhurst Rural District, and a little distance outside of that, had a surprising number of great houses, most of which were in private ownership in the 1930s. Initially, their owners could pay for necessary maintenance and services; they often had commercial interests producing diminishing income from their estates. For many, this was not their principal place of living or income generation. That they had the means to own these luxury estates it is to be expected that they wanted it that way: the district retained its rural nature

During WW2 many local estates were still in private hands. By 1950 the situation, however, was fast changing when many of these passed out of private ownership due to taxation and inability to keep paying for estate upkeep.

In terms of overall assets, it was a very wealthy district during the war having considerable disposable assets. This is discussed in later books; surprisingly large contributions came forth from this area in the national fund-raising weeks that were held in later years of the war.

We have covered the difficulties being tackled to keep these estates in good order as war approached. Because of social reform actions by the government, many owners were then teetering on selling up or gifting their property to the State. The war intervened, delaying that change for a while. Conversion into multiple accommodations was the new life to come for many of these places.

In a way, the war situation was fortuitous because most mansions, despite being run down in many instances, were requisitioned by the military to billet troops and officers, and as training establishments for commando, spies and possibly other low profile uses such as airfields and storage. For this use, they were obtaining compensation that they would not have had if peace had continued.

Chapter 12. Entertainment and Sport

12.1 Music and Film

As the 1930s decade moved on it was fast becoming clear, to those in the know, that war with Hitler's Third Reich was highly likely. That dampened things a bit but the general mood around was that it was not that likely or, at least, it would only take a few months to stop Hitler's advances.

People of the District largely must have continued much as they had before. Life, in general, was improving as the effects of the depression were diminishing. Contingency preparations for possible conflict needed more goods and services, resulting in a reduction in Britain's unemployed. Social programmes in housing and national infrastructure projects also assisted reduction of unemployment figures. Midhurst benefited from some of this increased spending, especially with new housing estates.

Music played a major part in the enjoyable side of people's lives in those heady, but worrying days. In 1877, the Edison *phonograph* was invented. It used tinfoil wrapped around a rotating cylinder. On that run a stylus that moved, by physical means, according to the sound going into its mechanical loudspeaker unit. The stylus formed an up and down record in the foil surface that could be played back. The wax-coated cylinder version soon came as it gave a more acceptable playback result.

The next decade saw a much-improved method invented by Emile Berliner. These versions started using a shellac coated, flat disk; that material was good for moulding copies from a master disk cut on a super quality transcription recorder. Today, this method still has a strong following under the title of a *vinyl* recording.

Vinyl record players need some fine mechanical mechanisms to reproduce quality sound. An essential requirement was a drive spindle that would turn the disk with a minimal of wobble and speed variation - called *wow* and *flutter*. The playback equipment needed a precision manufacturer. It was fitting that the British company, Garrard & Co, entered this market in 1915: they were jewellers. By 1930 their best models used direct-drive electric motors, Fig. 12.1, as that greatly reduced the pitch deficiencies of a belt drive from the motor to the turntable; that resulted in *rumble* being felt in the music.

Fig. 12.1 Direct drive Garrard record player of 1930: Model 201.

As is usually the case with inventions, a futurist artist had portrayed a fully electrical means for storing and recovering sounds in an 1878 Punch cartoon: but not how to make one! That took several new methods that gradually replaced mechanical methods with electronic ones.

Recorders using a metalised tape, or a wire, and electrical methods of playback were developed during WW2 but were not in common use then. The tape version came as the universal method that lasted until the 1980s.

That gave way to digital recording, in the CD form, in the late 1960s. Today the CD/DVD optical disk recording medium is rapidly giving way to using direct electronic memories in phones and players, the sound recording is there in digital format being stored in solid-state memory chips.

In quite a contrast, much pre-war entertainment was provided live from a piano or a piano accordion, or a group of musicians, such as a band or orchestra. Radio broadcasts provided a good supply of inexpensive music to the public that was performed live in the studio or played from recordings. Early radio broadcast methods did not provide top quality music fidelity because the radio transmission method (AM) was not up to that need as were not the electronic amplifiers and loudspeakers.

Chapter 12 Entertainment and Sport

It was essential to know to what radio station, and when to listen. First in the world to provide published programme listings was the British Broadcasting Company who published them in its weekly *Radio Times,* that commenced on 28 September 1923. That magazine for 4 September 1939 included a cartoon showing humour was still in force in the British psyche, Fig. 12.2. Note the sandbagging, record player, tin hat and periscope poking over the caller's sandbag enclosure. The gas mask is missing!

Fig. 12.2 Cartoon from BBC radio Times of 4 September 1939.

The caption says:

'It's rather hard to tell you who is winning, as all the horses are camouflaged.'

A sobering message was given as the editorial introduction:

'Broadcasting carries on! That is the slogan of the BBC in this hour of national endeavour, when the British nation is nerving itself for the greatest effort it has ever made. In every department of life, the British people are steeling themselves for their great task. Broadcasting intends to help in the work, whatever the difficulties may be. For nearly a year now the BBC has been making its plans. Recognising the part that broadcasting would play in the struggle, it could not afford to leave anything to chance.'

It goes on to say that the obvious use of broadcasting is that it can speak to the people - news can reach the remotest village - instructions can be issued by Ministries - warning can be given of approaching attacks. It also can:

'help take minds off of the horrors of war as nothing else can'.

Swing style music came into fashion in the mid-1930s. Black USA artists were gradually being accepted into previously only white person performing groups, and vice versa. They brought *soul music,* that evolved into *jazz.* These soulful blues melodies or high tempo and energy ones quickly arrived in Britain. Well before the US troops arrived these had been taken on in Britain. They were being played all over the country, including in local village halls, at the weekly dance. When the US troops arrived their genres of music took off.

Special public entertainment places for dancing catered for large numbers of participants. Spectacular ballrooms had big bands playing that filled the hall with voluminous, smooth melodious sound. These dance halls were a gathering place for a good evening out that allowed one to meet and converse with a partner during a dance. Some of these places do exist today, but many became bingo halls!

This was a Golden Age in British music. Notable British big band leaders included Stanley Black, Billi Cotton, Carrol Gibbons, Ray Noble, Harry Roy, Edmundo Ross, Victor Silvester and Cyril Stapleton.

These would often feature a star vocalist such as the very well-known Vera Lynn and Frances Day, Sam Costa, and Anne Lenner. Fig. 12.3 shows the Harry Roy band broadcasting from the Mayfair Hotel in London in 1934.

Fig. 12.3 Harry Roy's 1930s British big band.

Two singers of great significance over the war period were Gracie Fields and Vera Lyn.

Chapter 12 Entertainment and Sport

Gracie Fields 'Our Gracie' was born as Grace Stansfield, over a fish and chip shop in Rochdale, Lancashire in 1878. She was on the stage as a child star and went professional in 1910 at her local Rochdale Hippodrome, a generic name given then to theatres or concert halls. She performed dramatic roles in many revues as a talented performer.

The song, *Sally in Our Alley* of 1931, was adopted as her theme song and was worked into her first film. It was a box office hit. She made many films but preferred to perform to live audiences. Gracie declined to join the grand opera scene when given an invitation to follow that path.

She was made a Commander of the Order of the British Empire for "services to entertainment" in 1938, that being in recognition of her charity work.

In 1939 she had cancer surgery. That, and a need for serious rest, led to her moving to Capri, Italy. There she married her Italian-born film director, Monty Bank, in March 1940. At that time in the war, Italy aligned with the Axis nations. That new citizenship situation for Gracie led to difficulties with the British authorities who issued threats to intern her, as a person on the Axis side, for the duration of the war if she came back to her country of birth. Then Italy changed sides in mid wartime. She eventually received an official apology for the difficulties she had with the British Government.

For some of the war period, Gracie went to the US. There, her charitable work continued by raising aid for the Navy League of the United States, and the British Spitfire Fund that is discussed in a later book. Fig. 12.4 illustrates interest in her songs is still available today.

Fig. 12.4 'Our Gracie' hits Hollywood; also showing British troops getting refreshments, maybe on the journey home from Dunkirk.

During WW2 she toured the forces in the allied parts of France, playing from the back of army trucks and other impromptu stages; often with air-raids threatening. She also sang to troops as far away as in New Guinea and the South Pacific Islands.

Some of her so often heard and well-known songs are:
> *Sally*
> *Wish me Luck as You Wave me Goodbye*
> *Christopher Robin is Saying his Prayers*
> *The Biggest Aspidistra in the World*
> *Looking on the Bright Side*

'Now is the hour' has a poignant lyric. It has to be heard to experience her way of tugging the senses with her words and music:

> Now is the hour
> For me to say goodbye
> Soon I'll be sailing
> Far across the sea
> While I'm away
> Oh, please remember me
> When I return
> I'll find you waiting here
> Now is the hour
> For me to say goodbye
> Soon I'll be sailing
> Far across the sea
> While I'm away
> Oh, please remember me
> When I return
> I'll find you waiting here
> While I'm away
> Oh, please remember me...

After the war she continued a post-war career, still in charity and public events, like in the 1951 Festival of Britain, entertaining the rich and famous in her Capri home, taking parts in TV plays, films and theatre, and took part in no less than ten Royal Performances.

Gracie died from pneumonia in 1979 and is buried in Capri.

Chapter 12 Entertainment and Sport

Vera Lynn was born in 1917 in East Ham, England as the daughter of a plumber. Her talent was obvious and she was on the stage at age seven. Her 'call' came early; she left school at 11 years old to pursue an entertainment career.

Her first radio broadcast was in 1935. Soon she joined the aristocrat of British dance bands, Bert Ambrose and his Orchestra, in 1937. Some of her songs, written to reflect the mood of the time were:

> *There'll Be Bluebells Over the White Cliffs of Dover*
> *You'll Never Know*
> *I'm Sending a Letter to Santa Claus*
> *We'll Meet Again*

During the war, troop entertainment led to her touring Egypt, India and Burma. She was not only a singer but a friend and comforter to all who heard her. She had her radio programme, *Sincerely Yours,* through which were sent messages to troops overseas from their families back at the home front. Fig. 12.5 shows Vera Lynn helping out at a 'cuppa car' during WW2.

She continued to show her 'Courage and contribution to morale' to people all over the world. She remained the British 'Forces Sweetheart'. Vera recently suggesting that mantle be passed to Katherine Jenkins OBE who has a magnificent voice as a Welsh mezzo-soprano singer and songwriter. She was well-received during her tours of British forces in the Middle-East in recent times.

Fig. 12.5 Vera Lynn helping out at a YMCA cuppa car during WW2. (Sunday Express)

For her wartime contributions, Dame Vera was awarded the British War Medal and the Burma Star. Then came her OBE in 1969 for services to the Royal Air Forces Association. Later she was advanced to become a Dame of the British Empire in 1975.

The United Kingdom's *VE Day Diamond Jubilee* ceremonies in 2005 included a concert in Trafalgar Square, London. Dame Vera made a surprise appearance; she was then 88 years old.

Her speech praised the veterans and called upon the younger generation to always remember their sacrifice, and they then joined in with a few bars of "We'll Meet Again". She is reported as then saying:

> 'These boys gave their lives and some came home badly injured, and for some, family life would never be the same. We should always remember, we should never forget, and we should teach the children to remember.'   Wikipedia

She never really gave up her services to the community in some way or another. Honours just keep coming. She has even been honoured with a restored steam locomotive of the North Yorkshire Moors Railway being renamed, *Dame Vera Lynn*.

Her memoirs of the war years are published, Lynn and Cross (1989). Remarkably, at 92 years of age, she made a comeback with a No.1 British top seller recording. In March 2017 Decca Records released a compilation album to celebrate her 100th birthday.

She passed away on 18 June 2020. Wherever you go she will be heard singing for she epitomised the British spirit of WW2. It is already clear her songs and singing will still be listened too in the decades to come. I'll bet her spirit and recordings will still be there in force at the 100th anniversary of the start of WW2, in 2039.

In later years she did not like to sing to the public and spent time as a watercolourist using her garden in Ditchling, Sussex as her source of subjects; that is, when she was not needed for some event such as being President of the Dame Vera Lynn Trust for Children with Cerebral Palsy, a charity she founded in 2001, just 17 miles to the east of Midhurst.

You can still experience the emotions of the time through the *Vera Lynn Tribute Band* who perform in authentic uniforms of the wartime. One other of the touring shows about Dame Vera Lynn is *Sincerely Yours*; it covers her life story and is presented with a 7-piece band.

Chapter 12 Entertainment and Sport

Close by is her *Dame Vera Lynn Children's Centre* in Cuckfield, just a few miles from Midhurst. Today she is not only the 'Forces Sweetheart', but now the 'all peoples sweetie'.

Despite the dreadful events developing afar, life in Britain and thus Midhurst, went on much the same for the bulk of the population. It was still good for many in Britain.

However, they were still smarting from the past decade's events, but life was steadily improving in many of its facets: music, fashion, clubbing, ballrooms, cinema, theatre. They all had a firm fix on the just passing influence of the earlier *Arts & Crafts* period followed by *Art Deco*.

It was 'swing time' with the great new big bands of Tommy Dorsey, Harry James and Glen Miller giving people the chance of happiness. These bands and musicians came into their own in the late 30s, as if ready to keep up spirits when the war broke out.

As the 30s progressed, a tall dark and handsome young man was becoming ever popular in his circle of friends in Walworth, London. This 24-year-old, my Dad, Fig. 12.6, had that remarkable ability to play any of the musical hits after just one hearing of them on the radio. He could not read a note of music; a gift, that he sadly did not pass on to me.

Recorded music was, by then, affordable but a real-life 'piano jockey' was better at parties. He could switch from 'Knees Up Mother Brown' to Beethoven or Boogie in a twinkling.

Fig. 12.6 Henry Sydenham was the music maker for many a local get-together in 1932.

This young man never made it into the 'lights' but he did attract the attention of a pretty girl from a nearby suburb of South London. He was soon courted by my Mum, Violet. They married on 8 September 1935.

In Midhurst, however, then as now, to hear a sizeable band needed a trip to Chichester to listen to a visiting group; or to places further afield. These bands and singers made that distinctive 'sound' that one hears in the films about WW2. Midhurst had its music shop in 1939; Ron Jeans in Lamberts Lane. He sold instruments, sheet music needed to play instruments, records and ancillary items.

The 1930s experience can still be had today from several specialist groups via booking services such as www.warble-entertainment.com.

Big bands that offer their talents in West Sussex are *Conchord*, based in Crawley; *Harris Wheman Big Band* in Guildford; *James OC Big Band* also based in Guildford; and *Swing City* from London.

The military brought music with them when they started to trickle into Midhurst from the relatively close northern barracks at Aldershot, and later elsewhere, but that was yet to come from late in 1939.

Groups would perform in the local hotels and halls, but to make it pay they needed enough space to be able to accommodate a goodly sized audience. However, large halls were scarce in Midhurst. Smaller bands, of 2 to 4 members, or a lone pianist, would have to play their hearts out in the tiny bar rooms of the many pubs.

Dances were held in several village halls each Saturday evening. The influx of many soldiers to the District encouraged more dances. The then Easebourne Village Institute, now Cowdray Hall, was a popular venue, as would have been the Graffham Empire Hall, Fig. 12.7.

Fig. 12.7 Graffham's Empire hall today.
blog.ahsoc.org

Other dances were held at Lodsworth, in the Parish Room next to the Methodist church, and in the Drill Hall behind the Crown Inn (now a private home). Grander dances, the various Balls, were also often used to raise funds for worthy groups - the Hunt Ball, Golf Ball, Police Ball and Young Farmer's Ball.

Chapter 12 Entertainment and Sport

'The bands [in Midhurst], there were two of them, one of them was Ron Jeans and his brother Leslie who kept the record shop at the bottom of North Street, they had a band. Ron Jeans played the drums and Leslie, I think he played the piano, but I might be wrong about that but anyway they were a pretty good outfit and also, of course, later on, we had Reg Page and his band, they used to play down there as well. And we used to pack in there on a Saturday night'.
Tony Beck in Elsdon (2010).

Street musicians were also heard at times. A usual donation was just a halfpenny. As they might be taken as being a vagrant, they were not that common. In 1933, somewhere in North Street:

'It was a beautiful sunny day and I heard a very strange noise coming from the top end of the street and it was a Scottish piper playing his bagpipes. Now that's not all that unusual for that particular period because there were an awful lot of soldiers from the first world war who came out without any source of income whatsoever, so if they happened to be a bandsman or in this case a piper, they used to walk around the streets gathering whatever money they could'.
Tony Beck in Elsdon (2010).

The new wireless broadcasting medium for entertainment came of age in early 1920s. This took music to almost everyone.

Television broadcasting came to Britain in the early 1930s, but not in a good enough form for widespread public acceptance until after the end of the war.

In 1936 Hitler ran a much-improved version of an Olympic Games event - the 1936 Summer Olympics in Berlin. He showcased the latest audio and television technology: the first live television coverage of a sports event. Some 72 hours of live transmission of the event was beamed out.

Over 160,000 people saw these early TV broadcasts; along with 2500 radio broadcasts. It was impressive.

Germany, however, did not eclipse Britain in this use of TV for in that year the BBC had changed from the inferior, spinning disk, television camera method of Baird to the vastly superior electronically scanned, cathode ray tube image capture method that emanated in the US.

It had been broadcasting Baird type scanned performances from Alexandra Palace in North London since 1932. It was shut it down in late 1939, commencing again for a short time in 1946.

Moving picture film created widespread attendance when the technology had matured enough to attract sufficient box office receipts. These showing places were first called *Picture Palaces* or *Electric Theatres*. Before these, film showing locations, as is still done today, were often held in the local village, town hall, or the Mechanics and other Institute buildings.

Fortunately, an extensive study has recorded the cinema history in West Sussex, Eyles et al. (1996). These notes draw on that information. British people were avid cinema-goers, preferring films made in the USA.

In the early 1930s what material could be shown in public, McKibbin (1998), was only controlled by vendors interpreting soft guidelines taken from the Cinematograph Act of 1909, then issued by the Home Secretary to Councils:

'No film shall be shown that is likely to be injurious to mortality or to encourage or to incite to crime, or lead to disorder, or to be offensive to public feeling, or which contains any offensive representations of living persons'.

Filmmakers, along the lines of freedom of speech, tested these issues greatly. Lawyers had steady incomes from this kind of work!

In 1937 the 'H' category was introduced for horror films. At that time the only other categories were 'U' for films suitable for universal showing, and 'A', for adults only viewing; but children could attend these if accompanied by an adult! McKibbin tells of children hanging around the cinema waiting for an adult to take them in. The shortcomings of the rating allowed one woman to accompany 45 children into an 'A' rated film!

Many felt the people should be able to choose what they wanted to see, but that was not working well enough; the controlling elite instituted stricter censorship. Cinemas 'could not be allowed to operate unshackled', McKibbin (1998).

Chapter 12 Entertainment and Sport

Between 1928 and the outbreak of Second World War the Board of Film Censors banned, by not classifying them, 140 films. Several thousand more had to be altered, and many proposals were discussed with the Board being adjusted to suit their suggestions. Lord Tyrrell proclaimed in 1937:

'We may take pride in observing that there is not a single film showing in London today that deals with any of the burning questions of the day'.
McKibbin (1998)

The privileged few were still able to decide issues for the less fortunate! Even Mickey Mouse was once censored, in Denmark, Fig. 12.8. as being too macabre.

DANES BAN 'MICKEY MOUSE'

Censor Calls the Film Creation of Disney Too Macabre.

Wireless to THE NEW YORK TIMES.

COPENHAGEN, Feb. 23.—Walt Disney, American creator of the "Mickey Mouse" cartoon films, has run afoul of the Danish film censor.

The censor insists that the Danish public must not be allowed to see one of Mr. Disney's "Silly Symphony" films which shows dancing skeletons and ghosts in a graveyard. The topic, in the censor's opinion, is too macabre to be put on the screen.

This is the second time Mr. Disney has been in trouble with a censor. In Germany a "Mickey Mouse" film was prohibited for allegedly holding German soldiers up to ridicule.

Fig. 12.8 Danish censorship tried to stop Mickey Mouse in 1930.

Mind you, I confess when aged 7, that the 1937 film *Snow White and the Seven Dwarfs* scared me so much in one part that I ran out of the Midhurst cinema halfway through it. I was so frightened when the trees all bent down to reach her as she ran through the wicked witch's wood! And that had a G, for General, rating.

When war approached there was an important need to control the content of virtually anything, on the grounds of national and military security. An example of the failure of not censoring news material well enough was when a poorly managed situation caused the death of several Australian soldiers.

Midhurst WW2 Memoirs: 2. 'Evil' Rising: 'Good' Awakening

A distant photographic view, taken from an observation post overlooking Japanese lines in New Guinea, was published in an Australian newspaper. The Japanese rapidly worked out where it was and obliterated the post, killing its occupants.

Censorship during WW2 is taken up in the next Book 3.

By the late 30s many cinema specific buildings, easily reached by people of the Midhurst Rural District, had been built in Arundel, Bognor, Chichester, Horsham, Midhurst, Petworth, and Worthing. In larger cities, there were many outlets. For example, Bognor had six cinemas before 1934, with two more openings in that year.

London cinemas could be attended on the same day by car. Getting 'up to town', by the local trains from Midhurst, would most likely have needed an overnight stay after the show.

The cinema in Midhurst High Street was built as the Midhurst Public Hall in 1882; well before movies were in common use. By 1922 it had become the *Midhurst Electric Cinema.* It was soon changed to be the *Cinematographic Theatre*.

It was a grand ornate building that could seat 700 people! Pantomimes, musical events, London theatre group performances, and meetings of any kind took place there.

It seems the first regular use of it as a moving picture cinema was in 1910. In 1913 Gaumont film titles began to be shown on regular programme times.

In 1938 it became part of the *Moderne* Cinema chain owned by Harry Mears of Bournemouth. It was then renamed the Town Hall Cinema. (Midhurst never had a purpose-built town hall, but did have the Town Council Office there.) He modernised it by widening the proscenium (the decorative stage) to 35 feet and reduced the seating to 380 capacity. A cafe was attached.

In 1943 it was sold on again, being upgraded significantly to catch up with safety rules, and to provide seating for 560 persons - needed for the considerable increase in attendances by the many soldiers posted around the district by then.

After the war, audiences rose significantly for a while, but then slowly diminished as national television broadcast programmes became available across Britain.

The Midhurst cinema took on its last name, the *Orion,* in 1947. Sadly, it was demolished in 1966 to become the current, most uninspiring, supermarket building that is easily identified in North Street.

In 1933 the UK General Post Office GPO was then responsible to the Empire Marketing Board Film Unit. Its main purpose was to produce documentary films on the activities of the GPO. Screenonline.org.uk tells its history.

It was a game-changer in that this unit 'attempted to direct towards a socially useful purpose'. One aim was to present it 'as it is' in terms appropriate for public understanding, this being needed to make up for the stern norms of Civil Service designed communications.

When war came, being a well organised film unit in Government control, it was ready-made to become a propaganda film unit. In 1940 it became the *Crown Film Unit,* within the Ministry of Information. When one views films made within the WW2 time, it is interesting to look for the subtle, almost subliminal, messages given in its patriotic films; messages of working together, of the fact that lives will be lost and how the Brits will win through. It had a readymade morale-boosting presentation!

These did not engender racial hate, as did films issued by the Nazi propaganda machine under control of Joseph Goebbels, Head of their *Ministry of Public Enlightenment and Propaganda.*

'Propaganda' has Latin roots, wherein it initially meant simply, 'to propagate'. The Nazi use of it led to the common meaning now of it is about giving out information, usually of a biased or misleading nature, and being used to promote a political cause or point of view. They say 'the first casualty of war is the truth'.

As are mentioned at times in these Memoirs, the GPO films have left us with a truthful record of how the British lived in the immediate pre-war years and how they were being prepared for its start.

Thirty-six of their films have been re-released in 2008 and 2009, by the *British Film Institute;* as three collections; covering 1933 - 1935, 1936 - 1939 and another set on 1939 covering *If War Should Come.* These are thought-provoking; they illustrate the technology being then used, and how the less fortunate lived and were soon to endure the start of the war period.

Its wartime job over the Crown Film Unit became part of the *Central Office of Information* in 1946.

There was then a need for weekly news stories in motion picture form. Short documentaries, called *Newsreels,* usually ran in cinemas along with two major feature films.

There were also dedicated *news cinemas*. These kept the public up to date, often including global wartime imagery of the day - or at least as the censors wanted you to see and believe it. The first British newsreel was the 1910 Pathe's Animated Gazette, Fig. 12.9.

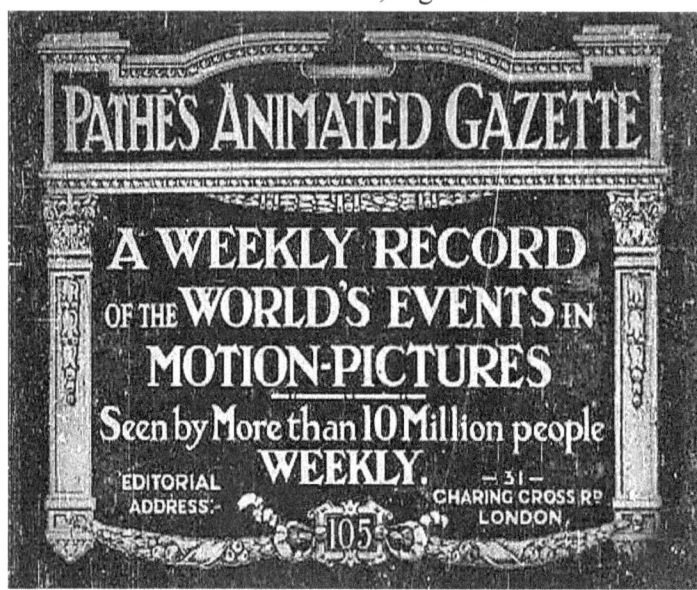

Fig. 12.9 Title page of the 105th Pathe's Animated Gazette showing in Charing Cross Road.

People were constantly reminded of the horror of war. These started to appear in Britain, with sound, as the *British Movietone News* showing in June 1929. Newsreels often included short films of very graphic conflicts. The *History of the Newsreel* website lists one:

'The Chinese-Japanese War provided some of the grimmest but most spectacular footage of the 1930s. The brutal bombing of Shanghai civilians was photographed by several American cameramen'.
14 August 1937, Pathe's Animated Gazette.

Chapter 12 Entertainment and Sport

In the early 1930s, technological modernisation and implementation were going at a fast and useful pace in peaceful application: but by 1938 it was, again, supporting the development of war machines having greater kill capability in European countries, England and Japan. Concerning war equipment, the US was not keeping pace to begin with, but did develop many of the new technologies that were so useful later.

12.2 Art Collecting

We have already seen in Book 1 the Midhurst District has had a centuries-old pull for people of greatness. One person of such distinction was American multi-millionaire, Peggy Guggenheim, a great *modern art* supporter of her time. She was not an artist herself, but championed many a struggling artist who was part of the new genre; that people either liked or disliked! She spent some tragic years of her life in the local Midhurst area.

This small window into her life in the District is framed from short Internet sources, her autobiography by Guggenheim (2005), and biographies, Gill (2002) and Dearborn (2004). Other biographical accounts exist that further describe facets of her intriguing and successful life outcomes.

A recent 2015 film by the Dakota Group, *Peggy Guggenheim: Art Addict* provides an excellent overview of her, her family, her place in the art world, and her life.

It, however, merely mentions that she once lived in the South of England. Here, I try to show how that rather sad time of her life was a key part in her movement into art exhibitions and collecting in support of budding artists needing a patron.

Marguerite "Peggy" Guggenheim was born on August 26, 1898. Her father, Benjamin Guggenheim, died in the sinking of the Titanic in 1912. He had not amassed such a massive fortune as had his siblings, but he had done very much alright by most people's standards.

When Peggy turned 21 in 1919, she inherited 'only' US$2.5 million - about US$50 million in today's currency. At the age of 21, she then had an income of $25,000 a year. In today's equivalence, that is $2 million a year to spend. She was, however, regarded as the 'poor little rich girl' of the

Guggenheim dynasties.

Interestingly, Peggy was often very frugal, even miserly or stingy, in circumstances that did not warrant it. But she was also extremely generous with regard to supporting her less fortunate friends in the art world of the 1930s and 40s. How she looked in 1940 is shown in Fig.12.10; taken when she was in Paris.

Fig. 12.10 Peggy Guggenheim in Paris, 1940. (Gill)

How did a strong link develop for a wealthy American woman of such distinction to come to live, in the pre-war years, in a somewhat run-down, Elizabethan cottage in South Harting, just west of Midhurst town? For what reason did she go there?

Despite her wealth, her first job was quite menial; working in an avant-garde bookshop in Central Station, New York.

That opened her heart and mind to the Bohemian lifestyle that enticed her to Paris in 1920. There she mixed with the free-thinking community becoming very friendly, in fact very often much more than just friendly, with avant-garde writers and artists, many of which were living in poverty as struggling artisans.

She picked up on their work, later being a patron, promoter and supporter to many of them; today many of these *modern* artists are now highly acclaimed in the art world. Peggy often invited artists to stay in country places she rented for British summers – one being Warblington Castle in England. That sounds grand, but it was actually in a pretty house

Chapter 12 Entertainment and Sport

in the Castle ruin's grounds.

Fig. 12.11 shows, on the left side, what is left of the gateway tower of the once large fortified house built by Lady Margaret Pole. It had a moat, staterooms, a chapel, apartments, and an armoury, all being surrounded by a large courtyard. That house rented by Peggy with its 4acre grounds is now restored and modernised.

Fig. 12.11 Grounds of Warblington Castle. built by Lady Margaret Pole between 1515 and 1525; with a later 17th-century house. (Daily Mail)

That location in Hampshire, was ideal for Margaret Pole's family to maintain their Catholic resistance in the 16th century. There is a connection for her to the history of the Midhurst District.

The tragic end of Lady Margaret's life began when she was incarcerated, under detention by order of Henry VIII, in the grand Tudor manor house at Cowdray. She was executed in the Tower of London a few years later. Her story is given in a later book when I discuss the naming of the Catholic Convent school that once existed in Petersfield Road.

Despite her potato-shaped nose, or perhaps because of it, Peggy

Guggenheim had a lurid sex life that she, her contemporaries and those who have written about her since, enjoyed embroidering.

When asked by an interviewer how many husbands had she had, Guggenheim replied: "Do you mean mine, or other people's?" She was said to have 'slept with 1000 men'.

Marriage for love, twice, provided some pegs in the ground of family life for her, these being between her numerous affairs. Her first, maybe serious liaison was to Laurence Vail in 1922; they begat Michael Cedric Sinbad Vail and Pegeen Vail Guggenheim.

Sexual spontaneity was typical of Peggy. She started her post-virginal life of lovers when she was 23 years old, that first time being with Laurence Vail who helped her, clearly as an obliging partner, to experiment with many of the positions she had seen on the pictures she had of the walls of pleasure houses in the old Roman town of Pompeii.

That marriage ended in 1928, due to the supposed outcome of an affair of Laurence with the writer Kay Boyle.

Peggy soon fell into her first truly seriously deep love affair with John Holms, Fig. 12.12. Until then Holms had been living with Dorothy Holms, who had taken his name without marriage.

Fig. 12.12 John Holms.

In her autobiography, Peggy candidly tells pretty well all about how that particular affair came about, Guggenheim (1979).

'all I remember now is that he took me to a tower and kissed me. That certainly made an impression on me, and I can attribute everything that followed to that simple little kiss'

They soon reinforced their new relationship:

'Later I asked the Holmses to come to visit us at Pramousquier (near St Tropez in France). They came overnight and we went in bathing in the moonlight, quite naked. John and I found ourselves alone on the beach and we made love'

Peggy analysed Holms' disposition and 'extraordinary mental capacity:

'being in his company "was equivalent to living in a sort of fifth dimension"'

She said that booze enhanced his conversation considerably. He could hold listeners spellbound for hours:

'Since no one else shared his extraordinary mental capacity, he was exceedingly bored when talking to most people. As a result, he was very lonely. He knew what gifts he had and felt wicked for not using them. Not being able to write, he was unhappy, which caused him to drink more and more. All the time that I was with him I was shocked by his paralysis of will power. It seemed to grow steadily, and in the end, he could hardly force himself to do the simplest things.'

Talk of her sexual life may seem to be right out of character in these memoirs but from the point in her life when she met Holms, her story moves on the saga that drove her life - modern art. Her love lives, and that 'in the office' life, both combined to take her to a cottage in Sussex for a while; to me, that was a most important juncture in her art life.

She found many other things she needed in Holms. He became her constant companion for the next two years, including millions of miles of travel in numerous countries. This real and deep love match, however, came to a tragic end in 1934.

John Holms fractured his wrist when horse riding on Dartmoor with Peggy. Despite being reset, the bones were not realigned correctly so he was advised sometime later to have a simple operation. He was a very heavy drinker and on the morning of 19th January 1934, he went onto the operating table with a terrible hangover; he died under the anaesthetic.

Peggy needed her unusual kind of companionship. An attractive man was ready in the wings. Previously, in March 1933, she had met Douglas Garman, Fig. 12.13, in a pub in Trafalgar Square. He was 5 years her junior; as she then had grey hair that made her self-conscious. Peggy said he was a 'frustrated poet', spoke beautiful English and several other languages, and was slow in his deliberations that often infuriated her.

Fig. 12.13 Douglas Garman.

  Douglas was the son of a family doctor with a large practice in Birmingham. As a present for his gentlewomen mother, he bought her a cottage in the South Harting area, the aim being to visit her more than he had in the past. One day Douglas drove Peggy to see this home and to meet his mother.
  Whilst at Douglas Garman's mother's house Peggy felt the need to have her own place nearby - for the convenience of her daughter Pegeen to attend local schooling with Douglas's daughter, Debbie.
  Not being able to find a place to rent Peggy was encouraged, by Douglas, to buy one instead - *Yew Tree Cottage*, as it was known then. It was in secluded spot in the lovely countryside of South Harting. As it turned out, Pegeen went to live with Mrs Garman anyway to begin with.

Chapter 12 Entertainment and Sport

Peggy and Garman soon moved into this cottage and remained there for several years – the most isolated time of her life. She became quite introverted and domesticated, even learning to cook.

The initial time in the cottage was probably the saddest down-side in her life; the grief of her loss of Holms made her seriously contemplate suicide. It was a vital 'recovery' period for her; as Garman nurtured her back to good health. It was a turning point in her life ambitions.

The ambience of this rural setting must have been beneficial for her. Later in that period of mental darkness, she began serious collecting and planning to exhibit the works of the new 20th-century art movement.

An excursion on her exotic cars! Peggy was several times, given gifts of 'top of the class' motor cars.

One of her first cars was a V8 Hispano-Suiza with its massive *Hisso* 18 litre, very elegant, aircraft engine - needing a massive body sufficient to carry it; she would have got her car as a chassis and had an open-top, silver body built on it - as you do if you have the cash.

She had a number of different cars over the years. She drove herself. From her autobiography it seems she made her first visit to Yew Tree cottage in a new, smaller car, a Delage. Perhaps hers was the D8 model with a 4 litre, 8 cylinders engine shown as Fig. 8.24 in Book 1.

It must have been quite a task manoeuvring them around the back lanes of the Hartings. Later she sold the Delage to get a still smaller car, a Talbot; another car with a top European heritage. Somehow, I expect this one to have been something like the 1938 T15, a modern restoration being shown in Fig. 12.14. It was well suited to those winding lanes.

Fig. 12.14 1938 Talbot T15 baby roadster. (Car & Classic)

Midhurst WW2 Memoirs: 2. 'Evil' Rising: 'Good' Awakening

When she bought the Elizabethan farmhouse cottage it only supported relatively primitive living. It had 'two living rooms, four bedrooms, a bathroom, kitchen and larder.'

Hovering over its roof were the spreading branches of the, according to Peggy, perhaps 500-year-old, yew tree. Being partly covered by the yew tree branches made the house damp, dark; and always very cold. The underside of the living foliage of yew trees also drops considerable black fungal and other decaying material that covers everything external on the house.

Inside the cottage was more tolerable at times; it had a charming chocolate-box room with exposed Elizabethan oak beams and a cosy feeling if the massive fire was burning strongly. Initially, however, when she moved in, a burning fire filled the room with acrid smoke. Perhaps crows had built a nest in the chimney, thereby blocking it?

Cows grazed right up to the windows. The acre of land needed development to make it a pleasant garden that seamlessly merged into the countryside. A gentle stream flowed across the sloping garden.

All the good it had was balanced by the down-side of a property that was much overdue for modernisation. Water was pumped from a neighbour's lake by an unreliable, kerosene fuelled, pumping engine situated by the lake.

Electricity was supplied by a noisy, 'pom-pom-pom', oil engine-driven generator situated in the house's garage. She comments little on the toileting situation; only that the cottage did have an inside bathroom, and that indicates it did have an inside toilet. If not, one can presume that was in an external hut somewhere outside in the garden.

Heating the house, especially in the first winter there, was an almost impossibly hard task. For her, it was a matter of wearing many layers of clothing. She used portable oil heaters and stayed in bed a lot to keep warm. This side of her showed her frugality. She was far from broke then! Hardly a millionaire's home!

Using the builders, Peacock and Waller, Douglas came to her rescue by upgrading the house and garden.

In that work, however, an annoying mistake was made. It inadvertently entrapped a large Venetian chest inside when a room was reshaped. It had to be sold with the house.

Chapter 12 Entertainment and Sport

12.15 Yew Tree Cottage as it is today, now called *Badgers*, in Hurst, South Harting

Fig 12.15 is of the house as in 2014. A local real-estate sales website had, as this account was written, a set of inside photos. In these, it was easy to recognise the oak beams and the large fireplace in the living room, perhaps the studio Garman built for his writing in the garden, and the sloping lawns.

The kitchen and general appearance are modernised but in the same country style as it must have been in Peggy's days there. Just where the extension was built for the house-help and his new bride, is uncertain.

There is no mention today of a cricket pitch, tennis court or swimming pool. And there is no Delage or Talbot car there to complete the imagery of Peggy with her family and friends enjoying the house in her darker days.

The real estate blurb tells of the yew tree 'reputedly being 2000 years old' – that means it was sown around the time of the birth of Christ. That sounds a little exaggerated! But yew trees have this romance of extreme age associated with them, partly because their age cannot be determined from rings as the shape of the limbs and trunk morphs over time as parts regrow again and again. That tree does not appear to be there now.

Peggy lived there with Pegeen and an Italian, live-in, young girl house-helper. She often went to a rented London flat over the winter months, perhaps to get warm and to entertain her many friends and colleagues.

It was in this period, from 1938 - 1940 that she began serious collecting, and then again over 1941 to 1946. She collected modern artwork pieces from the soul; not for investment. Her compulsion of acquisition was also directed to artists whose works were not selling, or who were being shunned by the establishment.

She just knew, as a *divvy* - an old slang term, meaning someone who guesses the unrevealed value of something without being an expert, that is which works had potential in the future. And she had the money to buy them.

This wild, bohemian 'drop-out' lifestyle for Peggy continued until 1936 when three significant events foreshadowed the rest of her life. They set in place her main destiny as the fierce and resolved patron of Modern Art: she later called herself, an *art addict*.

French Surrealists held a wildly successful show in London in the summer of 1936. Peggy declined to attend, at that time considering *Surrealism* to be a fad that was being replaced.

Second, she spent ten delightful days vacationing alone in Venice, becoming enchanted with the ambience and the lifestyle there. It was where she decided to settle for the rest of her life.

Lastly, she and Garman began a lengthy path to full separation, much brought on because Garman had become obsessed with communism and mostly entertained only party members at Yew Tree Cottage. Visitors there were numerous; but not to Peggy's liking. They had little in common now that Peggy had started on the dramatic art journey of her destiny.

Bertrand Russel, the eminent British philosopher, lived nearby; at that time, he was an anti-war activist, giving lectures across the country on the horrors of war. His line of thought was that acceptance of Hitler's ambitions was better than moving on to all-out global war. He was still preaching this in 1943!

This jolt in Peggy's life led her to consider how to have an occupation of merit that fitted with her main interest in life - *modern art*. A gallery in London would start to fulfil that need. Her first gallery, *Guggenheim*

Jeune, opened there in January 1938.

Peggy was never long without a man in her bed; often for a day or so. She, however, did sometimes occupy her time doing other things than making love in her bed. Samuel Beckett was there with her for a day and night; he taught her the basics of modern art – in between getting more champagne as needed.

Fig. 12.16 Deborah Garman, Pegeen Vail and Samuel Beckett at Yew Tree Cottage ca 1936.

They had many pleasant family days in the cottage, Fig. 12.16. In 1936 it was agreed between Douglas and his partner Jeanne, that she would have responsibility for her daughter Deborah during term-times, but Debbie would stay with Douglas and Peggy during the holidays.

This worked well as Peggy's daughter, Pegeen, was of the same age. Peggy recalled:

> 'Garman and Debbie moved into Yew Tree Cottage, and I found myself once again the mother of two children. I loved Debbie. She was just the opposite of any child I had ever known. She was so mature, calm, sensible, self-contained and well behaved, and so little trouble. She was intellectual like her father and loved to read, and to be read to. She had a wonderful influence over Pegeen, and Pegeen over her. She became less priggish in our home. They got on marvellously and were soon like sisters.'

By 1938 Peggy had made good progress in collecting the work of many avant-garde artists. These artists were still very much out in the cold - as were then the two emerging art genres, *Surrealism* and *Modern*. She was working to set up a gallery in Paris; much of her stock was held in that city.

Midhurst WW2 Memoirs: 2. 'Evil' Rising: 'Good' Awakening

Her interest was, however, falling on sterile ground due to the impending war. When the Nazis were close to occupying Paris, she looked for some safe place to store her artworks. The Louvre declined to give her space in their secret depositories, regarding them as 'worthless' and 'not worth saving'!

The Tate gallery in London defined them as 'not-art'. A leading British expert tried to prevent their entry into Britain. Even today there is much mystery around about this genre, Fig. 12.17.

Fig. 12.17 Modern art still mystifies many who see it.

The Emperor's New Clothes

These negative comments probably helped her a lot. They would have suppressed interest by investors in keeping these kinds of art; and that kept her purchasing prices low. In her later film interview, she said she never paid more the £600 for a piece, most costing only pocket money. In her autobiography, however, she says some cost in the tens of thousands of dollars.

Today one index of art worth is that given in *Art Market* reports of a total of sales of contemporary art made in a year. In the first six months of 2016 some 252,000 fine arts works sold for over $6billion.

Chapter 12 Entertainment and Sport

When Peggy found him, Jackson Pollock was working as a maintenance man in a USA art museum in 1943. His works were then barely of interest. *Blue Poles*, by Jackson Pollock, was bought by the Australian National Gallery for £0.73 million in 1973. Today there is talk that its market value may lay between £11-56 million. In 1950 Peggy owned a remarkable 23 Pollocks in her collection!

Her London gallery/museum was enjoying successful operation; in August 1939, she had moved to set up one in Paris. To stock this proposed new gallery, she took with her a recommended list of pieces to borrow or buy; it had been provided by Herbert Read, Fig. 12.18.

Fig. 12.18 Peggy with her adviser Herbert Read, 1939. *The Sun in its Casket* 1937, by Yves Tanguy, is in the background. (Freund Gisele)

Read was a prominent English art historian and writer on the role of art in education. Peggy then decided:

> 'to buy paintings by all the painters who were on Herbert Read's list. Having plenty of time and all the museum's funds at my disposal, I put myself on a regime to buy one picture a day'

'When finished, she had acquired ten Picassos, forty Ernsts, eight Mitros, four Margrittes, three Man Rays, three Dalis, one Klee, one Wolfgang Paalen and one Chagall among others. In April 1940 she had rented the proposed home for her museum.'

Just before the Germans reached Paris on 14 June 1940, Peggy had to abandon her plans for the Paris museum, fleeing to the south of France where the German-controlled Vichy government still permitted travel in and out by Americans. With difficulty, she obtained the necessary paperwork allowing her to escape France and freight the massive art collection to the USA.

After months of safeguarding her collection and her artist friends, she left Europe for New York in the summer of 1941. At one stage much of her art collection was temporarily stored in a barn in the French countryside. German soldiers missed seeing them on their journey from France! On the deck of the ship transporting her collection to the US, were several thousand crates of artworks!

Being an American citizen with American society connections, Peggy could easily find collector respectability in US circles. She had the drive, money, appreciation of the upcoming 'non-art' work, and a healthy disregard of the British and European, straight jacket establishments of the time that so limited acceptance of her kind of art in Britain.

In the USA, she opened her *Art of This Century* Gallery in 1942; it was 'short-lived but played a key role in launching the careers of many *Abstract Expressionists'*. The following year she married Max Ernst, as her second and last wedded husband. However, that marriage rapidly ended in 1946.

That is when she decided to make her home in Venice. There she lived, exhibiting her collection for the rest of her life in *The Peggy Guggenheim Collection,* one of the world's most foremost modern art museums that is still in the Palazzo Venier dei Leoni, on the Grand Canal in Venice. Fig. 12.19 shows the 18th-century palace on a canal in Venice, that she made into a gallery to show her modern art collection.

Fig. 12.19 Venetian gallery of her modern artworks in 1950.

Chapter 12 Entertainment and Sport

There are to be seen some 360 works from some 100 modern artists. Her collection defines the break-way, revolutionary aspect of 20th-century art.

Peggy died on December 23, 1979, aged 81. Her ashes are interred in her garden memorial at that Venetian museum, Fig. 12.20. Next to her, are also resting fourteen of her faithful dog companions.

Fig. 12.20. Memorial to Peggy Guggenheim in Venice. (Atlas Obscura)

What did she leave for posterity during in her time in that Yew Tree Cottage? What did Harting do for her?

She left very little of her life and works in Harting. No local bequests. No grand property was left to the community - not like the West Dean estate that became an art and restoration, teaching, and studio college. There seems to be no monument, or blue plaque, to her life to be found in Harting today; just a brief mention of her having living there in a real estate advertisement.

She did, however, find time to record, in her autobiography, her life in Yew Tree Cottage in some detail; that suggests it meant a lot to her!

That period was a time of out-pouring grief and mental recovery for her. It was a time for introspection, from which emerged a most important talent; her art collecting addiction. She left a great legacy of 20th-century art to the world...but, sadly, it is in Venice, not England.

Another important local person concerned with art, and its use to society, was Adrian Hill. His story is for a later memoirs book when I discuss my time living in Easebourne.

12.3 Sport in the District: Stoolball

Sport is a keen topic for many. As war approached serious competition became much harder to organise as many men and women went off to serve. Here, concerning sport, we are interested with a lesser-known activity, particular to the south of England.

It has a small stationary target at which a bowler throws a ball. A batter person stands in front of the target to try and stop it hitting the target. There are two team sides of 11 players who take it in turns in trying to get the other side out for fewer hits than the other had managed to get.

Sounds like cricket! But it has a square target held at waist height on a pole, and the bowler is only allowed to throw the ball underarm.

It is, in fact, *stoolball*, a serious bat and ball team game played almost exclusively in Sussex. Some suggest it originated at least before the 15th century, and may well be the forerunner of the games of cricket, baseball and rounders. Stoolball is sometimes called 'cricket in the air'.

Tradition says it was first played by milkmaids using their milking stool as the wicket and their milk bowl, called a *bittle*, as the bat. That seems to have been the origin in its oldest name of *bittle-battle*. Whatever the source, it has been played in Sussex for a very long timeall.

A fascinating poem on stoolball is that given in In *Poor Robin's Almanac of 1744*:

> 'Now milkmaids' pails are deckt with flowers,
> And men begin to drink in bowers,
> Sweets, sillabub, and lip-loved tansey
> For William is prepared by Nancy.
> While hobnailed Dick and simpering Frances
> Trip it away at country dances,
> At stoolball and at barley break
> Where they their harmless pastimes make.'

'It is played with similar equipment on any grass area with a ninety-yard diameter boundary. The pitch is sixteen yards long, bowling is underarm from a bowling crease ten yards from the batsman's wicket and teams consist of eleven players.

Wickets are wooden boards on stakes and the ball, aimed at the wicket, does not hit the ground before reaching the batter. The bat is the shape of a table tennis bat, made of willow with a long, sprung and spliced handle.

Chapter 12 Entertainment and Sport

Scoring and rules are similar to those of cricket with the batting side defending the wickets. There are runs, boundaries, catches and run-outs and also body-before wicket dismissals. Unlike cricket, however, there are eight bowling deliveries in each over.'

Sue Yates, Dicks et al, (2012).

'I started playing stoolball when I was quite young. They used to have juniors and seniors. We always went to away matches in a double-decker bus with the seniors downstairs, and us upstairs. All the Mums went as well so it was a big party. Stoolball is particular to Sussex although I have read a recent chat that it was played in Yorkshire as well. I think of it like cricket but with a wicket up in the air instead of on the ground.'

Sally Page, Dicks et al (2012)

During WW1 stoolball was used to assist the recovery of wounded soldiers. Major William Grantham was serving with the 6th Royal Sussex Regiment. His eldest son was seriously injured. *Military massage* was one form of treatment including playing physical team games, but most of the men's games were fraught with the possibility of worsening their wounds.

Grantham used his powers of persuasion to get it adopted. A demonstration match was played at Lords in 1917 and onward for the following decade. It was also played for decades in the Buckingham Palace gardens. Grantham used to appear in Sussex country folk dress; to portray its rural village origins, Fig. 12.21.

In the 16th and 17th centuries, it was banned by church officials from being played in churchyards, or on

Fig. 12.21 Col Grantham in a round frock and beaver felt hat. (Sussex County Magazine)

Sundays because 'several spend their time at stoolball.' It was deemed to have 'dangerous popularity'.

In 1919 Grantham published *Stoolball Illustrated and How to Play it*. That is available as a download, at www.stoolball.org.uk.

> 'The reason of my reviving the game in 1917 was on account of my meeting so many officers and men who had "done their bit" (had lost a leg, or arm or otherwise been disabled), and for whom cricket or football was too strenuous. It, therefore, occurred to me that Stoolball might be the game to fill a void for their benefit.'

That book by Grantham mentions an 18th-century booklet for children, *A Little Pretty Pocket Book* of 1767, that is held in the British Museum. There, a three-legged milking stool is called a 'cricket'. The illustration is accompanied by a poem:

STOOLBALL
"The Ball once struck with Art and Care,
And drove impetuous through the air;
Swift round his course the Gamester flies,
Or the stool's taken by surprise."

The booklet contains the rules of the game, its advantages over playing cricket and football; a load of supposition about its origin; hints on playing it; details of that first match at Lords on May 18th, 1918; and a lengthy bibliography including citations back to the 17th century.

Originally the batter simply had to defend the stool from each ball with one's hand and would score a point for each delivery until the stool was hit. The game later evolved to include the concept of runs and use of a bat.

One of the listed advantages is that it can be played on rough ground. That was the case in the '30s, for then the Midhurst area lacked a well-kept sports field.

That Lords game was not the first time in the records for these matches. A stoolball game being held locally in Horsham Park was sketched in the 1870s, Thomas (2003). It was then held to be a lady's game, with player's families sitting in attendance, Fig. 12.22. Grantham started up the *Stoolball Association of Great Britain* in 1923. Since his days the sport continued, but after a period in the of low interest, it spread from Sussex to Kent, and Surrey resulting, since 2008, in recognition by the Sports Council as *Stoolball England.*

Fig. 12.22 Stoolball being played in Horsham in the 1870s.
(Thomas 2003)

The simplified rules, from Wikipedia, for Stoolball are that it is: 'Played on grass with a 90-yard (82-metre) diameter boundary, and the pitch is 16 yards (15 metres) long. Each team consists of 11 players, with one team fielding and the other batting. Bowling is underarm from a bowling "crease" 10 yards (9.1 metres) from the batsman's wicket, with the ball reaching the batsman on the full as in rounders or baseball rather than bouncing from the pitch as in cricket. Each over consists of 8 balls. The "wicket" itself is a square piece of wood at head or shoulder height fastened to a post. Traditionally the seat of a stool hung from a post or tree was used. Some versions used a tall stool placed upright on the ground.
As it is played today, a bowler attempts to hit the wicket with the ball, and a batsman defends it using a bat shaped like a frying pan. The batsman scores "runs" by running between the wickets or hitting the ball beyond the boundary in a similar way to cricket. A ball hit over the boundary counts for 4 runs if it has hit the ground before reaching the boundary, or 6 runs if it landed beyond the boundary upon first contact with the ground. Fielders attempt to catch the ball or run out the batsman by hitting the wicket with the ball before the batsman returns from his run.'

In the 1930s it was being played in Midhurst and is still followed to this day, playing in the Cowdray Ruins Sports Ground for outside matches and in the Grange Sports Centre in Midhurst for those played indoors. The

Midhurst WW2 Memoirs: 2. 'Evil' Rising: 'Good' Awakening

Midhurst Sports Ground is leased to clubs. It was refurbished starting in 1984 to have modern facilities.

John Holland played stoolball on the ground opposite Russell's garage at the beginning of Bepton Road, behind the pub and the then existing Congregational Church that was bombed flat in 1943, see the later book:

> 'The, well you would hardly call it playing fields - but the field over behind the Pub, there was a pond then but there isn't now, it sloped and we boys used to play football and cricket over there. At the top we had allotments and we used to have a gardener come on Monday afternoons and we used to be taught gardening. But the girls for their playing fields they went up onto the Bowling Green at Midhurst and we older boys used to have to carry - on a Wednesday afternoon, their Stoolball posts and what have you up for them and they played up there - because this playing field, as I say, it just sloped down - but that's all we had.
>
> John Holland, in Elsdon (2010)

'My husband worked for Cowdray for 28/29 years - and he used to love football and cricket. I used to do the cricket teas, help with the cricket teas – I wasn't so involved with the football, that wasn't my scene. But I did enjoy cricket, I still do. I used to play stoolball for Easebourne. We played Stoolball and Cricket. We lived right opposite the Rother Field so that was where we played a lot, and down by the river when nobody knew we were there, Fig.12.23, we weren't allowed there in case we got into trouble.'

June Page, Elsdon (2010).

Fig. 12.23 June Page with little friends in Egmont Road, before it had houses built on the grassy meadows, 1938.

Chapter 12 Entertainment and Sport

The usual, nationally played, mainline sports of cricket, (soccer) football, rugger, and tennis were all played locally. These all suffered the lack of really suitable facilities until long after the war ended. The Rugby Club started up around 1980 as part of Sussex RFU (Rugby Football Union). There was a pavilion by the Cowdray Ruins that was made suitable for the various sports clubs; that helped matters along.

> 'After that the Rugger Club slowly grew in strength, and it's now an impressive sight on a Sunday morning to see - must be getting on for a hundred youngsters being taught the basics of rugger across that lovely green sward at the back of the Ruins'
> Keith and Beryl Moores, in Elsdon (2010).

> 'In 1981, I hope that's the right date, David West called a meeting of the Stoolball Club, the Rugby Club and the Cricket Club to institute what was to become the Midhurst Sports Association. This was to coordinate the 3 clubs, and particularly their use of the Ruins Ground and for the maintenance of the Pavilion.'
> Dr Peter Davis and Mrs Peta Davis, in Litchfield (2011)

John Holland, Fig. 12.24, has provided a good record of his pre-war childhood in Midhurst:

Fig. 12.24 John Holland, b.1922, taken in 2007.

'There were three Football Clubs in Midhurst - Midhurst (Saturday), Midhurst (Wednesday) and Midhurst Whites from the Brickyard. The first two played on the Whip Hill ground in Lamberts Lane. Cricket was played at Cowdray Ruins, that also had five grass Tennis Courts. Behind the Ruins was the Archery Club. Bowls was played at

June Lane, still the present site. Stoolball was also played at Cowdray Ruins. A sport which is long since gone is "Quoitts", this was played on a piece of ground down Blackiston's Yard in Midhurst'

'There were no playing grounds for children's swings or see-saws. The whole of the area became one huge playground for small boys. We roamed the Common which had two huge disused sand-pits off Carron Lane, just before the Cemetery. Here with vivid imagination we played Cowboys and Indians and First World War Battles with homemade guns and swords. Children did not have all the toys that are around now. Town Hill (St Ann's Hill) was another favourite place with the Castle Ruins and the river, Close Walks (now an estate) and in the Cowdray Ruins. These were the days of complete freedom; parents did not have to worry if we were gone for hours on end'.

'Schools did not have proper playing fields as they do today. Once a week, boys played Football or Cricket in a field to the other side of June Lane behind the Half Moon Pub. The girls played Stoolball or Netball on what is known as the Bowling Green on the Common. At the top of the field, we had allotments where the older boys were taught gardening by an old retired gardener. No doubt he was a good gardener but his control over unruly boys was sadly lacking'.

John Holland, in Elsdon (2010)

Fig. 12.25 Lurgashall today.

Chapter 12 Entertainment and Sport

'Ann Harfield was a keen sportswoman. She played hockey and rounders for the school, and stoolball and table tennis for the village.' Litchfield (2011).

She was in the Lurgashall stoolball team in 1952, Fig. 12.26. Ann is in the centre between the girls holding the bats. The wicket is behind. The team was photographed on the village green with the Webber's house in the background.

Fig. 12.26 Lurgashall stoolball team, 1952; see text.

Villages often had their stoolball team that would have played on their own recreational ground. Fig. 12.27 is of the heritage Fernhurst sports pavilion.

Fig. 12.27 Fernhurst recreational ground with its heritage timber pavilion. (Fernhurst Society)

Stoolball was played on village grounds across Sussex. Many a cricket match would also have been witnessed there, its pace being just right for leisurely watching when one is seated in a comfortable reclining deck chair, placed under a large oak tree to catch the shade. An occasional 'howzat call', or spectators clapping a player for a good catch of a ball or a 'hit for six', would interrupt one's rest.

During the 30s and wartime, formalised sports programs were suspended because men and women were serving in the war effort. However, sport was still played informally, as and when it could be arranged. Troops needed diversions from training and downtimes. They played much the same games as before the war for the soldiers were British and Canadian in the main - until the US troops arrived in increasingly larger numbers; bringing their interest in baseball with them.

With the back-story detail covered, this study of the Midhurst District memoirs during WW2 can get closer to the detail of what the District was like to live in as war was coming. But first it is necessary to record the exploits of one particular person, a dairy farmer as WW2 broke out who has earned the Victoria Cross.

Chapter 13. Some Local Memories

13.1 Heroes of WW1 - in Submarines

The following remarkable story must not be forgotten. It is of the exploits of a man who became a humble dairy farmer in Stedham after WW1.

In the mid-30s a person in the Midhurst Rural District who understood how things were progressing toward the growth of evil power, was submarine commander Norman Douglas Holbrook; awarded, in WW1, the first naval VC.

He did not leave us much of a record of his time in Stedham but his early life story cannot be left out of these memoirs. His experiences of such a dangerous and scary side of the war, would have left him well aware of the horrors to come in another major war.

Norman was born in Southsea, Hampshire in 1888. Of his schooling time at Portsmouth Grammar School his Headmaster James Priory said:

> 'young Norman's reports showed "some room for improvement" but that he made his mark on the sports field, including a win in the 100-yard dash "in the face of a stiff breeze" and came third in an obstacle race – an early indication of skills which stood him in good stead in the war'
>
> www.submarinersassociation.co.uk

He became a midshipman in the Royal Navy in 1905 at the age of 17. He, then, surely could not have imagined how the up-coming first World War would make him a most famous person - as the first British naval recipient of the highest British war honour, the Victoria Cross; and even more, with his family name given to a country town in far-away Australia.

His submarine service started early in 1905 and he was given command of the RN submarine HMS B11 in late 1913. Life on the submarine for him at that time would have been on training and, more training, without much everyday pressure - not that living on them was in any way luxurious - the crew seemed to be the last element accommodated in the highly mechanical system design of a submarine.

When on a mission it was a very dangerous kind of war service.

He was then a young 25 years of age, Fig. 13.1, and, apart from trips out in a submarine for a few days of exercises now and then, was probably enjoying a pleasant land-based RN lifestyle with its formal dinners, parades and socialising.

Fig. 13.1 Lieutenant Norman Douglas Holbrook, here, was just 26 years old in 1914 when he sunk a Turkish warship. (DVA Australia)

A report that Lieutenant Norman Holbrook had been wounded was published in the Canadian *Colonist* on 21 August 1915. It was, however, not a major wound.

Following his exploits that earned him the V.C., he left the submarine service in 1918, continuing in the Royal Navy to be promoted to Commander rank in 1920. He retired from the navy in 1928,

After his naval career, he became almost unknown in his native country - but certainly not in Australia where he had never been, as we shall see later. At some time later he went to live for the rest of his life in Stedham, as a dairy farmer raising Guernsey cows, Dicks et al (2012).

It is highly likely that I, and other little evacuees, drank lovely creamy milk from his Guernsey cows at our preschool in the Drill Hall, situated at the rear of the then Crown pub. They say he enjoyed gardening and fishing but little else is known of his later life. Perhaps he just wanted to live a quiet life after his most hazardous days in the Royal Navy.

At the age of 51, during WW2, he again served in the Admiralty. He was a reluctant hero who helped his country again in its time of need.

He married his first wife, Viva (b.1882) in 1919; she passed away

Chapter 13 Some Local Memories

in 1952, aged 70. His son with Viva, Lieutenant Geoffrey Norman Holbrook, was in the 12th Regiment of the Royal Horse Artillery (they had changed from horses to mechanical vehicles in 1939!). He, sadly, was killed on 10 April 1945 when he was just 24. He is buried in the Ravenna War Cemetery, Italy.

Douglas married Gundula (b.1914), who is still with us at the time of writing, then being 102. She lives in Austria.

He died on 3 July 1976 in Midhurst, Sussex and was buried at St James Old Churchyard, Stedham, Fig. 13.2. The headstone reads:

> (Inserted at the head is a VC medal replica)
> In memory of my beloved husband
> Commander
> NORMAN DOUGLAS
> HOLBROOK. V.C.
> Royal Navy (Retired)
> 9th July 1888 –3rd July 1976

Fig. 13.2 Grave of Norman Douglas Holbrook VC. (Ian Wegg)

Norman left no children, but over 120 relatives attended the memorial reunion of his death, held in Stedham on 25 July, 2014. Gundula was not present for the re-dedication, presumably her age of 100 years at the time, made it impractical for her to attend.

This re-dedication was organised by the Victoria Cross Trust that was then carrying out restoration work on the graves of Victoria Cross holders throughout Britain.

Many graves had become quite neglected. Responsibility for a grave is placed upon a living relative who usually must pay a tidy sum for its 'ownership' over the decades ahead.

419

This system of care for a grave can have difficulties for three major reasons. First, there may not be any next of kin to notify about the need to continue its support. Second, the sum of money needed can be prohibitive. Last, the person owning the lease might simply neglect its upkeep.

(As is mentioned elsewhere in these Memoirs, several important local graves seem have been 'lost' and are being rediscovered through this research work.)

The re-dedication service took place in the church, and around the grave, being attended by senior politician Eric Pickles, senior ranks of the Royal Navy, and members of Commander Holbrook's family including a great, great nephew Matt, and a great-nephew Alan. A few Stedham villagers who knew him were also there.

Returning to Norman's post-WW1 life, Geoff West in Dicks et al (2012) tells us that at some stage after he came to live in the District, Commander Norman Holbrook knocked down a big barn on the road to the Stedham Mill, that being at the end of the lane running down to the river by the Stedham church. Fig. 13.3.

Fig. 13.3 Stedham Mill c, 1928; the actual mill is no longer standing. (Gravel Roots)

He used the stone to enlarge Mill House; to make it match the Mill. The entrance is said to have looked like a mill-stone.

The mill was once used to make blotting paper but was

Chapter 13 Some Local Memories

demolished, after a fire in 1901, being rebuilt and then taken down in 1927.

Derek Christmas in Dicks et al (2012) tells us that Norman, when at the Woodgate Farm (now a modernised family home), ran his Jersey and Guernsey milking cow farm from the Mill House. Still apparent is a concrete slab where the milk churns were placed. It is stated there that Commander Holbrook extended the milking parlour when he enlarged the herd.

Additionally, Geoff West recalls the Commander also ran a mink farm inside the Walled Garden in Stedham, later moving it to behind the Mill Lane Cottages.

That is Norman's life in a nutshell. What did the somewhat reticent Norman do in WW1 to earn his prestigious VC award? How come he had sunk a Turkish ship?

When 26 years old he was a lieutenant in the Royal Navy and on December 13, 1914, he was stationed in the Dardanelles in command of the ageing Royal Navy submarine, HMS B11, Fig. 13.4.

Fig. 13.4 Submarine HMS B11 in 1917.

First, some history. Istanbul, then called Constantinople, was a major location in the crumbling Ottoman Empire in the early 1900s. It was the division between the Western and the Eastern world. This port was used to provision the Turkish troops fighting in the Gallipoli region.

As a key action to destroy the remnants of the Ottoman Empire, the British War department of WW1 had decided that Constantinople must be taken by the Western Allies.

Access to the port, refer to Fig. 13.5, was either overland, across the Gallipoli Peninsular from the Aegean Sea coast; or else through the *Dardanelles*. This stretch of sea is a narrow strait that connects the

Aegean Sea at its southern end, with the Gallipoli town at its northern end where the Marmara Sea begins. These narrows allowed large ships to connect Constantinople with the Mediterranean Sea, via the Marmara Sea.

A sea attack on the Dardanelles by the Allies was intended to break through the Dardanelles passage to capture Constantinople. Simultaneous attacks on land and at sea were needed.

This narrow straight, at Chanak in Fig. 13.5, can be likened to a fierce unpredictable river. It is 38 miles long, with a width that varies between 3/4 to 3 3/4 miles.

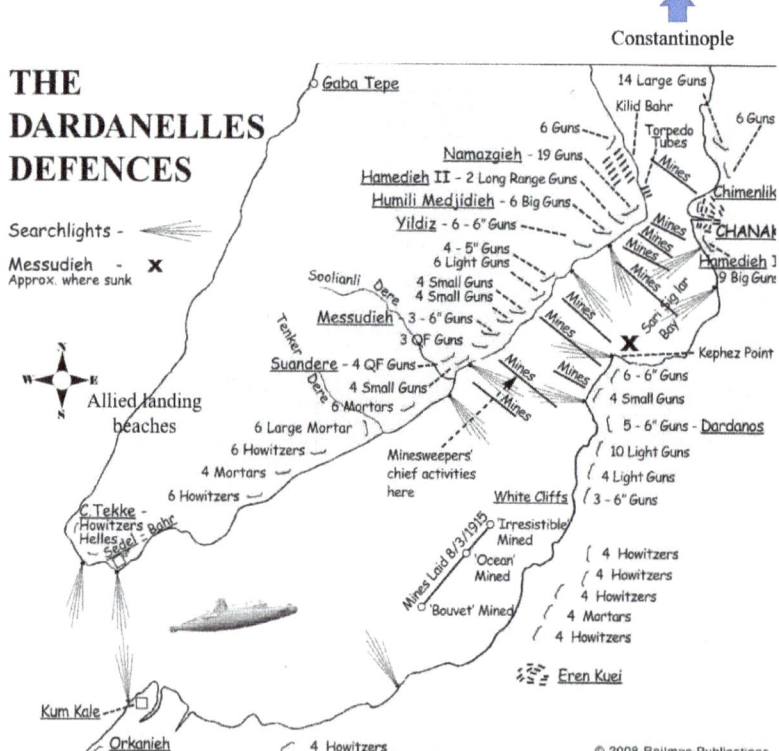

Fig.13.5 Dardanelles defences, at its lower area, were strong indeed. (Modified from Railmac Pubs.)

At that time the coastal land and underwater profile are rugged and they were mostly uncharted, or incorrectly recorded. The depth was as much

Chapter 13 Some Local Memories

as 338 feet, with many uncharted shallows. A most unusual feature is that water flows outward into the Aegean Sea in the top layers and is a reversed, problematic undercurrent flow in the depths below. It was an area of treacherous waters, so narrow at one spot that it could, seemingly, be solidly defended by mines, submarine nets, land-fired torpedoes and shore guns.

As can be seen from Fig. 13.5, the Turkish defences were most formidable at that point and others. Large artillery guns sent crossfire over the narrows. Layers of sea minefields and anti-submarine nets were thought to be too formidable for surface ships or submarines to pass.

The land assault aspect was carried out at the now well known 'Gallipoli' campaign landing by the ANZACs. The Allied Powers of British, Australians, New Zealanders, Indians and Newfoundland troops were committed there. They landed, incorrectly, on a coast - marked 'Allied Landing Beaches' in Fig. 13.5. Gallipoli town, situated off the map, north up the narrows, was where Turkish troops were being reinforced by ships coming down from Constantinople.

A major battle fleet of French and British warships attempted to break through the Dardanelles defences, but many (*Bouvet, Ocean* and *Irresistible*) were soon sunk by mines. That idea was abandoned. The Campaign was then to be carried out only over the land, and under the sea. French, British and Australian submarines attempted to get under the nets, past the mines and shore batteries, to sink ships in the harbour at Constantinople.

An important thing about these submarines needs to be understood. Simple electrical technology at the start of the 20th century had no satisfactory way to use the very sensitive underwater detection methods we now associate as crucial in submarine warfare.

The invention of the thermionic valve (tube), and thus the beginning of the electronic technologies, was then just starting to add this ability as electronic amplifiers could detect minute acoustic sounds. It also enabled faster, i.e. much higher frequency, signals to be generated and detected. These technologies did come into operational use at the end of WW1, but they were not available to the submarines of the Dardanelles campaign.

The early 20th century submarines, however, did have a distinct advantage; when submerged under the right conditions they were virtually undetectable as long their internal requirements for life support were met, and they kept very quiet. Sound travels very well in water so each side of a conflict could gain information on the other's position by what is called *passive* detection - simply by listening to noises made by external sources with mechanical headphones connected to their submarine shell. Without amplification, the ear's ability was useful for detecting loud noises but inadequate to detect the very weak sound 'pings'- the *active* methodology. A submarine could detect a low-level short ping. When an intense short burst of acoustic sound sent from the submarine hit a metal object, such as the other submarine's hull, a small part of these generated pulses of sound would return to the sender. The time it took to travel there and back gave the distance: the signal loudness, scanned across the front of the receiver gave the direction to the target. But this active method also worked in reverse; the vessel receiving a 'ping' return could to likewise to the other submarine.

Without improved sonar methods, the first submarines of the 20th century could, relatively easily, come to position and rise to carry out damage mostly at their will. Mechanical methods, sea mines and nets, shore batteries and patrol boats were the physical barriers. It was their periscope breaking the water surface to leave a small wake, that mainly gave their position away.

Sonar (SOund Navigation And Ranging) was not then feasible without improved electronic technology. When this developed to be a useful capability, the submarine contest with the defensive methods became better matched.

Starting with a position fix on the enemy boat the game, made with a quick periscope sighting, was to stay with that boat. From around 1913 arrival of electronic methods made sonar systems feasible, but not practical, in a submarine environment. By the end of WW1, the British name was changed to ASDIC, coined to keep British research and development work secret.

Thus, submarines used in the 1915 Dardanelles campaign had a considerable advantage over the Turks for they were hard to detect underwater - but that was counteracted by the poor reliability of the designs of submarine boats at the time, especially of the British B11 submarine commanded by Lieutenant Holbrook; theirs was an obsolete 1903 design.

Chapter 13 Some Local Memories

A submarine could not detect the presence of mines before reaching them. They learned of their presence when the wire holding a mine to a set depth screeched its way across the hull, hopefully without exploding if the wire became caught by some kind of protuberance on the submarine. That pulled the mine down to explode when its horn detectors were triggered. B11 was modified with protection rails to reduce this problem by letting the wire slide over the hull.

Submarines are propelled underwater with electric motors. Another limiting performance factor of this submarine was that it had to surface periodically to charge its electrical storage battery with an air-aspirated petrol engine driving an electricity generator.

These factors need to be taken into account when considering the several historic attempts by Allied submarines to get through to Constantinople.

The large naval fleet began the Dardanelles Naval Campaign by probing the shore batteries with naval fire on 3 November 1914.

Several interactions by the Allied Fleet with the Turkish shore defences and mines built up confidence for a major all-out support naval attack to be executed. That was expected to take the Allied forces rapidly up to Constantinople without needing a land assault. But that was not to be!

To assist the safer passage of the fleet, submarines were intended to get through when the full attack started. To gain confidence that the Dardanelles could indeed be passed through by the Allies naval battle force, in the early hours of 13 December 1914, Holbrook and his small crew, Fig. 13.6, were sent, in submarine B11, to get through the straights.

Fig. 13.6 Crew of B11 with, then Lieut. Holbrook. (DVA Australia)

They were in difficult waters - recall the fact that B11 was an obsolete craft. It was also a poorly set-up attempt. Despite upgrades in design from the former A class, B11 still was prone to dive unexpectedly in heavy seas. It, also, had no separating compartments to keep the fumes of its petrol engine away from the crew, who usually had to remain below when the boat was running on the surface.

Furthermore, no dedicated accommodation was provided for the 12 men and 2 officer crew. They dossed down where ever they could amongst the various technical environments inside a submarine. And that was not all. The boat had a mere 3-4 days of endurance time at sea and could only stay submerged for around 9 hours at time due to the limited oxygen that was available. Being 142 feet long and of 200 tons surface weight, it was, by today's submarine standards, quite small.

The defences of that entrance to the Dardanelles were considerable and considered to be impregnable, refer back to Fig. 13.5. The Turkish shore batteries had naval guns, large mortars, and close-up machine guns. Fast armoured patrol boats and shore searchlights probed the darkness all through the night.

Despite the treacherous currents and poor depth charts already mentioned, B11 dived under rows of mines, to start a journey up the Straight. On 13 December Holbrook torpedoed and sank the heavily armed Ottoman ironclad ship, *Messudieh*, that was guarding the minefield. The ironclad kept up the heavy fire as it sank. Many of its crew were extracted through a hole cut in the hull.

Holbrook reached the San Sighlar Bay that, (as is shown in the above figure as point X by Kephez Point), was still some way from breaching the full length of the Dardanelles. They had not passed through the narrowest, most defended, pinch point at Canakkale (also known as Chanak).

Despite being attacked by gunfire and torpedo boats, Holbrook succeeded in bringing the B11 back out of the straights through the minefield. By the time they got back to safety, the B11 had been submerged for nine hours, nearing its limit of oxygen.

Ryan (2008) provides more background of this spectacular engagement. A long local description of this event is found at the *Middle East Institute Editor's Blog* of 12 December 2014.

Not to be left out of this challenge to be the first to get right through to

Chapter 13 Some Local Memories

the Sea of Marmara, and then to Constantinople, French submarine *Saphir Q44,* commanded by Lieutenant de Vaisseau Henri de Fornier, attempted a passage on 15 January 1915. He got as far as Chanak but was forced to surface due to serious leaks in its casing, going aground as the result. Under fire, with no chance of escape, they scuttled the boat. The surviving members of the crew - the officers did not survive - were taken to become Turkish POWs.

Another underwater mission had failed, this time with prisoners being taken. Again, the Ottomans had been victorious.

Within hours of sinking the *Messudieh* by B11 on 13 December 1914, the good news of this limited success reached the war department in London. The British Admiralty was over the moon for it was then (partially!) shown that submarines could enter the Dardanelles and return without loss of crew, or submarine.

Regardless of the reality of the incident as not nearly achieving its military goal; within days the sinking event went viral in the newspapers of the Western World. For example, it was in the *British Times* and the *New York Times* on 15 December 1914; in the *Auckland Star*, New Zealand on 17 December; and in the *Brisbane Courier* of Queensland, Australia on 18 December 1914.

The normal process for making the award of the VC at that time was as follows; usually quite slow.

A recommendation for an award was proposed at the local naval action level. It then went up through Royal Navy channels starting with consideration by Commodore RN, after which it was passed to the Vice-Admiral RN, and then on to the Admiralty. The Honours Committee at the Admiralty would debate the case and pass their recommendation on to the Secretary of State for Navy – who, in turn, would present his recommendation to King George V for final approval.

One would expect that process to take months to carry out. Not surprisingly, Holbrook's award deliberations took only 7-8 days: heroes were so badly needed to boost the public's expectations.

Holbrook's was the first naval Victoria Cross of WW1 to be officially published in the London Gazette on 22 December 1914. Now that was fast; just over a week!! The British war and propaganda machine wanted a spectacular win to promote to the nation.

Holbrook had sunk the first battleship in WW1 and shown that the Allied fleet should be able to reach Constantinople. Fig.13.7 shows Commander Norman Holbrook's medals, donated to the town of Holbrook in NSW, now being on show in the Australian War Memorial, Canberra. Why they are in Australia will shortly be revealed.

Fig 13.7 Medal group of Commander Norman Holbrook.

Not meaning to detract from Norman's exploit his, however, was not the first naval event to be awarded a VC. That record went to Commander Henry Peel Ritchie RN. In November 1914 he led a commando-style harbour raid in Dar-es-salaam. It was not, however, gazetted until April 1915 - the bureaucratic process was held up deciding what medal was appropriate for his case.

On the exact day of Holbrook's epic mission, that is on 13 December 2014, a 100th-anniversary celebration of Norman's exploits took place at the Royal Navy Submarine Museum in Gosport, UK. Attending were 115 members of the Holbrook family.

Meanwhile, in New South Wales NSW, Australia, a very small town was seeking a new name for its original, strongly Germanic one.

Accounts of his success in the local newspapers (in late 1914), must have assisted the choice of his name for that inland country town. His name was in their shortlist before April 1915.

W D & H O Wills issued their 1st series set, of 25 cigarette cards, called *Victoria Cross Heroes (The Great War)* in 1915. As the last date

Chapter 13 Some Local Memories

of action in that set is in late August 1915 it seems they were not published until the end of that year, and thus were not instrumental in assisting the town's folk of Holbrook in selecting Norman's surname for their new name.

Two differently worded sets of cards were published, another being by Gallaher, Fig. 13.8. The card numbers in these two series do not match, nor does the text of the account given on the reverse side.

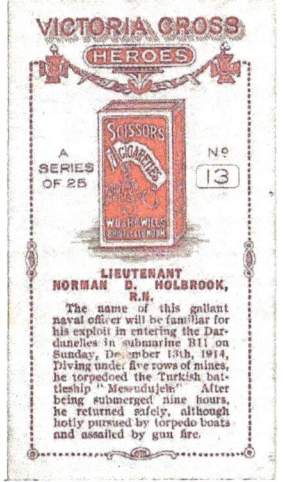

Fig. 13.8 Holbrook's WW1 submarine story was rapidly told to all in a 'Wills' cigarette card series issued in Australia in late 1915.

LHS Face side

RHS Rear side

A town named after him on the other side of the globe! How did that happen? Tell me more you say.

In the 1840s, at a developing set of crossroads in the NSW outback at Ten Mile Creek, there was an inn named, around 1858, after a German pioneer that spot being called Germanton.

The outbreak of WW1 led to serious discomfort with that name by the residents. Government propaganda then was much about hating the Germans:

'Hate the Hun', 'Destroy This Mad Brute', 'How the Hun Hates', 'Hun or Home?'

In September 1914 the Germanton Shire Council started proceedings to decide a kinder name for the town. Patriotism for the British Empire led to many names of famous British persons being put forward. By April 1915 their list was down to Asquith, Jellico, Kitchener, and Holbrook, the little-known submariner. On 5 December 1915 Holbrook became the name of a town and later a municipality, Ryan (2008).

How did Holbrook even get into the list? He had been a hero in action just months before; but he was only a young unknown lieutenant, not a Prime Minister, a Commander of a naval fleet, or a hero of long-standing as were the others.

He was, however, 'a brave face of the British Empire' Ryan (2008). As seems to be too often the case, Lieutenant Holbrook only found out about his name being adopted from newspaper articles, and after that from direct communication by the Town Council. He was honoured by the choice. It was, however, to take some 40 years before he made his first visit to the town with his second wife, Gundula.

'Submarines', as a topic, just would not go away in the Holbrook town – it is situated far from the sea. The locals subsequently worked to make it a draw-card for tourists. In the 1960s Holbrook town commenced its identification with submarines in a big way.

The APEX club created the Commander Holbrook Memorial Park in which a physical representation of B11 was needed, Fig. 13.9.

Fig. 13.9 Replica of B11, at 1/5th scale, in aluminium.

It took several years to raise the funds, but on 11 September 1971 the half-ton, 28-foot-long, aluminium model was lowered onto its prepared mounting blocks. The Turkish Ambassador was present, among

Chapter 13 Some Local Memories

the many dignitaries. Holbrook town was on the tourist map but Commander Holbrook was not able to attend. Over the years ahead he made several visits to the town.

Norman died in 1976; the tradition of being a submarine town being continued with more submarine initiatives that transformed the town into a major tourist attraction. They including a scholarship in 1965 for young high school students, a submarine museum, and placement there, starting around 1995, of the above-water line, full size, salvaged shell of the 1950 HMAS Otway, an Oberon Class diesel engine submarine. Its 12ton fin (the conning tower) and much internal machinery are also there.

Getting these over-size tons of Otway material to the town, needed considerable funds. This move and reassembly task rapidly ran out of funds before completion. Mrs Gundula Holbrook came to the rescue with a major donation to help make Holbrook THE submarine history town in Australia.

In 1997 Mrs Gundula Holbrook was the guest of honour at the dedication of HMAS Otway in its new place of rest at Holbrook; saved from the scrap metal market!

To end this thread, Holbrook town is 270 miles from the nearest seashore; an unexpected place for a historic submarine centre. It epitomises the theme of Commander Holbrook's military life - to take on, and win over, the seemingly impossible.

A bronze statue of Holbrook stands in Germanton Park, Holbrook, but nowhere in the UK where he is almost forgotten. A complete account of this transformation is available, Ryan (2008).

Before we move on from Commander Norman Holbrook's submarine contribution a misconception needs to be corrected. One report on the Internet suggests that he held a senior rank in the Australian Navy. Incorrect!

Norman Holbrook never had any direct active naval service connection with the Australian Navy, only a post-retirement connection as the result of the naming of Holbrook town. There was, however, also in the Royal Navy of that time one Leonard Stanley Holbrook, a brother of Norman Lindsay Holbrook. The family were known as 'the fighting Holbrooks' - five of Norman's 10 siblings fought in WW1 and were each decorated. His father, Arthur, was knighted for his service in the Army Service Corps, becoming the Member of Parliament for Basingstoke in 1920.

Leonard took a quite different career path to Norman, rising to hold a most senior rank of the RN. His naval life duties were more about management, control and command; all contributed at some distance from the battle front line. That was the situation for the majority of those in military service. Of all enlisted military personnel in a large war, a very low proportion take front-line fighting roles. Guestimates of the ratio ranges from 5:1 to 30:1, the latter ratio including the civilian support also needed.

Leonard Stanley Holbrook was born in Portsmouth on 1 January 1882, a few years before Norman. In 1896 he joined the Royal Navy, receiving naval rating two years later, Fig. 13.10.

Fig 13.10 Rear Admiral Leonard Stanley Holbrook. (Walter Stoneman NPG)

This was at a particularly quiet global time for the Royal Navy. An important early career role - he was just 19 years of age - for Leonard was to be chosen in 1901 as a member of the Honour Guard at the Funeral of Queen Victoria.

The following years in the Royal Navy saw him mainly carrying out protective duties of the British Empire protectorates. From 1900 - 1913 there were no major British naval battles listed in the chronology given in Wikipedia. Many heavy battleships of this period never fired a shot in anger! Was this the reason why the Allied Fleet performed so poorly in the Dardanelles engagement, discussed above?

This pre-WW1 period saw the Royal Navy became the world 'policeman' ensuring *Pax Britannica* (British Peace) was in place. To

Chapter 13 Some Local Memories

counter the growing strength of several other nations, larger - and still larger - gunned battleships were built to make it clear that 'Britannia Ruled the Seas'. She maintained a policy of having a naval force just greater than the sum of the two next best nations! She was rarely challenged; such was her sea power.

When WW1 broke out Leonard, then 32 years old, was a gunnery officer on HMS Devonshire, an armoured cruiser launched in 1904. Devonshire served centrally with the Grand Fleet; it never saw combat in its life, its role was as an escort for convoys, Fig. 13.11.

Fig 13.11 HMS Devonshire, armoured cruiser; in service 1904-1921.

Whilst on the Devonshire he was progressively promoted to Commander, and then as Flag Commander to several Vice Admirals. He became a naval Captain in 1920. HMS Devonshire was sold for scrap in 1921.

At this stage, another notable Australian link to the Midhurst District existed. Previously, in August 1914, an agreement had been signed that the Royal Australian Navy (RAN) would come under British Navy control; at least until August 1919. That kind of relationship lingered on after WW1 with RN involvement in top RAN posts.

In 1929 Leonard was seconded to the Royal Australian Navy to command the original HMAS Canberra, a newly built heavy cruiser with eight 8inch guns, and many smaller gunnery pieces. It could steam at some 32knots, that is, at 36mph.

In Australia, Leonard was rapidly appointed as Commodore First Class to command His Majesty's Australian Squadron between 29 May 1931 and 7 April 1932, by then meaning RAN, not RN, ships. The Commodore rank was one step below Rear Admiral.

After that, nearing retirement age, Leonard became an Aide De Camp to King George for short periods in 1932. His naval career ended in that year when he was 50 years old, having been appointed to Rear Admiral on the day before he was placed on the Retired List.

He would have retired on a generous naval pension and be given a highly respected place in civilian society, being permitted to carry his rank in everyday life. However, as is so often the case, as his lind of service was not of the kind that captures the public imagination, he would most likely have dropped out of the public eye on retirement.

Leonard died at home in August 1974, his funeral being held on 6 September, followed by cremation, in Bury, West Sussex, 12 miles SE of Midhurst and just over the borderline of the Midhurst Rural District.

Unlike his brother Norman, who had retired as a Commander to become a farmer, Leonard had made a strident and significant career in the Navy; not being able to go much higher in rank at its end.

What Leonard did for the 42 years left of his life seems to not be recorded. Attempts at identifying a memorial to his death anywhere were not successful.

Returning to the Dardanelle's submarine campaign, all the publicity and follow-on about Norman Holbrook's Dardanelles Campaign submarine incursion, masked the valour and daring of other similarly brave and harrowing submarine experiences in that action.

The first fully successful passage of an Allies' submarine past all of the minefields, was a made in a more modern submarine of that time. This is now described: it is another Australian connection.

The main Allied fleet of 10 battleships (six British, the others French) plus many support vessels, began the main Dardanelles Naval Campaign assault mid-morning on 18 March 1915.

Chapter 13 Some Local Memories

Within hours it was a major naval failure. The Allied fleet met with the massive, highly effective, Turkish land and sea defences and soon lost three of its 10 battleships from shore battery fire and undetected sea mines.

It retreated. This was a significant victory for the Ottoman Empire: and a major blow to British prestige. Perhaps too many years without high-level real action had not helped the RN when it came into this kind of real warfare?

It had become clear that a land assault was badly needed - the Gallipoli Land Campaign - that commenced on 25 April 1915. The fact that Norman Holbrook in the B11 had been able to breach some of the Dardanelles protection seems to have garnered the notion that submarines should be able to take some of the heat off of that invasion, making it still a possible winner.

Enter the experiences of the crew of HMAS AE2, commanded by Henry Stoker! Lieutenant Henry Dacre Stoker, Fig.13.12, was in command of HMAS submarine AE2.

Fig. 13.12 Henry Stoker - submariner, actor and sportsman. (Bramstokerestate.com)

The B11 mission showed that submarines should be able to get right up to Constantinople, but B11 did not make it that far. That is where Lieutenant Stoker enters this submarine account.

HMAS AE2 was one of two contemporary design E-class submarines built for the Royal Australian Navy by Britain: it was commissioned into the Australian Navy in February 1914, becoming part of the Dardanelles invasion fleet, Fig. 13.13.

Fig. 13.13 Submarine AE2 of the Royal Australian Navy. 2014 postage stamp.

Being 181 feet long with a displacement of 759 long tons, this class was the latest design and was much larger than the ageing B series submarines. It had a longer surface range (3000nmi), increased submerged endurance (65nmi), and a larger crew of 34 officers and ratings. It used diesel engines, that were far less pollution was generated inside the submarine than there has been in the petrol-driven B11. It was much more spacious and accommodating for its crew. The captain even had a padded armchair in the control room!

Australia had not had submarines before then. Consequently, there was no submarine staffing experience within their command. AE2 was commissioned at its berth in Britain so an experienced commander was needed.

Lieutenant Henry Stoker, an Irishman in the British Royal Navy, was chosen to command the boat for its maiden voyage over the 15,000 miles to Australia; a record endurance feat in itself.

Henry was born in Dublin in February 1885. He became a Royal Navy cadet when he was 12 years old, that is, in 1897. He knew what he wanted to do for a career!

Chapter 13 Some Local Memories

Promoted to acting sub-lieutenant in 1902 - to get more pay - he volunteered for the submarine service. When just 23 he was given submarine command, later being posted to Gibraltar.

His interest in playing polo in Australia had some bearing on him applying for a posting to the RAN's new submarine service - see www.awm.gov.au/people/P10676826/

In 1913 he took command of AE2. The crew were appointed from the existing RN and RAN navy personnel. In March 1913 he, and the sister submarine AE1, left for Australia, arriving there in May. They were at sea for 60 of the 83 days taken for that long surface journey.

Upon arrival, AE1 and AE2 were put to work in the areas of New Guinea and Fiji. In this period AE1 mysteriously disappeared - another story!

Stoker was back in Sydney on 16 November 1914. Now that the German naval presence near Australia had been beaten back, he suggested his submarine could be used more effectively in the European theatre.

After another long sea journey – under tow this time - AE2 arrived in Port Said, Egypt on 28 January 1915. Leaving from Albany, Western Australia she travelled there with the Australian Imperial Force (AIF) convoy that was taking the bulk of the men and stores to be deployed at the ill-fated Gallipoli land assault, shortly to come.

AE2 carried out patrol work at the Dardanelles. Being under repair in Malta she was absent on 18 March 1915; that was when that Allied Naval force suffered their drubbing whilst attempting to breach the Turkish sea defences.

On the 17 April another British submarine, the E15 under command of Lieutenant-Commander Brodie, tried to make a run through the Dardanelles. It was forced ashore by strong eddies and was fatally fired upon. Again, a naval failure had occurred resulting in deaths and crew being taken as Turkish POWs.

The British Allied High Command was getting desperate for a naval success. Stoker, with his crew of 34, was approved to attempt to get through the Dardanelles. His first run on 23 April failed very early in its run due to mechanical difficulties.

Midhurst WW2 Memoirs: 2. 'Evil' Rising: 'Good' Awakening

On the next day Stoker pressed for another go, and was again approved. The ANZAC Cove troops were, on the next first light, then to be put ashore on the beaches on the other side of the Gallipoli Peninsular, see back to Fig 13.5.

He was told if he got through "There is nothing we will not do for you". His orders were 'To sink any mine-laying ships and to generally run amok around Cannakale to cause maximum disruption'

As had B11 needed to do, to succeed AE2 had to run the gauntlet of the straight at full speed making two sharp turns on the way. Stoker, like Holbrook had to contend with, had only sparse periscope sightings to get measured angles for setting positions. These were then calculated using measured run/speed times and mechanical gyroscope headings, to make runs; all this being done in uncertain currents.

They also, could not accurately gauge their clearance from underwater ground surfaces with any certainty. And then there were the many mines floating on top of cables that might catch the AE2s structure causing the mines to be dragged down to explode on her hull.

After a night of careful surface movement, including an attempt to sink a small Turkish cruiser, AE2 was compelled to dive to escape being rammed. That day Stokers' submarine succeeded in breaking right through the straights. A radio message was sent by 22-year-old William Falconer, in Morse-code, advising of this success on 26 April 1915, Fig. 13.14.

Fig. 13.14 The actual Morse key used to advise the allies that AE2 had broken through the Dardanelles. (RAN)

Chapter 13 Some Local Memories

The Allied Navy and Army commanders then knew it had been achieved. However, Dacre did not know they had received his message because their radio was not functioning properly.

Many suggest this success played a key part in the decision to keep the Allied land force in place at Anzac Cove. In theory, Turkish troops would be cut off, by an Allied naval presence inside the Marmara Sea, preventing reinforcement and re-provisioning. The ANZAC troops were told not to retreat:

'there is nothing for it but to dig yourselves right in and stick it out'.

Inside the Sea of Marmara, for 5 days, AE2 rose and dived in many locations to give the impression of many submarines being present. Stoker set up several sights for torpedo runs but most failed to run, or missed their targets. On 29th April AE2 met with E14, one of the other submarines that had also then entered via the straights following AE2's example.

When exploring a possible target on the 30 April, AE2 unexpectedly broke the surface – a common defect for that class. That began a chain of incorrect mechanical events that allowed the Turkish guns to hole her pressure hull. Stoker ordered her to be scuttled. That was her last dive. Fig. 13.15.

Fig. 13.15 HMAS AE2 submarine surrenders to the Turks. (Curmo)

The crew were all picked up alive and taken prisoner. Over the many months ahead they had a tough time; during their confinement four of them died in captivity.

Fig. 13.16 shows the crew at the Belemedik POW camp in the remote Taurus mountains.

Fig.13.16 Crew of AE2 in POW captivity, as 'guests' of Turkey.

Their epic POW experience is written up in Brenchley et al (2001). AE2 was eventually located under the sea, being identified in October 1998. Details of that passage and its difficulties are well described by Stoker (1925) and Brenchley et al (2001) and on-line at:

www.gallipoli.gov.au/submarines-in-the-dardanelles
www.submarineinstitute.com/userfiles/File/AE2%20_THE_SILENT_ANZAC.pdf
www.navy.gov.au/hmas-ae2

Stepping back a little in time, on the day after Stoker got through on 27 April 1915, the Royal Navy's Lieutenant-Commander Edward Boyle also took his submarine, E14, through the Dardanelles and into the Sea of Marmara.

Boyle's E14 submarine moved around the Sea of Marmara for two weeks sinking three ships and causing panic and confusion among the enemy naval forces there. The most important sinking being of a Turkish troopship with the loss of 2000 troops of the 4000 souls on board. That event influenced the Turks to stop reinforcing the Gallipoli land campaign by ship.

On this assignment, E14 returned without loss of the submarine, crew deaths, or anyone being taken prisoner. Edward Boyle was also awarded the VC; it being gazetted on 21 March 2015.

Other British submarines also passed through to assist create havoc inside the Sea of Marmara. E11 being commanded by Martin Nasmith sank, or disabled, 11 Ottoman ships. He, also, was immediately awarded the VC and promoted to Commander as a result of his contribution.

As we will soon see, the presentation of three naval VC medals for commanders of British flagged boats was in sharp contrast to the Australian AE2's boats award of the DSO to each of its crew members.

As this class of submarine was equipped with a powerful wireless communication system, they were all able to keep the British Admiralty up to date with their activities throughout their time in the Dardanelles campaign.

Controversy still exists about the decision to keep on fighting at Gallipoli, for, as it turned out, the army troops hung on for months there pinned down in their landing place, sustaining massive losses for no gain at all.

Using various subterfuges to make the Turks believe they were still present, all troops of the France, Britain, Australia and New Zealand expeditionary force withdrew under darkness over days, the last man leaving the beachhead at 4 am on 20 December 1915.

What became of Henry Stoker? On his return from captivity by the Turks late in 1918, he and his crew were each awarded the DSO medal described as being awarded as 'just short of deserving the VC'.

Many people considered his case to be worthy of a VC and that one was waiting for him when he returned to Britain at the end of the war. He must surely have wondered why he was not awarded the same honour as the commanders of B11, E11 and E14!

For the first time, his was the boat that had gone all the way through the straights, more than B11 had managed to do. They had sunk one, perhaps two, Turkish ships.

On the other hand, however, the AE2 was lost and the crew all captured. It was a British made, but Australian owned; the submarine was led by an Irishman in the British navy, crewed by Australian and English submariners. Perhaps it was seen to not be 'English enough'.

Furthermore, Stoker's exploits were not entirely known at the time of his capture for no member of his crew returned to the allied territory until well after the war ended, them having been taken, prisoner.

One other reason for lack of award of the VC at the time, was possibly that the Australian and British governments did not want publicity for the Stoker raid at the time. It was not sure how successful it had been and also feared for how the crew might be treated if the Turks were badly mentioned in the British press.

The accounts of this heroism and bravery waited for many years to be told, first in Stoker (1925) and then by Australian researchers in Brenchley (2001). The latter account strongly makes this case and asks the question regarding the VC, pointing out that Stoker's contribution was all but lost in Australian military history.

The matter brewed for a decade. On 21 February 2011, the Parliamentary Secretary for Defence, in Australia requested that a Tribunal inquire into, and report on, unresolved recognition for past acts of military gallantry and valour.

The Valour Inquiry was duly set in place in April 2011. Among the several cases put forward was ID No 19, that of Lieutenant Commander Henry Hugh Gordon Dacre Stoker.

An extensive report was released covering facts of the case; many written and oral submissions; how honours were decided then; a precis; and links to the many for and against points submitted for consideration.

The final recommendation in Dacre's case was:

> 'Tribunal recommendation 19-55. The Tribunal recommends no action be taken to award Lieutenant Commander Henry Hugh Gordon Dacre Stoker a VC for Australia or other further forms of recognition for his gallantry or valour.'

Surely this case has not been put to rest! After all, he was not an Aussie and did it for Britain. Again, citizenship may have won the case - 'not Australian enough' either!

Even though Stoker was in command of an Australian submarine, the chain of command in that war was through the Royal Navy, not Royal Australian Navy channels. A recommendation for an award, had it been

Chapter 13 Some Local Memories

raised at the time, would have gone through Commodore Keyes, RN, to Vice-Admiral de Robeck, RN, then on to the Admiralty. The Honours Committee at the Admiralty would then pass it to the Secretary of State for the Navy and then on to the Sovereign for approval. Upon royal approval, the award was listed in the London Gazette, after which it became official. That leaves lots of room for 'pride and prejudice' to enter the decision making.

The Naval authorities had looked into the situation in 1916 but a decision, for fear of Turkish reprisal, was made then not to do so while the AE2 crew was in captivity. It was not until just after the war ended in 1918 that Stoker and his crew's situation for battle honours were deliberated upon.

The Australian Navy Board credited Stoker with being the first Australian submarine to pass through the Straits. The British Admiralty declared he had made the passage - but did not mention he was the first to do so - did they not want to admit that?

The VC is awarded for 'gallantry in the face of the enemy'. Surely, Henry and his crew performed that requirement. If Henry felt an injustice had been made, he did not seem to have said so.

After a period in captivity by the Turks as a POW, in which their treatment was not all good, Henry returned to civilian life in 1920 becoming a successful British actor, writer and theatre director. He served again in the navy during WW2. There, like Norman Holbrook, he was recalled to serve the British WW2 effort, as a base commander, public relations man and one of the many planners of the 6 June 1944, D-Day landings at Normandy.

He was retired to the British Navy Retired List as a Captain in 1946 - not as a Commander! Just before he died in London in February 1966 he became the Irish croquet champion. He was 77 years old.

Fig. 13.17 Medal group of Dacre Stoker. (RN)

His medal group, Fig. 13.17, is on display in the Australian Naval Heritage Collection in Sydney.

Finally, where did he get that name, *Dacre?* It seems he needed to adopt it early in his life in order to be given an inheritance!

So! Was the Allied forces sea campaign successful? By the end of that long engagement, the seas part was deemed to be have had a 'significant outcome', regardless of the bad start.

It was, however, the submarines that made the difference; and it seems certain the many sunken Ottoman ships led to the Turks giving up re-supply of their Gallipoli land campaign by the sea route.

The Wikipedia account of the 'Naval operations in the Dardanelles Campaign' tells us that:

'Nine British and four French submarines sank one battleship, one destroyer, five gunboats, eleven troop transports, forty-four supply ships, and 148 sailing vessels at a cost of eight Allied submarines which were sunk'.

The next topic in this chapter brings back to life, other close-up personal memories of the Midhurst District.

13.2 Experiences of Nearby Persons

Those living in the Midhurst area, when asked to talk about their past experiences, recorded a different perspective about the war period to those people living just a few miles further south.

Of the several 'memory' books published by MRD villages and Midhurst town, only one, Harting Residents (1995), targets the wartime period, but not just before it. Others include snippets about their pre-war wartime experiences, but only as a small proportion of content.

As war approached the South Coast saw considerably more presence of the military than did Midhurst villages; and of the enemy, who bombed them mercilessly until the Allies subdued the Germans soon after D-Day, 1944. The main reason for them being a target was the presence of

Chapter 13 Some Local Memories

several key RAF airfields, such as Tangmere just 12 miles south of Midhurst.

In 2005 the WSRO carried out a major audio history project called the *Home Front Recall* as part of the *Wartime West Sussex 1939-45* project. This recorded 22 audio histories by Sussex persons covering their wartime experiences. Little, by definition, is included in their pre-war thoughts and memories. They need to be listened to for content, but that is very time-consuming. *Interview Summaries* are available that can be searched to identify what might be relevant.

Several books have been written on WW2 life on the coast so we can get an impression of the more hectic experiences of other English residents as the breakout of war began its path toward live conflict.

Clare Fordham Harriss, the solicitor living in Worthing 28 miles from Midhurst and introduced in Chapter 6.1, left us insights into the times, from his perspective. The compiler of extracts from his writings, Holden (2010), concludes that Clare was a bit of a snob. We must be thankful that he and his wife were 'curtain peepers' for that would have been needed to produce the 'historical gem' he left to us. They showed his lack of acceptance of many social habits such as women who 'smoked in public' and 'painted their lips red'.

He had a *classical* British education from which people of that time often emerged from their formative years acting as though they were a cut above the rest. In my youth I recall meeting people like this; a trait was the often quotation of Latin phrases and features taken from stories of Ancient Greek mythical characters, a very put-down way of communicating with those who just happened to not have learned that kind of history.

From that diary summary, on 6 February 1938, Mrs Harriss went to church and listened to a 'dismal discourse about the militarism and unrest in the world'. Clare recorded he had enough of this in the newspapers.

War was again the topic on 25 February when Lord Halifax, Foreign Secretary at the time, stridently said he was not afraid of Italy or any other Power. He would only go to war if it were 'right and inevitable'.

Hitler gets a mention in the diary when, on 12 March 1938, he had then marched into Austria without much of a whimper in the newspapers. 'Germany is, once again, making herself more and more intolerable'.

Mr Harriss's entries for 1938 almost always include a comment on the potential war to come. Gas masks came into the record in September. On September 29 he observed the digging of great trenches in the 'fine old turf' of Steyne Gardens; probably the start of the major air-raid shelter built into the ground there, Fig. 13.18. This picture was probably taken around 1944 for the three white rings around the tree are the marking used during the D-Day invasion campaign.

Fig 13.18 Air raid shelter in Steyne Gardens.

He records that the Royal Navy has been mobilised. Radio broadcast topics included the evacuation of children from London.

On September 30 his fears included personal financial calamity, and how could he volunteer for war service. A brief moment caused those thoughts to be reversed when the peace terms of the Munich agreement pointed to Britain not becoming involved with Hitler's European aspirations. But then common sense ruled as the character of Hitler made that utterance more a delaying strategy, than an honest contract with him. 'Peace in our time' had folks happy again with a 'feeling of holiday'.

By October the mood has reversed back to the gloom. At his barber's shop, it is again talking of gas masks. Appeasement is an item of discussion again between Mussolini and Lord Chamberlain. It was said that it was no good going first to Hitler direct, for his atrocious persecution of the German Jews show his real aims. What she reads of this persecution brings Mrs Harriss to tears!

On December 2, 1938, Harriss's entry reads:

'The newspaper, as usual now, full of alarm. Europe seems to be

Chapter 13 Some Local Memories

in ferment, and the Dictators grow so frantic that I fear a big war cannot be postponed. When the German man eater roars, the Italian jackal yaps - and we and the French run away. So it has been over the past five years. But some day we must stand at bay', Fig. 13.19.

Fig. 13.19 War becomes imminent.
[Musso, "It says. Light the blue paper & RETIRE IMMEDIATELY.]

At the end of that year his entry is most depressing:

'December 31, 1938
As this year ends, we are left wondering what will befall in 1939. For the heathens, in the persons of Hitler and Musso, rage furiously together, seeking whom they may devour next; whilst the British and the Gallic citizen sit in the valley of the shadow of hated war. Luckily, our rearmament has gone some way. We are no longer in the peril in which we stood a year ago. Nevertheless, owing to the development of the aeroplane, our very hearths and homes are no longer safe, as they have been through the centuries. Life seems more helpless than it used to do. We seem to be borne along like flotsam in a mill-race. What will be the event?'

Ordinary citizens were coming to understand that their lives were no longer their own. They could only wait and see how it all would turn out. They still believed that the differences between the Dictators and the British would soon be resolved; Britain was the superior power; at least, that is what they had come to fully believe and rely upon in their minds.

Southern defences were not developed to a major extent until the scare resulting from the retreat at Dunkirk in early 1940.

Harriss's 1 September, 1939 entry tells us on that day that Hitler had begun to suppress Poland. Harriss's retirement plans were on hold. Being bombed in force is to be the new and worrying factor in this war. That lesson had been observed in the Spanish Civil war as Hitler's trial air force developed its bombing methods. The complete armed forces of Britain were now being mobilised. Children evacuations had started. Military uniforms were now everywhere to be seen.

Harriss was asked to take two or three children evacuees; he and his wife were quite unsuited to that task. He managed to have that changed to billeting a lady teacher who would feed herself. I wonder if she had had a classic education and could have held good discussions with him!

And then there was another intrusion into their ordered life; blackouts. He had to cut out paper to stick onto his window panes. On that day they were overtired and very bewildered. Now he had to observe the blackout times shown in places, Fig. 13.20.

Fig. 13.20 Blackout time-clock.

Next day, it was business as usual as they ate in Khong's Cafe, to then saunter down the beachfront of Worthing for a couple of hours.

No one seemed to be unhappy, or expressing a case of the jitters over all that was happening over on the Continent. Holidaymakers were still holidayed. Planes were flying overhead out of Britain. Busloads of day outing 'old age pensioners'

Chapter 13 Some Local Memories

saddened them as it was a pathetic sight.

On September 3 the news was that Britain had declared war on Germany. There was no going back until it had been fought out. Panic actions were seen as people thought overhead inward flights might be enemy bombers. Life was often disrupted as air-raid sirens started their distinctive wailing imperative.

War had come! Over the next days, Harriss's entries covered many issues in which he was wondering what the result of all that was taking place would have on the British lifestyle.

He saw social change, as evacuees and soldiers had to live differently to before. The gloomy faces of old people were very noticeable. They already needed more care and support, and that could not get better in wartime.

Normal services became unreliable - milk deliveries, laundry services.

The previously pleasant environment had become tainted with trenches and a range of weird and wonderful types of military equipment. Fig. 13.21. shows a light tank and dispatch rider on the road near to Petersfield.

Fig. 13.21 Light tank and dispatch rider near to Petersfield. (IMW)

Soldiers were appearing:

'Everywhere there is marching around in companies. His wife observes them sadly, as lambs preparing to be slaughtered, but they seem to be in highest spirits.'

Foodstuffs were beginning to be in short supply in the shops. Things in demand, such as brown paper to put on windows, were running out.

On September 7 he sums it up:

> 'This war in its beginning is very different to the last. This time there are no patriotic concerts, no flags, no recruiting posters, nor speeches in public places, no long companies of newly-recruited heroes in mufti, marching along the streets.'

The plain fact was that those in power had not believed it needed much action - until these latest hours. War Department propaganda streams had not got going!

The public made the change to this wartime mood quite quickly. Harriss recalls it was but a week since the war was declared and things had already settled into a new, very annoying lifestyle, where excitement joined fear as an endless state of affairs for the mind.

Harriss had managed to avoid having his teacher billet. She had made his life miserable by her friends constantly ringing the doorbell! He, in turn, had not helped her circumstances. They parted.

The time period for this Book 2 of memoirs ends as war is declared. To round it out we need to find out what it was like at this uncertain period for folks in the Midhurst Rural District.

Being in the countryside without any important enemy targets, allowed it more to be comfortable. Lie low and not be seen was the way to go. "Wait for it to all be resolved, as it surely would by next Christmas," they said.

Another useful pre-war and wartime account is that of Petersfield, Jeffery (2004), just 7 miles to the west of Midhurst. There he presents, in his Introduction, a summary of life in a nearby town in the 1930s.

He provides a good overview of daily activity in a largely rural town in which there were also significant homes with servant staff. The upper-class people went their way; the farmers likewise. It was easy to take photographs with few people or cars; if you were allowed to take them - and had a film!

Chapter 13 Some Local Memories

The Petersfield town area in the country was different from the Midhurst District in 1939 for it was a commuter 'semi-urban' environment, whereas Midhurst was definitely 'rural'.

Petersfield had an ancient start going back to at least the 12th century. In 1895 its Urban District Council (UDC) was implemented, ending in 1974. It, too, had many church parishes.

The coming of the railway rapidly made it a commuter town. In contrast, the Midhurst District also had railway train routes, three in fact, but it did not have a station on the direct route from London. Nor were these lines ever electrified. Individually owned, small, farm holdings covered the perimeter of Petersfield. Whilst way back in time the area was once manorial there was, in 1938, no major aristocratic family estate with its landed gentry manor house, that dominated activity through the provision of tied cottages, leased farms, and direct employment of many farmworker families. Petersfield was still a market town, but by WW2 it had many homes of commuters. It had developed in early times 'on the sheep's back'.

In 1726 Daniel Defoe described Petersfield as 'a town eminent for little but being full of good inns'.

The town of Petersfield had approximately 5000 residents in 1939. Being larger than Midhurst it saw more activity in the town, but it was still generally country quiet. The presence of many more people at regular cattle and poultry market times overfilled facilities; but that influx was short-lived each time.

Commuters moving in led to substantial schools, family houses, public buildings and fine facilities existing by the end of the 1930s. They had built their Town Hall building in 1935. An advertisement for Mr W P Jacobs, Auctioneer, Valuer and Surveyor, and also

Fig. 13.22 W P Jacobs building in Petersfield, taken in 1938. (David Jeffery Collection)

an agent for Land, House, Estate and Insurance, shows an imposing, castle-like, three-story building of a very strong presence, Fig. 13.22.

By 1938 Southern Electric trains connected Petersfield to London (Waterloo). The railway had made this town attractive to commuters working in, or near London. They attracted middle and upper-class needs of schools, churches, hotels, shops, parks, and public working spaces such as a large market square.

In 1938 the responsible British government departments were almost suddenly 'waking up'. War was indeed coming: numerous physical preparations were needed.

Today, Midhurst has little to show on record that WW2 ever existed. Being so rural made the residents feel very remote from all those needs. Petersfield, however, has many records that illustrate these changes. Being also in a rural location we must look to how things were there, to 'feel' the times of Midhurst.

Basic planning information was being collected for supply, in 1939, of all of the new activities that were to take place. So many new issues needed data; in large ledgers, on cards, and in order books; data that had never been called for before. Many issues, not important before, were suddenly needed.

For example, there were no adequate central records of how many people of the different groups of age existed and how to contact them. Needed was their place of living, name, sex and age to facilitate military service call-up; ration books for distribution; and potential billeting spots for evacuees.

This urgently needed every man, woman and child in Britain to be registered and issued with a personal ID booklet. Acquisition of large buildings for war duty purposes had to be implemented before the war came.

Tasks also needing to be done were preparations for the arrival and billeting of evacuees; lists of civil support volunteers; supply and delivery of Andersen air raid steel shelters; supply and training in the use of gas masks; sandbagging of buildings; major improvements to fire brigade equipment; the issue of ration books; application of blackout materials to buildings - and more. Bureaucracy took over!

Chapter 13 Some Local Memories

The organisational support work to be done was gigantic....and it all had to be done on paper with pen or pencil, often with 6 or more copies being made using carbon paper between the pages as the records were hand written or typed with a clacking mechanical typewriter. Such features are covered in the later books of these memoirs.

In late 1938, to the eye, residents would have physically seen interviewers, notices and posters going up calling them to duty, to register, and to learn about air raid precautions. Orders and instructions came down from all high: Local Councils had new types of agenda items put upon them.

Seeing military uniforms gradually became the norm. Soldiers came from all directions to where their temporary camps were set up. Airmen and airwomen came up to the town from the nearby southern fighter plane airfields.

Road signposts were taken down to make it hard for fifth column spies to get around and make maps… and, later, to frustrate invaders.

Families were beginning to learn how to make do with less food and consumables. Rationing was about to begin in the local shops. The black market was starting up! Tinned food was being stocked piled.

Home gardeners were being asked quite firmly to grow food; to help reduce the need for imports, and to feed the hundreds of thousands of soldiers who were coming from Canada to assist Britain.

The Petersfield town area was large enough to have its own locally produced, type-set, and printed newsletter covering Petersfield and its local surrounding area. This was largely organised by Frank Carpenter, a man of numerous talents and a gift to the local society. Its official name was the *Hants and Sussex News*, colloquially called the *Squeaker*. During WW2 this became a 4-page broadsheet. It gave an account of Council meetings, Petty Court sessions, major local events and some adverts.

Frank's presence was so well felt that it was said there were only two permanent features in town: 'the King William statue and Frank'.

That statue is of such quality as to not to be expected to be found in a small town. It is of King William the Third, in triumphant Roman-style costume. It was commissioned around 1753. Being cast in lead it has done well to remain so crisp! It would have looked magnificent when it was originally gilded. Midhurst does not yet have any public statue – but has one coming at the time of writing.

The next section pulls together some memories of pre-war Midhurst times.

13.3 Local Midhurst Memories as War Arrived

Aural history projects concerned with the Midhurst Rural District include the major *Midhurst in Living Memory* MILM project of the Midhurst Society. Interviews were conducted in 2008. It resulted in some 100 audio recordings, that were then transcribed into digital format by hand-typing them to form Word files. Its published output was Elsdon (2010).

That book has some additional information not found in the transcripts. The original audio tapes and transcriptions are available in the WSRO. When all of these transcript files are joined into one Word file, of over 450 pages, that is 233,000 words, of aural record it forms a digitally searchable record that is often used in this project to find specific material.

Additionally, to that project are the published memory projects of Easebourne, Fernhurst, The Hartings, Stedham, Women's Institute of Sussex, and more. Some of it is repetitive in content and is often given from a childhood perspective.

Little is reported on the wartime daily situation, or on the troops. Presumably, most children were not that interested in such matters. An exception concerning the troops that were there, came from Richard Comber who has given this project accounts of the army presence around the Heyshott area. His mother said he was more interested in that at the time, than being at school! He has provided considerable detail of such aspects such as make, model and numbers of equipment used there, mainly by the RASC. That is covered in a later book when the military presence is dealt with.

Some of these published 'memory' reports, recorded around 2008, give us an idea of Midhurst town in the 30s. Here are included those situations in the pre-war years. The next Memoirs book includes daily life stories of evacuees that began to arrive when war was declared.

If you have the cost needed, a good start to seeing what Midhurst

Chapter 13 Some Local Memories

town was like just before WW2, is to access the hi-res files from *Britain from Above* series of *English Heritage*. Those presented here are only research copies. Two photos of Midhurst town were taken in 1928. Fig. 13.23 shows the town view from the west. Fig. 13.24 is taken from the south. Little would have changed by the wartime.

Fig. 13.23 Midhurst from the West, 1928.

Fig. 13.24 Midhurst centre, 1928.

One of the relevant MILM records, recorded in 2007, is that of Tony Beck who was born in 1928. He was 11 years old when war broke out, an age wherein comprehension, inquisitiveness and recollection can be reasonably relied upon.

> 'When I was growing up we had four gentleman's outfitters, Morleys, Hendersons, Gillhams and Packhams, and a haberdasher, Robertsons; we had two fish shops, Willshire's and Farnes; we had five grocers, Pescods, Stanfords, Pearces, the Co-op and the International; there were four greengrocers, Aylings, Goldring's and there were two in North Street, Churchers, and another, Gales, further down next to the cinema'.

There were a surprising number of the same kind of shops serving the District.

> 'We had three cycle shops, Dales, Daniels and Holdens, we had six butchers, Blackistons, Merritts, Marshalls, Farnes, Knights and the London Meat Co., and there was also a pork butcher (Porky Woods) at the top of Church Hill, we had three chemists, six sweet shops, we had our tailor – Eric Waller — we had three coal merchants, a sawmill, a saddler and a blacksmith. And we used to have a "proper" Post Office.'

Another person with good memories of pre-war times is Andy Robertson. He was born around 1929 so also has useful accounts to offer. His father, Robbie Robertson, had the draper's shop, (see back to Fig 10.14), next to the, now departed, Westminster Bank from 1927 onwards. The following is condensed from his MILM, ca 2008, interview.

> 'Charlie Bowyer had the chemist shop in North Street, and then between him and Barclay's Bank, where Harold Stone was the bank manager, was the entrance into Short's Bakehouse - and at the back there they had all the ovens for baking bread and cakes. Bill Poston worked for South Down buses; his wife had the hairdressers across the road.'

Chapter 13 Some Local Memories

Andy said they used to cook turkeys in Short's bread baking ovens over holiday periods; the ovens stayed hot for days. When you opened the huge oven door, a light let you see right into it. There were great big long poles, like an oar of a boat, to get the Christmas turkeys into, and out of, this oven. Several hours later they would all go back to take them out and baste them again; and later again.

Fig. 13.25 *Three Horses* pub in Elsted village, today.

During the in-between times, they went to the *Three Horseshoes*, Fig. 13.25, then Dick Lazell's pub, where they 'basted' themselves with plenty of the good brew. This pub is still there, some 5 miles west of Midhurst in Elsted village, on the Elsted Road.

Derek Mott's father and Andy's father were both in the London Scottish Regiment during WW1 war so whenever they got into Dick Lazell's pub, their dads would start fighting that war all over again. Andy continued:

> 'As you come up from Barclay's Bank, next door where Valentes is now, was a newsagents Birchnells, then there was a little cake shop; the next shop is now an ironmonger. It was then the Midhurst Post Office, and around in Grange Road where the sorting office is now, there were allotments. It was common knowledge that there were some who helped themselves to these fruit and veggies!'

Alfie Mordle was a hairdresser in West Street – but that place has changed dramatically. There were then just fields along Grange Road.
My own mother, Vi, made sure I always looked neat and tidy - when she could find me! I recall in the war years this was the location of my personal barber's shop in West Street. I did not know his name. One day he accidentally nicked the skin on my ear and it began to bleed. I recall his rush and bustle to cover it with a small piece of tissue paper that was dipped in alum to stop the bleeding.

The post office, according to Andy Robertson, moved from North Street to Grange Road around 1933. He recalled, when taken there for the first time, seeing the same faces in a nice new building.

Andy remembers that the dust cart, the coal merchant and the milkman all used horse-drawn vehicles. I remember horses very clearly in 1944 when beer barrels were delivered to the Spread Eagle; they were let down into the basement of the hotel through the West street footpath.

In my earliest London days, a horse-drawn carriage used to come with sacks of coal on the back. They had a little terrier dog that walked underneath the cart. Our local 'rag and bone' cart was horse-drawn. Horses were still in transition to petrol and diesel motors in Britain when war broke out.

Although motorised vehicles were quite prolific by the late 1930s the horse was still a viable, relatively inexpensive transport method in outlying places. They needed no petrol or diesel fuel. They only needed hay or grass to eat and that was much a-plenty most of the time in the country areas, even present at the roadside to eat whilst they waited, oh so patiently, for orders to 'walk on'.

Horses can traverse poor ground at a good speed quite well but they do not have the 'horsepower' output of trucks and all-wheel drive vehicles; 1-5 horsepower compared with 150 or more. They did, however, required good keepers, and rest periods when their limits were reached.

The German and Russian armies in WW2 used hundreds of thousands of horses to move artillery, supplies and men behind the front-line areas. Those nations did not have the same availability of oil-based fuel as did the Allies.

One German coastal defender, when seeing the invading troops swarm onto the land from the sea during the D-Day invasion, commented

Chapter 13 Some Local Memories

on the complete absence of horses coming ashore. To him, it was a clear sign that the Allies had modernised considerably and had no need for them.

Andy continued:
> 'There were many butcher's shops in the town. In West Street there was Blackistons. with Merritts next door. Up by the Midhurst church was Charlie Marshall's butchers' shop, which is now a Charity Shop opposite the Lloyd's Bank.'

> 'I think the first door around the corner from the bank is a solicitors office now, but next door there was one of these typical old-fashioned doors, you know, open top and bottom and it was Porky Woods the Pork butcher. He had a daughter, Rachel, who I seem to remember - she sort of ran a gang, and Ian Carpenter and myself and one or two others - if Rachel Woods was coming along, we were all scared and ran for our lives.'

> 'But then you come down Knockhundred Row and across the road, now where the fish and chip shop is - that was Ernie Knight's butcher's shop, and then you came up towards my father's shop, and on the left-hand side at the bottom of Duck Lane was the London Central Meat Company, so that was another butchers shop and they were all viable, they were all making money - and then coming up from that butchers shop you had Archie Steadman, who was a jeweller - and then next to him there is now a clock shop - that was his private house with steps up to the front door. Next to that was the International Stores, and then George Ayling's fruiterer's shop adjacent to Grandpa Rudwick's little cottage on Rumbold's Hill, that later became the Mida Restaurant.'

Another direct experience of that time was that of Marjorie Bishop, the oldest contributor to the *Midhurst In Living Memory* project. It gives us insight about her life at home when she was a child in Midhurst town:

> 'I was born in a little cottage in Market Square; I was the eleventh

child – I had five brothers and five sisters. We all had to go to Sunday School every week. We had no toys so we played on St Ann's Hill, Fig. 13.26], at whatever game – football, cricket or mums and dads.'

Fig. 13.26 St Ann's Hill; town square entrance today.

'On Saturday nights my mother used to get the bath out in front of the kitchen range and we used to line up for our hair to be washed first, and then step into the bath. Our nightdresses, or nightshirts for the boys, used to be on a line in front of the fire to get nice and warm'

Her description stands much the same as for myself and many other evacuees in the early 40s - except there were only me and Mrs Karn in our home at 343 St Ann's Hill buildings. Husband Sam was serving in the Royal Navy somewhere. I too would play on the Hill and have flannel washes out of a basin whilst sitting by the woodstove or coke burning fire.

There was in the District, a significant middle class who lived very much better, but often with little disposable income. Their houses often had some, but rarely all, of the desired utilities; running water inside, electricity, effective heating arrangement, inside toilet and a bathroom with running hot water. Chapter 11 gives an idea of the 'better life' enjoyed by a minority.

Chapter 13 Some Local Memories

Of course, the top wealthy classes, living there in small numbers, were still having a very good life in many cases. But that was fast declining for them as taxes, and now the effects of the war restrictions and house requisitions eroded their quality of life.

The poor, however, by then, certainly were getting a better deal in life. They still had money to pay for their level of luxuries, such as butter rounds that Prescod's boys, at the grocer on the corner of North Street and Knockhundred Row, would prepare using wooden moulds.

Evacuees, who had started to come to their new life in late 1939, usually found the countryside (if not their billet) very much to their liking. Fig. 13.27 shows one, Maureen Peacock, in a field at Egmont Road, today a housing estate.

Fig. 13.27 From the left: Beryl Orchard, evacuee Maureen Peacock and Hazel Orchard.

As still seen today, many of the local cottages had painted yellow window frames and doors, signifying they were owned by the Cowdray estate. At the time war broke out these were starting to be upgraded. War conditions stopped upgrades for the duration.

An example is the set of plans and application drawn up in January 1939 to modernise the facilities in two cottages; nos. 49 and 50 in Easebourne Street. I will talk more of these cottages in Book 3; I lived there for a while in late 1943, before it was modernised in the proposed manner. A Planning application was lodged in July 1939. However, these changes, to add a modern bathroom and inside toilet, were not then pursued because war broke out in September.

A later example, about another Cowdray cottage in Heyshott, Fig. 13.28: is recorded in Easebourne's memories book, Litchfield (2011). It is from the memory of Elsie Pack.

Fig. 13.28   Heyshott today.

'A Cowdray cottage was requisitioned for them (for the family of Elsie Cook then, now Elsie Pack said it was quite a shock coming to the country. Their flat in London had running water, gas and electricity, and an indoor loo. Their cottage had none of these luxuries. But it did have a nice big garden. There was a great big black cooking stove in the kitchen that did not cook properly, so they complained to the Cowdray estate office. Two men called round, and Elsie's mum, not being one to mince her words, declared, "I shouldn't think Lord Cowdray would have such a stove in his kitchen" Little did her mum know at the time that the two men from the estate were none other than Lord Cowdray himself and his agent. Shortly thereafter, they were given a new cooker.'

The 3rd Viscount Cowdray (Weetman Pearson) lived well in the Cowdray House until the war broke out, but then he had to make most of the grand house available to the Royal Army Service Corp, (RASC). By then, however, he was also engaged in war service readying to go to France with the British Expeditionary Force BEF. His polo fields were soon requisitioned to build an airfield. The Cowdray stables accommodated commandos; not polo horses. Playing fields had to be ploughed to grow food.

Chapter 13 Some Local Memories

Elsdon (2010) provides a set of useful sketch street maps that compare the uses of Midhurst's business buildings for the 1939 and the 2009 years. Fig. 13.29 is the fourth page of the four.

1939	2009
KNOCKHUNDRED ROW, CHURCH HILL & RED LION STREET	
NORTH WEST SIDE	
Old Surgery	Offices
Verralls, electrical shop	Open Country, ladieswear
Sargent & Stevens, dentist	St Oswald's Dental Surgery
Harper, cobbler	Macdonald Oates, solicitors
"Porky" Woods, pork butcher	Offices
House	Offices
C.Marshall, butcher	House
T.Charles, Blacksmith	Driveway
House	House
C.Mitten, chemist	Church Hill Dental Practice
Old Manor tea shop	House
House	Anthony Lodge, jeweller
Lyndale House, school	Houses
Ewens, sweets	Richard C Arnold, optician
House	Marlin Shipping
House	Comestibles, delicatessen
Holfords, cobbler	Dale White, barber
Carver, tailor	Wheelers Book Shop
Stedmans, ladies & gentswear	Sussex House, ladieswear
M.Burnett, bikes/Nat.Provincial Bank	Bottle & Jug, wines and ales
The Swan, Pub	The Swan, Pub
Old houses	
WEST STREET SOUTH	
Spread Eagle Hotel	Spread Eagle Hotel
Willshires, fishmonger	" "
T.Merritt, butcher	Jefferson's butchers
F.Blackiston, butcher	Closed
Goldrings, greengrocer	Closed
" florist	Down to Earth, healthfood
E.Bannister, jewellers	Allnut & Co. Jewellers
Stanfords, grocers	Black Sheep, wool & woollen-wear
Frisby, shoes	Wine Etc. wine merchants
GRANGE ROAD	
Curtis, saddlemaker	Offices
Clarks, newsagents	Dummers, newsagents
Etheringtons/ Pearce, grocers	Michael Chevis, photographer
" "	Martyn Chevis, hairdresser
Gillhams, shoes	Violet Designs, bathrooms
Bradleys, menswear	" "

Fig. 13.29 A page comparing Midhurst shop uses for 1939 and 2009. (MILM project)

Some residents of the Midhurst District saw sons and fathers go into war service. Many, however, were not allowed to serve in the fighting force; their skills were needed in 'reserved occupations' keeping food, production and societal needs going on the home front. Being a productive rural community, the Midhurst District would have had many men, and some women, in this class.

Normal daily life was much like it had been before war broke out, but then went under more difficult conditions. This need for rural productivity may well be the reason why Midhurst and its surrounding parishes stayed relatively immune to there being a war on; until the massive build-up of troops and equipment arrived to service the D-Day Normandy landings.

Getting about was mostly by bus or train, or walking or cycling as much as 5 miles or more. Few people had a motor car. Wartime rationing of fuel severely limited private use.

The memories provide little about the mental mind mood of locals, regarding the effect of the war. They often recall it being a time of growth and improved prosperity as some new suburbs of Midhurst were built to provide more and better accommodation. The entries in MILM are clearly skewed, reflecting children's lives of that time.

We need to look elsewhere to find adults reporting on the mood to see the effect of the impending war that soon became a reality in the District.

Chapter 14 War Begins in Britain

14.1 War is Declared: September 1939

At the time war was declared, Midhurst was a much smaller town than it is now. The urbanised area then was almost the same as reported in 1947, Howell (2005). It was:

> 'effectively confined within a perimeter bounded by Carron Lane, Sussex Terrace in Bepton Road, South Pond and the Methodist Church.
> There were no June Meadows, Pretoria Avenue, Orchard Way, Guillards Oak. No health centre, WI room, Youth Club, Midhurst Grammar School facilities to the south of Lamberts Lane. Where the Wharf development is now was the gasworks; the river site of the MGS was open fields. In surrounding parishes, there was no Taylor's Field or Rise, No Holmbush, or Fairway, Little Midhurst or Close Walks development in West Lavington. In Pitsham Wood, it was just becoming into use as a rubbish tip. In Easebourne, Cowdray Road was still to be built and Canada Fields were garden allotments.'

The top of Midhurst was a nodal defence point in the national anti-invasion defences: to be held at all costs when ringed with barbed wire entanglement, gun emplacements and tank traps. Hence the recognition of a tank trap as a historic might-have-been place in the town.

By the end of 1938, it was painfully clear that everyone who reads a newspaper, looked at publicly displayed posters, listened to the radio or perhaps looked at a television set, went to the cinema, or talked it all over in the local pub, knew about the coming of the *Evil* period.

War for Britain was coming without any doubt. The previous Great War had taken place some 20 years before so most families were still smarting from the accounts they had seen, or perhaps suffered in the trenches of the Great War. They could only see that it was not going to be much *Good* ahead. Whilst many commentators suggest the government was too slow to realise that war would come, Cabinet had started the processes needed for civil protection in early 1937.

Under secret memorandum instructions a range of *Air Raid Precaution* manuals was issued, McCutcheon (1938). Fig. 14.1 shows that for home protection.

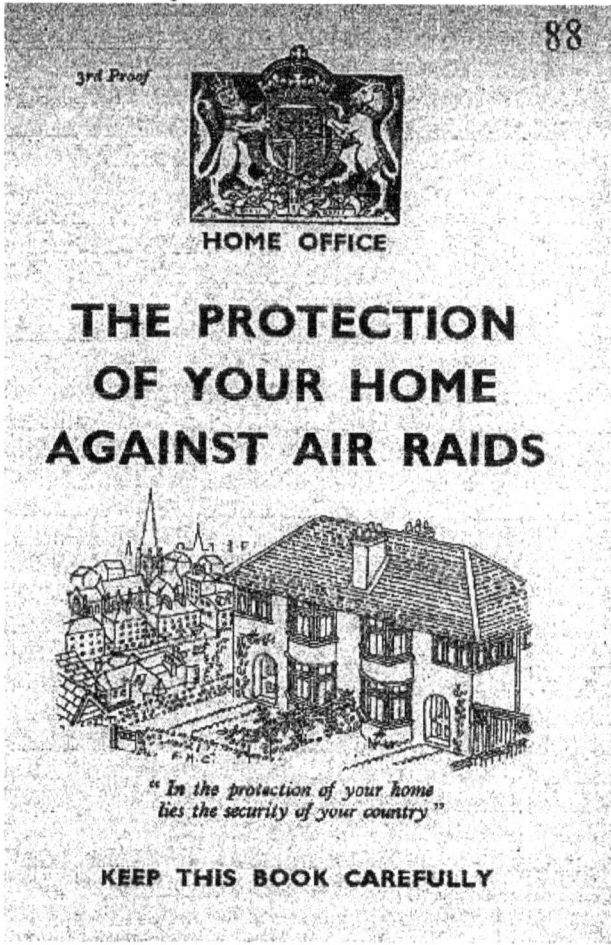

Fig. 14.1 Home protection manual.

It took the best part of 12 months to compile it for many agencies had to be consulted. The cover-note with its internal issue, says it is to be issued free of charge to every household or be at Post Offices for 1d per householder.

Now that's a massive print run in the tens of millions. They were reported as then costing around £35,000 to print so the use of paid advertisements should be able to raise £5000 net to defray costs. It also pointed out that this issue would:

'awaken attention to this most vital and important part of our

Topics in the household 42-page booklet covered what to do as soon as the manual was received; how to prepare your home as a refuge from bombs and gas attacks; essential first aid; managing things during an air raid, and what to do for hurt people.

There was a similar booklet for employees in business premises and more specialist prints on strengthening buildings, personal protection against gas, and other titles.

Some of the needs stated in these manuals must have taxed people and shop supplies considerably: gas proofing of rooms with sealed brown paper; plugging holes everywhere whilst making sure the glass of windows would not shatter and split the paper. Every detail seems to be well covered. If you did all that it was suggested your refuge area would resemble a building site.

Reading these instructions must have put fear into people's minds. If you lived in a major town or industrial area these would seem truly necessary; but in Midhurst, and its surrounding villages, I would expect they would have been somewhat neglected in private homes for a rural area with such low a population density would surely not be a target?

Back in town, the War Cabinet had its first weekly Home Security Report on 8 September 1939. (Secret C.P. (R) (39) 4.) It was to be kept under lock and key.

It told of Air Raid Precautions A.R.P. staff all being called up to be over strength; that their equipment was still understrength, but adequate. Distribution of babies' gas masks for those not evacuated from large towns was behind in supply. Shelter deliveries had slowed, and non-galvanised black steel sheets had to be issued to some people for their shelters.

Air Raid warning systems were working effectively, but with difficulties in identifying aircraft and sifting reports. One wonders how they tested them for at that time enemy aircraft were very sparse. Black-outs were working well. Charts giving aircraft silhouettes helped.

The Auxiliary Fire Service was efficiently mobilised on the 1st of September. Over 450 extra fire pumps had been distributed.

To increase the availability of hospital beds, 5000 existing casualties were moved by road and rail away from London hospitals. That needed 34 evacuation trains. Some 18,000 were taken from larger provincial towns. Additional to that, new beds resulted in a total of 200,000 beds being ready and waiting for casualties. Doctor's availability was increased by 2,500 and reserve nurses joined up to provide 16,000 of them ready for action: another 60,000 were in training.

The report told of the children evacuations starting on 1st September. Many, however, were already at their safer locations. The problem in London was exceptionally large but was 'completed by the following Monday.' Over 2 million children and their teachers had been moved to presumed safety!

New rail timetables were to come into force on 11 September. Sea traffic in the English Channel was reduced by diverting vessels.

Addition of extra armed forces vehicles on the roads, and the need to conserve fuel imports, led to numerous local difficulties with fuel rationing starting on 16 September.

Government departments were evacuated to most unexpected secret locations - see section 14.5. The places chosen were considered to be safe enough to not need air raid protection.

From these records, it is clear that the nation was well and truly ready for war coming to the home front by bombing and gas raids. Fortunately, poison gas was never used on London.

The government officials may have been satisfied with all that progress but some civilians were not. Nevil Shute wrote the future fictional history *What Happened to the Corbetts* in 1938, it is published in January 1939. This was his response to his reckoning of the inadequacy of the precautions being taken for protection against gas and the spread of disease from the lack of clean water. These issues were poorly covered in manuals.

To try to bring better awareness to the public, he distributed 1000 copies of that book, for free, to ARP wardens.

Everywhere across united Britain, people were listening intently on the radio to the broadcast that announced the war was declared on Germany. They sort of knew what Lord Chamberlain would say.... but it was now becoming real.

At 11.15 a.m. on 3rd September 1939, Mr Chamberlain broadcast to the nation the following statement announcing that a state of war existed between Britain and Germany, Fig. 14.2.

Chapter 14 War Begins in Britain

Fig. 14.2 Headlines of *Daily Mail*, 4 September 1939.

"This morning the British Ambassador in Berlin handed the German Government a final Note stating that, unless we heard from them by 11 o'clock that they were prepared at once to withdraw their troops from Poland, a state of war would exist between us.
I have to tell you now that no such undertaking has been received, and that consequently, this country is at war with Germany"

He ended with:

"Now may God bless you all. May He defend the right. It is the evil things that we shall be fighting against - brute force, bad faith, injustice, oppression and persecution - and against them. I am certain that the right will prevail."

What a catastrophe! What a waste of people's lives and their collective past industriousness. Oh, the trauma of pain and horror of what that meant! And it would have to take place in the very streets of Britons. Never before had war impacted on their homeland as this one could.

Britain was just becoming a better place in which to live for many - not just the wealthy. A national health scheme was being built. Housing estates with attractive designs, and full of modern appliances, had been popping up all over the country. Jobs were becoming more plentiful. More people were owning motor cars; and lovely looking ones at that. It was all looking quite rosier. Roads and public utilities were given major strides in improvement.

What would have been going through the minds of the British people? Going into the war meant all that would change; very much for the worst. Their very existence was coming under threat. London, indeed, might become a massive burning metropolis - a Crystal Palace fire thousands of times larger. Lives would be lost at home and in places foreign. All manner of restrictions would be in force!

Heaven forbid! If it were lost the country might, in a short number of years, be speaking German; surrounded by Swastika laden flags and banners. The steady, all-powerful, British Empire might not be able to subdue this mad man Hitler, and his ambitions.

Hitler's ambitions were to form a *Greater Germanic Reich of the German Nation*.

Fig. 14.3 Berlin, as Hitler was planning it to be. (Reddit.com)

Fig. 14.3 is an artist's rendering of how Berlin, to be called *Germania*, would become once Hitler had conquered the world. Using masses of slave labour, he had already had parts of this built by 1943 - including the central, grand East-West, city boulevard that is 3 miles

Chapter 14 War Begins in Britain

long. It was also to have a huge domed building that could house 180,000 people.

The *Grosser Platz,* of 350,00 sq metres, would allow Hitler to speak to massive audiences. From 1935 - 1939 he had been preparing for this step. He was not going to change his intentions just because Britain did not agree with his ambitions.

His intentions and ways of achieving them by human oppression are now seen in their entirety today; but then they were just beginning to be witnessed in parts, the invasion of Poland being a strong sign.

On August 22, just over a week before the onset of war, Hitler had delivered a speech to his military commanders at the Obersalzberg:

> 'The object of the war [with Poland] is ... physically to destroy the enemy. That is why I have prepared, for the moment only in the East, my 'Death's Head' formations with orders to kill without pity or mercy all men, women, and children of Polish descent or language. Only in this way can we obtain the living space we need'

Hitler is also said to have decided these sentiments on his pan-Germanic plans:

> 'The most notable exception [for assimilation into the Reich] was the United Kingdom, which was not projected as having to be reduced to a German province but to, instead, become an allied seafaring partner of the Germans'

> 'Britain was thus a nation created by struggle and the survival of the fittest among the various Aryan peoples of the isles, and was able to pursue global conquest and empire-building because of its superior racial heredity born through this development.'
>
> en.wikipedia.org/wiki/Greater Germanic Reich

Dramatic and penetrating words indeed. Many who heard it felt their hearts drop with a sinking feeling in the pit of their stomachs - 'Oh hell! It is on again'

On the other extreme, life just went on for many as though the situation would not affect them. The stoic nature of the Brits came to the fore.

'We knew it would come'. 'Let's get on with it. Put the kettle on and make a cuppa'

Hitler was eventually to find that that the British heritage he chose to try to suppress, was not compliant, or weak in its resolve to defeat him. The *British Bulldog*, with the help of its Empire countries, had been prodded hard enough to start to respond.

In 1937 British opposition to the Fascists had already been demonstrated in the Spanish Civil war by a group of volunteers from England who joined the *International Brigade* fighting against the 'dark threat of fascist dictatorship in Spain'.

At Jarama, near Madrid, they achieved the first victory against Franco's army. All but forgotten today, it was a crucial military turning point in the fight against Fascism. Hughes (2011) reconstructs the battle that showed Fascist force was not always instantly victorious. A memorial to these brave fighters stands in Lambeth. Fig. 14.4.

Fig. 14.4 Memorial to the International Brigade in Lambeth.

'Six hundred poorly-trained, ill-equipped "city-bred young men" were attacked by an overwhelming force comprising the cream of Franco's professional army, backed up by German armour. That the

Chapter 14 War Begins in Britain

British Battalion managed to hold the line – just – was a feat of both stubborn defiance and astonishing bravery. But the cost was substantial. After the three days of fighting of 12-14 February 1937, less than half the Battalion remained.'

http://www.richardbaxell.info/ben-hughes/

The Wikipedia account tells us about the growing experience and war hardening of the German forces that the French and the British soon would be facing. The all-out war had to come. Hitler was intent on military conquest and had surreptitiously built up a massive and very modern fighting force that would afford him a considerable unbeatable head start before the Allied nations could catch up.

As we will see later, he nearly succeeded. If he had beaten Britain by the end of 1940 he might well have been left alone to get on with his aims for Europe. The only force that could challenge him - the USA - was still in its isolation mood and on a poor war footing. Being on another continent, Hitler's plans would not affect them!

Despite its horror, some looked forward to the excitement and opportunities a major war offered. Remember, only a relatively few of the nation's population would see the horrific side of all-out war.

I recall, in 1951 a storeman I worked under in Australia, kept saying how sorry he was that the war was over. He did not go into service because of his age and he had done well out of the situation.

Sue Hogg in Midhurst recalls what her mother felt at that moment:

'After Mum died, we found lots of her diaries some of which I read. On the day war was declared (I guess she would have been in her late teens) she wrote "War was declared. Went to Aunt Clara's for tea."!! Other than the mention several times of the sound of lots of lorries passing her home (Half Moon Cottages) during the night (one of which contained my Dad), there wasn't much mention of activities after that! I suppose boys found it more exciting than the girls.'

The sinking of the passenger liner SS Athenia by German U-Boat torpedo is said to be the first hostile act between Britain and Germany in WW2.

Mrs Barbara Wilson reported her experience of that event in an article by Ian Johnson of the Telegraph, on 2 September 2014.

She was sailing to Canada and at the time was suffering badly from *mal de mer*. The ship's captain knew of the declaration of war so had begun zig zag manoeuvres. The captain of German submarine U-30 mistook the ship for an armoured merchant one. He ordered a torpedo to be launched at 1740 hours, that being on 3 September.

The first torpedo hit at midships, stopping the ship instantly. A second one missed.

The sea state was calm, the sun had not yet set and SS Athenia was sinking very slowly with her laying in the water without much of a slope. She stayed afloat until the next morning. Rescue ships were able to reach her; passengers were able to leave in a reasonably orderly manner.

Mrs Wilson and others managed to board a lifeboat and after 10 hours she was rescued, returning to Scotland, Fig. 14.5. The ship was carrying 1400 people, of which 117 were killed; many in the panic to leave it when 'a rescue ship chewed up a lifeboat with its propellers during the rescue.'

Fig. 14.5 Passengers being assisted to leave the SS Athenia. (IMW)

Some assert the first shot of WW2 was really that in Poland, for that invasion started WW2. That was when the German Battleship *Schleswig-Holstein* began to shell the Polish garrison at Westerplatte, that being on 1 September, at 0445 hours. The garrison was valiantly defended by just 182 soldiers, who endured 6 days of heavy shelling, bombing and then flame-throwers, before having to surrender.

Previously, on 31 August, German soldiers posing as Poles, and

Chapter 14 War Begins in Britain

carrying a Polish flag, attacked a German radio station - yes, a German one! - at Gleiwitz in Poland. That was a deceitful action to be an incident that would show that Germany had to invade Poland for its protection!

Far away in the State of Victoria, in Australia, a shot was fired over the bow of an unidentified ship at 1.30 am Eastern Standard Time in Australian on 4 September, that being in GMT the day before, and thus very close to the time that first torpedo was fired.

That ship was steaming in toward Melbourne and passing Fort Napean. It was, in fact, an Australian ship; presumably then quick to advise its credentials!

This could well have been the first shot! War was on for Britain and it Allies of that time.

14.2 Plans go into Action

For all of his beneficial achievements by 1939, Neville Chamberlain's policy of appeasement of Germany's ambitions had not brought the British nation to a safe place. To some extent, it had delayed preparation for war. His appeasement-based foreign policy was no longer suited to the circumstances being faced for Britain's survival.

His time since becoming Prime Minister in 1937 had been much devoted to improving the lot of the workers in British society - paid holidays and more reasonable working hours for children and women. He also had started the path to the welfare state with its National Health Scheme, overhauled government finance, improved conditions of factory workers, much reduced the national debt remaining from WW1, and sped up modernisation of British industry.

All that was for the good; indeed, many of those issues were beneficial to winning the war. However, his desire and actions for home front improvement had been completely overshadowed by Hitler's actions of aggression.

A more suitable leader for wartime was needed. In May 1940 Churchill had replaced him. Neville Chamberlain died later in that same year. He was then still a highly regarded politician with a great record, apart from his stance toward Hitler. It is a pity that people go on being remembered by a single, often negative, event in their life; ignoring the considerable good they have done.

That announcement by Chamberlain was a critical path point for the Government; many processes had been in preparation for deployment if this happened. The nation now had no option but prepare to push back Hitler by use of extreme force and to protect those likely to feel the force of bombing. It would only take a few months to subdue the Nazis - they thought! Churchill 'cocked his snook' at the Nazi regime, Fig. 14.6.

Fig. 14.6 'Heavy firing squad at the Western Front'.

The issue of creating a large enough British army with urgency had been aired in the Daily Mirror of 26 April 1939. If all men of 18-21 age were conscripted into war service it would have raised about 1 million strong. Raise that limit to 25 years of age would get to a 3 million strength, but they would be impossible to train sufficiently in time. The all-services

Chapter 14 War Begins in Britain

number of the *Wehrmacht* of Germany had managed to amass and train over 2 million strong by 1939.

Using the newly introduced British National Registration cards it was possible to send out the compulsory call-up papers for young men. As well as the armed forces there was a need for supporting services. These were voluntarily given, to begin with, some becoming directives later in the war. Volunteers were recruited using colourful and enticing posters.

The poster, given as Fig. 14.7, calls young women to join the Women's Land Army.

Fig. 14.7 One on many kinds of a poster seen everywhere in the early days of the war.

Overall Germany committed around 7 million men to their army for the whole war and they were well equipped, with many being battle-hardened.

With the French and Polish forces combined, the Germans were outnumbered - but their experience, readiness, equipment and tactics were much superior.

Getting the British Expeditionary Force BEF ready to go to France to push Hitler back needed much effort and more time. Such action had not been considered to be needed until late 1938!

Churchill's prior warnings in Parliament of the rise in size and better design of the military equipment of Germany had not found many supporters in the years up to 1939.

On the equipment aspect, the need to carry out research and design, and then take new designs into mass production, needed long lead times. The BEF would not go to war in September with the sophistication of the Germans.

Sending the BEF to France would take almost all of the home-based fighting capability out of Britain. The Empire colonies sent military support to help fill this gap.

1st Division Canadian soldiers began to arrive in Scotland on 17 December 1939, Fig. 14.8.

Fig. 14.8 1st Division Canadian soldiers arrive for Christmas 1939. (Longstaff-Tyrrell 2002)

The Canadian 2nd Division was arriving in the country by late summer 1940. These came down to the South Coast in July 1941 to take over beach defences, Ockenden (2009). There would have been few Canadians in the Midhurst District before then. But then they came in force!

The first Royal Canadian Air Force squadron arrived a little later in February 1940. Over the first years of the war, thousands of Canadians

Chapter 14 War Begins in Britain

had been in the South of England; the South Downs was a major training ground.

It has been estimated that over 7000 Canadians found wives there. And they all wanted to own a British pub! Longstaff-Tyrrell (2002). A detailed, almost contemporary, account of the 1939 arrival of a Canadian soldier is Clegg (1942). He had to be discharged early in the war, then setting his mind to recording his, and fellow soldiers, experiences for the 1938-1940 period.

As one ship was getting close to Scotland, and close to their port of arrival - a report came in of a German submarine torpedoing a ship nearby. That ship managed to reach port. They had noticed their escort ships had lessened in number, presumably to chase that submarine. Onboard, increased surveillance was set in place and they manned the guns in readiness for what did not come.

Below decks, they were polishing their gear ready to disembark next morning. On December 30, 1939, the ship berthed in the Clyde. They received a rousing welcome from the many ships they passed.

Those British people not deemed to be suited for call-up were persuaded to provide auxiliary civilian service for fire services, air raid patrols, farming labouring, nursing, and more.

A formal soldier Home Guard contingent would also be needed; but that was not considered until mid-1940 - when invasion by the Germans was then highly likely.

All of this involved the organising, training and equipping of many millions of people - and it now had to be done with great urgency.

One issue that then arose, was that of those British citizens with German or Italian backgrounds or interests. They had to be interned in secure camps. As the authorities could not be sure if these persons are loyal to British interests, the policy was to overdo the numbers put into the camps. Fascist politicians in Britain fled to other countries when their British Fascist party was banned just before war broke out.

The only military strength Britain still had that was greater than the Germans, was the Royal Navy; but that was unable to give much support

Midhurst WW2 Memoirs: 2. 'Evil' Rising: 'Good' Awakening

to a land insurgency by the, tested and tuned in Spain, modernised Germany Air Force and Army.

Britain had the big guns at sea. However, the British navy was not properly prepared to combat the cleverly constructed German submarine attacks on the essential supply convoys from Canada, the USA and Australia.

It was expected that the Germans would immediately bomb London when war was declared. That had been foreshadowed and remedies had already been implemented. Over a million bomb shelters had been distributed for Londoners to assemble and dig into their back gardens. It seems that was an official wearing a bowler hat, Fig. 14.9, as men delivered the steel to make shelters.

Fig. 14.9 Delivering the materials of Anderson bomb shelters.

Then there was the task of sending over two million children to safety from London. The number varies to as high as three million; they were not easy to count! Those children had to be moved in a matter of days, not weeks - and they were.

In peacetime, Britain had an insufficient home supply of agricultural products. It relied on a very large amount of imports, especially from its Empire countries. It now would soon need to feed those at home, an army overseas and also the additional troops coming

Chapter 14 War Begins in Britain

from the Empire countries.

As these import lines of support would be a definite target of German submarines it was necessary to entice the British nation to grow more basic foodstuffs. Plans for securing food supply in time of war had been created in 1936.

The War Agricultural Executive Committee, *War-Ag*, set up for WW1, had been set in place again early in 1939, to be operational by September. Growing more food was a matter that had to be set into place rapidly to prepare for the 1940 spring plantings, a few months ahead. It was locally dubbed the *Spring Offensive.*

The Royal Air Force had to be improved, especially those aircraft still with WW1 designs features - biplane wings being wooden frames covered with doped cloth and using tensioning wires.

The German fighter planes had been much improved by the mid-1930s. Fortunately, there were British designers, notably Reginald Mitchell (Spitfire) and Sydney Camm (Hawker Hurricane) who were leading the world in single-engine, metal frame aircraft design. The advent in 1933 of the privately developed, Rolls Royce *Merlin* engines was also a major factor in these improved designs.

Whilst Mitchell was convalescing in Germany in 1934, after an operation to remove cancer, he spoke to many Germans about their new fighter aircraft designs. He returned with the will to ensure Britain could do better. To him, it was a matter of life or death of a nation. This mandate was soon to be proven with the fights for life in the air in 1940.

The Chief Test Pilot for the Spitfire in 1939 was Alex Henshaw. In 1938 he toured Europe and saw, first hand, the quality and capability of the best German fighter plane - the Messerschmidt Me109. It is said he was later invited in 1939 to view the new German fighters and heard of the German disdain for British designs. The Germans said of one that it 'was a pretty little toy.'

Initially, as Hitler gained power from the start of the 1930s, there was not much of a rush to replace British warplanes. However, the threat of Hitler's obvious build-up of his air force after 1934 led to British contracts for the supply of 600 Hawker Hurricanes and 310 Spitfires in June 1936.

The prototype test of the first Spitfire, K5054, in 1936, under the control of "Mutt" Summers showed it was a winner.

> 'When you were strapped in it was like adding a plane to yourself; not you to the aircraft'.......' It slipped along as though sliding on ice', Fig. 14.10.

Fig. 14.10 Captain "Mutt" Summers in the cockpit of K5054, the prototype Supermarine Spitfire, 5 March 1936. (BBC)

Test piloting, at that time, was a particularly dangerous occupation. These men were heroes in the old-world sense. There were no computer-driven mathematical simulators then. Stress calculations took hours, and hours, carried out by maths experts using a mechanical calculator to get values at a single point, the whole individual stress pattern needing hundreds of thousands of points.

The prototype built, a test flight was then run to find out deficiencies, as well as its performance parameters. The test pilot was part of the design cycle. Think; design; draw; make some physical models for physical testing; built a first of type, basic aircraft; and then fly it to see if it was acceptable. That cycle is then repeated, and repeated until it is good enough - or, until time runs out, or the design is abandoned when some kind of unwanted latent parameter is found that cannot be fixed. Whoever gets all that done the fastest, and in reasonable

Chapter 14 War Begins in Britain

numbers, will have the best chance of winning a battle with the enemy's best.

Today a major air-liner build is so supported by an almost unbelievable amount of computer-aided design and off-line testing of components that collectively show it will fly - with only a handful of simple issues to fix. So good is the modern process that, in fact, the first built is often then put into service after its verification flight.

The Germans were more ruthless than the Allies with their test pilots. As the war progressed Hitler needed his rocket-propelled aircraft in service as soon as possible. A long line of test pilots died trying out each next prototype plane made. Most deaths occurred on the launch pad when the oxygen of the rocket exploded, oxidising everything in sight. Those pilot's lives had little priority: they just had to do their duty!

The Hurricane, being built with a metal frame and covered with fabric, was easier and cheaper to build than the all-metal Spitfire. Fig. 14.11 shows the prototype of these; it first flew in November 1935.

Fig. 14.11 K5083, the prototype Hurricane fighter aircraft, 1935.

It was first off the production rank in numbers. Delays took place in building the Spitfires; at one stage Alex Henshaw began to think they would be discontinued.

The enormous importance of these two aircraft in the Battle of Britain of 1940 is covered in the next book of these Midhurst Memoirs.

WW2 was a time for many advances in technology. Science was applied more than ever before. It is easy to argue that it was the science that won the war for the Allies!

An example, in February 1935, Radio Direction Finding RDF, (also then known as radio beam systems) was being tested for the first time in Britain at Upper Stowe, Northamptonshire. Two beams, sent out at different known locations, could be used to ascertain the position of distant objects that reflected some of the sent beam energy back to the source.

In its defining test, a Handley Page bomber was flown using a ground-based test set for locating it in flight: the so-called *Daventry Experiment*. It was so clearly successful that its R&D was rapidly taken to the next step; building a prototype system.

'It is historically correct that, on June 17, 1935, radio-based detection and ranging was first demonstrated in Britain. Watson-Watt, Wilkins, and Bowen are generally credited with initiating what would later be called radar in this nation.'

The use of physical sciences to create new means of detecting aircraft, just before and into wartime, has been examined in depth in the recorded memoirs of that time of a scientist attached to the Air Ministry for the duration, see Jones (1978), and Chaline (2016), Fig.14.12.

Fig. 14.12 Professor "RV" Jones.

Reginald Jones, Chaline (2016), was the Assistant Director, Air Intelligence (Science) from 1941. He was usually known as just RV.

He was an especially talented person who had a real hold on using mental perception of situations. Guided by an underpinning of sound experimental science, he was able to come to good conclusions with just a few really clear facts.

He could decide what the Germans were likely to be doing when a mere fragment of intelligence of a German message, or aerial photograph, was given to him to advise upon. This was often in the face

Chapter 14 War Begins in Britain

of superiors who did not always agree with his conclusions.

Perhaps my link to him was predestined for we were both born at Herne Hill, SE London - but some 26 years apart. We had our first professional link in 1968 where he showed me utmost patience and understanding - that I badly needed!

As said at the start of this book, our working relationship began when it I visited him in Aberdeen in 1968. There, he so politely told me that he had been the Assistant Director of Air Intelligence during WW2. To him making decisions about grades for his students was far easier than many decision he had to take part in during that time in the war.

Near the end of 1940 he was been recruited as an Intelligence Officer and was asked about the particularly high accuracy of the German bombers. He worked out, from the available intelligence scraps, that they had a better method than the British then had. From then on, he was a key person in the *Battle of the Beams,* as this electronic method became known as, Jones (1978).

To him the bombing raid on Coventry during the 1940s blitz was the hardest decision he was involved in. As the raid was developing and German bombers were on the way he said he had realised where one raid was targeted from by listening to the actual signals of the Germans version of RDF – to Coventry! If the RAF had been redirected to defend that attack in major way it would have alerted the Germans that their Enigma code system had been broken by the Allies. It was decided to let it take place! A hard decision had to be made. That is how he put it to me at the time. However, that Churchill having RVs advice, let the raid go on is still in debate!

Over the years we became scientific colleagues - at a large distance for I was working in an underground observatory I set up in an old mine in the bush of New South Wales. I had written a scholarly book on the history of measuring instruments, Sydenham (1979), for which I invited him to provide a Foreword. After stating pleasant things about the need for the book and my accomplishment he wrote:

'.... It is testimony both to him and to the University at Armidale that enthusiasm and understanding support, in the preparation of this work, have so signally triumphed over geographical remoteness from the historical centres of instrument development.'

Midhurst WW2 Memoirs: 2. 'Evil' Rising: 'Good' Awakening

Distance did seem to make Australia remote then. At that time desktop computers were still more than a decade away; email and Internet for on-line retrieval were still to come. The fastest electronic method of image and text communication was Facsimile, Fax!

In 1988 I enticed him to write a book on his personal career's scientific contributions for John Wiley, Chichester; other book invitations to him were almost always directed to his WW2 contributions, Jones (1988).

Back to his WW2 contributions! In June 1939 it was becoming vital to be able to protect Britain from German bombings. Radar and other Radio Direction Finding RDF equipment were needed: but they were primitive then. These were not yet compact enough for use in an already, filled, aircraft. Much smaller and lighter electronic components were needed. Whilst it was later taken into general war use, it was the pre-war years of development that gave British advanced capability by the time it had become essential when the Germans sought to bomb Britain into submission.

As war broke out it was not expected by the British War bureaucrats, that Britain could be successfully invaded by the Germans. The meant the southern coast defences had not been given the attention needed. Britain was ill-prepared at that time.

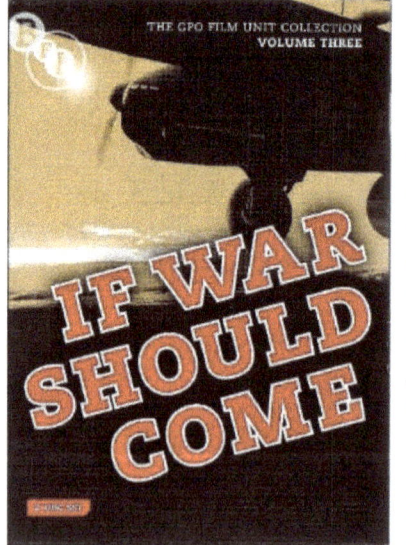

It was fortunate for Britain that Germany did not immediately start to bomb Britain in force. The country needed time to develop its military capability. The last months of 1939 was a time when those who knew about such matters were becoming jittery about success in beating off the aggressor.

Fig. 14.13 Cover of the GPO collection.

486

Chapter 14 War Begins in Britain

The GPO Film Unit was commissioned to make a collection of short films *If War Should Come - Volume 3* for distribution across London, and other likely enemy bombing targets. Fig. 14.13 shows the cover of the two-CD set including the following short films.

Disk 1	Disk 2
The City (1939)	Squadron 992 (1940)
The Islanders (1939)	La Cause Commune (1940)
Spare Time (1939)	French Communique (1940)
A Midsummer Day's Work (1939)	The Front Line (1940)
SS Ionian (1939)	Men of the Lightship (1940)
If War Should come (1939)	London Can Take It (1940)
The First Days (1939)	Spring Offensive (1940)
War Library Items 1, 2 and 3 (1940)	The Story of the Air Communique (1940)
	War and Order (1940)
	Christmas Under Fire (1941)

These entertaining shorts told viewers what might happen and how to be ready if war comes. It opens:

'No one in this country wants war. If war shall come, we will not be beaten. Democracy will triumph. Not everyone will be in the fighting forces but all have a vital part to play. There are some things you can and should do at once. The warning may be short. Prepare now!'

- It showed people erecting an Andersen bomb shelter in their back gardens.
- It urged people to not panic by overbuying food; there was plenty in the country. Also do not use emergency food up.
- To reduce the danger of fire, clear out the loft and set up buckets of sand, or dry earth. These were needed to cover small incendiary bombs to keep them from activating.
- Gas masks should be to hand at all times, as should a pencil and paper be ready by the wireless set, to take down important messages.

- Keep off the phone unless needed.
- Tie labels on kids to help them be identified if lost.
- Do not let your evacuation arrangements to leave London interfere with government plans; in the country, kids are safe and happy.
- Be ready to obscure all lights in the house and extinguish street signs. Take cover when air raid sirens wail up and down, or police give 3 blasts on their whistle.
- A hand rattle sound means gas. Put on your gas mask fast and keep it on.
- Do not be alarmed at the noise of an air raid; most of it is our guns at work.
- No one wants war. But if war should come don't be alarmed - keep a good heart. Whatever happens, Britain is prepared; the film shows comforting shots of factories, farmers, and ships unloading.

What it was like to be in an air raid is described in the next book - being my own experience in 1940s London. Hitler must have been feeling so supreme as his war machine gobbled up countries by deceit and brute force. They had taken Austria, March 1938: Sudetenland, October 1938: Czechoslovakia, March 1938 and the rest of it in March 1939, and Poland in September 1939. It was to take a year of fighting Hitler's forces before the tide started to turn in favour of the Allies. A lot of fighting had to happen to get there, Fig. 14.14.

Fig. 14.14 Britain begins to take on the Nazi monster.

Chapter 14 War Begins in Britain

14.3 BoB Pilots in the Making

It was very clear by 1937, that with several hundreds of these new, high-performance Hurricane and Spitfire fighter aircraft coming into service, many more pilots were needed for this specialised duty. They needed to be trained in a dogfight type of battle in the air, at airspeeds not known before, and with greater firepower. It took time to select and train them.

Hurricanes went into squadron service on Christmas day, 1937. The first two production Spitfires came off the production line in July 1938. The first went into service at Duxford airfield in RAF 19 squadron in August 1938. By the start of the war 306 of these were in service. Pilots had been in pre-war training getting flying hours up, in readiness for the expected war that came.

To begin with RAF aircrew were all volunteers. To train a Spitfire pilot normally had a requirement that they have flown around 300 flying hours over 18-24 months. To man the many new planes, and to meet with the need as war broke out, that training was often done with only 150 hours, flown over six months. Required flight time of trainee pilots, to be given command of a Spitfires, went down to just 10 hours as the Battle of Britain wore on. They often carried out many sorties per day.

Finding enough suitable people to train up was a problem. Fortunately, many young men already could fly... in their small planes...who wanted to have a go on these new aircraft. The first of these mostly came from wealthy young men looking for adventure.

There were many Americans who wanted this experience. However, the USA was a neutral country at that time so it was internationally illegal for them to do this. Some joined the Canadian Air Force as a path to the RAF. Some American's citizenships were simply ignored.

Other pilots came from Australia and New Zealand, and later from those French, Czechoslovakian and Polish pilots who escaped Hitler's invasion of their respective countries. Possibly the most celebrated *Battle of Britain* unit was the 601 Squadron. This had been formed in 1925 by wealthy amateur aviator aristocrats. Called the 'millionaire's squadron', their sense of God-given privilege made many of them colourful in their contempt for rules and instructions that needed to be observed.

They even altered their uniforms with colourful linings and had their own designed blue ties. Many stories resulted about their exploits, at times stupidities. Their ages ranged from 18 to 30 years plus. Examples of the brave actions taking place in 1940 are covered in the next book.

Fig. 14.15 is a still image from colour footage taken by William "Willie" Rhodes-Moorhouse, who got his civil pilot's licence before leaving school at Eton. After showing his skill at flying and getting many confirmed kills, he was killed when shot down in September 1940. He was just 26 years old.

Fig. 14.15 'Millionaire' BoB pilots taking a break. (BBC)

Once the Squadrons came into live battle action with the new aircraft, there was an urgent need for many more pilots, that making the pilot cohort more cosmopolitan in composition.

'The first dogfight combat firing at a German fighter was that of Peter Ayerst, in October 1939; he was 19 years old. As it was not an intended action, he avoided a close-by Messerschmidt he had come upon as many other German and British fighters arrived to create the first WW2 dogfight.'
Daily Mail, James Rush, 20 May 2014.

Chapter 14 War Begins in Britain

Some of these fighter pilots were buried near to the Midhurst Rural District; RAF Tangmere, a major Battle of Britain airfield, being just south.

The size of a fighter squadron 'flight' is in the range of 12 - 22 aircraft with a similar number of pilots. Additionally, there were also the unsung, important ground support staffs. By January 1940, some 500 Hurricanes and Spitfires were in service, rising to over 1000 by August.

On the 16th October 1939, the Luftwaffe carried out what seems to be the first 'raid' on Britain by Germany. They were equipped with reconnaissance cameras, being sent to collect tactical information, including weather states relevant to them sending bombers to attack ships at berth in the Firth of the Forth.

Some twelve Junkers Ju88 German bombers, loaded with 1,100lb bombs, then set off to attempt to sink warships there. The raid was on the Rosyth Naval Base at the Firth of the Forth.

Only just *embodied,* Auxiliary Air Force Squadrons, No. 602, Fig. 14.16, and No 603 flew up in defence. These Spitfires were yet to go into full service, still only being allowed to engage the enemy in the day time. They could be considered to be the first in combat over Britain for the Battle of Britain.

Fig 14.16 602 Squadron, City of Glasgow. (Wordpress)

The raid was foiled by the Spitfires and anti-aircraft shells. Three German bombers were shot down by the 603 Squadron, piloted by Auxiliary (Reservist) Airmen. Some 16 RN personnel were killed from shrapnel of a bomb that just missed hitting their ship. This lengthy engagement episode included the first shot made in combat over Britain.

Fig. 14.17 shows Spitfire "Stickleback" just after its pilot, Flight Lieutenant Pat Gifford had returned to base after the bombing raid had been repulsed.

Fig. 14.17 "Stickleback" after the first Spitfire combats on home soil. (Queensferry Museum)

A blow by blow, but inadequately verified, account of this action is available on Wikipedia. Other reports wrongly claim this attack was to destroy the Forth Bridge, but photographs show the bombers were there to sink ships.

Deployment of Spitfires and Hurricanes in the Battle of Britain BoB was a very important engagement to bring about the turning point of the war; but that was only a small part of their use in many WW2 campaigns, and countries, Ward (1989) and Smith (1989).

Life as a BoB pilot, in the making, has been described in one of the articles run in the *Midhurst and Petworth Observer* by David Coxon, the Tangmere Military Aviation Museum curator. From his article, the early years of a pilot are condensed here.

Frederick Rosier was born in Wrexham in 1915. He entered the RAF as a commissioned pilot with No 43 Squadron at RAF Tangmere. Rosier described his first two years at Tangmere as:

"carefree – I belonged to one of the most exclusive flying clubs in the world".

Chapter 14 War Begins in Britain

His logbook for 1936 listed some of the training a pilot undertook; camera gun attacks on other aircraft, instrument and formation flying, cross-country flights, slow-flying and spinning, message bag dropping and battle climbs to 25,000 feet.

Back on the ground, in the officer's mess, he was required to wear mess kit (blue waistcoats) at dinner on three nights of the week. On Thursday of each month, full mess kit had to be worn and every Friday, dinner jackets.

Tweed jackets were allowed for dinner in the mess on Wednesdays and at the weekend. During his third year at Tangmere, the squadron exchanged its Furies for Hurricanes and prepared for a war that seemed inevitable.

At the outbreak of war, Rosier joined No 229 Squadron at Digby. On May 18, 1940, two days after he had arrived in France, Rosier destroyed a Luftwaffe Messerschmidt Bf 109 fighter plane, before being shot down himself. Fig. 14.18 shows one shot down in over Ilford, NE London, in 1940. It was put on display around the country.

Fig. 14.18 Messerschmidt Bf (or Me 1090) fighter shot down and on display in Maidstone. (Burgess and Saunders 1990)

When he attempted to bale out of his burning Hurricane, his cockpit hood jammed. He only survived because his aircraft exploded and he was thrown out of the wreckage enabling him to parachute to safety.

Badly burned, he was hospitalised and later repatriated, arriving at Southampton a week later. Three months later, after recovering from his injuries, he re-joined No 229 Squadron as commanding officer and flew in the last few weeks of the Battle of Britain.

Midhurst has its own, homegrown, Battle of Britain hero - Arthur William Eade AFC, Fig. 14.19.

Fig. 14.19 Arthur William Eade AFC: Midhurst's BoB hero.

Arthur was a pupil of the Midhurst Grammar School leaving it in 1929 to join the RAF as an Aircraft Apprentice, becoming an Aero Engine fitter - probably then not thinking he would become a commemorated Spitfire pilot.

His next role in 1937 saw him become an Air Observer; an aircrew member with mainly reconnaissance duties, who is also expected to be a gunner. At that stage, he was entitled to wear a 'half wing' with a 0 on it.

He was posted in July of that year to 90 Squadron at Bicester as a Corporal-Observer. He then applied to do elementary training as a pilot and began that on 13 March 1939. By Guy Fawkes night, 5 November 1939 he had joined at Sutton Bridge as a fighter pilot.

His battle record started on 15 August 1940 when he had become a Battle of Britain pilot - with full wings then. After several kills of German aircraft, he was eventually shot down on 15 March 1941. That appears to be the end of his combat fighting period.

During the remainder of the war, he carried out ground duties on training and maintenance. He was awarded the AFC (Air Force Cross) medal in 1943. He left the RAF on September 1947 as a Warrant Officer, the highest level attainable as a non-commissioned airman.

His circumstance reeks of class attitude. He became a pilot on active duty, many times under direct, close up fire. Yet he never got to be a Commissioned Officer.

Class attitudes to him being a hands-on person may have been the reason. I know what that felt like! I first trained as an electrical tradesman. When I had completed my Bachelor of Engineering with Honours as a mature student, I applied to read the Master of Engineering.

Chapter 14 War Begins in Britain

The elderly professor of the day, and the Head of Department, said of me to my supervisor "Once a technician, always a technician!"

A plaque commemorating Arthur's wartime contribution exists in Midhurst. Fig. 14.20.

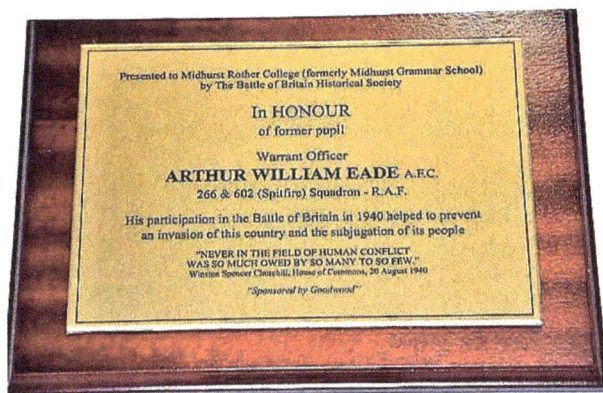

Fig 14.20 Memorial to Warrant Officer Arthur Eades at the Midhurst Rother College.

It was unveiled by Her Majesty's Lord-Lieutenant of West Sussex, then Mrs Susan Piper, on July 2013, at the school that absorbed the MGS - the Midhurst Rother College.

We have seen here an introduction to the lead up to the Battle of Britain. It began well before the brave pilots of the Allied Forces resisted German attempts to subdue Britain in late 1940. More stories of that BoB time are included in the next book.

14.4 The Midhurst District sends Sons and Daughters

Many women already had their husbands or sons away in service somewhere by September 1939. Britishers started to get call-up notices from 29 September 1939 onward. Some 300,000 had already enlisted voluntarily. Announcement of war had resulted in more volunteers, swelling the total force to over 800,000. Still more were needed.

Choices facing young men were, first, to volunteer for a named unit in your preferred service branch; that being where you felt you and possibly your friends would be, see Fig. 14.21.

Fig. 14.21 Signing on for service in the Royal Fusiliers, in Fleet Street.

Next, you could sit tight and wait for conscription to find you, in which case you were told the force name and type of duty you had to do.

You could also be a conscientious objector, being called a 'conchie'. It has been said there were 16,000 registered this way. The definition was:

> 'An individual who has claimed the right to refuse to perform military service on the grounds of freedom of thought, conscience, or religion.'

It did not mean they gave no service to the war effort. They just did not have to combatants; many went into ambulance services.

By that time, this attitude could be accommodated in law but was not always accepted by everyone as a choice, by even your own family or by your family friends. Opposition to these people could be quite fierce.

A delay in conscripted call-up was much due to the fact the government did not have accurate data on who existed, where they lived and or if they were already in, or eligible for war service.

Chapter 14 War Begins in Britain

The newly created National Registration Bill requirement was given Royal assent on 5 September 1939, just two days after war was declared on Germany. That then called for an almost instant national census to be carried out. The bill was completed in just 2 days - all with paper only records! At last, the Government was moving its plans along at top speed.

In the mean-time, food ration books were being prepared in October 1939 for release soon after January 1940, Fig. 14.22.

Fig. 14.22 Food ration books being prepared for distribution.

The task was gigantic; everything had to be on paper with each document authorised for a specific person - tens of millions having to be designed, printed, marked up, and then taken to issuing points.

The person then had to decide which retailer to register with.

There must have been an issuing depot on Midhurst but its location is yet to be established. Comments in the MILM records mention rationing, but more because of its nuisance at times. In the country there was plenty of non-rationed food available in the district - pigs, chickens, vegetables and rabbits were also hard to ration completely.

One might ponder on why so late? This information was going to be needed from at least early in 1938. Perhaps they still thought the Hitler would go along with British requests to be non-aggressive. National panic was not needed!

A special evening edition newspaper was run when war was declared on 7 September 1939, Fig. 14.23.

Fig. 14.23 Special Edition Newspaper.

One can feel certain that the MRD residents responded positively when calls for volunteers went out in 1938, or to the compulsory call-up that began in late 1939.

However, just how many men and women served in the Armed Forces from the Midhurst Rural District is problematic for no easy to use record seems to exist on this statistic?

A District roll of honour is available in Royal British Legion (2000) with names by village, but it is not clear if the list is of those that died or all that served. It also may not be only of local people at the start of the war. Furthermore, the locally published village memories rarely tell of people of the district who went to war. They must have gone quietly!

Chapter 14 War Begins in Britain

The BEF had already been established, following Hitler's annexation of Austria in early 1938.

It was set up then as a hopeful deterrent against more territorial ambitions by Hitler. Troops started to move to France, Fig.14.24, and assemble along the Belgian-France border with Germany after the war was declared.

Fig. 14.24 The BEF in France 1939.

An estimate of the build-up in France follows:

'The plan for the deployment of the BEF to France was called *Plan W*, and was the responsibility of Maj-Gen L. A. Hawes. The advance parties left for France on September 4th 1939, with the first major contingents arriving at Cherbourg on September 10th, and at Nantes & St Nazaire on September 12th. The first 2 Corps of the BEF were in France within 37 days after mobilisation. I Corps took up its positions by October 3rd, whilst II Corps took up its positions by October 12th 1939.'

Andy H on forum.axishistory.com

Two more Corps were still to arrive. Out-fitting them all was a problem; many did not have the uniforms, weapons and field support equipment needed. Some trained initially with sticks and pipes as rifles and carried small flags to represent themselves as imagined vehicles. To get so many troops into a defensive position in France was a real accomplishment.

'By the end of April [1940], the strength of the BEF in France had reached 394,165. Of this total:

237,319 were within the main fighting formations/units.
18,347 were TA [Territorial Army part timers] divisions undertaking labour and training duties.
17,665 were reinforcements held at area bases.
78,864 were on LOC [Logistic Operations Centre] duties, whilst a further
23,545 were stationed on other duties
9,051 were in drafts en route
2,515 were yet to be allocated, and finally
6,859 were with the AASF [Advanced Air Striking Force]'

Andy H has another list; that being of the Royal Navy deliveries to France by 27 September 1939:

152,031 Army Personnel
9,392 Air Force Personnel
21,424 Army vehicles
2,470 Air Force vehicles
36,000 tons of Ammo
25,000 tons of motor spirit
60,000 tons of frozen meat
  Andy H on forum.axishistory.com'

So, who did go from the Midhurst District? One person we can be sure of having gone to France was the 3rd Viscount Lord Cowdray. He was a captain in an artillery regiment of the 98th (Surrey & Sussex Yeomanry Queen Mary's) Army Field Regiment, Royal Artillery, 1 Corps, under General Sir John Dill when it first entered France.

He soon returned to Dunkirk, but had lost his left arm at the shoulder, in the retreat. That loss did not dampen his enthusiasm for playing polo. 'A *'contraption'* was made with the help of the Roehampton Limb-Fitting Centre and his gun maker, Purdey, enabling him to ride on the kerb and play up to medium goal, later to umpire.'
  Russel-Stoneham and Chatterton-Newman (1992)

Chapter 14 War Begins in Britain

In 1947 he resurrected the game in Cowdray Park, Fig. 14.25.

Fig. 14.25 Polo at Cowdray Park, Summer 1947. From left: John Lakin, Lord Cowdray (third Viscount), Daphne Lakin, Peter Dollar.

Russel-Stoneham and Chatterton-Newman (1992)

He then used his prosthetic arm, but not that much in public. Polo was not played formally during the war years for many of the men players were then serving in the armed services. Some Cowdray polo fields became a naval airfield, Pons (2017), supporting small planes used to rescue downed pilots in the nearby English Channel; carrying out sea mine spotting, invasion attempts; and sinking German navy ships.

Lord Cowdray expected he would retain the small hangars erected by the RN, but in the end, he had to buy them after the war, Russel-Stoneham and Chatterton-Newman (1992).

Another Midhurst man who served for sure was Sam Karn, husband of Edith Karn, the lady I was billeted with from 1940-1943. He was in the Royal Navy. Several times he came home on leave in his sailor's uniform; to give me a good time.

I recall being with him, in his shed somewhere, wherein he let me help him make me a little wooden toboggan. That came about as the result of a really cold winter. We were then ready for the next winter; but before it snowed again, I had left that home.

In the centre of Church Hill is the war memorial for Midhurst's fallen. It was originally erected in honour of those who made the sacrifice in WW1. Names of those who died as the result of WW2 war service were added to the south, and north-facing, sides of the base of the obelisk, Fig. 14.26 shows one side.

The shortlist below, is of 11 names of local people who died in WW2 giving war service. It is available on the Midhurst Town War Memorial Honour Board website. It may not be complete and some name spellings do vary.

Fig. 14.26 North side of the Midhurst WW1 and WW2 memorial.

Charles, Arthur Eric. RASC. POW Singapore and Burma.
De La Coze, John Rushbrook. RAF 270 Flying Boat Squadron.
Foard, Richard William Charles. Lance Bombardier. The Royal Artillery 144th Field Regiment.
Jennings, Mike. RN.
Madgwick, William. 1st Battalion, Ox and Bucks Light Infantry. Normandy D-Day force?
Pett, Donald Andrew. 5th Battalion, The Cameron Highlanders. [Normandy D-Day force?]
Sutton, William Charles. RAF Pilot officer. 149 Bomber Squadron.
Tack, George. Sub Lieutenant RN V.R. H.M.L.C. Tank.
Trusler, Ralph. 2/6th Battalion, The Royal West Surrey Regiment.
Weller, Leslie Herbert George. Sgt RAF 460 Bomber Squadron.
Willshire, Raymond Venables. Sgt Engineer, RAF 102 Bomber Squadron.

Another WW2 Roll of Honour, for part of the Midhurst Rural District, is given in Royal British Legion (2000). It lists 67 names of persons, for the Parishes of Bepton, Cocking, Easebourne, Graffham, Heyshott, Iping, Lodsworth, Midhurst and Stedham, who may have lost their lives in war service, with 15 being from the Midhurst parish. It is not clear that this honour list is of all of those who served, or those who died in service.

That Midhurst list contains some extra names to those on the Midhurst Memorial, namely Ronald Buchman, John and James Fairweather, and Frederick Jennings.

From the honour list website details, it is clear that local lads went into a wide range of services - bombers, seaplane, D-Day assault period as infantry and in the special beach clearance landing craft. These stories need to be researched! Contributions made by the Midhurst Rural District were significant indeed.

These lists can only be used as starting points, for names do not always get recorded for the district they came from, and some are simply too hard to identify.

According to the multiple sources discussed earlier, when war broke out, the MRD population was around 10,000. Assuming 30% were less than 18 years old and 30% were above 25 years old, the shorter list is then some 2000 who were of age to be called up. Of these, say, 50% are women, then that leaves 1000 in a likely male group. Of these let 40% be in reserved occupations and 10% unsuited - medically unfit, objectors, etc.

We are left with a very rough guestimate of a few hundred men possibly went to serve. There would have been some women as well, especially at late times during the war. Presumably many men would have gone into the Royal Sussex Regiment.

At present a Midhurst University of Third Age U3A team is researching and making available the stories of local people who are honoured on WW1 War Memorials around the District. Maybe, one day, the numbers and names for WW2 will be also researched with as much care! However, names of those who died in service only is a but a small part of those who went into war service of all kinds.

Midhurst WW2 Memoirs: 2. 'Evil' Rising: 'Good' Awakening

The Royal British Legion of Midhurst collected 33 accounts of WW2 service lives, Royal British Legion (2000). The accounts were, however, mostly by people who lived in the area around the year 2000; almost all had come to live there from somewhere else after the war. It does not help us to understand how many local people went into war service from the Midhurst District.

In those cases, just two people listed left the district to serve, and then came back to stay. They are Betty Simmonds, and John Ainsworth, see below.

Those at home, who were sufficiently able, joined the Home Guard, the Royal Observer Corps, Land Army, the nurses, fire brigades, Air Raid Precaution ARP personnel, other support services. Young and old took up as many duties where they could.

Women not in employment in the District, as at other suitable locations, were extolled to do their bit as their wartime duty by taking in Evacuees and refugees, Fig. 14.27. More of that issue is given in the next book.

Fig. 14.27 One of the posters calling women to take in evacuees.

The war impacted local living had to also cope with the influx of evacuees and their teachers; with government officials housing and their work accommodation. These swelled the need for staff in the hospitality industry and the food and clothing shops thereby increasing the need for employment.

The contributions of this background support are easily forgotten. Life in one branch, the *Home Guard* was immortalised in the TV film series, *Dad's Army*. The Home Guard (HG) was begun after the war had started; when it was highly likely the war for Britain, might be lost to the Nazis!

Chapter 14 War Begins in Britain

We appreciate the humour generated at their expense today. With such sincerity, they were ready to carry out that great responsibility to defend the country to their death. Fig. 14.28 shows, however, that with all that devotion they would have stood little chance of beating back a German land attack using Blitzkrieg methods and advanced machinery.

Fig. 14.28 Home Guard unit mid wartime; they stood tall, with dignity. (Green 1989)

By Summertime of 1940 over 1 million men had joined the HG service; but with such speed that they often had no uniform, no rifles, no ammunition. We make fun at their antics today, but we should give them the recognition of what they were prepared to do to defend the British way of life!

Women also played their part joining as volunteers, one of the many organisations that worked alongside the men in the Armed Services, see Royal British Legion (2000).

Fig. 14.29 LACW Betty Simmonds in her blue uniform. (Royal British Legion 2000)

Betty Simmonds, Fig. 14.29, was born in Lodsworth in 1917. She left school at 14 becoming a domestic worker. In 1941 she was called up to join the

Women's Auxiliary Air Force (WAAF).

She said she was not suited for khaki dress. Betty was sent to Gloucester to live with 30 others in a hut. She served, doing many tasks at various locations as a nursing orderly. Sarah Churchill was in the next hut. Betty rose to be a Leading Aircraftswoman (LACW). It was a man's type world for her – tough living, but full of companionship. She was demobbed in December 1945. Returning to village life, with its still pre-war living conditions and few friends, was hard to take at first.

Major J F Ainsworth, Fig. 14.30, was another person from Midhurst who was part of the BEF - in the Royal Sussex Regiment, Royal British Legion (2000).

He was born in 1917 at *Hollist*, Midhurst, with the surname of *Combe.* A name-change to *Ainsworth* took place in 1926; his family left the district. His army career commenced in 1937, soon becoming a fully commissioned officer.

Fig. 14.30 John Ainsworth, sketched in 1941 whilst he was in the OFLAG VII-D POW camp in Germany. (Royal British Legion 2000)

At the time of the Munich crisis, in late 1938, when Hitler took over Czechoslovakia, John went into the 2nd Battalion of the Royal Sussex Regiment. There he received training, moving on to Belfast. He spent time at several placements until the war was declared wherein, he

Chapter 14 War Begins in Britain

then became an Intelligence Officer and Assistant Adjutant; that meant office desk work for the while.

This life of constantly moving from place to place was very typical for most of the defence force people. There would be heightened times of joy, and much sadness, but the hard to take times were usually short to endure in WW2. Only a few campaigns took place in which Allied troops were under enemy fire for a long period.

John's battalion left for France on 8 April 1940. His story is continued in the next book. He survived the war!

To round out this pre-war period, and to end this Book 2 of the Memoirs, the next part of this chapter summarises the changes that had started to be made in the District; many that would not be restored when the war ended.

14.5 Life will Never be the Same Again

War has been declared. Britain begins to stir, but still with disbelief that it happening. Hitler is holding the handle of his large mixing spoon. He has, so far severely disrupted the people's lives in many Eastern European nations. Now he is directing his evil mind to the West of Europe. Stirring still more vigorously, he is trying to scoop inside Britain with his recipe for chaos.

Hitler is so confident of Britain becoming a kind of partner, the result being Britain is left largely alone for a few months. The *Battle of France* has started but those at home probably only gave it scant attention. The BEF would do their job and tell Hitler to buzz off with his tail between his legs. They will all be home by Christmas 1939!

Hitler's actions brought mistrust, fear and severe hardship to the peaceful British Isles. This time, however, it will be soon, if not a little tardily, be shown that Britain could rally the forces needed to rid the world of him.

By November 1939 it was becoming the coldest winter for half a century. The river Thames froze over for 8 miles near Teddington. It snowed in central London! To make matter worse, there was soon upon the land freezing winter rain, sleet, lightning, frosts, frozen fog, snow flurries, and cold driving winds resulting in lack of good and timely sleep: with it came with the need to perform strenuous outside activity under many layers of heavy clothing.

The British would rapidly 'grow up' - see Fig. 14.31.

Fig. 14.31 Just wait until the little feller grows up. (WordPress)

For my family's part, as war broke out, Dad was fully 'embodied', serving in the RAF operating barrage balloons in the so-called 'ring around London'. He was located within the area of the underground tube system so could get home to West Norwood on leave, but that was rarely given.

It was not, immediately, a dangerous task because Germany had not commenced its bombing campaign on Britain. However, just being on duty at a balloon site in that 1939/40 winter was tough. Despite his RAF issue woollen great-coat, chronic asthma started to take its toll on Henry.

I suppose at that time, I just ran around making baby talk non-stop and asking loads of questions; that is, being a real nuisance as they dug in the Andersen shelter in our back yard, or were preparing the house for blackout with crossed tapes on the windows to hold any breaking glass.

Mum had me, and her parents, to look after in our West Norwood family home. I grew up a bit more, but without remembering what was happening to us. I was just 2 years 9 months old when the war started in

Chapter 14 War Begins in Britain

earnest for Londoners. By then I had some teeth, could climb stairs, pull myself up to things, eat by myself, use crayons, and was most likely to have been potty trained.

I was becoming able to make a kind of talk and understand mum's talk to me. I loved listening to her reading me books, but suspect that did not happen that much. The experts tell us that children remember things from age 2-3 but most of those early memories fade over time. I can recall some things from around 3 years old. The amusing ones are discussed in the next book.

Petrol was the first commodity to be rationed. On September 8, 1939 ration books were distributed. That did not affect my immediate family's lifestyle. Only much better-off Uncle Charles had a car... and he rarely used it, except for annual and bank holidays.

It was not until 8 January 1940 when food rationing began, that Mum would have to think carefully what she needed and how to cope with the smaller portions and very limited choice. She would also have to learn how, when, and where, to join a queue for food items when a shop announced that some kind of goodie was available - until it ran out. Sometimes it could take hours of queuing to get just one banana, or a tin of peaches.

The wealthy did not escape the above new restrictions and they carried on, for as long as they could, in the lifestyle they had enjoyed: but not for much longer.

Goodwood ran in July 1939. Polo at Cowdray went on, Fig. 14.32, as before, for the first half of that year. Lord Louis Mountbatten captained the local Committee, having joined the Navy in 1936 and been given command of the destroyer HMS Kelly in June 1939.

Fig. 14.32 Polo went on, as the war was impending.

Midhurst WW2 Memoirs: 2. 'Evil' Rising: 'Good' Awakening

The 3rd Viscount Lord Cowdray was already a member of the British Expeditionary Force BEF for it had been established following Hitler's annexation of Austria in early 1938. The BEF was set up then as a deterrent against more ambitions by Hitler. The force started to move to France and assemble along the Belgian-France border with Germany soon after war was declared.

At first, little action happened for far longer than expected, to the point of some humour, Fig. 14.33.

Fig. 14.33 BEF life on the French front, Dec. 1939. (Punch)

But first things must get worse; to the point where all seems about to be lost to the Nazis. This war will bring itself right into the homes of Britain. By the end of the next year, 24,000 civilians will be killed and hundreds of thousands made homeless in the bombing Blitz on London; with major losses in other major cities, such as Coventry.

Chapter 14 War Begins in Britain

Civil projects just started would not all be mothballed for it was seriously expected by many that the war would all be over soon, with life returning to normal. One such project was the new Anglican, *Church of the Holy Cross,* being built for Greenford, Middlesex.

By the mid-1930s the greatly expanding population of the new dormitory suburb of Greenford Magna in West London badly needed a larger Anglican church. The existing one, dating back to the 12th century still had charm and religious presence but it was far too small to take the expanding number of worshippers.

The first design, by Professor Sir Albert Richardson, was set down and physically modelled in 1937. His vision was not strictly adopted, it being adapted into that now built. A 1/8th scale architectural model of his design was auctioned in London when his collection was sold through Christie's in September 2013.

On 10 July 1939, the foundation stone was set into the wall of the new church. When war broke out a few months later the dilemma was 'to build, or not to build?'. In a show of local defiance, that work carried on through the war. It was ready for worship in 1942. The dedication took place in 1944.

The original church has been kept. *Songs of Praise* featured its war-time history showing many period photographs.

A valuable insight into those times, provided by Henry Vollam Morton, Fig. 14.34, was his long walk around England in 1939. He reported on his findings in two time periods; just before, and just after when the war started, Morton (1942).

Fig.14.34 Henry Canova Vollam Morton (or just H V Morton), 1892-1979 Journalist and Writer.

When he called in on the Fotheringhay village in Northamptonshire early in 1939 he came upon this notice:

'PROCEEDINGS ADOPTED ON PROCLAMATION OF A STATE OF WAR

The Church bells will not be rung or chimed during the whole period of a state of War for any ordinary or special services. The only bell to be used for such occasions will be the small five-minute bell.

In the event of an enemy air raid threatening the village, the **ALARM** will be sounded by two, or more, of the church bells being rung continuously for two, or more, minutes.

When the alarm has been sounded:
DON'T
Wander about the roads in the village.
Hinder by trying to help the ARP personnel in the performance of their duties.
Collect in groups in the fields.
Leave your gas-mask behind.
Walk into a gas-contaminated area, or get down-wind of a gas bomb, or go and look at the crater.
Step purposely onto any splash on the ground that maybe gas.
Rush to the spot at the sound of a bomb dropping to see what the damage is, or to see what it looks like.
Be surprised at anything that may happen.'

He had not seen such a notice before in any of the chocolate box villages he had just visited. He concluded the 140 plus residents of Fotheringhay had no faith in the Appeasement Policy working.

That notion was still being practised up to the very end of peace in Britain, that is, until the British Ambassador in Berlin, Sir Neville Henderson, passed over a formal communique to the German Foreign Minister von Ribbentrop - yes, to that person who may have visited Midhurst and who would like to be 'King of Cornwall'. The document

Chapter 14 War Begins in Britain

insisted Hitler withdraw from Poland.

Paul Schmidt was then a translator in the German Foreign Ministry, and present in Germany at the history-making events of those last days of peace in Britain:

> 'It might possibly be a real ultimatum. Ribbentrop in consequence showed not the slightest inclination to receive the British Ambassador personally next morning. I happened to be standing near him. "Really, you could receive the Ambassador in my place," he said to me. "Just ask the English whether that will suit them, and say that the Foreign Minister is not available at 9 o'clock." The English agreed, and therefore I was instructed to receive Henderson next morning - that is, in five hours' time, it being now 4 o'clock in the morning.'

He recalled the effect immediately had on Hitler as it was read out as a translation to those present:

> 'Hitler sat immobile, gazing before him. He was not at a loss, as was afterwards stated, nor did he rage as others allege. He sat completely silent and unmoving.'

This, and more detail, is available at "The Beginning of World War II, 1939," www.eyewitnesstohistory.com

Returning to Morton's stroll through Fotheringhay, he stated:

> 'How impossible - how fantastically beyond words - the notice was in that quiet, lovely, place.'

Morton likened the changed societal situation he was seeing, to that of the Elizabethan Tudor period:

> 'Danger produced fear, and fear produces unscrupulousness. Danger and uncertainty are two of the constant factors in human affairs. .... money and fear of Nazi Germany are the great factors of England today.'

Midhurst WW2 Memoirs: 2. 'Evil' Rising: 'Good' Awakening

Henry had plenty of contacts in the Ministry of Information, Admiralty, War Office and Ministry of Supply. These contacts got him into war support activities denied to the common man. He obtained a pocket full of petrol coupons and set forth to see some of these 'secret' places, now that the war had begun.

In one of the several instances he commented upon, he went looking in a rural area for the new wartime location of part of the Baltic Exchange, the operation where corn movements and distribution were controlled, Fig. 14.35; he found its location as the result of a whisper he had heard in Whitehall! Pre-war government offices moved to numerous, out of the way places that were hidden from public view.

Fig. 14.35 Corn Exchange memorial to staff who died in action during WW1.

Chapter 14 War Begins in Britain

From Morton (1942) we learn that he set off for an unnamed village (Note that this account was first published in 1942). He found the Surrey village looking as if it had come off of the cover of a chocolate box. It had the usual village pond, wide common, avenue of trees, pub, and small shops with virtually no inhabitants.

He had his letter of introduction to gain admittance but it had no address, just the name of the Chairman and the village name. He went asking around, imagining to see men there in striped trousers, black coats and the bowler hat and umbrella. He expected to see file clerks walking fast between cottages carrying piles of files. But it was just so silent!

First, he tried the Postmaster, a man in a blue apron and blue hat, weighing out tea. When asked if he knew of the whereabouts of the Cereal Imports Committee. He replied he had never heard of it.

As there were possibly other 'untrustworthy women' (the fifth column listening in?) in the shop he whispered: "do you know of Mr Blank". Oh, the Postmaster said quietly, "Go up the road a quarter of a mile and you will come to the lodge gates on the left".

Henry ventured up to the nominated driveway, finding there a mansion. A man in fine butler's dress answered the door. Realising, too late, he blundered into betraying his country by asked for the Office of the Cereal Imports Committee. The butler's demeanour changed from friendly politeness to the mood of repelling a boarder. "Are you expected. Sir?"

Morton had compassion for the butler, a man who prided himself with being so proper but now needing to be more of the manservant who ushers all of these kinds of society into his life's mansion.

In the background of the hall, with its numerous articles of landed gentry clothing, he saw hurrying figures. After some time, the impeccable butler found Mr Blank has just been in the swimming-bath. But it was no longer a fabulously expensive bath; it had been drained and now contained 'thirty clerks sitting at trestle tables, with their noses in ledgers or their mouths to the telephones.'

Mr Blank was eventually found in the squash court, also now converted to office space filled to the brim with clerks. Then they went 'into a splendid drawing-room, which had been heartlessly divided with matchboard partitions'. A grand piano stood forlorn with stale cigar butts sitting in ashtrays.

An explanation was then afforded as to what was happening. On the declaration of war, they came down with a 'bottle of ink and a pen'. "We started to buy millions of pounds worth of the stuff. The government was taking over the essential food commodity. The staff and furniture then came quite rapidly".

Their role was to ensure cereals were kept in good supply and that the price and quality were controlled to a reasonable level. He was told all buying of cereals is done there. No one else can. The situation was summarised by Morgan. "This is the most important room in the country".

That visit over, H V moved on to his next wartime investigation. His book is an amazing snapshot of how the country was coping when on the war footing. The whole book makes absorbing reading, especially as it records true circumstances as they were as the war started.

Somewhere in, or near to, Midhurst, similar unexpected changes were being made. In one of the *Foyles War* TV episodes was featured a secret engineering establishment based on a real hideaway; the local railway tunnels were used to store tons of naval ammunition; the Commando, led by Lord Lovat, carried out the development of many of their famous raids in Cowdray House grounds; and light military aircraft were stored locally in large garages and farm sheds.

In 1939 my cousin, Marjorie Sims and her brother Arthur were at school in South East London. Their school was possibly evacuated to Midhurst in early September. Teachers escorted the class to Midhurst, them being left in a Midhurst Grammar School hall to be billeted. Lizzie, their mother did not go with them. Their story is covered in the next book.

Being only two and a half years old I was not then going to school so it was up to my mother to decide when to leave our house in West Norwood in London. My Dad was then serving in the No1 Balloon Centre station at Kidbrooke.

Mum had moved back in with her parents in West Norwood, so it was logical to wait for events to worsen before she took me to safety. It must have been her connection with Lizzie, being Dad's sister, that suggested to her that we eventually moved to Midhurst.

Chapter 14 War Begins in Britain

September 1939 was looking like being a warm and pleasant month but on the day before war was declared, thunderstorms developed and a half-inch of rain fell on London. Perhaps it was a portent of things to come.

Everyone was waiting to see what horrors would rain on them from that day on. Their overnight kits were ready along with their gas masks. Their air-raid shelters were set up for nights sleeping a lot rough. Rationing has started. The main armed services call-up was soon to begin.

My father was being kept very busy when war broke out; he was one of those already operating the balloon barrage that Jonah Barrington described as

'A gigantic oval field of white, shimmering thistledown'.

Dad would have been standing on his balloon squad's 'sailing' location with their balloon deployed and being occasionally adjusted to a height suiting the weather conditions. Alternatively, after modifications or repairs having been carried out at RAF Kidbrooke, he might well have been driving an articulated lorry carrying a folded-down Spitfire out to Biggin Hill to re-join its squadron.

This would all have been a shock to those in Britain; but overseas, much greater horrific events and situations had become commonplace. Over twenty unsuccessful attempts, by many brave and determined people from his own country, had already tried hard to remove the *Evil* Hitler, usually losing their lives for not succeeding.

Civilians across the English Channel now had to live a life of constantly looking over their shoulder and having total mistrust of those around them - also knowing that it was pure chance if they got caught up with the dictatorial regime. We will visit several of those events in the following books.

The opening caption of GPO (1939*): The First Days* film segment reads:

'Four-fifths of our people live in cities. Here is a picture whose spirit is true of them all: A picture of the London Front'

Midhurst WW2 Memoirs: 2. 'Evil' Rising: 'Good' Awakening

Whilst it is best to see this film, it goes like this:

It is late 1939. The *London Front* is at peace. Its people are at the ready.
Kids innocently play on memorial guns from WW1. Their parents feel the good of peace. A State of War message is heard from a radio.

'London is calling. London calling to the World'

The air-raid alarm sounds and people, without panic, go to shelters. It is a false alarm! An unknown plane has arrived over the south coast and is spotted by the Royal Observer Corp personnel who phone its positional information to control centres. Other observers do likewise, obtaining the aircraft's position and height to be phoned to artillery guns, Fig. 14.36.

Fig. 14.36 Royal Observer Corp member *spotting* on a London roof, 1939.

Barrage balloons have already been sent up. Air Raid Precaution ARP men are at work, showing friendliness to those they help. All is very quiet.

Again, it is peaceful. Little noise is to be heard. People joke, but that alarm has now dragged out bad memories. Thoughts of devastation flood their thinking: that of WW1 and it's still being repaired memorials, not yet all in place.

People are working hard to make the city safe. Sandbag walls are rising like the tide. Sandbags by the millions are been made and placed

Chapter 14 War Begins in Britain

around buildings as protection from bomb blast. Everyone is helping prepare for the inevitable German bombs. When will they come?

Buildings in the Midhurst District got the same treatment at times. Fig. 14.37 shows a well sand-bagged entrance to the Midhurst and Easebourne Cottage Hospital, given by Lady Cowdray in memory of her husband 2nd Viscount Cowdray, Women's Institute Easebourne (1947).

Fig. 14.37 Sandbagging of Rotherfield House, Midhurst and Easebourne Cottage Hospital. (WI Easebourne)

Londoner's faces are hardening; peace is leaving Britain. For how long?

A generation of British young men born in the last war is training for arms. They also are being taught to outsmart the enemy and kill if necessary. Not like what Hitler has been doing to his youth, they have been, until then, enjoying a peaceful life - not one of pseudo-military training over their entire schooling. The defence of London is in the firm hands of the youth and their elders.

Against the obvious background of wartime many Londoners must still go to work on businesses of all kinds. The nation is still a living entity. More planning and production are needed.

White war paint is added along the edges of car's mudguards: they need to be seen in blackout times. The fire brigades are being enlarged and water fire-fighting pools are created across the city. Thousands of the familiar London taxis had been retrofitted with a pressure water pump to feed the many fire hoses.

Midhurst WW2 Memoirs: 2. 'Evil' Rising: 'Good' Awakening

The aged and the sick have been evacuated to safe places. Pets have been put down (said to be around 750,000) or evacuated. Some have made it to the Battersea's *Dog's Home* where they are building more kennels under railway arches to save some of the increased number of animals being taken off the streets. People will want dogs again once the war is over.

Some 750,000 children have been sent away from London over the first weekend, and more are to follow. Mothers have mostly stayed in their London homes but now have time to spare to help the war and civil aspects of life. Many have joined up and are now in uniform. Many just knit; socks, pullovers and all sorts else.

Army convoys are hiding under trees out of sight from enemy observation. Everywhere young men are in training.

It is now *Time To Say Goodbye* to men as railway carriages and ships take them to the coast on their way to France. Ships are being painted with camouflage colours by dusky crewmen. The song *Wish Me Luck As I Wave Goodbye* is being heard and sung by Gracie Fields in October 1939.

Behind the scenes in the National Gallery, and the British Museum, old masters and invaluable artefacts are being taken to country hides, such as the Welsh slate mines.

Notably, for us today is that most tasks then needing tough labour, were being undertaken by the sheer power of men. Electrically powered hand tools were then still to become a part of our easier and faster way of doing things today.

As it is on the days of filming, everywhere around the East End one sees a patient world. A large map of Poland in a shop window shows it is still not all in danger. Warsaw then was still untouched by enemy action as was London in that first week of the war. Overseas, however, many have lost their homeland to the rampaging Third Reich vision.

The night will soon fall. It is free of cloud; the snaking, gleaming and reflecting river Thames may betray London to enemy bombers! Throbbing night aircraft patrols can be heard droning overhead in the dark. The observers are ready, as are all civilian service. Hopefully, this night will be another boring, but safe one.

That night will result in more Spitfires being made as factories burn the midnight oil, Fig. 14.38.

Chapter 14 War Begins in Britain

Fig. 14.38 Creating the famous Spitfires in Birmingham. (Birmingham Mail)

At least one London theatre is staying open. Hospitals are residing in eerie darkness because of the blackout requirement. A search-light beam moves over the sky. It will be used to light up any enemy aircraft to guide gunners below. The *London Front* is apparent. It is ready.

> 'London Calling. London is calling to the world at war. Grass is still growing; babies still being born. Men still whistle at their work. When you hear that call phrase on the wireless you know Britain is still free.'

The BEF was soon to become seriously engaged with the German army in the Battle of France. For several months at home, nothing much was happening. It became known as the *phoney war* period.

The way the war was going then made it look like Van Ribbentrop might just get the St. Michael's Mount Castle in Cornwall. Hitler's henchmen might set up home in the Midhurst District!

That description is of London, but is that a good representation of life in Midhurst? War had come to people a few miles away.

On the South Coast below Midhurst, are the towns of Bognor Regis, Worthing, Brighton and Easebourne; and along a little further to the west, Portsmouth. The larger houses in these towns were soon to be used by the Canadian military. Fig. 14.39 shows *Highmead* in Easebourne, as it is today. This was first used as the RHQ of 23 Fd Regiment, Canadian Army, later being used for 'other ranks' accommodation and film entertainment, Ockenden (2006).

Fig. 14.39 *Highmead* in Easebourne; used by the Canadians.

For these places, their daily life was just like that in London. As they had the strategic front-line airfields, factories making aircraft and shipyards, plus troops and materials flowing in and out of the docks there, they were perceived to be targets for bombings.

Troops appeared in the streets unexpectedly, as did many evacuees - this location was, however, not to be a safe haven! Blackout rules were enforced. and call-ups had begun. Fewer cars were on the roads. Roads were often blocked with barriers. The entry in the diary of Harriss for 6 September says:

'Another fine hot day. At 8.15 am the air-raid warning sounded, rather to our consternation......'

And on the next day:

Chapter 14 War Begins in Britain

'This war in its beginning is very different to the last. This time there are no patriotic concerts, no flags. No recruiting posters, nor speeches in public places, no long companies of newly-recruited heroes in mufti marching along the streets.' [mufti is civilian dress.]

Trenches were being dug in the local gardens. A week into the war and Harriss states they had adapted to wartime living and already could hardly remember what peace was like.

Deliveries of ordinary shop items had started to become haphazard, or non-existent.

Move just north by some 20 miles as the crow flies and you find Midhurst town. A German bomber would take only 6 minutes to reach it from Portsmouth where it might be first seen by the Royal Observer Corp members and around 20minutes from an unseen airfield in France. That small distance, however, reduced considerably the direct impact of enemy action on the Midhurst district. Two major bombing incidents were to take place in the District, but apart from those, there were only sporadic enemy aircraft incursions.

For most of the wartime, the Midhurst district had no apparent strategic value to either side. It was as though it was not there; isolated as it had been for centuries before.

This observation was not confined to Midhurst alone. Morton (1942) says the same of many country areas he visited in late 1939.

The main activity in the villages and town of the Midhurst District as the war started, was the task of finding billets and carers for the large influx of evacuees. As a matter of record, I was not one of them; I arrived in late 1940.

The town had never seen such an upheaval in its centuries of history. Trenches were being dug. Blackout precautions were being followed. Rationing has started. The various auxiliaries forces were learning and tuning their tasks. Church bells had gone quiet. However, air-raid warning systems were a topic of hot debate there - as will be discussed in the next book.

Looking down Church Hill to Red Lion Street a Pathe film, dated 12 February 1939 (repeated from Book 1, Fig. 14.40), shows a couple of cars, a truck disappearing down to the South Pond, and the occasional pedestrian. It may well have been taken on a Sunday but it is very, very, quiet. War was still to start.

Fig. 14.40 February 1939, Church Hill and its lack of cars and people. (Pathe)

Unfortunately, views of the street on that day, or soon after the declaration, have not been located. Somehow, I would not expect them to differ much!

It was unimaginable that Hitler or Goering would take over Midhurst and have dinner in the Spread Eagle. Heck! This is Britain, where the British would not allow that to ever happen.

Changes to the District start their path to a new future. Some points are:
- There was little change in industrialisation; it remained a rural area. The canal returns itself to nature.
- Trains were still running into the three stations; but not for much longer.
- Mechanisation changes from using horse and steam power, to oil and petrol-driven engine power sources.

Chapter 14 War Begins in Britain

- New housing in the District was being developed on previously green fields.
- Many older public buildings will eventually become housing. The Workhouse, King Edward VII Sanatorium, and St Margaret's school all get a new life.
- The original Easebourne Primary school moves to newly build premises, the original building still being empty in 2020.
- Midhurst Grammar School students move to join other schools; its original buildings going into public use.
- The new catholic church will be built. By then it is realised, however, that the need has greatly diminished. Several small churches will close and be demolished.
- Easebourne Village Hall becomes Cowdray Hall.
- The ICI research establishment closes.

General Lord Gort was appointed to the command of the BEF on 3 September 1939 and the BEF began moving to France on 4 September 1939. The BEF assembled along the Belgium and France borders. Serious fighting, as the start of WW2 for Britain, would soon erupt, Fig. 14.41.

Fig. 14.41 British soldiers under fire. (Artist's impression)

By the standards of the time in Britain and Canada, the BEF was regarded as a strong force, especially when joined by France. The German army, however, had effectiveness that superseded all Britain and France had on the ground; as we will see in Book 3.

Midhurst WW2 Memoirs: 2. 'Evil' Rising: 'Good' Awakening

I end this second book of Midhurst WW2 Memoirs with some serious questions that were on Britisher's minds at the end of 1939.

- Would Hitler get to rule Britain, and how soon?
- What would happen to the Jews in Britain?
- What would it be like to be under the rule of the Nazis?

Appreciations and Acknowledgements.

With the Covid-19 impositions hanging over us all at this time of completing this Book 2, I was fortunately still able to carry on largely unimpeded.

These Memoirs, being wide-spread in their subject material, rely on the availability and existence of relevant facts, and the cooperation of many people.

Serious preparation work began in 2013. Major research was needed to set up the content for the Midhurst Memoirs series of planned books. The first book, *Memoirs of WW2 Midhurst: 1. A Place Close to My Heart* took several years to complete; it was published in May 2018.

As a living far away visitor to Midhurst, I have continued to find generous support by residents; for this, I am again most appreciative and much encouraged.

The several village and town histories compiled and published by local historians continue to be invaluable. They are stepping stones that help me mine deeper into topics.

My unique home collection of printed material and recordings related to these memoirs continues to grow, now numbering over 250 books, documents and DVDs. Internet accessed films and other downloads have also been useful sources, especially those released soon after the war ended.

So many people have assisted me. Book 1 contains the initial list of people who assisted me get going. Constantly helping since, have been Tania Pons, Sue Edwards, Ian Wegg, Andy Robertson, Tina Litchfield and Dave Rudwick.

Others who have also responded to my calls for help with the content of this second book include:

Barry Hinton, Harvey Tordhoff, Ken Mordle, Betty West, Bridget Howard, Colin Hughes, Sue Guile, Dave Rudwick, Dawn Ades, Fr. Peter Newsam, Judy Fowler, Judy Rich, Marie and Dennis Merritt, Marjorie James (nee Sims), Martin Hayes, Peter Garwood, Tony Weston, Martin Postranecky and others of the BBRClub, Peter Nightingale, Richard and Sue Comber, Robert and Talei Strick, Sanchia Elsdon, Sandy Ryrie,

Midhurst WW2 Memoirs: 2. 'Evil' Rising: 'Good' Awakening

Sheila Ryan, Ken Mordle, *The Observer* staff, and more.

I was pleased to find that *Jacquie Lawson* e-cards business is hosted from Lurgashall; that service fits well for me to send greetings to people in the District.

My associated www.midhurstmemoirs.com web site continues to find use. *GoDaddy* staff in the US are so helpful to me in keeping this up to date and when I had to rebuild it in October 2019.

To those I have may have overlooked to mention here, please accept my apologies. It has not been intentional.

A very special event for me took place in Midhurst in April 2018; that was the launching of Book 1, and at the same time celebrating the start of publishing output of my *Midhurst WW2 Memoirs Project*.

The South Downs National Park SDNP kindly provided use of the Memorial Hall for an evening where people could gather to see Book 1 finally released. The weather was foul - but the attendees made up for that.

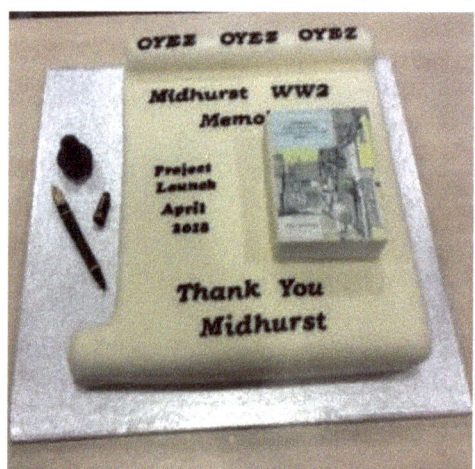

Professor Dawn Ades CBE, Easebourne resident and internationally acclaimed historian, was just the person to launch Book 1. I am most grateful for her kindness in accepting my invitation to do this task. In that week, Midhurst Society members also gave Book 1 a good push off at their AGM.

Again, Pauline Sherman of the *Creative Cookies Company* crafted one of her magnificent specials for the cake cutting ceremony of this special occasion; my way to show appreciation.

I think some wondered if this evacuee would ever deliver again! With Book 2 now ready, I only have 2 more books to go! The problem is that I have gathered so much material that I will have to be very selective and

Appreciations and Acknowledgements

speed up my technique! At least the material is set up and ordered in *Scrivener* as a searchable database, of which much is already written.

I aim to ensure that anyone in the Midhurst District, now and into the long future, will be able to obtain access to the material as part of its historical assets. The West Sussex libraries network help here by carrying copies for reference use. Reference copies are being provided to the WSRO.

Local distribution for sales was always going to be a difficult issue: Ian Wegg came to the rescue by holding stock of Book 1, and its companion guide *The Evacuee Story;* and in getting books to outlets. The Midhurst Museum has given the project essential central support by holding books at the ready for sale. It is foreshadowed that The Midhurst Society will be the supplier for local supply in the near future.

Material for the *Memoirs* has come from numerous sources. Many items, especially pictures, arise in multiple places often making it practically impossible to know if anyone has valid copyright on them.

Where no acknowledgement is given, I have come to the understanding that the image is in the public domain. Whilst a concerted effort has attempted to contact copyright holders there have been times that has not succeeded. Where the source is clear, it is acknowledged in the caption. Where I am advised, omissions will be corrected in future editions.

The on-line technical email support afforded to writers using *Scrivener* is very effective when a new tool, or trick, is needed of it.

Producing one's book required me to learn many new methods and skills with software applications. David and Daniel Beale, formerly of Stallard & Potter, printers of the deluxe version of the first Book, were my mentors is helping me reach a high standard of production. Their untiring help is much appreciated.

Apart from any fair dealing for research or private study, or criticism or review, as permitted under the Copyright, Designs and Patents Act 1988, this publication may only be reproduced, stored or transmitted, in any form or by any means, with the prior permission in writing of the publisher, or in the case of reprographic reproduction under the terms of licences issued by the Copyright Licensing Agency. Enquiries concerning reproduction outside those terms should be sent to the publisher.

Fortunately, I learned in the Book 1 cycle, of the remarkable advantages of being an independent publisher, making books available by the Print on Demand POD process. I use Ingrams-Spark, who also make my memoirs books available on-line through numerous sales outlets all over the world. I would have had to cease this project without this method as there would have been costs I could not sustain. Staff of my Sydney office of *Ingram-Spark* are also so responsive when it is time to move on to a Print-on-Demand release. The outcomes expected here do not include making a financial profit - that is just not possible for low demand works - but to ensure the information, as hard copy and e-book versions, is there for all to reach well into the future.

It was that certainty of POD assistance that led to me suggesting, as a member, that the Midhurst Society move to that method of publication to provide an upgraded modern magazine with considerable colour. It also is less costly because large stock holdings are not needed for each print run ordered.

You can guess what resulted! I got the job of assisting that transition. With resident, Harvey Tordoff, we jointly edit the new look digital magazine - that is continuing to get a great reception.

Proofing the pages is a most demanding task. My wife Pat, and Sue Edwards in Midhurst, have assisted this for me. This book should be close to being error-free but do let me know of errors that need correction.

Finally, to my dear wife, Pat, who has had to cope for so long with my Midhurst obsession, that results in numerous absences of my attention, if not my physical presence. I ask her to keep enduring for a while yet.

Peter H Sydenham, Adelaide, July 2020.

About the Author - **Peter Sydenham**
sydenham@senet.com.au   www.midhurstmemoirs.com

Born in London in 1937, Peter was evacuated to Midhurst in West Sussex. With his family, he migrated to Adelaide, South Australia in 1951, where he still lives. His working life began in Australia as an electrical trades apprentice, merging into an academic career in Engineering from 1961. Upon gaining the BE (Hons) and ME at the University of Adelaide, with his wife and baby daughter, he moved to Warwick University for a PhD research period in the early 1960s.

After a decade as an academic in geophysics at the University of New England, he returned to Adelaide as a Professor of Electronic Engineering. In 1986 he was awarded the DSc, in Engineering, by the University of Warwick. He took early retirement in 1998 to allow him to follow writing and handicrafts. He and Pat then spent five pleasant years in the Cotswolds.

Peter has always been attracted to non-fiction writing. His background led him in the 1980s, into freelancing popular technical articles in the monthly magazine, *Electronics Today International.*

During his 35year academic career, he has also authored or edited, over 20 text and research books, and the usual 100 plus scholarly papers. He was a book-series Editor for John Wiley, in Chichester.

Writing far away in Adelaide, Australia, has not been a problem; the Internet, and its email, provide most of what is needed today. He has visited Midhurst many times, the latest being in 2014, 2015 and 2018 to build up research on the Midhurst District during WW2, and to launch his Midhurst Memoirs project and Book 1.

His interests have covered numerous handcrafts - with mixed successes. He completely rebuilt and modified an Amilcar racing car in 1954. His 1958 electronic base-guitar was an experience; his several house building extensions were well done. His 2017 classic decorated wrought iron balustrades received unsolicited craftsman acclaim (but wore out his shoulders)! He has constantly been building onto their homes to provide for their 6 children - who now live in Adelaide, Dubai and Melbourne. Pat and he, now have 11 grandchildren.

List of Illustrations
for Book 2. 'Evil' Rising: 'Good' Awakening

Frontispiece: Map of the Midhurst Rural District, c1967.
Chapter 1
Fig. 1.1 Squad getting a barrage balloon under control. Dame Laura Knight's famous painting *Balloon Site at Coventry*.
Fig. 1.2 The British Empire kept the Peace for the World during the 1930s.
Fig. 1.3 Hunger march of unemployed men somewhere in Britain c1935.
Fig. 1.4 Primary School class in 1931. Joachim is the top row, fifth from the left.
Fig. 1.5 Brownshirts parading, as people *Heil Hitler*.
Fig. 1.6 *Jungvolk* members were being converted to be fighting soldiers.
Fig. 1.7 "The German Student Fights for the Führer and the People".
Fig. 1.8 Synagogue burning; buildings around were hosed, but not this one.
Fig. 1.9 Joachim Liebschner, centre rear, age 16, with his Youth camp colleagues.
Fig. 1.10 Hitler's apartment was rented in this building in Munich: as it is today.
Fig. 1.11 East German stamp in memory of Lion Feuchtwanger.
Fig. 1.12 *Jud Süß* poster. The worst antisemitic film made by the Nazis.
Fig. 1.13 Hitler appointed Chancellor in 1933. Absolute power!
Fig. 1.14 Lawyer Michael Siegel being forced marched in a street in Munich, 1933.
Fig. 1.15 Decimating the dignity of the German nation was not the way to go.
Fig. 1.16 Depiction of the Battle between *Good* and *Evil*.
Fig. 1.17 Every 1930s home had its set of WW1 history books.
Chapter 2
Fig. 2.1 1935 'Come to Germany' travel poster.
Fig. 2.2 Adolf Hitler; early Party Day held in Nuremberg, 1927.

List of Illustrations

Fig. 2.3 A cover of *The Jewish Peril: Protocols of the Learned Elders of Zion.*

Fig. 2.4 The ruins used as the Dachau Concentration Camp in 1933.

Fig. 2.5 Hitler's 1938 *Times* cover; 2 January 1939.

Fig. 2.6 Artist's view of Germany's 1936 stadium and Hindenburg airship.

Fig. 2.7 Broadcasting network created by the Germans for their hosting of the 1936 Olympic Games.

Fig. 2.8 Did he, or didn't he? This artist's impression shows Hitler congratulating Jesse Owens.

Fig. 2.9 Hans had years of 'marching and heiling' to become a good Nazi soldier!

Fig. 2.10 Hitler's young soldiers at the Eastern Front, 1942.

Fig. 2.11 The Holy Lance (Spear of Destiny).

Fig. 2.12 British 1936 cartoon sums up the thinking of Hitler.

Fig. 2.13 Dietrich Bonhoeffer's statue at Westminster Abbey.

Fig. 2.14 By the mid-1930s, Dietrich Bonhoeffer had become the target of Nazi oppression.

Fig. 2.15 Admiral Wilhelm Canaris. Master spy for the Allies whilst heading up German military intelligence.

Fig. 2.16 Cell 92 in the Tegel Military Prison.

Fig. 2.17 1995 postage stamp commemorating Bonhoeffer's life.

Chapter 3

Fig. 3.1 Nicholas 11, captive after abdication c1917.

Fig. 3.2 Joseph Stalin, 1937. General Secretary of the Communist Party of the Soviet Union.

Fig. 3.3 Digging the *White Sea-Baltic ship* canal in 1932.

Fig. 3.4 In 1939 and 1943, Stalin was *Man of the Year* on a *Time* magazine cover.

Fig. 3.5 Russia fights back to defend Moscow in late 1941.

Fig. 3.6 Mussolini as *Time Man of the Year,* 1923.

Fig. 3.7 Mussolini is pleased with his little *Sons of the She-Wolf.*

Fig. 3.8 Mussolini's racial attitude, 1936.

Fig. 3.9 Mussolini saved at Mount Sasso in 1943 - to lead again in the *Evil* Axis.

Fig. 3.10 'The Fascist Beast is Vanquished'; WW2 poster after the fall of Mussolini.
Fig. 3.11 General Primo de Rivera. Prime Minister in Spain, 1923-1930.
Fig. 3.12 A beaming Franco with Hitler, 1st April 1939.
Fig. 3.13 Hitler and Mussolini wooing Franco.
Fig. 3.14 Spanish Civil War poster suggesting Hitler was the real leader in Franco's clothing.
Fig. 3.15 Bombing of Guernica city in 1937.
Fig. 3.16 Cartoonist David Low's portrayal of the *Good* shrinking from the *Evil* Bully.
Fig. 3.17 French cartoon of 1898. The China pie is being divided up by the global powers.
Fig. 3.18 The Battle of Yalu in October 1894 showed up the weakness of China to combat Japan.
Fig. 3.19 Chinese recruitment poster, c1937.
Fig. 3.20 *Flying Tigers* in formation over China in 1942.
Fig. 3.21 Romantic image of 1930s Japan.
Fig. 3.22 Emperor Hirohito - *The Son of Heaven,* 1928.
Fig. 3.23 The *Tripartite Pact* is signed by the Axis members in 1940.
Fig. 3.24 Children of their nations dancing in unison for the Axis leaders in 1938: Japanese propaganda poster.

Chapter 4

Fig. 4.1 *Shape of Things to Come*: Dust jacket of First Edition in 1933.
Fig. 4.2 The LN was intended to be the muzzle holding the mad dog in control.
Fig. 4.3 Pavement street artist in London. 27 August 1939.
Fig. 4.4 Artist's impression of Athenian Greek democracy at work.
Fig. 4.5 Memorial to the sealing of the Magna Carta in 1250.
Fig. 4.6 Birth of Democracy in the new United States of America, 1776.
Fig. 4.7 Mussolini shows contempt for the League of Nations.
Fig. 4.8 Poster for HG Wells film, 1936.

Chapter 5

Fig. 5.1 British Empire and Commonwealth countries in 1939.
Fig. 5.2 Sir Francis Drake. A Privateer of Queen Elizabeth 1.
Fig. 5.3 *Planting the Sugar Cane*, Antigua, 1823, by William Clark.

List of Illustrations

Fig. 5.4 Recruitment poster for the British Indian Army in WW2.
Fig. 5.5 *Let's Go Canada.* Poster for WW2.
Fig. 5.6 Canada joins the Allies in September 1939.
Fig. 5.7 Canucks helping out with farming in the early years of the war.
Fig. 5.8 Artist's impression of Captain Cook taking possession of Australia, 1770.
Fig. 5.9 Sydney Harbour Bridge celebrations poster, 1932.
Fig. 5.10 *The Japanese are coming.* Australian poster ca 1942.
Fig. 5.11a Early expansion of the USA - up to 1861.
Fig. 5.11b Expansion from 1861.
Fig. 5.12 Sinking the RMS Lusitania increased resistance against the Germans in WW1.
Fig. 5.13 USA poster based on the Lusitania sinking.
Fig. 5.14 USA isolationism in the late 1920s.
Fig. 5.15 Caption: Hitler ordered to his macabre crew "Remember! Women and Children first".
Fig. 5.16 US troops arriving in Derry, Ireland in 1942.
Fig. 5.17 Just one of the forts of the *Maginot* Line, 1934; the world's greatest underground fortification!
Fig. 5.18 *Siegfried* line along the Western Germany border.
Fig. 5.19 Polish forces fight hard to defend the Hel Peninsular, October 1939.
Fig. 5.20 Hitler, victorious in Warsaw, 5 October 1939.
Fig. 5.21 German Calendar of the *Racial Politics Office* Rally 1938.
Fig. 5.22 Norwegians being trained in Sweden for resistance service.
Fig. 5.23 Neutral Sweden was surrounded by Axis countries by 1942.
Fig. 5.24 US troops and Coast Guardsmen on patrol in Greenland, 1943.
Fig. 5.25 *Operation Fork* in progress, 1940.
Fig. 5.26 Chinese army in WW2.
Fig. 5.27 *Pincers for Pincers.* Nazis meet Russia,1941- 45.
Fig. 5.28 Combatants of WW2.
Fig. 5.29 First part of the *Operation Foxley* document, SOE 1944.

Chapter 6

Fig. 6.1 Hitler and Mussolini walk through Munich with some of the Nazi High Command in September 1938.

Fig. 6.2 *Stepping stones to Glory*.
Fig. 6.3 6-inch coastal defence gun at Sheerness, November 1939.
Fig. 6.4 Royal Artillery parading in Cowdray Park. 1937.
Fig. 6.5 THE BANDITS FEAST "I've said it once, and I'll say it again, the British are starving Europe". (LHS, Goering; centre, Hitler; RHS, Ribbentrop).
Fig. 6.6 Ribbentrop, (right) with his lawyer, at the War Trials in 1946.
Fig. 6.7 *Bollards*. Said to be what Ribbentrop would take when the Nazis took over Britain.
Fig. 6.8 One-time example of a four-poster suite in the Spread Eagle Hotel.
Fig. 6.9 Portion of Aliens Register page of the Spread Eagle, including a Ribbentrop signature.
Fig. 6.10 Ribbentrop signatures.
(a) With family photo in 1937, from Schwarz (1943).
(b) On Spread Eagle Hotel register page.
Fig. 6.11 The Eagle purported to have been Goering's.
Fig. 6.12 Graffiti drawing on Cowdray Ruins wall.
Fig. 6.13 The Cowdray Ruins register book consulted in May 2018.
Fig. 6.14 Rudolph von Ribbentrop in London, 1937.
Fig. 6.15 Goering is easily recognised in caricatures.
Fig. 6.16 Ribbentrop forcing a politician to sign (1939?).
Fig. 6.17 Jutta Sorge and Helmut Cords, pre-war.
Fig. 6.18 Once well-to-do, German Jews leaving Germany without their possessions.

Chapter 7

Fig. 7.1 *Kindertransport - the Arrival* memorial outside Liverpool railway station, by Frank Meisler.
Fig. 7.2 Kindertransport - arrivals at the Warner's Dover Court Holiday Camp in Essex.
Fig. 7.3 Munich Jewish orphanage, c.1936.
Fig. 7.4 The Jews were increasingly sent to camps after Ernest Vom Rath was assassinated.
Fig. 7.5 Susi Bechhofer's British entry card of May 1939.
Fig. 7.6 Fred and Audrey Mann, foster parents with Susi and Lotte, age 8.
Fig. 7.7 Susi Bechofer, celebrating 70 years of the Holocaust c.2007.

List of Illustrations

Fig. 7.8 He came to Midhurst as Karl Hartland but left as Charles Hannam.
Fig. 7.9 1938 leaflet on hosting refugees before the war was declared.
Fig. 7.10 Hand puppet given to Stephie Leyser, as she left Germany in 1939.
Fig. 7.11 Australian Citizenship Certificate for the author, 27 November 1975 (front).
Fig. 7.12 Record of Oath of Allegiance for Author, 6 February 1976 (rear side).
Fig. 7.13 Alfred Bader, a much-acclaimed scientist and philanthropist was a *Kindertransport* child.
Fig. 7.14 Herstmonceux Castle, now the Bader International Study Centre in Hailsham, East Sussex.

Chapter 8
Fig. 8.1 Dunford House: 1860s.
Fig. 8.2 Publishing logo of the Cobden Club, used from 1881.
Fig. 8.3 Dunford House today.
Fig. 8.4 Francis Hirst.
Fig. 8.5 Bureaucracy at work.
Fig. 8.6 Barbara Ward, in her 20s, later to become Baroness of Lodsworth.
Fig. 8.7 Barbara Ward, with son Robert, c1958.
Fig. 8.8 The rock-filled, Volta River, *Akosombo* dam is one of the largest man-made reservoirs on the globe.
Fig. 8.9 St Peter's church in Lodsworth, where Barbara Ward is buried.
Fig. 8.10 Barbara Ward, Baroness Jackson of Lodsworth postage stamp, 2014.

Chapter 9
Fig. 9.1 The Fascist way was brutal.
Fig. 9.2 Development of Fascism in Britain.
Fig. 9.3 Sir Oswald Mosley, with men and women Black-shirts in London, 1936.
Fig. 9.4. "How much will you give me not to kick your pants for, say, twenty-five years".
Fig. 9.5 Lloyd George visiting Hitler at the *Berghof.*
Fig. 9.6 BUF rally in Olympia, 1934.

Fig. 9.7 New Jersey, US. March past by fascists of the America-Germany Bund on 18 July 1937.
Fig. 9.8 German-American Bund rally; Madison Square Garden, New York, 1939.
Fig. 9.9 A family listening to Lord Haw-Haw during the early war years. Note the gas masks at the ready.
Fig. 9.10 Jonah Barrington, ca 1945.
Fig. 9.11 Cyril Dalmaine's gravestone in the Midhurst Cemetery - also using his pen-name of Jonah Barrington.
Fig. 9.12 Joyce was easily identified from his facial scar.
Fig. 9.13 Joyce's German ID.
Fig. 9.14 Cartoon of Lord Haw-Haw.
Fig. 9.15 Joyce's freedom ends; no more Lord Haw-Haw hilarious broadcasts!
Fig. 9.16 The lecture that started these memoirs.
Fig. 9.17 Sir Oswald Mosley inspecting followers at a Sussex summer camp.
Fig. 9.18 Charles Bentinck Budd c1930.
Fig. 9.19 Jorian Jenks 1938 booklet. Food imports were undermining home agriculture.
Fig. 9.20 Dame Rebecca West DBE b.1892: d.1983.
Fig. 9.21 Myrtle Cottage, on the left, was an orphanage run by a member of the Scrimgeour family.
Fig. 9.22 Great British Union Countryside Campaign, September 1936.
Fig. 9.23 1942 US poster. 'The world now knows that Fascists have nothing to offer the youth but death' Franklin D. Roosevelt.

Chapter 10
Fig. 10.1 Midhurst Town's WW1 memorial erected in 1923.
Looking South side.
Looking North side.
Fig. 10.2 1930s. One very poor family trying to cope with unemployment in South Wales.
Fig. 10.3 Soup kitchens existed in Britain.
Fig. 10.4 Postcard marked 'Mrs Elliot, Crown Hotel, Edinburgh Square'.
Fig. 10.5 Hindenburg's last trip ended in disaster in May 1937.
Fig. 10.6 Girls out for lunch in a London park.

List of Illustrations

Fig. 10.7 House of Lords sitting c1810.
Fig. 10.8 Today, membership of the House of Lords is more democratic.
Fig. 10.9 The local Hunt and Hounds in action.
Fig. 10.10 Archery underway for guests to Cowdray.
Fig. 10.11 Lady Beryl Cowdray (centre) serving tea in July 1939.
Fig. 10.12 Historic map of the Brighton railway system; still in Victoria Station, London.
Fig. 10.13 Regular train on the LBSCR line to Brighton.
Fig. 10.14 Robertson's Shop in North Street.
Fig. 10.15 Cash carrier in a 1930s restored shop.
Fig. 10.16 Both Bros. portable ECG machine 1932.
Fig. 10.17 Totalitarianism was fast becoming a prospect for Britain and the US under Nazi rule.
Fig. 10.18 British made Philco radio model 70, ca1933. Left: Front view of controls and loudspeaker vent.
Right: Inside view of electronic parts; the glass envelopes are the electronic valves.
Fig. 10.19 Finding the location of a person; idea of the 1920s.
Fig. 10.20 How people could have thought about an invasion from outer space in the 30s!
Fig. 10.21 Orson Welles broadcasting in 1938.
Fig. 10.22 Hitler's invasions were a joke, but the *War of the Worlds* radio programme instilled the deepest fear in millions of listeners.
Fig. 10.23 Reporters being told that the radio station did not think the play would cause so much panic.
Fig. 10.24 Who would have thought the radio hoax would be so frightening?

Chapter 11
Fig. 11.1 1st Viscount Cowdray, c1917.
Fig. 11.2 Sheer Wealth! The appearance of oil-rich development in Southern California in the late 1800s.
Fig. 11.3 Cowdray House in the 1930s.
Fig. 11.4 Wedding of 3rd Viscount Cowdray to Lady Anne Bridgman in July 1939.
Fig. 11.5 Lord Lovat at work in Newhaven, 1942.
Fig. 11.6 Stedham Hall on the Rother.

Fig. 11.7 George Chatterton D.S.O, O.B.E., Brigadier, British Glider Pilot Regiment, British Army; in WW2.
Fig. 11.8 Wispers/St Cuthman's School, converted to student accommodation in 2006.
Fig. 11.9 Duchess Russell and personal pilot Captain C D Barnard back from India, 1929.
Fig. 11.10 Fitz Hall main house, with extensions.
Fig. 11.11 Gatehouse at Fitz Hall, today.
Fig. 11.12 Bignor Manor, 1933.
Fig. 11.13 Barbara and Anthony Bertram, 1930s.
Fig. 11.14 Bignor Manor drawing-room during wartime.
Fig. 11.15 Bohunt Manor.
Fig. 11.16 Uppark House, from the front.
Fig. 11.17 Sir Herbert in full ceremony dress, with Lady Meade-Fetherstonhaugh.
Fig. 11.18 Uppark House was gutted in a matter of hours.
Fig. 11.19 *Deadly Nightshade* is a poisonous, commonly found, weed.
Fig. 11.20 Standsted House.
Fig. 11.21 Vere Ponsonby, 9th Earl of Bessborough and his wife, Roberte.
Fig. 11.22 Flying Officer Justin Clermont died when his aircraft crashed in Stansted Park.
Fig. 11.23 Parham House.
Fig. 11.24 Clive and Alicia Pearson in 1956.
Fig. 11.25 Long Room of Parham House, where some records of WW2 events are on display.
Fig. 11.26 Memorial stone for Clive and Alicia Pearson in Parham village.
Fig. 11.27 Leonardslee Estate.
Fig. 11.28 Sir Edmund Giles Loder in 1947.
Fig. 11.29 Leonardslee gardens in full bloom today.
Fig. 11.30 Woolbeding House.
Fig. 11.31 Grimm's 1782 record of the Fountain when in the Tudor Cowdray House.
Fig. 11.32 Petworth Park and House: (Artist Jean Courtauld)
Fig. 11.33 Charles Wyndham in 1908, owner of the Petworth Estate in WW2.

List of Illustrations

Fig. 11.34 West Dean House before WW2.
Fig. 11.35 Young Edward W F James and wife, Tilly Losch.
Fig. 11.36 Edward James in Xilitia in later life.
Fig. 11.37 Edward James is buried in a modest grave at the grounds of the estate he left to the nation for a useful purpose.
Fig. 11.38 Goodwood House.
Fig. 11.39 Frederick Gordon-Lennox, 9th Duke of Richmond.
Fig. 11.40 Young pilots under training in 1940.
Fig. 11.41 The QA Nursing unit stationed at Goodwood during the early part of June 1944.
Fig. 11.42 German pilots marched off to Goodwood.
Fig. 11.43 South Downs Hotel.
Fig. 11.44 Park House Hotel.
Fig. 11.45 Ariabelle Manor today.
Fig. 11.46 Aldworth House today.
Fig. 11.47 Dunford House being resurrected in 1952.

Chapter 12

Fig. 12.1 Direct drive Garrard record player of 1930: Model 201.
Fig. 12.2 Cartoon from BBC radio Times of 4 September 1939.
Fig. 12.3 Harry Roy's 1930s British big band.
Fig. 12.4 'Our Gracie' hits Hollywood; also showing British troops getting refreshments, maybe on the journey home from Dunkirk.
Fig. 12.5 Vera Lynn helping out at a YMCA cuppa car during WW2.
Fig. 12.6 Henry Sydenham was the music maker for many a local get-together in 1932.
Fig. 12.7 Graffham's Empire hall today.
Fig. 12.8 Danish censorship tried to stop Mickey Mouse in 1930.
Fig. 12.9 Title page of the 105th Pathe's Animated Gazette showplace in Charing Cross Road.
Fig. 12.10 Peggy Guggenheim in Paris, 1940.
Fig. 12.11 Grounds of Warblington Castle. built by Lady Margaret Pole between 1515 and 1525; with a later 17th-century house.
Fig. 12.12 John Holms.
Fig. 12.13 Douglas Garman.
Fig. 12.14 1938 Talbot T15 baby roadster.

Fig. 12.15 Yew Tree Cottage as it is today, now called *Badgers*, in Hurst, South Harting.

Fig. 12.16 Deborah Garman, Pegeen Vail and Samuel Beckett at Yew Tree Cottage ca 1936.

Fig. 12.17 Modern art still mystifies many who see it.

Fig. 12.18 Peggy with her adviser Herbert Read, 1939. *The Sun in its Casket* 1937, by Yves Tanguy, is in the background.

Fig. 12.19 Venetian gallery of her modern artworks in 1950.

Fig. 12.20 Memorial to Peggy Guggenheim in Venice.

Fig. 12.21 Col Grantham in a round frock and beaver felt hat.

Fig. 12.22 Stoolball being played in Horsham in the 1870s.

Fig. 12.23 June Page with little friends in Egmont Road, before it had houses built on the grassy meadows, 1938.

Fig. 12.24 John Holland, b.1922 in Midhurst; taken 2007.

Fig. 12.25 Lurgashall today.

Fig. 12.26 Lurgashall stoolball team, 1952; see text.

Fig. 12.27 Fernhurst recreational ground with its heritage timber pavilion.

Chapter 13

Fig. 13.1 Lieutenant Norman Douglas Holbrook, here, was just 26 years old in 1914 when he sunk a Turkish warship.

Fig. 13.2 Grave of Norman Douglas Holbrook VC.

Fig. 13.3 Stedham Mill c 1928; the actual mill is no longer standing.

Fig. 13.4 Submarine HMS B11 in 1917.

Fig. 13.5 Dardanelles defences, at its lower area, were strong indeed.

Fig. 13.6 Crew of B11 with, then Lieut. Holbrook.

Fig. 13.7 Medal group of Commander Norman Holbrook.

Fig. 13.8 Holbrook's WW1 submarine story was rapidly told to all in a 'Wills' cigarette card series issued in Australia in late 1915.

Fig. 13.9 Replica of B11, at 1/5th scale, in aluminium.

Fig. 13.10 Rear Admiral Leonard Stanley Holbrook.

Fig. 13.11 HMS Devonshire, armoured cruiser; in service 1904-1921.

Fig. 13.12 Henry Stoker - submariner, actor and sportsman.

List of Illustrations

Fig. 13.13 Submarine AE2 of the Royal Australian Navy. 2014 postage stamp.

Fig. 13.14 The actual Morse key used to advise the allies that AE2 had broken through the Dardanelles.

Fig. 13.15 HMAS AE2 submarine surrenders to the Turks.

Fig. 13.16 Crew of AE2 in POW captivity, as 'guests' of Turkey.

Fig. 13.17 Medal group of Dacre Stoker.

Fig. 13.18 Air raid shelter in Steyne Gardens.

Fig. 13.19 War becomes imminent.

Fig. 13.20 Blackout time-clock.

Fig. 13.21 Light tank and dispatch rider near to Petersfield.

Fig. 13.22 W P Jacobs building in Petersfield, taken in 1938.

Fig. 13.23 Midhurst from the West, 1928.

Fig. 13.24 Midhurst centre, 1928.

Fig. 13.25 *Three Horses* pub in Elsted village, today.

Fig. 13.26 St Ann's Hill; town square entrance today.

Fig. 13.27 From the left: Beryl Orchard, evacuee Maureen Peacock and Hazel Orchard.

Fig. 13.28 Heyshott today.

Fig. 13.29 A page comparing Midhurst shop uses for 1939 and 2009.

Chapter 14

Fig. 14.1 Home protection manual.

Fig. 14.2 Headlines of *Daily Mail*, 4 September 1939.

Fig. 14.3 Berlin, as Hitler was planning it to be.

Fig. 14.4 Memorial to the International Brigade in Lambeth.

Fig. 14.5 Passengers being assisted to leave the SS Athenia.

Fig. 14.6 'Heavy firing squad at the Western Front'.

Fig. 14.7 One on many kinds of a poster seen everywhere in the early days of the war.

Fig. 14.8 1st Division Canadian soldiers arrive for Christmas 1939.

Fig. 14.9 Delivering the materials of Anderson bomb shelters.

Fig. 14.10 Captain "Mutt" Summers in the cockpit of K5054, the prototype Supermarine Spitfire, 5 March 1936.

Fig. 14.11 K5083, the prototype Hurricane fighter aircraft, 1935.

Fig. 14.12 Professor "RV" Jones.

Fig. 14.13 Cover of the GPO collection.

Fig. 14.14 Britain begins to take on the Nazi monster.

Fig. 14.15 'Millionaire' BoB pilots taking a break.

Fig. 14.16 602 Squadron, City of Glasgow.

Fig. 14.17 "Stickleback" after the first Spitfire combats on home soil.

Fig. 14.18 Messerschmidt Bf (or Me)109 fighter shot down and on display in Maidstone.

Fig. 14.19 Arthur William Eade AFC: Midhurst's BoB hero.

Fig. 14.20 Memorial to Warrant Officer Arthur Eades at the Midhurst Rother College.

Fig. 14.21 Last minute volunteers signing on for service in the Royal Fusiliers, in Fleet Street.

Fig. 14.22 Food ration books being prepared for distribution.

Fig. 14.23 Special Edition Newspaper.

Fig. 14.24 The BEF in France 1939.

Fig. 14.25 Polo at Cowdray Park, Summer 1947.
From left: John Lakin, Lord Cowdray (third Viscount), Daphne Lakin, Peter Dollar.

Fig. 14.26 North side of the Midhurst WW1 and WW2 memorial.

Fig. 14.27 One of the posters calling women to take in evacuees.

Fig. 14.28 Home Guard unit - mid wartime; they stood tall, with dignity.

Fig. 14.29 LACW Betty Simmonds in her blue uniform.

Fig. 14.30 John Ainsworth sketched in 1941 whilst he was in the OFLAG VII-D POW camp in Germany.

Fig. 14.31 Just wait until the little feller grows up.

Fig. 14.32 Polo went on, as the war was impending.

List of Illustrations

Fig. 14.33 BEF life on the French front, Dec. 1939.

Fig. 14.34 Henry Canova Vollam Morton (or just H V Morton) 1892-1979. Journalist and Writer.

Fig. 14.35 Corn Exchange memorial to staff who died in action during WW1.

Fig. 14.36 Royal Observer Corp member *spotting* on a London roof, 1939.

Fig. 14.37 Sandbagging of Rotherfield House, Midhurst and Easebourne Cottage Hospital.

Fig. 14.38 Creating the famous Spitfires in Birmingham.

Fig. 14.39 *Highmead* in Eastbourne; used by the Canadians.

Fig. 14.40 February 1939, Church Hill and its lack of cars and people.

Fig. 14.41 British soldiers under fire.

Referencesa
for *Book 2. Evil' Rising: 'Good' Awakening*

Anon. *Surrealistic Prince: Of Two Continents,* The Esoteric Curiosa, 2011.

Balfour, Michael. *The Spread Eagle Hotel,* Spread Eagle Hotel, Midhurst, rev. ed. 2007.

Barrington, Jonah. *Lord Haw-Haw of Zeesen*, Hutchinson, 1939.

Barrington, Jonah. *And Master of None*, Walter Edwards, London, 1948.

Beaven, Brad., Manchester University Press, 2016. *Leisure, Citizenship and Working-class Men in Britain, 1850-1945*

Bloch, Michael. *Ribbentrop*, Bantam Books, 1994.

Bonhoeffer, Dietrich. *The Cost of Discipleship*, Broadman Holman Publishers, United States. 2001. Many editions. First Ed 1937.

Boxall, Ronald E. *A Midhurst Lad*, Red'n'Ritten, Steyning, 2003.

Boyd, Julia. *Travellers in the Third Reich: The Rise of Fascism Through the Eyes of Everyday People,* Elliot and Thompson, 2018.

Brady, Frank. *Citizen Welles: A Biography of Orson Welles*, Charles Scribner's Sons, 1989.

Brecht, Berthold. *The Resistible Rise of Arturo Ui,* a play, Arcade Publishing, 1957.

Brenchley, Fred & Elizabeth. *Stoker's Submarine*, Harper Collins, London, 2001.

Bud, Robert and Warner, Deborah Jean. *Instruments of Science – an Historical Encyclopedia*, Science Museum, London, 1998. p201.

Buxton, Andrew. *Cash Carriers in Shops*, Shire Books, 2004.

Campling, Christopher. *I Was Glad: The Memoirs of Christopher Campling, (Dean Emeritus of Ripon Cathedral)*, Janus, 2005.

Chaline, Eric. *Secret Heroes of World War II*, Pier 9 Books, 2016.

Chatterton, George. *The Wings of Pegasus*, MacDonald, Battery Press, 1982.

Cheek, Richard and Gannon, Tom. *Newport Mansions: The Gilded Age,* Foremost, c 2008.

Christopher, John. *Balloons at War*, Tempus, Stroud, 2004.

Clegg, Howard. *A Canuck in England*, Harrap, London, 1942.

Cobden Club. *A History of the Cobden Club by members of the Club*, Cobden-Sanderson, 1939.

Collins, Marie, *Caxton. The Description of Britain*, Wiedenfeld & Nicholson, 1988.

Danziger, Danny & Gillingham John. *1215: The Year of Magna Carta*, Touchstone, 2004.

De Courcy, Anne. *The Husband Hunters; Social Climbing in London and New York*, Orion, 2018.

Dearborn, Mary V. *Mistress of Modernism: Life of Peggy Guggenheim*, Houghton Mifflin Harcourt, 2004.

Dickens, Charles. *The Life of Our Lord*, Associated Newspapers, London, 1934.

Dicks, Christine; Dunne, Colin and Elsdon, Sanchia. *Stedham & Iping Remembered*, Kerry Type, Midhurst, 2012.

Disney studios. *Education for Death - The Making of the Nazi,* Disney Studios, 1943.

Eckhertz, Holger. *D DAY Through German Eyes - The Hidden Story of June 6th 1944,* Sprech Media, [Kindle Edition], 2 books, 2015.

Edwards, Sue. *The Cowdray Estate: past, present and looking into the future*, Midhurst Magazine, Issue 26, Midhurst Society, 2017.

Elsdon, Sanchia. *Midhurst in Living Memory*, Midhurst Society, Midhurst, 2010 - or in its e-file transcripts collected into one file for research use in the Memoirs project - see MILM (2010).

Eyles, Allen; Gray, Frank; and Readman, Alan. *Cinema West Sussex: The First Hundred Years*, Phillimore, 1996.

Fernhurst Soc. *Voices of Fernhurst*, Fernhurst History Group, Fernhurst, 2006.

Ferry, Tom. *Georg Elser: The Zither Player*, Create Space, 2016. Amazon e-books 2018.

Feuchtwanger, Lion. *Jud Suss*, Roman, München: Drei Masken, 1925.

Feuchtwanger, Lion. *Erflog,* Knaur, Berlin, 1930. English Translation as *Success,* Martin Secker, London, 1930.

Gartlan, Jean. *Barbara Ward: Her Life and Letters*, Continuum, London, 2010.

Gill, Anton. *Art Lover: A Biography of Peggy Guggenheim*, Harper Perennial, 2002.

GPO. *The First Days*, a segment in *'If War Should Come: The GPO Film Unit Collection Volume 3*. 1939, British Film Institute BFI, DVD. London. 1940. http://www.bfi.org.uk/

Green, Benny. *Britain at War,* Coombe Books, 1989.

Guggenheim, Peggy. *Out of This Century: The Autobiography of Peggy Guggenheim*, Carlton Books Ltd, 1979, 2005 paperback, Andre Deutsch 2005.

Guske, Iris. *Trauma and Attachment in the Kindertransport Context: German-Jewish Child Refugees. Accounts of Displacement and Acculturation in Britain*, Cambridge Scholars, 2009.

Guy, John. *Elizabeth: The Forgotten Years,* Viking, 2003.

Hannam, Charles. *A Boy in Your Situation,* Scholastic, 1988. First published by Deutsch, 1977.

Hannam, Charles. *Almost an Englishman*, Andre Deutsch, 1979.

Hannam, Charles. *Refugees: Silver Box Collection,* Nelson Thornes, 1988; or Macmillan, 1989.

Hardy, J. *Park House Hotel: Resurrection,* The Midhurst Magazine, Issue 30, 20-23, 2019.

Hare, Chris. *Worthing Under Attack: Eye Witness History of Worthing During the 1930s and 40s.* Guild Care, 2011.

Harting Residents. *Wartime Memories 1939-1945, by Residents of South Harting, East Harting, West Harting and Nyewood,* One Tree Books, Hampshire, West Sussex, 1995.

Hill, Maureen and Alexander, James. *The Blitz on Britain*, Trans-Atlantic Press, Daily Mail, London, 2010.

Hirst, Francis W. *Gold, Silver and Paper Money*, Cobden Club, Midhurst, 1943.

Hitler, Adolf. *Mein Kampf*, Eher Verlag, vol 1 1925, vol 2 1926.

Holden, Paul. *Worthing at War*, Phillimore, Chichester, 2010.

Hope, Sir, William Henry St. John. *Cowdray and Easebourne Priory in the County of Sussex*, Country Life, 1919, and ReInk Books (poor miniature copy!) 2017.

Howard, Bridget. *Cobden Country*, Midhurst Society, 2004.

Howard, Bridget. T*he Market Square*, Midhurst Society, 2006.

Howell, Leslie. *Midhurst in 1947,* Midhurst Heritage, No 3, 2005.

Hughes, Ben. *They Shall Not Pass!*, Osprey, 2011.

References

James, Lawrence. *Aristocrats: Power, Grace and Decadence? Britain's Great Ruling Classes Since 1066: A History of British Lords, Ladies and Landowners from Medieval Times to the Present,* Little, Brown & Co, 2009.

Jeffery, David. *Petersfield at War*, Sutton Publishers, 2004, also Kindle and Google e-books.

Jones, Reginald Victor. *Most Secret War*, Hamish Hamilton, London, 1978.

Jones, Reginald Victor. *Instruments and Experiences*, Wiley, London, 1988.

Josephs, Jeremy and Bechofer, Susi. *Rosa's Child*. Tauris, 1996.

Kenny, Mary. *Germany Calling: Biography of William Joyce*, New Island, Dublin, 2003.

Kirk, Jayne. Parham: *An Elizabethan House and its Restoration,* Phillimore, 2009.

Liebschner, Joachim. *Iron Cross Roads*, Athena Press, London, 2006.

Litchfield, Tina. *Easebourne Village Vignettes*, Tina Litchfield, Easebourne, 2011.

Loder, Sir Edmund. *19th Century Tour of the World; A Visit to the World's Astronomical Observatories*, publisher unknown, ca 1880. A very rare book.

Longstaff-Tyrell, Peter. *Maple Leaf Army*, Gote House, Polegate, 2002.

Lynn, Dame Vera, and Cross Robin. *We'll Meet Again*, Sidgwick & Jackson. 1989.

MacDougall, Philip. *If War Should Come*, History Press, 2011.

Magorian, Michelle. *Goodnight Mr Tom*, Kestral Books, 1981. Later eds. Penguin/Puffin Books.

Manvell, Roger and Fraenkel, Heinrich. *Goering: The Rise and Fall of the Notorious Nazi Leader,* Skyhorse Publishing, 2011. Also, on Google e-books on-line for free.

Maxse, Lady. *Petworth in Ancient Times,* Petworth Parochial Church Council, original articles in Petworth Parish Magazine over 1925-1930, Revised version 1972.

McCutcheon, Campbell. *Air Raid Precautions*, Home Office, 1938.

McKibbin, Ross. *Classes and Culture: 1919 – 1951*, OUP, USA, 2000.

Mearns, David L. *The Ship Wreck Hunter*, Allen & Unwin, 2017.
Minear, Richard, H. *Dr Seuss Goes to War*, New Press, New York, 1999. Also, as Kindle version.
Morton, H. V. *I Saw Two Englands*, Methuen. London, 1st ed 1942, 7th ed 1947 seen.
Neve, James. *The History of Cowdray House & the Visit of Queen Elizabeth 1 to Cowdray*, Scribd e-books, 2011.
Newing, F E and Bowood, Richard. *Magnets, Bulbs and Batteries,* Wills & Hepworth, Loughborough, 1962.
Newman, Janet; Crouch, Colin; Fischer, Edward and Newman, John. *Midhurst Grammar School Remembered: A Souvenir*, privately published, 2010.
Nilus, Sergei. *The Jewish Peril: Protocols of the Learned Elders of Zion*, Eyre and Spottiswoode, 1920. Many later editions.
Ockenden, Michael. *Canucks by the Sea*, Eastbourne Local History Society, Eastbourne, 2009.
Pons, Tania. *A Midhurst Flying Field, 1941-1945*, Selham Airfield Project, Sussex, 2017.
Ratcliffe, Bob. *Sweet Bessy Come Over to Me; a Community Play for Midhurst*, Midhurst Town Council, c. Jun 1991.
Ratcliffe, Bob. *A Patriotic Duty - a Community Play for Midhurst*, Programme. Kerry Type, Midhurst, 1995.
Ribbentrop, Joachim. *The Ribbentrop Memoirs*, Wiedenfeld and Nicholson, 1954; from German vs of 1953.
Roundell, Julia Anne Elizabeth. *Cowdray; The History of a Great English House*, Bickers, 1884 or Gyan Books, 2016 - a scan of 1884 edition.
Rowell, Christopher and Robinson, John Martin. *Uppark Restored*, National Trust, 1996.
Royal British Legion. *They Also Served*, Royal British Legion Midhurst, Midhurst, 2000.
Russell-Stoneham, Derek and Chatterton-Newman, Roger. *Polo at Cowdray: The Home of English Polo from 1910,* Polo Information Bureau, London, 1992.
Ryan, Lawrance. *Holbrook the Submarine Town*, Greater Hume Shire Council. NSW Australia, 2008.

Salzman, L F. *A History of the County of Sussex: Volume 4, the Rape of Chichester*, originally published by Victoria County History, London, 1953.

Schwarz, Paul. *This Man Ribbentrop: His Life and Times*, Julian Messner, 1943.

Smith, Robert. *Against All Odds: The Battle of Britain Experience. 50th Commemoration,* Battle of Britain Ltd and Royal Air force Museum. 1989.

Snyder, Louis L. *Encyclopedia of the Third Reich*, Paragon House, New York, 1998.

Stoker, Henry. *Straws in the Wind*, Herbert Jenkins, 1925.

Strachan, Hew and Sturmer, Corinna. *The First World War, Episode 10 'War without End'* BBC, April 2014.

Sydenham, Peter Henry. *Measuring Instruments: Tools of Knowledge and Control,* Perigrinus, 1979.

Sydenham, Peter Henry. *Midhurst WW2 Memoirs: An Evacuee Story*, Ingram POD, 2018.

Thomas, Spencer. *West Sussex Events: Four Centuries of Fortune and Misfortune*, Phillimore, 2003.

Urquhart, Brian. *A Life in Peace and War*, Weidenfeld & Nicolson, 1987.

Wake-Walker, Edward. *A House for Spies*, Robert Hale, London, 2011.

Walker, Sally. *Report on the History of Woolbeding House and Grounds,* Sussex Gardens Trust, 2006.

Ward, Arthur. *A Nation Alone: The Battle of Britain – 1940*, Osprey, 1989.

Women's Institute, Easebourne. Easebourne: *Our Village scrapbook; 1938 -1947*, WSRO Inv No. AM239/3/1. 1947.

WSFWI, *West Sussex Within Living Memory*. West Sussex Federation of Women's Institutes, Country Side Books, 1993.

Ziemer, Gregor. *Education for Death - The Making of the Nazi*, OUP, 1941. Indian reprint 2015 used.

Index
for
Book 2. 'Evil' Rising: 'Good' Awakening
The text of this book can be fully searched in its e-book edition of the same title.

1st September 1939 52
1st Viscount Cowdray 323,200,248, 446
229 Squadron 493
266 Squadron 494
3rd Viscount Cowdray 298,462,500
602 Squadron 491
603 Squadron 492

A

Abstract Expressionists 406
Abwehr 61
Acoustic sound 424
Adolf Hitler 31,53
Advanced Air Striking Force 500
Africa 81
Against the Wind 339
Aide De Camp to King George 434
Air Force Cross 494
Air Raid Precautions 467
Air-raid shelters 517
Akosombo dam 241
Albania 81
Aldworth House 373
Alexandra Palace 388
Alfred Bader 228
Aliens Register 184
Allies 27,121
American Heiresses 321
Ancient Rome, 111
Andy Robertson 302,458
Ann Harfield 414
Anne Bridgeman 297
Annexation 175
Annie Weaver 283

Anthony Bertram 337
Anti-Comintern Pact 102
Anti-Semitic 19,42,211
ANZAC Cove 438
Appeasement 171,176,475
Archery 295
Archery International 296
Ariabelle Manor 373
Aristocracy 250,321
Armistice 6
Armistice agreement 24
Arms race 174
Art 404
Art Collecting 393
Arthur William Eade 494
Arts & Crafts period 385
Aryan 156,171,207
Aryan Law 207
Aryan Paragraph 57
Aryan peoples 471
ASDIC 424
Assassinations 54,166,285
Athenia 146
Australia 132,240,437
Australian Citizenship Certificate 227
Auxiliary Fire Service 467
Avanguardista 78
Axis countries 27,159

B

B11 replica 430
Bader International Study Centre 230
Baird's TV 289
Balilla 78
Balloon Command 3

Index

Baltic Exchange 514
Barbara Ward 237,241
Barrage balloons 1,177
Bath night 287
Battersea's Dog's Home 520
Battle of Births 80,164,495
Battle of the Atlantic 146
Battle of Yalu 92
Beamish Open-Air Museum 303
Bechhofer 218
Beer Hall Putsch 198
BEF 499,507,510
Belemedik POW camp 440
Belgium 152
Belladonna 344
Berlin Opera House 199
Berlin-Marzahn concentration camp 40
Bertold Brecht 20
Beryl Orchard 461
Betty Simmonds 504,505
Big bands 386
Bignor Manor 337
Birth of Democracy 115
Bittle 408
Black Shirts 187
Blackout rules 522
Blackout time-clock 448
Blackshirts 60,77,196,247
Blitzkrieg 119,150
Blue Max 198
Board of Trade 236
BoB Pilots 489
Bohemian lifestyle 394
Bohunt Manor 340
Bollards 183
Bolsheviks 50
Bomb shelters 480
Bombing of Guernica 88
Bonhoeffer 54,65
Boston Tea Party 114
Bottle of ink and a pen 516

Brigadier George Chatterton 332
Brighton Railway Works 300
Britannia Ruled the Seas 433
British Allied High Command 437
British Broadcasting Corporation 310
British Commonwealth 90,291
British Empire 67,116,118,121
British Expeditionary Force 129 171,174,477
British Fascist party 479
British Film Institute 391
British Foreign Office 203
British India 124
British Indian Army 127
British Mandate of Palestine 211
British Movietone News 392
British music 380
British North America 128
British Parliament 116,246
British Raj 126
British soldiers under fire 525
British spirit of WW2 384
British Union of Fascists 60,187,247,249
Broadcasting network 41
Brownshirts 10,32
Buck Hall 326
Bullion Report 234
Bureaucracy 235
Business buildings 463

C

Canada 127
Canada Memorial 132
Canadian Air Force 489
Canadian soldiers 478
Canadian troops 130
Canadian troops 350
Canadian war Children 130
Canucks 129
Captain "Mutt" Summers 482

553

Captain Claire Chennault 94
Captain Cook 133
Carinhall 199
Case White 51
Cash carrier system 302
Cat's whisker 309
Cattle 302
Caxton 114
Censoring news 389
Central British Fund 219
Cereal Imports Committee 515
Chamberlain 60,176,476
Chanak 422,426
Chancellor 11,20
Charles Hannam 222,225
Charles Wyndham 360
China 161
China pie being divided 91
Chinese army 163
Chinese monarchy 162
Chinese recruitment 93
Christopher Campling 295
Christopher Clark 22
Church Hill 1939 524
Churchill 117,142,304,475
Cigarette cards 428
Cinemas 388
Clare Fordham Harriss 169
Classical British education 445
Clive and Alicia Pearson 348,350,353
Coastal defence gun 177
Cobden 233
Cobden Club 231,232
Code of Hammurabi 111
Combatants of WW2 165
Commander Henry Peel Ritchie 428
Communist Party 68
Confessing Church 57,61
Congregational Church 412
Conscientious objector 496
Conscription 128
Contraption 500

Corbetts 468
Corn Exchange memorial 514
Council for German Jewry 211
Cowdray cottage 462
Cowdray dynasty 323
Cowdray empire 329
Cowdray Estate 321,324
Cowdray Heritage Trust 193
Cowdray Ruins register book 193
Cowdray House 325
Cowdray Hunt 292
Cowdray Park Polo Club 294
Cowdray Ruins Sports Ground 411
Crew of B11 425
Croquet Champion 443
Crown Hotel 286
Crown pub 418
Crystal Palace 2
Crystal Palace 305,320,470
Cuppa 472
Currency Guidance 231
Czechoslovakia 153,189

D

Dachau 36
Dame Mary Russell 333
Dardanelles 421,422,424,432,437
Dardanelles Campaign 444
Dardanelles Naval Campaign 434
David Coxon 492
Dawson's 303
D-Day Normandy landings 463
Declaration of Independence 114
Defence of the West 239
Democracy 108,110
Democracy 284
Denmark 158
Derry Naval base 148
Deutsches Jungvolk 10
Dictator 109,248
Dieppe Raid 131

Index

Disasters of epic dimension 287
Dispatch rider 449
District roll of honour 498
Dogfight 490
Domesday Book 112
Dominion Drama Festival 346
Douglas Garman 398
Dovercourt Holiday Camp 212
Drang Nach Ostenor 74
Drill Hall 418
Duelling 11
Dunford House 233,375
Dunkirk retreat 327

E
Eagle 191
Early memories 509
Early radios 309
Easebourne Street 461
East India Company 124
Economist 239
Education for Death 43,45
Edward Gerald Hollist 190
Edward James Foundation 364
Edward James grave 365
Edward W. F. James 362
Egmont Road 412
Electric Spark-Screen Broadcaster 312
Electrocardiograph 306
Electro-Episoded 311
Elizabethan reign 123
Elsie Pack 462
Elsted village 457
Emancipation Proclamation 125
Emperor Hirohito 95,98
Enabling Act 37
Endurance time 426
Englebert Dollfuss 285
English Heritage 455
Englishness 228
Enlightenment and Propaganda 35

Entertainment 377
Erfolg 20
Erich Koch 156
Ernst Vom Rath 14,215
Ethiopia 78,80
Eunice Mann 217
Evacuation trains 467
Evacuees 504
Evangelical Church 57
Evil 26
Evil Camp 67
Experiences 444
Explorers 133

F
Fascism in Britain 247
Fascist Beast 83
Fascists 9,245
Fatherland 15
Ferdinand Foch 24
Fernhurst 181
Fernhurst recreational ground 415
Fernhurst Women's Institute 181
Festival of Speed 368
Feuchtwanger 16, 21
Fighting Hitler's forces 488
Figli della Lupa 78
Film 377
Finland 157
First Days film 517
Fitz Hall 335
Fitzhall Lodge 336
Flying Tigers 94
Food ration books 497
Football Clubs 413
Fort Napean 475
Four-poster suite 182
Fox hunt 292
France 149
Francis Hirst 234,375
Franco 85
Frank Carpenter 453

555

Frederick Rosier 492
Free Settler pioneers 132
Free trade 231
Freedom of speech 388
Freikorps 33
French front 510
French Generals 150

G

Gallipoli 421,422
Garrard record player 378
Gas masks 171
Gas Works 302
General Hideko Tojo 96
General Lord Gort 525
General Primo de Rivera 84
Gentlemen scientists 355
Geoffrey Cox 246
Geoffrey Norman Holbrook 419
Georg Elser 285
George Bell 59,65
George V1 189
German Ambassador 197
German ancestry 144
German bomber 491,523
German coastal defender 458
German Empire 6
German Honour 213
German Jewish Aid Committee 216
German Jews 446
German Reich 205
German Resistance 55,63
German school 44
German submarine 142,177,479
German troops 76
Germania 14
Germanness 228
Germanton 429
Germany 31
Gestapo 60
Gestapo police records 220
Gilded Age 299,323

GIs 148
Glider pilot 332
Glory parades 45
Goebbels 202
Goering 179,183,191,197,200
Goethe Gymnasium 222
Good 26
Good Contributors 165
Goodnight Mr Tom 351
Goodwood 183,186
Goodwood Aerodrome 367
Goodwood horse races 369,509
Goodwood House 366,369
Goodwood Motor Circuit 368
Goodwood Revival 368
GPO collection 486
GPO Film Unit 487
Grace Mann 217
Gracie Fields 381
Graffham's Empire hall 386
Graffiti 192
Great Court of Cowdray 358
Great Depression 17,23
Great Genocide 69
Greater Germanic Reich 470
Green Sussex 374
Greenland 158
Gregor Ziemer 44
Grosser Platz 471
Guernsey cows 418
Gulags 70
Gundula Holbrook 419
Gutenberg 113

H

Half Moon Cottages 473
Hans 46
Hans von Tschammer und Osten 42
Harold Pearson 281
Hartland Trilogy 223
Heil Hitler 194,203,209
Heinkel bomber 371

Index

Heinrich Himmler 48,54,36
Helmuth Cords 206,209
Henchers 190
Henry Stoker 435,441
Henry Sydenham 385
Henry Vollam Morton 511
Herbert Read 405
Hermann Goebbels 19, 54
Herstmonceux Castle 230
Heyshott 232,462
H.G. Wells 105
Highmead 522
Hindenburg airship 288
Hispano-Suiza 399
Hitler 117,147,170,513
Hitler Directives 167
Hitler Jugend 10,12
Hitler Youth 11,12,15
Hitler's apartment 17
Hitler's grand plan 167
Hitler's Henchmen 204
Hitler's regime 179
Hitler's British admirers 250
Hitler's Time cover 38
Hitler's young soldiers 47
HMAS Canberra 434
HMAS Otway 431
HMS Devonshire 433
Hofburg Treasure House 48
Holbrook 424,429
Holbrook's medals 428
Hollist 506
Holocaust 212
Holodomo 69
Holy Grail 48
Home Front Recall 445
Home Guard 479,504,505
Home protection manual 466
Hosting refugees 223
House of Lords 290
Hunt balls 293,294
Hurricane 481

I

Iceland 160
If War Should Come 391,487
IIED 242
Imperial Sun Lineage 97
Incendiary bomb 301
Information and Propaganda 311
Inherited titles 324
Inner Circle of Evil 53
International Brigade Memorial 472
International Brigades 87,89
International Coin 235
International Communications 289
Iron Cross 8,196,201
Iron deposits 155
Isolationist policy 143
Italian Social Republic 83
Italy 76

J

Jackson Pollock 404
James Joyce 181
Japan 90
Japanese 136
Japanese military leaders 95
Japanese propaganda poster 103
Jesse Owens 41
Jewish Experience in Australia 43
Jewish people 13
Jewish Peril 33
Jewish Polish migrants 37
Jim Turcan 245
Joachim Liebschner 7
Joachim Von Ribbentrop 53
John Ainsworth 504,506
John Churchill Pearson 327
John Holland 411,413
John Holms 396,397
Joseph Goebbels 54,391
Joseph Stalin 69
Jud Süß, 19

June Page 412
Junk 96
Justin Clermont 348
Jutta Sorge 206,209

K

Kantaro Suzuki 96
Karl Hartland 222
Katyn massacre 154
Kindertransport 211,213,219,222,228
Kindertransport memorial 212
Kinds of shops 456
Kingdom of Great Britain 126
King George V 427
King William statue 453
Kingdom of England 228
Knockhundred Row 459
Korea 95
Kristallnacht 37,214

L

Lady Anne Bridgman 327
Lady Beryl Cowdray 298
Lady Emma Barnard 352
Lady Margaret Pole 395
Last minute volunteers 496
Laurence Vail 396
LBSCR 300
League of Nations 24,40,80,106
Leignitz 8
Lend-Lease 146
Leonard Stanley Holbrook 432
Leonardslee Estate 354, 356
Liberty, equality and fraternity 115
Liebschner 206
Lieut-Cmd Edward Boyle 440
Life of Discipleship 54
Life with War Imminent 281,299
Light tank 449
Lion Feuchtwanger 18,55

Little feller grows up 508
Liverpool Street station 216
Local Midhurst Memories 454
Lodsworth 242, 238
London Front 518,521
London Season 296
Long Room of Parham House 352
Lord Charles March 367
Lord Egremont 361
Lord Halifax 173,445
Lord Lovat 328
Luftwaffe 198
Luftwaffe 356,414
Lusitania 140

M

Maginot line 150,151
Magna Carta 112
Magnificent hoax 314
Major General Robert Clive 126
Major William Grantham 409,410
Man of the Year 72
Manchuria 93,99
Mao Zedong 162
Marjorie Bishop 459
Marjorie Sims 516
Market House 114
Martin Borman 54,198
Measuring instruments 485
Medals of Dacre Stoker 443
Memorial Honour Board 502
Messerschmidt Me 1090 481,493
Messudieh 426
Mexicans 144
Michael O'Brien 373
Michael Siegel 21
Mickey Mouse 389
Midhurst 178,196
Midhurst and Easebourne Cottage Hospital 519
Midhurst and Petworth Observer 359
Midhurst Catholic church 243

Index

Midhurst Grammar School 221
Midhurst in Living Memory 454,497
Midhurst Public Hall 390
Midhurst Rural District 2,376
Midhurst stations 300
Midhurst town 455
Midhurst WW1 memorial 281
Mien Kampf 306
MILM transcripts 299
Minimax Fire Extinguishing Company 338
Modern Martyrs 56,65
Moloch 49
Molotov-Ribbentrop Agreement 74
Moorish troops 246
Morse key 438
Mother Country 134
Motorised vehicles 458
Mount Sasso 82
Mr Blank 515
Mr Chad 192
MRD population 503
Mrs Karn 460
Mrs Susan Piper 495
Munich 16,171,286
Music 289,377
Mussolini 77,82,107,118,170,174,

N

Napoleon Bonaparte 15
National Defence Schemes 466
National Registration Bill 497
Natural Philosophers 233,485
Naval blockades 25
Nazi Final Solution 213
Nazi oppression 58
Nazi rule 308
Netherlands 152
Neutral countries 121
Neutrality Acts 145
New Australians 225,226
Night of the Broken Glass 13,215

Night of the Long Knives 37
Nissen huts 351
No 348 and 393 222
No1 Balloon Centre 516
Nodal defence point 465
Non-Aggression Pact 73
Non-Intervention Sub Committee 188
Nordic Countries 155
Norman Douglas Holbrook 417,420
Northern Ireland 148
Norway 157
Now is the hour 382
Nuremberg 32,36

O

Oath of allegiance 226
Obituary 329
Office of Information 392
Old-money wealthy 322
Opening of Parliament 291
Operation Barbarossa 75,163
Operation Fork, 160
Operation Foxley 166
Operation Valkyrie 62,65
Operations against England 53
Orion cinema 391
Oswald Mosley 187,249
Ottoman Empire 435
Ottoman ships 441
Overseas development 238
Owen Tweedy 245

P

Pantechnicon 296
Parham House 348
Park House Hotel 372
Paul Schmidt 513
Pax Britannica 3,432
Peace Pledge Union 59
Pearl Harbour 43,146
Pearson family 297

559

Peggy Guggenheim 393,394
Peggy Guggenheim memorial 407
Penicillin 306
Persecuted Jews 199
Persecution of Catholics 239
Persons Without Essentials 211
Petersfield 451
Petronella De Wharton Burr 295
Petworth 359
Petworth House 358
Philco radio 310
Phoney war 521
Plan of Attack of Poland 51
Plan W 499
Plum-coloured Mercedes-Benz 194
Poland 153,520
Polish forces 153
Politburo 73
Polo at Cowdray Park 501
Pommie bastard 225
Port Moresby 101
Pound House 242
Pound Sterling 283
Poverty 290
Prescod's boys 461
President Franklin Roosevelt 77
Privileged estates 237
Prized art possessions 199
Propaganda posters 143
Proscribed 250
Protecting Germany 50
Protection of German Blood and Protocols 35
Prototype 482
Prototype Hurricane 483
Purges 71
Push to the East 74

Q

Queen Alexandra's Imperial Military Nursing Service 370
Queen Elizabeth I visit 295
Queen's University, Ontario 229

R

Racial Politics Office Rally 156
Scandinavian countries 156
Radio broadcasting 312,378
Radio Direction Finding 483,486
Radio hoax 319
Radio Times 310,379
Radio Towers 1
RAF Kidbrooke 517
Rail timetables 468
Rationing 522
Razor Blades 236
Red Lion Street 182,523
Refugee Children Movement 211
Reginald Jones 484
Reparation 6
Reserved occupation 299
Restrictions on Jews 208
Rev. Mann 217
Ribbentrop 201,204
Ribbentrop signature 184
Rich Play On 290
Richard Barwell 345
Rivalry 149
RNAS 328
Road signposts 453
Robert Jackson 240
Rocket-propelled aircraft 483
Roll of Honour 503
Romulus and Remus 78
Ronnie Boxall 4,304
Rosa Bechhofer 213
Rotherfield House 519
Rotterdam 153
Royal African Company 124
Royal Army Service Corps 295
Royal Artillery parading 178
Royal Australian Navy 433
Royal British Legion 498
Royal Canadian Air Force 131

Index

Royal Canadian Air Force 478
Royal Navy 122,177,417,509
Royal Navy Submarine Museum 428
Royal Observer Corp 518
Royal Society 134
Rudolph von Ribbentrop 193,195
Rumbold's Hill 459
Runnymede 112
Russia 163,67
RV Jones 297

S

Sam Karn 501
Samurai 97
Sandbag walls 518
Scarlet Finders 370
Schleswig-Holstein 474
Scrimgeour 331
Sea of Marmara 427,439
Second Sino-Japanese war 93, 99
Secret Intelligence Service 338
Seuss 144.308
Shape of Things to Come 105,119
Sieg Heil 40
Siegfried Line 151
Silesia 9
Singapore 136
Sino-Japanese War 91
Sir Albert Richardson 511
Sir Arthur Grant-Duff 71
Sir Aston Webb 326
Sir Edmund Loder 353
Sir Francis Drake 123
Sir Matthew Fetherstonhaugh 341
Sir Nevile Henderson 187512
Sir Simon Sainsbury 357
Slave Trading 124
Soft underbelly 82
Solid earth tides 485
Sonar 424
Soup kitchens 284

South Downs Hotel 372
South Downs Training Area 350
Southern Electric trains 452
Soviet offer 72
Soviet POWs 76
Spain 76,84
Spanish Civil War 85,118,448
Spanish Civil War poster 87
Spear of Destiny 47
Spitfire 481,520
Sport 377
Spread Eagle 180,182,187,293,366
Spring Offensive 481
SS Athenia 473
St Ann's Hill 414,460
St Cuthman's 334
St Michael's Mount 180
St. Michael's Mount Castle 522
St. Petersburg 68
Stalin 73
Stansted House 345
State of war 469,512
Stedham Hall 330,420
Stephie Leyser 224
Stepping stones to Glory 175
Steyne Gardens 446
Stoolball 407,415
Stoolball Association 410
Stoolball at Horsham 411
Sturmabteilung 9
Submarine 417
Submarine B11 425
Submarine E15 437
Submarine HMAS AE2 436
Submarine HMAS AE2 439
Submarine HMS B11 421
Sudetenland 153,175,318
Sue Hogg 473
Summer Olympics 1936 39
Surrealism and Modern 403 Modern
Susi Bechhofer 221
Sussex Yeomanry 178,328,346,360

561

Sweden 158
Swing style music 380
Sydney Harbour bridge 135
Synagogue 14

T

Talbot T15 baby roadster 399
Tangmere 145,368,491
Tegel prison 63,64
Television broadcasting 387
Tennyson 374
Ten-pound pom 225
Thames froze 507 l
Thermionic valve 423
Third Age U3A 503
Third Reich 170,520
Thomas Clarkson 125
Thomas Thistlewood 124
Three Horses pub 457
Tilly Losch 362
Titles by birthright 292
Tony Beck 456
Tony Blair 291
Totalitarianism 308
Town Hall Cinema 301
Treaty writing 102
Tripartite Pact 100
Triple Entente 97
Tsar Nicholas 11 67,68
Turkish reprisal 443

U

Undesirables 154
Unemployed 5,283
United States of America 137
Universal Documentation 106
Uppark House 341,343
Urbanised area 465

V

VC award 419,427,442

V-E day 101
VE Day Diamond Jubilee 384
Venetian chest 400
Venetian museum 406
Venice 407
Vera Lynn 383
Veronica Tritton 349
Versailles Treaty 144
Victoria Cross Trust 419
Vinyl recording 377
Viscount John Cowdray 297
Viva Holbrook 418
V-J Day 101
Von Ribbentrop 179,183

W

W. P. Jacobs building 451
Wait and see approach 145
Wall Street crash 281
Wallace Collection 297
Walled Garden in Stedham 421
War Approaches 169
War becomes imminent 447
War Begins 465
War Cabinet 466
War Department propaganda 445
War Guilt clause 7
War memorial 501
War of the Worlds 311,313,315,317
War reparations 25
War was declared 498
Warblington Castle 395
Wars between nations 284
Weetman Dickinson Pearson, 322
Well-to-do German Jews 208
West African Conference 22
West Dean House 361,363
West Norwood 508

West Wall 151
Western Front 476
Westminster Cathedral 243

Index

Westminster School 194
Whingeing poms 226
White Horse pub 339
White Sea-Baltic Ship Canal 70
White supremacy 100
White war paint 519
Whittle's jet engine 289
Wilhelm Canaris 62
William "Willie" Rhodes-Moorhouse 490
William the Conqueror 111
Wispers 332
Woermann 188
Woman's Hour 219
Women's Auxiliary Air Force 506
Women's Land Army 477
Woodgate Farm 421

Woodrow Wilson 140
Woolbeding House 357
World Brain 106
World is Invaded 307
World Order 22
World War II, 23
Worthing 448
WW1 history books 29

X
Xilitia 363

Y
Yew Tree Cottage 398, 403
YMCA 234, 383

Epilogue

This book took far too much time to get it to print. Let's hope the next two will be speedier now that much has been learned - the hard way – on how to find a smooth and reliable way to carry out the final preparation stages.

It is fitting to record that this preparation period took place across the initial time of the great global Covid-19 2020 pandemic. Its effect came into force to us in Adelaide with lockdowns and job losses starting in late February of 2020. This event will surely go down in history along with the other great hard-times of mankind, the most recent one being WW2 of the 1940s.

The pandemic is not over by far. But as yet it, fortunately, has not had much impact on us as this book finally goes to print for online availability. It is a suitable lockdown this task!

By Patrick Chappette, at www.Chappette.com

There is a parallel here with similar early frightening radio programme hoaxes: see page 313 for the Adelaide one of 1927 and page 315 for the USA one of 1938. It is so amazing that a particle, far too small to be seen by eye, can bring the human race to its knees! Our appreciation goes out to those battling its front line.